THE PRIDE THAT WAS
CHINA

SIDGWICK & JACKSON GREAT CIVILIZATIONS SERIES

THE PRIDE THAT WAS
CHINA

MICHAEL LOEWE

SIDGWICK AND JACKSON
LONDON

ST. MARTIN'S PRESS
NEW YORK

First published in Great Britain in 1990 for Sidwick & Jackson
Limited, 1 Tavistock Chambers, Bloomsbury Way. London
WC1A 2SG
First published in the United States of America in 1990 for
St. Martin's Press, New York

ISBN 0 283 99648 X (Sidgwick and Jackson)
ISBN 0 312 03739 2 (St. Martin's Press)

Library of Congress Cataloging-in-Publication Data
Loewe, Michael.
The pride that was China / Michael Loewe.
p.   cm.—(Sidgwick & Jackson great civilization series)
Includes bibliographical references.

1. China—Civilization.   I. Title.   II. Series.
DS721.L717   1990
951—dc20   89-70042   CIP

Printed and bound in Great Britain by
Butler & Tanner Ltd, Frome and London

For
Carmen

CONTENTS

CONTENTS

PLATES

1. Court life in the Shang kingdom; from *Kodai Chûgoku* (*Sekai rekishi* series no. 3), Tokyo: Sekai bunkasha, 1968, p. 37
2. Wine vessel (*zun*); see *Hunan sheng bowuguan*, Beijing; Wen wu Press, 1983, Plate 15
3. Wine vessel, in stoneware; see *Nanjing bowuguan*, Plate 84
4. Lamp, in shape of actor or shaman; see *Treasures from the tombs of Zhong shan guo kings*, Plate 41
5. Lamp, in shape of goose and fish; see *Wen wu* 1987.6, 26 and Colour Plate
6. Seven Sages of the bamboo Grove; see *Nanjing bowuguan*, Plate 92
7. Stoneware animals, used to denote the years; see *Zhongguo lishi bowuguan*, Plate 134
8. Screen of lacquered wood, with 51 animals; see *Archaeological treasures excavated in the People's Republic of China*, National Museum Tokyo, 1973 Plate 21
9. Bronze tiger; see *Shaanxi bowuguan*, Plate 199
10. Table of bronze, with gold and silver inlay; see *Treasures from the tombs of Zhong shan guo kings*, Plate 4
11. Monthly return of stores and equipment, AD 93–95
12. Buddhist Reliquiary, from Famen si; reproduced by courtesy of Wen wu Press
13. Śākyamuni; see *Nanjing bowuyuan*, Beijing: Wen wu Press, 1984, Plate 126
14. Pavilion in courtyard of a Confucian Temple; photo by author
15. Tang wrestler; reproduced by courtesy of the Los Angeles County Museum of Art (gift of the Michael J. Connell Foundation)
16. Seated Apsaras; reproduced by courtesy of the Los Angeles County Museum of Art
17. Zhong Kui; a spirit in Taizong's dream; see *Liaoning sheng bowuguan*, Plate 116
18. Bodhidharma's visit to China; see *Shaanxi bowuguan*, Beijing: Wen wu Press, 1983, Plate 159
19. Host bidding farewell to his guest; *Nanjing bowuguan*, Plate 144
20. The Temple and Altar of Heaven; photo by author

FIGURES

MAPS

TABLES

NOTE ON PROPER NAMES AND PRONUNCIATION

THE ROMANIZATION OF CHINESE NAMES

For a number of years the government of the People's Republic of China has approved the use of the Pinyin system for romanizing Chinese names and terms, and it is this system which is in general use in many contemporary Chinese publications, including news-papers and official announcements. In addition, outside China Pinyin has largely supplanted the Wade–Giles system and a number of variants that have been in use, and for these reasons Pinyin has been adopted in this volume. Older readers, however, may be more familiar with the Wade–Giles system, which has been used regularly in many of the works of the early pioneer sinologists, without whose contributions few studies of China could be written today. For their convenience, cross-references are given to the Wade–Giles versions in the index, unless the two forms are closely similar.

However, no system of romanization is free from ambiguities, and the following conventions have been adopted in order to avoid confusion:

(a) *Hann*, for the name of one of the states that existed in the pre-imperial period from 424 to 230 BC; *Han* for the name of the imperial dynasty that reigned between 206 BC and AD 220.

(b) *Jin* (*Tsin*) for the name of the reigning dynasty between 265 and 419; *Jin* (*Kin*) for the reigning dynasty between 1115 and 1234.

(c) *Shanxi* for the modern province whose capital is at Taiyuan; *Shaanxi* for the modern province whose capital is at Xi'an.

PROPER NAMES

Chinese surnames consist usually of one and sometimes of two units (e.g. Wang or Sima) and these precede the names (sometimes of one but usually of two units) that are given to an individual at birth (e.g. Wang Anshi, Wang Bi, Sima Qian, Sima Xiangru). Traditionally, it was sometimes customary to adopt a secondary name, often termed the 'style', to define or draw attention to a particular aspect of an individual's interests or career. As a result it may sometimes be necessary to identify two different names as belonging to one and the same person (e.g. Wang Yangming and Wang Shouren). Where possible, such causes of confusion have been eliminated from these pages.

A distinction must be drawn between the names of early Chinese teachers and the written accounts of their precepts, whose compilation was usually completed after their own lifetimes as an anthology in which certain interpolations may have been added; for example, the works ascribed to Han Fei, the man, are denoted as the *Hanfeizi*.

Confusion may also arise in connection with the titles of Chinese emperors, whose personal names were never used. They have been designated in several ways:

(a) By their posthumous titles. These consist of two units of which the second (usually *di, zu* or *zong*) is a term which denotes 'progenitor' or 'ancestor', and the first is drawn from a list of conventional epithets such as 'August', 'Magnanimous' or 'Mighty' (e.g. *Shizu, Taizong*). As some of these titles were adopted on several occasions in imperial history, for precise definition it is necessary to precede them with the name of the dynasty in question, for example *Tang Gaozong* (reigned 650–83) or *Qing Gaozong* (1736–95).

(b) Beginning with the Ming dynasty (founded 1368), it became customary to refer to an emperor by means of the title adopted to enumerate the years of his reign (e.g. Ming Taizu, reigned 1368–98, has been referred to, incorrectly, as 'the emperor Hongwu'; Qing Gaozong as 'the emperor Qianlong'. Practice today is to use the form 'the Hongwu emperor'.

GUIDE TO PRONUNCIATION

Roman letters are used in the Pinyin system to convey the sounds of Modern Standard Chinese as: (a) an initial, consonantal element; and (b) a final element, consisting of a vowel, which may be followed by *n* or *ng*. Equivalents, as usually expressed in southern English, may be suggested as follows (for distinctions of tone, see p. 69 below).

(a) Initial elements:

b as in	b[ath]		p as in	p[aint]
c	[oa]ts		q	ch[ip]
ch	ch[at]		r	r[ye]
d	d[eep]		s	s[un]
f	[trou]gh		sh	s[ugar]
g	g[un]		t	t[eam]
h	h[ow]		w	w[ait]
j	j[ingo]		x	s[ing]
k	c[oat]		y	y[ear]
l	l[and]		z	[a]dz[e]
m	m[an]		zh	[dan]g[er]
n	n[ight]			

(b) Final elements. An apostrophe indicates a division between two component parts which together form a unit and which must be pronounced successively; for example, distinguish *Xi'an* (two component parts) and *xian* (a single unit):

a as in	[f]a[ther]
ai	[b]uy
an	[f]un; if after y as in [h]en; distinguish *ian*
ang	[st]ung
ao	[n]ow
e	[h]erb, ling[er]; if after i, u, y, as in [y]e[s]
ei	[w]ay
en	[col]an[der]
eng	[b]ang
i	ea[ch]; if after c, ch, r, s, sh, z, zh as in [s]u[pport]
ian	*yen*
in	[t]in
ing	[st]ing
iong	the German name *Jung*
iu	[J]ew or yeo[man]
o	[b]o[re]
ong	the German name [J]ung
ou	[t]oe
u	[t]oo; if after j, q, x, y as in French [t]u
ü	French [t]u
ui	way
un	as in the German [B]un[destag]; if after j, q, x, y as in French une
uo	[s]wor[d]

ACKNOWLEDGEMENTS

My sincere thanks are due to many of my friends and colleagues who have encouraged me to proceed with this work. With deep gratitude I name but a few of the many colleagues who have assisted me with suggestions and who have been kind enough to read some of the early drafts: Carmen Blacker, Hugh Cortazzi, Christopher Cullen, Hilda Ellis Davidson, Paul Kratochvíl, Max Payne and Gay Robins. Sebastian Chan supplied written forms for some of the Chinese characters; Miles Litvinoff saved me from a number of editorial errors; and Neil Hyslop drew the maps and some of the line drawings. The character index was made with the help of Paul Thompson's system and Miss Lillian Chia's typesetting.

I am glad to render my deep thanks to the following institutions for kind permission to reproduce illustrations from their collections or publications: Asahi shimbun, Tokyo (for Plate no. 8); Birkhäuser Verlag, Basel (for Plate no. 26); Los Angeles County Museum of Art (for Plates nos 15 and 16); Sekai bunkasha, Tokyo (for Plate no. 1); the Tokyo National Museum (for Plates nos 4, 8 and 10); and Yomiuri shimbun, Osaka (for Figure no. 2).

INTRODUCTION

China's achievements have been unique. Just as the glory that was Greece and the grandeur that was Rome have left their indelible mark on Europe, so have the features of China's traditional way of life nurtured the cultural growth of East Asia; for it was largely the ideas, beliefs and ideals of China that shaped the humanities of the east, with their counterparts to the spirit and grace of Greece and the dignity and organization of Rome.

The tale is one of experiment and evolution, of destruction and suffering. Resilient recovery followed the catastrophes wrought by nature; values that at times faced extinction survived the turbulence of man's own making. A long evolutionary process unfolded within the cycle of creation, decay and renewal, and subject to the conflicting influences of two attitudes. One of these sought to integrate man with the world of nature; the other hoped to discipline his mind and to regulate his activities in the interests of the community.

The themes are wide-ranging. Ancient religious rites that stemmed from an untamed way of life shed some of their crudities and came to serve lofty ideals. Mystics sought to comprehend the permanent values of the universe; teachers endeavoured to define its truths. Literature served as an expression of human emotions, as a record of individual or communal experience and as an instrument of instruction. Respected institutions were founded to organize the government of man, to recognize the different sections of his society and to restrain its unruly tendencies. Accepted principles persisted throughout the centuries with a remarkable degree of continuity, subject to the modifications and adaptations that changed circumstances demanded.

Evolutionary processes were at work throughout the imperial ages (221 BC to 1911), but it was in the Song period (960–1279) that many of the most significant departures took place, or that the way was prepared for new development. In 200 BC the idea of imperial government was as yet unproven and might even have seemed to be experimental; by AD 700 it had become accepted as the norm, to which ambitious challengers to power would aspire, and which statesmen and civil servants would be proud to serve; but it was in the centuries after the rather weak governments of Song that some of the emperors of the Yuan (1260–1368), Ming (1368–1644) and Qing (1644–1911) dynasties were able to assume a personal grasp over affairs of state that was marked with a new strength. The Former Han emperors (202 BC to AD 9) started by exercising their direct rule in the limited areas of central and western China; by the Tang dynasty (618–907) officials of Chinese government were operating on a far wider scale, and their control extended over a considerably higher proportion of the inhabitants of the south than hitherto. In the twelfth and thirteenth centuries alien dynasties ruled in the north, and a native Chinese house exercised authority only in the south; by 1368 it had become possible, for the first time, for a dynasty that was based in the south to claim imperial rule throughout the subcontinent.

In the early empires the Yellow River valley and the lands to the east formed the focus of economic activity; along with a rudimentary appreciation of some of the problems of supply and demand, certain measures were taken to collect produce and to organize the use of labour corporatively. By 700 imperial governments had recognized that the north required supplies of food from the south; and they had initiated schemes to control the use of resources with a view to the more effective benefit of the state. From the Song period onwards the valley of the Yangzi River was taking its new place as the centre of economic activity; the population had been increasing markedly, and the growth of the trading emporia was preparing the way for brisk commercial contacts with venturers from Europe.

Significantly new advances took place in China's technology during the Song period, such as the development of printing and shipbuilding, and the manufacture of porcelains of new quality. When the Han dynasty had been founded, the shortage of trained men of letters who could staff the offices of state posed a severe administrative problem; and the complex systems of education and examination of the Sui and Tang governments were designed to overcome these difficulties. The new degree of professionalism which had entered into the civil service by the Song period was destined to characterize the higher reaches of Chinese society in a new way, affecting the growth of cohesion and stability, and the successful application of governments' rule. The age of a landed and hereditary aristocracy had finally, after many centuries of transition, given way before the acceptance of new criteria; social privilege was now firmly linked with the traditional respect for learning.

At the outset of the empires, no approved canon of classical writings had yet been recognized. From Han times onwards, the adoption of certain works as vehicles for training produced a series of commentaries and interpretations that moulded the minds of officials; those of the Song scholars took count of religious and philosophical developments of the years that had intervened since the original texts had taken shape, and showed how they could be applied to the intellectual, social and political needs of the contemporary world. In the early days, prose had been used for didactic writing, be it historical record, philosophical treatise or technological manual; the centuries that preceded the Tang dynasty had seen the growth of certain forms of literary experiment and embellishment, where form counted for more than matter. By Song, many writers were aiming, above all, at clarity rather than contrived elegance. In the new age of printing, literature circulated on a far wider scale than previously; a new literary genre, that of the long novel, reached the bookshelves; the scholars of the Song, Ming and Qing ages attained newly advanced standards in their philosophical tracts, their historical comments and the newly emerging exercises in textual criticism.

Chinese sources and writers tend to concentrate on the contributions of the palace and the court; to ignore the practices of the less privileged members of society and to scorn the more populous walks of life. It is however from those levels, and from origins that have rarely received their due recognition, that many of China's characteristics have emerged; and a number of achievements that were of an exceptional nature have likewise been denied the praise that was their due. It was by reliance on the hard labour of those who gathered fuel and stoked the furnaces that master craftsmen could create the bronzes of Shang or the porcelains of Song. The messianic cults and untamed religious practices of the secret societies drew the frowns of Confucian dignitaries; but they excited the passionate interest of the populace. In the first century of the Christian era Wang Chong sought a rational explanation of the natural world that lay around him; but in doing so he had perforce to depart from some of the accepted ideas of the day and thus to forfeit the acclaim that he deserved.

From the tales told by the story-teller in the market-place there developed certain genres of literature, imaginative and appealing, but long denied the respect accorded to the writings of tradition. Above all the part played by women in formulating the Chinese achievement was rarely recognized. Their virtues may be idealized in some official writings, but there are few authors who acknowledged the influence with which they moulded the unity of clan and family or the skills with which they fashioned some of China's most beautiful products, in silk.

*

A wide selection of books, some in series of several volumes, treat the different periods of Chinese history in straight chronological sequence; and the monographs of recent decades have attempted to handle individual personalities or subjects with the depth and detail that they deserve. This book, whose subject-matter rarely extends beyond the middle of the nineteenth century, is in no sense intended to be yet another comprehensive history of China within the scope of a few hundred pages.

Most of the chapters that follow below are devoted to a single theme, whose development is treated in chronological sequence. They set out to explore the main achievements of the Chinese heritage that have left their mark on the humanities of East Asia. But while they attempt to depict some of the noblest and finest products of Chinese civilization, they may also remind the reader from time to time of the price necessarily paid for such results, such as the constant tension between an individual and his or her soul on the one hand and the community with its demands on the other. Nor can the contrast between ideal and practice be ignored. If much of China's culture derived from the efforts and imagination of members of the lettered class, it was they too who could be tempted to practise oppression or who were open to corruption. China's achievements must be seen against a background of arduous effort and fighting, of poverty and civic turmoil; for the effective organization of China as a unit has been a rare phenomenon; Chinese society has been anything but stable.

Of necessity, the choice of subjects to be treated within the scope of a single volume must be limited and arbitrary, and it has been possible to accord no more than a passing glance, if as much, to a number of topics that deserve considerably greater attention: education, music and drama; medicine and acupuncture; the impact of Buddhism on daily life; or esoteric Daoist practices – these spring to mind as obvious examples. Nor has it been possible to consider the impact of the non-Chinese confederacies and their leaders, or the effect of the introduction of ideas from Europe and America. In some instances the existence of recent monographs that are available without undue difficulty has suggested that curtailment of a topic here can be remedied by reference to a full study. The 'Notes for Further Reading' at the end of the book suggest where further information may be obtained or a subject taken to greater depth. They will also enable readers to find translations of some of the works of Chinese literature and the published conclusions of other writers. Limitations of space prevent the inclusion of such material here in a manner that could be representative and fair. The modicum of proper names and technical matter that has been included in the text recurs with supplementary information in the tables, which record the principal events and developments in chronological sequence.

I

THE GIFTS OF NATURE AND
THEIR PROBLEMS

China is a land of variety, contrast and surprise. Variety is seen in the diversities of landscape and climate, and in the different products of the fields, north and south. Contrasts abound between the ways of life of country and town, and between the sophisticated elegance of the few and the squalid suffering of the many. Surprise lies in the reflection on the continuities of much of China's achievement, the survival of order despite chaos and the maintenance of a civilized way of life in the face of repeated incidents of violence and destruction.

THE LIE OF THE LAND

Major differences of terrain, climate and occupation separate China from the hinterland and steppes of Central Asia. In certain areas, particularly the west, high mountain ranges mark the distinction abruptly; elsewhere the change is more gradual, with one way of life merging through intermediate zones into the next. As a result there may be little uniformity in the use of the name China to designate a geographical area; the term may cover different adjoining regions as they were absorbed into or separated from an established political authority. Sometimes a distinction is drawn between inner and outer China with various implications; sometimes the term 'China proper' is used to denote the central provinces, as distinct from areas known sometimes as Mongolia, Tibet or Manchuria.

Eight or more different climatic zones are sometimes distinguished, ranging from the frozen conditions of the north-east to the subtropical south, and including the desert conditions of Xinjiang province in the north-west. Similarly the extent of the rainfall varies dramatically, from an annual precipitation of 8 cm in the extreme north-west to 150 cm on the southern seaboard near Hong Kong. A particular feature that marks much of north-western and parts of central China (the provinces of Shaanxi, Gansu, Shanxi and Henan) is seen in the deposits of silt, or loess, which have been blown in from

1

Central Asia and may lie in depths of up to 90 metres. Friable in drought, loess can be moulded together when moist to form the upright walls of habitations; in the farmsteads it can be dug to act as sties or pits in which to pen animals. With its rich mineral qualities, loess land can give a good return to the farmer for a comparatively small effort; but once moist and slippery, all too easily it can bring his carts to a halt and delay his transport.

To the west of China stands that great massif of the world's highest mountains, bounded on its southern edge by the Himalayan range. To the north-west of that range the Hindu Kush forms the extreme westerly limit of territory that has ever been subject to Chinese authority. From the Hindu Kush rise the Tian Shan and the Kunlun ranges, stretching in an easterly direction around the Taklamakan desert and featuring in Chinese mythology as a home of the gods, or as land's end. At the foot of the massif, in the south-west, there is a particularly fertile region, low lying and bounded by lesser hills on all sides. Known now as the Sichuan basin, this is one of several areas where centres of Chinese culture have been able to arise and be sustained independently.

Elsewhere mountains have likewise formed natural lines which separate large regions. Thus the Qinling and Taihang ranges form barriers on the southern and eastern sides of an area that saw the rise of some of China's earliest cultures, and which persisted as the seat of government of Chinese kingdoms and empires until the tenth century. Over on the east coast the Wuyi mountains have isolated the coastal belt from the lands of the interior; likewise the Nanling has formed a barrier preventing easy access from the north to the modern provinces of Guangxi and Guangdong.

Among the great number and variety of mountains that China boasts, five peaks have been singled out for special attention as being sacred sites where intermediary or prayer can provide access to the gods. Situated in different parts of the land, they include Emei, in Sichuan province, Taishan, in Shandong, and Huashan, in Shaanxi.

Rivers are of no less importance than mountain ranges in determining the shape of the land and defining regions where cultural growth takes root or communities settle. Springing from the great massif of the west the Huang He, or Yellow River, charts its tortuous path to the sea. Its flow is sluggish, choked with the deposits of silt from the loess territory. As it nears the coast the river loses momentum and its banks their purpose, and its course becomes subject to the press of mighty waters that force their way down from the interior. From time to time the banks burst and the river charts a new course to find its outlet to the sea. In this way a delta has taken shape, whereby the Yellow River has reached the coast sometimes north and sometimes south of the Shandong peninsula. Such changes of course have been recorded for some 2,000 years, being accompanied by violence and disruption in one of China's most populous and highly cultivated regions.

Despite its vagaries the Yellow River has formed the principal artery of the northern part of China. Some of the first known traces of man's presence were found near its banks, and its valley was long termed the 'cradle' of Chinese civilization. Thanks to subsequent discoveries that description has required modification; but it remains true that the area long formed the central focus of much of China's culture and saw the establishment of many of China's kingdoms and imperial dynasties.

The second of China's best-known rivers, the Yangzi Jiang (also known as the Chang Jiang), is fed by a number of tributaries that rise from that central massif that lies to the west. Crossing the Sichuan basin, the Yangzi strides across succeeding provinces in an easterly direction, finally reaching the sea close to Shanghai. The landscape through which the river flows comprises some of China's most beautiful scenery, including a series of gorges through the flanking mountains. Unlike the Yellow River, the Yangzi is not subject to the wind-blown sands of the loess area. The press of water that it carries varies considerably in volume according to the seasons, following the melting of the snows of Central Asia. As a result the level of the river and the speed of the current are subject to marked change from season to season, and at times passage upstream depends on well-organized corporate labour or mechanical aids.

Fortunately two extensive lakes that have formed on the south bank provide the necessary scope for the drainage of excess water at certain seasons of the year, and the surrounding countryside is usually not subject to the floods that mark the lowest reaches of the Yellow River. Occasionally, however, a heavy press of water could demand stern measures, as happened in 1065. In that year a local official named Shen Gua (1031–95) constructed a barrage to resist the oncoming dangers. Shen Gua is known principally as a keen observer of the world around him who took care to describe with great clarity and precision the natural phenomena that he witnessed and the mechanical contrivances devised by man for his better living.

The Yangzi Jiang is so situated that it forms a natural dividing line between the northern and southern parts of the subcontinent. For many centuries the seat of government and the centres of cultural activity lay in the north, and for that reason there was for long a tendency to regard the Yangzi valley, and especially the lands that lay beyond its southern bank, as the home of peoples who practised an inferior style of life. Officials sent from the north to serve in these

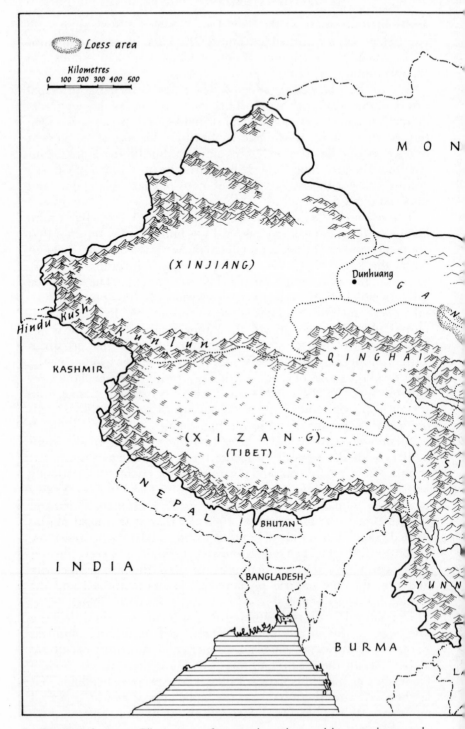

1. *Physical features. The names of mountains, rivers, cities, provinces and other features, which are given in their modern forms, are in general limited to those mentioned in the text*

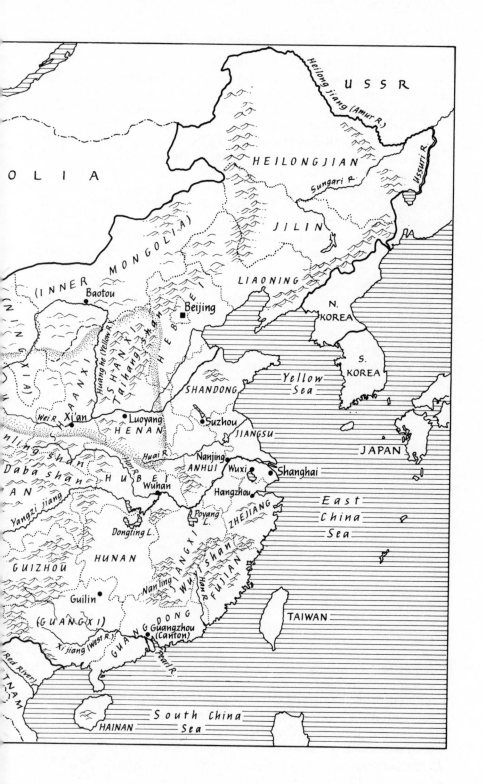

areas could sometimes express dismay or shock at the conditions that they found, in lands where primeval customs, long eliminated elsewhere, still lingered.

A number of other rivers have played a distinctive role in the development of Chinese civilization, providing water for the fields or carrying the craft that conveyed travellers and staple goods across the provinces. Joining the Yellow River to the east of Xi'an, the Wei River would seem to form an ideal link from east to west that would also irrigate lands that housed the capitals of kings and emperors; but thanks to the silt of the loess territory its current is sluggish and its channel somewhat shallow and ill defined. Nevertheless the Wei River has sometimes featured in dramatic incidents of history, seeming to form a final defence line against the onrush of an invader.

At times when the full force of the Yellow River has sought its way to the sea south of the Shandong peninsula, it has done so by taking over stretches of the Huai River. This is one of several streams flowing in a south-easterly direction which water one of China's major grain-producing areas. On occasions when the government of the land has been split among several authorities, the Huai River valley has formed an area under dispute between a northern and a southern regime, acting as a prize worthy of hard fighting.

The Yangzi is fed by four tributaries that give the province of Sichuan its name and ensure its fertility. Further east the Han River joins the Yangzi, at the modern industrial complex of Wuhan. In the deep south a number of rivers which rise in the western hinterland eventually merge to form the Xi Jiang (West River), whose estuary, near Guangzhou (Canton), is known as the Pearl River. By these means a line of communications was sometimes formed with the interior. In the extreme north-east, where the rivers are frozen for up to six months in the year, the Sungari flows north to join the Amur (or Heilong Jiang); the latter, which is joined by the Ussuri at Khabarovsk, forms the boundary between China and the Soviet Union.

THE FRUITS OF THE EARTH

It is hardly surprising that types and methods of production vary to a point of extreme in an extensive land which is subject to major differences of climate and terrain, and to extensive flooding or severe drought. In general a dividing line passes through the modern provinces of Jiangsu, Anhui, Henan and Shaanxi, whereby the north produces millet, wheat and sorghum, and the southern fields are sown with rice. Different styles and methods of irrigation and fieldwork are needed in each case. Unpredictable rainfalls can wreak havoc with a farmer's labours, and imperial governments or local officials were frequently beset with the problem of alleviating distress or crisis, when the water supply was either too profuse or else too scanty. Surviving fragments of documents show that manuals which prescribed procedures for successful work in the fields were being written from at least the start of the Christian era in the west.

Chinese farmers have been wresting a living from the land since perhaps 5000 BC. Artificial means of raising water to irrigate the paddies had been evolved by the second century AD, and have since then required countless hours of back-breaking toil; in recent decades electrical devices have saved the farmers from much of this. Different patterns of fieldwork are exemplified in two cases; in the plains the land tends to be delineated regularly in rectangular, somewhat elongated plots; in mountainous country terraces have been constructed with great skill, in such a way that the water may pass from upper to lower levels as may be desirable. In the favourable climate of the south the fields yield two or more rice harvests annually.

Cultivation of tea had started some centuries before the Tang dynasty (618–907), when its use had become widespread and it was being praised for its medicinal properties; it is grown mainly in the south-east (the provinces of Hunan, Jiangxi and Fujian). For long the annual crops of hemp formed the principal material for China's textiles, but this came to be replaced by cotton, cultivated since the eleventh century, and is now sown extensively in the Yangzi area. Its growth has also been encouraged in the north, and may be observed close to Beijing. From perhaps 1500 BC some Chinese had mastered the skilful art of nurturing the silkworm, timing the process needed for unravelling the delicate threads from the cocoons, and weaving the much-prized rolls of fabric that were reserved for the clothing of the noble and the rich. Archaeology has recently revealed some splendid examples of polychrome and patterned silks fashioned in central China early in the second century BC. The best-known mulberry orchards on which the silkworm thrives, and whose product depends on long-term land tenure, are concentrated in the centre of the land; the textile industry has developed extensively in cities such as Hangzhou, Suzhou and Wuxi.

Despite considerable destruction of forests throughout the ages, whether for use as building material or as fuel, China still possesses rich sources of timber. The climate and soil of Hunan province give rise to cedar; the south-east yields conifers and bamboo – nature's gift to farmer and builder alike, in addition to its use as writing material or as a table delicacy. Bamboo's luxuriant growth forms a conspicuous feature of the landscape of Sichuan; Manchuria produces rich supplies of pine. From Sichuan there also come precious woods such as catalpa, long prized as choice timber for coffins, owing to its properties of endurance. Guilin, or 'Forest of Cassia Trees', which is the name of a city in the south, tells its own tale of the provenance of spices, including pepper, in those parts.

The Chinese have for long emphasized the contrast between their own sedentary and agricultural way of life and the mobile, nomadic conditions of the stock-breeders of the steppes of Asia. Throughout the historical period, and perhaps from earlier times, the Chinese have concentrated their effort on the production of cereal crops, rearing animals such as oxen or buffalo for ploughing or other farmwork. While chicken, sheep or pigs have been reared for the table, their nourishment has usually derived from the farmyard and its scraps, rather than from verdant pastures. Such grounds are difficult to find in China; partly as a result horses have been prized as animals that are in short supply, and dairy products have not formed an important element of the Chinese diet.

China's Bronze Age started at about 2000 BC, and the Iron Age followed some thousand years or more later; workings started independently in the west, east and south (the pre-imperial kingdoms of Qin, Qi and Wu). More recently, both copper and iron have been mined in a number of widespread areas, with rich supplies of copper being available in Sichuan and Yunnan. Sources of iron are found in Manchuria and near the modern cities of Wuhan and Baotou, and it is in precisely these

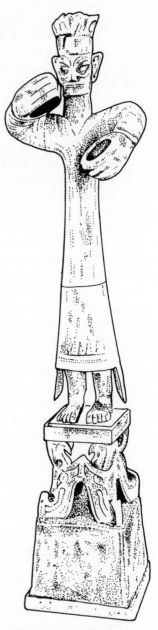

1. *Bronze figure of newly found type with local characteristics, from Sanxing-dui, Guanghan (Sichuan province); c. 1000 BC; height: 2.62 metres*

regions that modern industry has been concentrated. Of precious metals, silver deposits have been worked in the south-west; gold has been forthcoming from Heilongjiang and Xinjiang provinces.

Iron and salt soon came to be recognized as necessities of life for a people whose main occupation was that of tilling the soil and for whom cereals formed the staple diet. From about 120 BC the imperial government imposed a monopoly of state on both of these products in the hope that the goods would be distributed more fairly and efficiently, and that any profits that were forthcoming would accrue to the government rather than to the few private mine-owning magnates of the time. These monopolies operated sporadically rather than regularly, being revived in succeeding centuries from time to time; central or provincial governments were by no means always able to prevent evasion of the regulations or to control the practice of smuggling.

Salt was made both from the salt-pans of the Shandong coast and from deep mines situated in various parts of the interior. Coal has been found and worked in many areas, including Henan, Shaanxi, Gansu, Sichuan and the provinces of the north-east.

No reference to the gifts of China's soil can omit mention of jade, long prized as a life-giving substance whose enduring properties assure the presence of blessings both in this life and in the world to come, and whose soft beauties challenge the ingenuity and skills of artist and craftsman. Jade is found in two major forms, nephrite and jadeite. Nephrite, which is of superior quality, derives from sites in the extreme north-west, such as Khotan (Xinjiang provinces); this area lay long beyond the confines of Chinese territory, and was brought under the direct control of a Chinese government only from the eighteenth century. Jadeite is found in the south-west, principally in Yunnan province.

China's natural resources have seemingly been extensive, to the point that there has often been difficulty in exploiting the land to the full or finding the labour needed to collect all the fruits of the earth. But despite the proud claims of Chinese emperors that their domains are self-sufficient and require nothing from external sources, occasions of dearth have occurred only too frequently throughout the long history of the land.

The earliest surviving count of the registered population of the empire that is available is dated for AD 2, and from that we learn that the government reckoned that it could control some 60 million persons. As at later times, so then, the spread was anything but even, and a few centres of density could already be discerned (for example, in modern Shaanxi and Sichuan, and between the Yellow River and the Huai River). By c. 1000 the figure had risen to 100 million, and by the middle of the nineteenth century it had probably reached nearly 450 million, with new areas of concentration in the south. In the meantime the government of the land had moved from one dynasty to another, and long periods had intervened in which it had been split among two or more regimes. But throughout the centuries there had been no corresponding growth of material resources or of sources of energy; privation, famine and all too frequent death by starvation have marred the history of much of the countryside.

COMMUNICATIONS AND THE CENTRES OF GRAVITY

It has been seen how the major mountains and rivers separate the face of China into different regions; on a smaller scale isolated communities have survived to wrest a living from the soil in clefts lying between the hills, or in spots where an oasis can support a small number of families. In large areas it has at times been possible to establish an independent political regime, ruled by its own king or warlord and based on local supplies. In historical times it has been possible to do so in the basin of Sichuan with its well-watered rice field, its supplies of timber, salt-wells and iron, and the protection of its encircling hills. The peninsula of Shandong has likewise possessed resources such as salt, iron, grain fields and a capacity for manu-facturing cloth, which might well support an independent ruler. But it is further to the north-west, in the modern province of Shaanxi, that nature had provided protection of a type that attracted kings and emperors to establish their capital cities, whence they could extend their domains in an easterly or southerly direction. This area lay within the Qinling and Taihang mountains that surround Shaanxi on two of its sides; access lay by way of a few defined passes through the hills, and the area has been known as Guanzhong, or the 'Land within the Passes'.

Communications and the need to distribute staple goods have posed one of the major difficulties that governments have had to face. For comparatively short journeys the ox-drawn cart, the mule, the pack-ass and the Bactrian camel have rendered yeoman service; without such stalwart accomplices the peasant has necessarily should-ered these burdens on his own back. Small craft, manoeuvred with ease in many of China's lesser waters, have been in use up and down the land.

Grave drawbacks have limited the value of many of the major rivers. Until the tenth century, when the centres of authority were established in the north-west, it would seem that the Yellow River might well have constituted an admirable link with the east. However, the course of the river was highly unreliable, nor could it reach as far as would be desirable. Major floods, and major shifts of course, effectively prevented passage below Puyang, the point where the main channel could abruptly turn, either to the north or to the south of the Shandong peninsula. Further upstream the carriage of goods was severely hampered by a series of rocks or islets that lie athwart the river, often forcing the boatmen to unload their cargoes and carry them over land for reshipment for the final stages of the journey into the Guanzhong area. This obstruction, known as the Sanmen ('Three Gates') gorge, lay upstream from Luoyang.

When, from perhaps 1150, the centre and south came to assume greater importance than the north, the Yangzi, with its strong currents and dramatic changes of level, could prove to be equally intractable for cargo-laden craft; stretches of the river that lie locked between cliffs cannot serve as a link between the fertile basin of Sichuan and the cities that were growing apace downstream towards the sea. In addition, there was no viable natural link between north and south that could join Shaanxi with the rice-fields of the Yangzi River valley, or with Sichuan. Nor could effective communication be made by way of the Han River, between the north-western fortress of Guanzhong and the fertile reaches of the middle Yangzi; for the Qinling mountains lay between the two.

It is in such circumstances that canals came to be dug, to supplement nature's waterways. One of the earliest examples, the Honggou canal, was cut to link the Yangzi with the Huai River and was in use perhaps during the fifth century BC. Doubtless construction of this and other canals was eased by the use of iron tools which enabled a passage to be drilled through rocky terrain. But the greatest achievements of China's man-made waterways are seen in the two systems known as the Grand Canal.

These projects arose owing to two major shifts of balance that took place in imperial times (221 BC to 1911). The two systems of the Grand Canal served strategic considerations and economic needs as these developed during the centuries, and as successive dynasties established their imperial capitals in different situations. Each of these shifts of balance, the one from the north to the south and the other from the north-east to the north-west, was a long drawn-out process.

In AD 317 the pressure of non-Chinese peoples from the north forced the native dynastic house of Jin (Tsin), which had been centred in Luoyang and Chang'an (modern Xi'an), to seek refuge in the south, and found a new capital at Jiankang (near modern Nanjing) on the lower reaches of the Yangzi River valley. Thereafter the government of the subcontinent was split between two or more authorities for nearly three centuries, and a move had started whereby the south was eventually to grow more populous than the north, and the south was to become the main scene of economic experiment. As a result the significance of the south began to grow, both as a centre of administrative importance and as a rice-producing area whose supplies were required in the north. When, in 589, imperial rule was re-established under a single dynasty, that of Sui, the new government was able to conscript a large force of manpower to construct a system of waterways that would connect its government, at Chang'an, with the granaries of the middle Yangzi region.

It was in this way that the first version of the Grand Canal was built, partly on the basis of natural waterways and partly by means of digging artificial links to connect them. The main course of the canal, which was completed by c. 600, drove in a north-westerly direction, so as to reach the metropolitan area of Guanzhong. Construction and maintenance presented considerable problems, with the need to provide for the different levels of the terrain that was traversed; effective use depended on a series of locks, and on a readiness to co-operate in a systematic plan for the passage of all craft. Towards the middle of the ninth century the canal conveyed the Japanese monk and diarist Ennin on a religious mission to the north-west. In the meantime the canal had served to improve the government's hold on the adjoining territories and the population that lived along the banks of the Yangzi River. The Tang emperors (618–907) could reflect that some quarter of their subjects came from these parts, as contrasted with the tenth that had been registered there during the days of the Han governments (206 BC to AD 220).

As in 317, so in 1127, a native house fled south in the face of foreign invaders, and the Song government was established at the city known now as Hangzhou. Amid the intellectual initiative and brilliance which characterized the period, agriculture, communications and commerce developed steadily, thanks partly to the introduction of new technology. Cities arose on the banks of the Yangzi and elsewhere to house the increasing population of the area, much of which was now engaged in city life rather than the work of the fields. Imperial governments were imposing more intensive control on the provinces of the seaboard than had been possible previously. It was from the Yangzi River valley that for the first time an imperial dynasty, that of Ming, arose in the south to establish its hold over the whole of China (1368); by the middle of the nineteenth century at the latest the south had achieved economic dominance as compared with the north.

In the meantime a second shift of balance had been taking place.

Until the end of the ninth century the empires had been founded in the north-west and had established their capital cities there. But the non-Chinese peoples and leaders who forced the Song house to a southern exile in 1127 had originated in the north-east. Their ties lay with their original habitat in Manchuria, and their incursion into the Chinese plain took the form of an advance in a south-westerly direction. They therefore chose to establish their seats of power in China close to their original habitat, at sites whence they could communicate with their base and co-ordinate their military plans. In this way the city now known as Beijing was chosen as the capital of the Liao and Jin (Kin) rulers, who could command the northern part of the subcontinent (between 947 and 1125, and 1115 and 1234). The city next served the Mongol emperors of the Yuan dynasty (1260–1368), once they had secured their rule over the whole of the land; and shortly after the foundation of the Ming dynasty (1368) Beijing was again adopted as the imperial capital, remaining thus until the end of the imperial era.

In economic terms a new situation had arisen. No longer was it of prime priority to supply the north-west with grain and rice from the south; along with the change of capital there had occurred an increase of population, and it was now necessary to transport supplies to the north-east. It was in such circumstances that the masters of the Yuan dynasty embarked on building the second version of the Grand Canal, which was completed c. 1290. To reach the neighbourhood of Beijing the course followed a northerly direction from south of the Yangzi river, crossing the Yellow River at right angles and skirting the foothills of the Shandong peninsula. The waterway brought north the grain that the cities needed and the silk that the palace demanded by way of taxation. It also carried the Earl of Macartney, an emissary of the British government, on his journey from Guangzhou (Canton) to seek an audience with the Qianlong emperor in 1793.

The choice of the site for the capital city, the changing needs of the economy and the value of communications may be exemplified in three situations, each pertaining to a time when a single dynasty claimed to govern the land. During the Han dynasty, when the capital lay behind the defences of the Taihang and Qinling mountains, the problem lay in transporting grain from the east, despite the difficulties of the Yellow River and its vagaries. In the Tang dynasty, when the seat of government likewise lay at Chang'an, or Luoyang, it was necessary to bring supplies from the south-east to the north-west, and in the absence of natural links the first version of the Grand Canal served the capital's needs. By the Yuan, Ming and Qing dynasties the second Grand Canal enabled the governments to call on the rice grown in the Yangzi River valley and to maintain contact with the wealthy emporia whose newly developing prosperity and technical achievements were stamping new characteristics on the economy.

Officials, merchants and bandits would need to make their way by land as well as by water. Imperial carriageways, ordered to a specified width, and roads designed for military purposes were known from the earliest days of the empires, either to convey the emperor on a progress to distant parts of his realm, or to ease the movement of troops to danger spots in the north. Official couriers carried their reports on foot or, if express, on horseback; for the latter there was established ·a system of post-stations and inns where the travellers could change horses and spend the night. By 100 BC routines existed for the conveyance of mail to the outlying posts of the defence lines, near Dunhuang, and surviving records testify to the efficiency of the system. From such beginnings there started the postal service of China, which has been operated with varying degrees of success throughout the centuries, reaching a high point during the Yuan dynasty of the Mongols. Schedules that have been worked out for the nineteenth century show that messengers from Beijing reached Guangzhou after fifty-six days on foot, or thirty-two days on horseback. In the eighth century fresh fruit from the extreme south was being delivered regularly for the delectation of the emperor's favourite, feasting happily in Chang'an, regardless of the human suffering involved in the transport of her delicacies.

*

The rich and varied face of China's landscape bears witness to the problems that have beset man in his struggle to wrest a living from the earth and the ingenuity with which he has devised techniques to solve them. The results are seen in the terraced platforms, sown with rice, that gird the hills (Sichuan); in the folds of loess territory, bare and brown in winter, ready to sprout with fresh growth come the new season (Gansu); in the dazzling fields of rape-seed, reaching their full brilliance as early as March and demanding a never-ending supply of labour at harvest time (Sichuan); in the stubble left after the second rice harvest has been lifted, perhaps in November (Hunan); and in the timber floated down the Gui River, winding its course through the limestone crags that stand like towers against the skyline. Boatman and porter, drover with his cart and ploughman with his ox, symbolize the work spent over the centuries in mastering the difficulties of the land.

II

KINGDOMS AND EMPIRES: MOMENTS OF DYNASTIC CHANGE

Changes of religious faith, intellectual outlook or economic practice may well affect the lives of men and women with a far sharper impact than those of a political nature. Nevertheless, the traditional historians of China, who were writing to serve their imperial masters, had perforce to compile their officially commissioned histories within the framework of the rise and fall of dynasties. As their work forms the basic primary material that is available for study, such a framework, faulty and misleading as it may be, has remained the standard means of dividing Chinese history into discrete periods. Dynastic titles, such as Han, Tang, Song, Ming and Qing, have thus been used as catchwords in much the same way as Plantagenet and Tudor, Middle Kingdom and Quatrocento.

Some dynastic periods lasted for only a few decades, others for perhaps up to three centuries, and they can hardly be treated as separate units of history, each worthy of the same degree of attention. Nevertheless, reference by means of the dates and titles of kingdoms and empires retains considerable value in so far as it may form a benchmark against which innovations in philosophy, government and social structure may be set. But before such events are considered, the story must reach back to the earliest traces of mankind in China's prehistory.

THE STAGES OF PREHISTORY

The dramatic discoveries of archaeology of the last few decades have transformed our knowledge of these early stages. Perhaps 800,000 years ago, man's ancestors (*Sinanthropus lantienensis*) were shaping choppers and other stone tools at Lantian (Shaanxi province). Other finds at Yuanmo (Yunnan province), which were at first thought to have been from about a million years before that, are now dated at some 600,000 years ago, thus predating the activities of *Sinanthropus pekinensis* (Peking man) by perhaps 100,000 years. Discovered at Zhoukoudian (near Beijing) in 1918, the remains of Peking man

TABLE 1

DYNASTIC SEQUENCES

Pre-Imperial History

Xia	? ?
Shang (traditional dates)	1766–1122 BC
Western Zhou (trad.)	1122–771
Eastern Zhou	771–256

(The following terms are also used:

Spring and Autumn:	722–481
Warring States:	481 or 403–221)

The Early Empires

Qin	221–207
Former (Western) Han	206 (202) BC to AD 9
Xin (Wang Mang)	AD 9–23
Later (Eastern) Han	25–220

The Centuries of Disunity

Wu 222–80   Shu-Han 221–263   Wei 220–64

(The period 221–80 is known as the Three Kingdoms)

Western Jin (Tsin)	265–316
Eastern Jin (Tsin)	317–419

Song 420–78	North Wei 386–535		
Qi 479–501	West Wei 535–56	East Wei 534–50
Liang 502–56	North Zhou 557–80	North Qi 550–77
Chen 557–89			

(The period 386—589 is sometimes termed the North and South Dynasties, or the Six Dynasties)

The Medieval Empires

Sui		589 (581)–618	
Tang		618–907	
Ten Kingdoms	907–79	Five Dynasties 907–59	
Song	960–1127	Liao 947–1125	
Southern Song	1127–1279	Jin (Kin) 1115–1234	Xi Xia 1038–1227

The later empires

Yuan	1260–1368	(dynastic title adopted 1271)
Ming	1368–1644	
Qing	1644–1911	

The Post-Imperial Period

Republic	1912–49
People's Republic	1949–

were long taken to be the earliest surviving traces of man to be found. The complex site of this cave, which comprises twenty-two localities, yielded remains of at least forty individuals, including some complete skulls. Peking man stood erect; he controlled fire with which to cook the meat that he had caught and dressed with his stone implements; and, with a cranium that was two-thirds the size of that of modern man, he was capable of meaningful speech. The many other sites of the palaeolithic stages of mankind include that of Kehe (close to the Yellow River) with artefacts that had been reshaped during the course of use, and Sjara-osso-gol (Inner Mongolia) with its characteristic Ordos culture.

Several hundred thousands of years later came the neolithic revolution. Man was tilling the earth, and with the spread of agriculture there came his need to husband his hard-won produce in storage vessels. On the basis of most of the evidence which was then available, mainly from the north-west, archaeologists of the 1930s regarded the Yellow River as the 'cradle' of Chinese civilization, and distinguished two principal cultures, of Yangshao and Longshan. Yangshao, in Henan, is the name of one of many sites of that province which yielded characteristic wares of black and red, often decorated with geometric or linear patterns. Similar sites are known in Shanxi and Shaanxi. The Longshan sites from further east (Shandong) produced, more rarely, examples of altogether different wares, made of a black lustrous pottery.

More recently the large number of sites found scattered throughout China, together with the realization that agriculture may be traced to the sixth millennium BC, has forced a complete review of the subject. Sites found in the east and the south must be regarded as originating independently of the culture of the Yellow River valley, and can in no sense be identified as outcrops of the types previously distinguished as Yangshao and Longshan. Altogether five major stages can be discriminated, ranging from an incipient neolithic, of perhaps before the sixth millennium, to late neolithic, of the third millennium and perhaps later. Each of these major stages is further subdivided, and any scheme that may be suggested can only be subject to revision in the light of newly forthcoming evidence. One particular discovery worthy of mention concerns the early cultivation of rice, now placed at c. 5000 BC, at a site named Hemudu (Zhejiang province).

The wealth of new evidence prompts a number of questions; of the relation between technical innovations and social differentiation, or whether the production of luxury artefacts, such as bone ornaments, sprang from religious causes. In general, the identification of types of China's neolithic cultures must take account of the choice

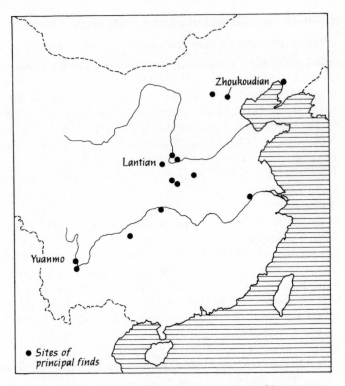

2. *Principal palaeolithic sites (after K. C. Chang)*

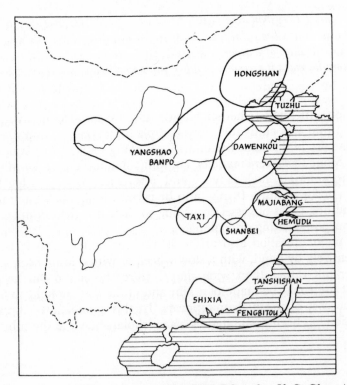

3. *Neolithic cultural zones 4000–3000 BC (after K. C. Chang)*

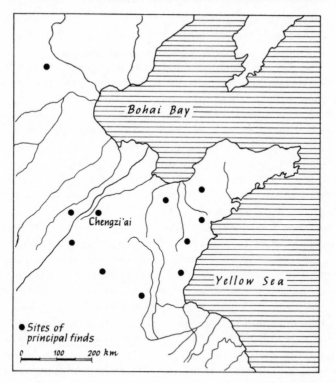

4. The coastal Longshan area (after K. C. Chang). At one time some of the particular finds at Chengzi'ai, such as wares of a lustrous black pottery were regarded as evidence of a separate characteristic culture. More recent research and discoveries make it necessary to allow for a much more complex situation

of site for settlement (whether hillside, forest clearance or cave); of the crop that was cultivated, for example millet or rice; and above all of the use of different materials for making tools (horn, bone or stone). Stone tools were made by chipping, hammering or polishing; precious materials, such as ivory and jade, could be used either for luxuries or for utilities. It may also be asked whether a community distinguished types of vessel according to their use, for example for ritual purposes, eating or cooking.

The major question also arises of whether pottery vessels were made entirely by hand, with a slow wheel, or with a fast wheel; and whether tall rather than wide shapes were chosen, so that more efficient use could be made of a kiln and of the fuel brought to fire it at the cost of so much manpower. In this connection a broad distinction has been postulated by some scholars between the culture of the north-west, where vases were fashioned in one piece with broad bases, and those of the east with their slender vessels in which several component parts had been joined together to form an articulated whole. Possibly the difference may reflect the growth of two different attitudes to life, the one of easy acceptance, the other of shrewd calculation.

Chinese mythology refers frequently enough to named monarchs who were alleged to have reigned in the remote past. It is hardly surprising that such accounts, which arose at different times, are far from consistent, and that the names of the rulers who are cited are not identical. The somewhat standardized references of later times may mention these heroes collectively as the 'Three Sovereigns' (*San huang*) or the 'Five Monarchs' (*Wu di*).

In addition, Chinese traditionalists of later times looked back with nostalgia to the three eras of the Xia, Shang and Zhou kings, as a golden age which had witnessed just government, popular contentment and material prosperity. There is no doubt of the historicity of the kings of Shang and Zhou, but no direct evidence supports a claim that these had been preceded by an earlier kingdom, named Xia. However, recent finds that are datable at the close of the neolithic period but before that of the Shang kingdom show traces of a markedly sophisticated way of life that may have depended on the control of a leader or king. Early metallurgy and the use of signs in writing may even be present. In chronological sequence such sites would correspond with the existence of a kingdom which had preceded Shang, but positive identification as settlements of the Xia kingdom still awaits demonstration.

PRE-IMPERIAL HISTORY

With the kings of Shang we may claim to leave prehistory and enter history; for contemporary records survive to tell of their way of life and religious practices, and such records are consistent both with archaeological discoveries and with references to the Shang kingdom in histories that were written some 1,500 years afterwards. Royal attention to religious practice, the earliest attested examples of the Chinese script, the manufacture of bronze vessels and the use of horse-drawn carriages distinguish the Shang age sharply from its predecessors.

Kings of the house of Shang, later termed Yin, reigned from perhaps the eighteenth to the twelfth centuries BC. Accession followed a complex system, being at one time from brother to brother and eventually from father to son. The kings were settled in a comparatively small area around the middle reaches of the Yellow River, as is known from the situation of the principal sites excavated so far, at Anyang and Zhengzhou. Gradually their centre of control moved from the south to the north bank. They could command the services of scribes or officials who could write, and of their many subjects, who were put to work at building houses, by stamped earth methods, digging ditches for irrigation or campaigning against an enemy. Above all, the kings could co-ordinate the work of a large force of manpower for fashioning precious objects whose religious significance was of paramount importance, but whose immediate benefit in material terms was by no means obvious.

Believing in the power of occult forces to reveal guidance to man, the kings of Shang practised a characteristic form of divination with the use of turtles' shells or animals' bones. The engraved inscriptions which survive on such pieces and which first came to the attention of scholars in c. 1900 constitute an archive of the Shang royal house. The system of writing was already comparatively far advanced, and had probably followed stages for which no or little evidence survives. The inscriptions tell of the regular and frequent performance of sacrifices and services to the gods, accompanied sometimes by music and dance. They refer to the work of the fields, on which the majority of the population were engaged, and to that of domesticating animals and fashioning vessels of pottery or implements of stone or bone. There are references to the king's hunting expeditions and his plans for warfare.

Sites identified as the tombs of kings supplement the evidence of the shells and bones. Eleven large chambers, carefully dug and constructed to be the resting place for leaders of the land, reveal the practice of honouring them with an escort of human sacrifices and burial of horses and carriage in the same tomb. Above all the contents of the tombs demonstrate the high degree of artistry and technical ability of the bronzesmiths of the age. They turned out weapons of war and equipment used in the carriages, and they fashioned vessels designed for religious purposes, in a rich variety of types. Many examples include a mark or sign, of either ownership or manufacture, which relied on the use of moulds. The intricate décor of these vessels was of an exceptionally high order, often incorporating a stylized face or mask, which evidently acted as a talisman, invoking a blessing or forfending a curse.

In the middle of the twelfth, or perhaps the eleventh century BC the kings of Zhou replaced those of Shang as the leaders of a centrally recognized authority. They may well have made their way into China from the west, to found their kingdom within the fastnesses of the Guangzhong area.

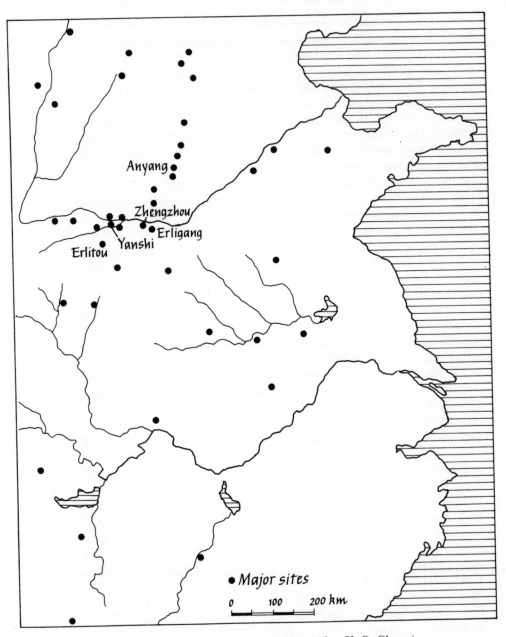

5. *Sites of settlement in the Shang period (after K. C. Chang)*

With the passage of the centuries the people over whose lives these kings presided attained new cultural standards. Organs of government, social distinctions and political aims came to be identified with greater clarity and significance, and new relationships developed between a sovereign, his assistant ministers and his subjects.

There can be little certainty regarding the character of these kings or the extent of their authority. Formulated considerably later, the Chinese tradition has singled out Wen Wang and Wu Wang, the first kings, as the exemplary successful founders of a blessed dispensation. Similarly the Duke of Zhou has received repeated adulation for selflessly presiding over a regency at a time when a young king still in his minority (Cheng Wang) had acceded, rather than choosing to exploit the situation in his own interests. Two other kings, Li Wang (tenth in the line: reigned 878–827 BC) and You Wang (twelfth in the line: reigned 781–770 BC), stand out in the tradition as examples of monarchs whose weak dispositions and frail characters led to dynastic ruin.

From perhaps 500 BC the kings of Zhou – with the exceptions just named – were regarded as ideal monarchs whose dispensation over all civilized humanity rested on ideal institutions. This view was nostalgic, and there was little hard evidence available to support it at the time when it was being propagated. Nevertheless it came to exert a profound influence on the subsequent forms and institutions of China's governments which persisted until the close of the nineteenth century. The view owed much to the teachings ascribed to Kongfuzi or Confucius (traditional dates 551–479 BC). It was thanks largely to this that the kings of Zhou were seen as reigning under the blessing of Heaven, and in accordance with a code of behaviour that ensured the stability of human society.

The line of the Zhou kings survived until 256 BC. But however lofty their ideals had been, or were believed to have been, their strength as ruling monarchs had been in no sense pervasive throughout the land for the eight centuries in question. It was claimed that their authority extended over wide areas north of the Yangzi River, and that in the domains that lay beyond their immediate centre locally established leaders owed fealty and homage to those kings. How far the leaders at the perimeter received their initial authority or title to rule from the kings of Zhou, how far they were bound by contract to serve those kings or how far their rise was completely independent are questions that may well remain subject to controversy. The description of China as 'feudal' at that time can only be accepted with reserve.

The decline of Zhou's strength forms a constant theme in these

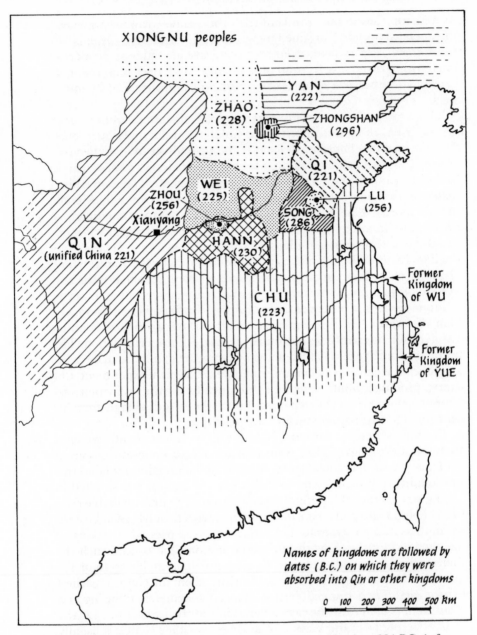

6. *The kingdoms of China on the eve of the first unification, 221 BC (after Ōba)*

centuries. Traditionally the king's move to a new capital in the east near the later city of Luoyang in 771 BC was seen by Chinese historians as a humiliation forced upon him by weakness. Thereafter a number of political groupings, independent kingdoms and confederacies arose, and claims that the kings of Zhou exercised a unique rule in China could not be supported in fact. In the course of the major economic developments and social changes of the eighth century BC and later, *de facto* rulers arose with their own royal courts and attendant ministers, relying if they could on the independent sources of supply that could be found, for example, in east China. In time some of the smaller units merged together, or were united by conquest. The surviving chronicles for the years 722–481 BC relate tales of alliance and warfare, of solemn compact and intrigue between the states, and of attempts to form a confederacy independently of the kings of Zhou.

By 403 BC the rule of China was divided between Zhou, whose territory had been severely contracted, a few other small units and the self-styled kings, with a system of hereditary succession, of seven major states. The names of those states – Qin, Wei, Hann, Zhao, Qi, Chu and Yan – were to recur in later times, being often re-adopted as dynastic titles at times of disunity during the imperial period. The fifth and fourth centuries BC witnessed the growth of some of the most significant elements in Chinese thought and political experiment; but they were marked and marred by alliance and intrigue, by plot and counterplot, as one kingdom sought to wrest advantage from its neighbour and to take over its territories.

The terminology used to describe these centuries is at first sight somewhat confusing. The term Western Zhou denotes the period starting with the foundation of the Zhou kingdom, taken traditionally at 1122 BC, and lasting while the capital was situated in the west. It is for this period that we possess the first verifiable date in Chinese history, thanks to the eclipse recorded for 841 BC. 'Eastern Zhou' is used to designate the remaining centuries when a king of Zhou was enthroned, with his capital lying to the east; as such the term accords greater political significance to that house than the situation warranted. Following the title of one of China's earliest chronicles, *The Spring and Autumn Annals*, the expression 'Spring and Autumn' is used for the years covered in that book, that is, 722–481 BC. The period 481–221 BC, or sometimes 403–221 BC, is usually described as that of the Warring States.

THE EARLY EMPIRES

It was from this situation that there emerged the first empire, the first regime which could claim to being the sole effective authority in the land. Qin had been one of the seven contending kingdoms of the Warring States period. By dint of resolution, discipline and courage it had extended its domain by conquest or annexation, first over the rich lands of the Sichuan basin, thereafter over those of Qin's neighbouring kingdoms to the east. By 221 BC the process was complete; all the other kings had yielded to *force majeure*, and their lands had been incorporated as administrative units of Qin. As a mark of his newly acquired status, the king of Qin adopted the new title of *Huangdi*, usually translated as 'Emperor'. Until 1911 the subsequent rulers of all China, or the masters of part of its territories, all laid claim to the exclusive use of this same title.

TABLE 2

THE EARLY EMPIRES: RELATIONS WITH NON-CHINESE
PEOPLES AND THE EXTENSION OF IMPERIAL AUTHORITY

Major Dynastic Developments

221 BC	Foundation of the Qin empire.
210	Death of the first Qin emperor.
206	Liu Bang accepts the title King of Han.
202	Liu Bang assumes the title of Han emperor.
141–87	Reign of Han Wudi.
111–104 BC	Han influence extended by the establishment of twenty-four commanderies in the north-west (to Dunhuang), Korea, the south and south-west (in modern Guangdong, Yunnan, Hainan and Vietnam).
AD 6	Death of Pingdi; Wang Mang as regent.
9–23	Wang Mang as emperor of the Xin dynasty.
25	Accession of Guangwudi, first emperor of the Later Han dynasty.
220	Abdication of Xiandi, last of the Han emperors. Start of the Three Kingdoms period.

Relations with the Xiongnu

221–214 BC	Qin's construction of the first 'Great Wall' as a defence against the Xiongnu; Meng Tian's campaigns against the Xiongnu.
166	Xiongnu penetration close to Chang'an.
121, 119	Han defeat of Xiongnu forces; varied relations with Xiongnu follow for three centuries.
51 BC	Visit of Xiongnu leader (Shanyu) to Chang'an.

first century AD	Han policy of *divide et impera*, with two groups of Xiongnu (north and south); settlement of some southern Xiongnu in Chinese territory.
73, 89	Northern Xiongnu defeated by Han.
311–17	Xiongnu penetration of north China; flight of Jin (Tsin) court to the south.

Extension of Influence to the North-West and West

130–120 BC	Zhang Qian's journeys to north India.
104–101	Li Guangli's campaigns in Central Asia.
c. 100	Extension of armed causeway and defences to Dunhuang; new trade routes (the 'Silk Roads') operative in the west; Han relations with oasis communities of Central Asia and beyond.
from *c.* 100	Incorporation of Qiang (proto-Tibetan) peoples in Han commanderies.
99 and 90	Defeat of Li Ling and Li Guangli by Xiongnu and others in Central Asia.
60 BC	Establishment of the Protector-General to co-ordinate colonization and Han relations with the communities of Central Asia.
AD 120	Embassy from Shan kingdom (Burma).
126	Successful extension of Han influence in Central Asia by Ban Chao and Ban Yong.
184–221	Rebellion by Qiang tribes of north-west against Han authority.

The North-East and Japan

108 BC	Han influence established in Korea.
AD 49	Incorporation of Wuhuan leaders and peoples of the north-east within Han authority.
57	Gift of a Han official seal to a leader from the Japanese islands.
107	Embassy from Japanese leaders.
150–80	Growth of Xianbi power and threats to China under the leadership of Tanshihuai.
187	Revolt of Wuhuan peoples in the north-east.

The South

AD 42–3	Ma Yuan's suppression of a revolt by the Trung sisters (in Vietnam).
166	Visit to south China by traders from the Roman world.

Following his successful unification of the land, the first emperor faced the task of organization on a far larger scale than that of any previous ruler. With the advice of Li Si, his senior minister, and

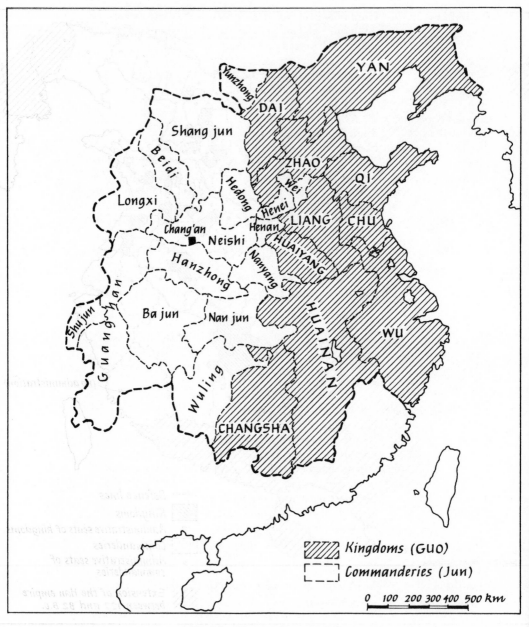

	Kingdoms (GUO)
	Commanderies (Jun)

0 100 200 300 400 500 km

7. *The Han empire, 195 BC*

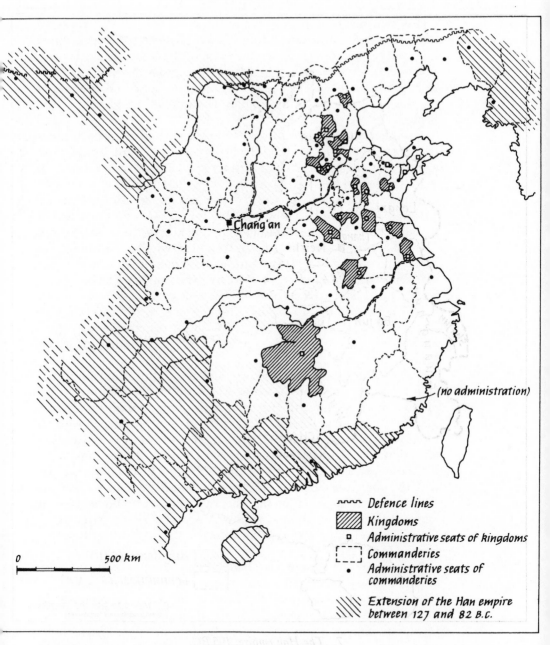

Chang'an

(no administration)

Defence lines
Kingdoms
□ **Administrative seats of kingdoms**
Commanderies
• **Administrative seats of commanderies**
Extension of the Han empire between 127 and 82 B.C.

0   500 km

8. *The Han empire, AD 2*

Comparison of these two maps shows how large areas, originally made over to kinsmen of the emperor to be governed as kingdoms within the empire, were in time reduced and finally absorbed within the lands directly under the central government. The names of some of the kingdoms are identical with those of the pre-imperial era (see map 6 on p. 24). These maps also show the extent to which Han territories had been increased during the two centuries others, new institutions were evolved whereby the administration of large areas, extending beyond the Yangzi River, could be controlled from the centre; measures were introduced to standardize economic practice, to implement imperial laws throughout the provinces and to co-ordinate defences against the Xiongnu, potential enemies of the north; in this way China's first 'Great Wall' was brought into being.

But the regime was short-lived. The political and dynastic disputes that broke out at the death of the first emperor (210 BC) ushered in a period of rebellion and civil warfare, amid attempts to re-establish some of the earlier kingdoms that Qin had eliminated. Of two principal protagonists, Xiang Yu and Liu Bang, who eventually emerged, it was Liu Bang, king of Han in 206 BC, who succeeded in founding the next imperial dynasty, named after his own kingdom (202 BC). Although dynastic unity and strength were subject to threat and political breakdown at frequent intervals during the next two centuries, the Former, or Western, Han empire survived until AD 9. It had improved considerably on Qin's organs of government; it had faced the threats of the Xiongnu and partly succeeded in establishing a secure frontier. Its officials were penetrating and operating in far wider areas, and trade routes had been established which led into Central Asia.

After some decades of weakness and instability, the rule of the Han emperors was interrupted in AD 9, when Wang Mang set up his own dynasty under the name of Xin. Wang Mang's family had long served the Han house. While his assertion of independence is usually described as an act of usurpation, and his dynasty came to an end in AD 23, he left his successors with an ideological precedent that no subsequent empire could ignore. He had linked imperial rule with the universal order of being, and by building on the work of his predecessors he had ensured that the ways of Zhou would henceforth figure as the ideal of Chinese empire. A period of civil war preceded the restoration of the house of Liu, known as that of Later, or Eastern, Han (AD 25–220).

By now greater complexity had been making its way into the organs of government and a professional civil service was emerging. New campaigns reasserted the force of the Chinese presence in Central Asia and elsewhere. But the dynastic story was marred by bitter quarrels among the rival families at court. Palace and government were subject to the ambitions of different families of imperial consorts; from time to time politics were liable to intervention or domination by eunuchs. Political factionalism weakened the unity of the empire and encouraged the growth of social instability. Although the house survived until 220, the revolt of the Yellow

Turbans in 184 may be taken as marking the effective end of Han dynastic strength. In the meantime, security had been threatened by a number of peoples, some of which had been exerting pressure from the north-east.

THE CENTURIES OF DISUNITY

The rise of independent leaders and their effective occupation of territories led to the formation of the Three Kingdoms: Wei (220), in the Yellow River valley and the north-west; Shu-Han (221), in the west (including modern Sichuan); and Wu (222), in the lower Yangzi valley and to the south. Each kingdom hoped to survive and to extend its power with the help of its own economic resources and military strength, and the period of the Three Kingdoms witnessed considerable fighting. The unification of China that was achieved by the Jin (Tsin) dynasty for a short period from 265 or 280 was disrupted by the pressure of Xiongnu leaders from Central Asia, who sacked Luoyang in 311 and captured Chang'an in 317. At this juncture the Jin (Tsin) court fled to the south, establishing its seat of government at Jiankang, close to the later city of Nanjing.

From now until 589 the government of China was divided among two series of short-lived regimes, which succeeded one another in the north and the south respectively. In general, the Yangzi River formed the natural division between the two, and the period is known as that of the North and South Dynasties, or the Six Dynasties. Most of the regimes which were established in the north were of non-Chinese stock; exceptionally the house of Northern (sometimes termed Later) Wei, founded by Toba peoples of the north-east, survived for 150 years (386–535), and adopted a number of Chinese characteristics and habits in the process of governing the country. The south-westwards move of the Wei capital in 493 to Luoyang, one of the traditional seats of Chinese empires, the adoption of a new system of land tenure on the advice of a Chinese statesman and the promotion that it gave to Buddhism mark stages in the assimilation of the Wei court to a Chinese way of life.

The rivalries of these many dynastic houses or soldiers of fortune frequently led to warfare, much of which was directed towards winning control of the grain-growing lands of the lower Yellow River valley and the Huai River valley. The period of disunity was brought to a close when one of the minor kingdoms succeeded in eliminating its coexistent rivals. Yang Jian established his dynasty of Sui in 581, and by 589 he was able to assert a claim to exercise sole authority as the single ruler of China.

THE MEDIEVAL EMPIRES

Short-lived and soon to be followed by a more successful house, the Sui dynasty has been denigrated as oppressive; its achievements lay in the co-ordination of waterways to form the first of China's Grand Canals, its adoption of new institutions that suited the political, scholastic and social developments of the preceding centuries and the inauguration of a new system of examinations for entry to the civil service; but the campaigns that it initiated in Korea were expensive and ineffective.

TABLE 3

THE MEDIEVAL EMPIRES: RELATIONS WITH NON-CHINESE PEOPLES AND THE EXTENSION OF IMPERIAL AUTHORITY

Major Dynastic Developments

581–604	Reign of Sui Wendi.
604–17	Reign of Sui Yangdi.
618	Foundation of the Tang dynasty.
626–49	Reign of Tang Taizong.
684–705	Wu Zetian dominant at court; empress from 690.
712–56	Reign of Xuanzong; Kaiyuan period 713–41; Tianbao period 742–56.
755–63	Rebellion of An Lushan and others.
907	Formal end of Tang empire.

Relations with the Turks and Central Asia

552 onwards	Emergence of eastern and western Turkish confederacies, operative from the Liao River (Manchuria) to the borders of Persia.
630	Taizong's pacification of the eastern Turks; Tang expansion into Central Asia.
657	Chinese defeat of western Turks (Issyk-Kul battle).
660–70	Chinese power established in the Tarim basin, Zungharia and Ili valley.
682–716	Reassertion of eastern Turkish strength and pressure on Chinese borders.
744	Rise of Uighur power from Central Asia (Orkhon River).
795–835	Height of Uighurs' power; economic pressure on Chinese court.

The West, South-West and South

634	Diplomatic relations between the Tang court and newly arisen Tibetan kings; rise of Tibetan expansive power.
696	Tibetan defeat of large Chinese army.
714	Tibetan invasion of China, followed by defeat.
739	Establishment of the independent kingdom of Nanzhao (modern Yunnan).
763	Tibetan occupation and looting of Chang'an for two weeks; Tibetan occupation of north-west China with continued pressure on Chinese.
842	Collapse of Tibetan kingdom; Uighur occupation of the north-west.
858	Exercise of strength by Nanzhao in Sichuan and Vietnam.
939	Independent state established in Vietnam.

Contacts with the East and North-East

598–613	Unsuccessful Sui campaigns of conquest in Korea.
607	First formal mission from Japan.
c. 680	Emergence of Silla as the dominant power in Korea.
696	Rise of independent Khitan strength in the north-east and Khitan rebels' defeat of Chinese near Beijing.
712	Emergence of independent kingdom of Bohai (Parhai) in the north-east.
894	Last formal mission from Japan until 1404.

Contacts with the Western World

635	Arrival of Nestorian monks at Chang'an.
638	Sassanid Persian envoy sent to Chang'an.
643	Byzantine mission sent to Chang'an.
651	Arab envoys in Chang'an.
751	Chinese forces defeated by Arabs at the battle of the Talas River.
781	Nestorian Tablet erected in Chang'an.

The Sui dynasty was brought to an end with the foundation of that of Tang, in 618, by a family whose roots lay in the north-west. Although his path to the throne lay by way of intrigue and bloodshed, Taizong, the second emperor (reigned 626–49), has often been regarded as one of China's most able rulers. But in later years the dynastic line failed to produce emperors of similarly strong character; the palace came under the domination of an empress or empress dowager, notably the empress Wu, who assumed her own dynastic title from 690 to 705, and the empress Wei who exercised considerable power for some years around 710. Of the other and later emperors, two deserve mention: Xuanzong, who reigned for over forty years (712–56), at a time which saw considerable cultural achievements; and Xianzong (806–20) for his determination, albeit unavailing, to restore the fortunes of a dynasty that had reached a period of decline.

In its early decades the Tang dynasty adopted or adapted a set of sophisticated institutions designed to co-ordinate and intensify the operation of central and provincial administration; to regulate and control landholdings and the collection of revenue; and to provide regular recruits for the armed forces. But it proved impossible to implement such measures over a long period of time and over the large and varied extent of the Tang dominions. For these had been widened considerably by the efforts of explorers, officials and diplomats, whose influence was now felt in lands that lay deep in Central Asia. Such extension is itself a mark of the strength that the Tang governments were able to deploy in face of the continual potential threats to security from confederations under Turkish, Tibetan or other leaders.

To achieve this degree of expansion the Tang governments had been obliged to delegate considerable powers, both civil and military, to a number of regional commissioners, often of non-Chinese extraction. From such circumstances there arose a highly dangerous situation, in which the central government could be denied control of the perimeter; and it was precisely in this way that a major rebellion, mounted by An Lushan, broke out in 755. Forced to flee from his capital city, Xuanzong abdicated his position; but it was not until 763 that the series of rebellions that had been started was brought to an end, largely thanks to the help of Uighur troops, from Central Asia.

Thereafter the Tang dynasty never recovered its strength, despite attempts to do so in the reign of Xianzong (805–20); of the further rebellions that occurred during the second half of the eighth century and the ninth century, at a time of growing economic weakness, that of Huang Chao (874–84) was one of the most serious, once again forcing an emperor to flee from his capital. It was on this occasion that a city which was the forerunner of the later Guangzhou (Canton) was sacked, to the great distress and suffering of the Arab population that had established its trading centre there. The last of the Tang emperors was deposed in 907.

The Tang capital cities of Chang'an and Luoyang had been sites of some of the most important and flourishing cultural centres of the world. They drew embassies from Japan to learn of China's way of life; they housed a cosmopolitan population, engaged in practising its trade or promoting its religions, be they of Manichaean, Muslim

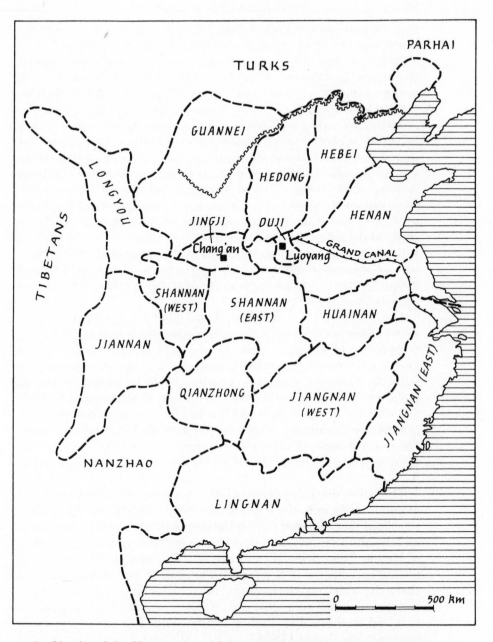

9. *Circuits of the Tang empire, AD 742. Administrative units were grouped together as circuits (dao) within which a single commissioner inspected the work of provincial officials, reporting directly to the central government. The circuits as such did not constitute provincial units with their own organs of government*

or Nestorian Christian persuasion. While Buddhism had enjoyed the sponsorship of some emperors, there came a time (845) when its wealth provoked envy and destruction. In the meantime the new outlook on government of the Tang age had led to the growth of a professional civil service, and to active official sponsorship of literature and the arts.

There followed a half-century of division (907–60), in which a succession of short-lived dynasties contended among each other. The period of the Five Dynasties (in the north) and Ten Kingdoms (in the south) was closed when Zhao Kuangyin established the Song dynasty, with its capital city at Kaifeng. Marked as this dynasty was by institutional innovation, the growth of professionalism and the exercise of intellect, it lacked adequate administrative strength or political determination and was unable to preserve the integrity of Chinese territory for long. Powerful leaders of non-Chinese groups had established themselves with strength in the north-east and adopted dynastic titles according to Chinese usage, thereby creating the Liao dynasty (also known as Khitan; 947–1125) and then the Jin (Kin) dynasty (1115–1234). The Song governments proved to be unable to withstand the thrust of these powers into north China, culminating in the Jin (Kin) occupation of Kaifeng in 1127 and their effective settlement in northern China.

In the meantime a separate group of peoples, known as Tangut, had taken control of lands in the north-west that had at times been administered as imperial provinces; and they too had set themselves up as a ruling authority under the name of Xi Xia (1038). In effect the rule of China was now divided among three masters, of whom only one was of native Chinese stock. This was the house of Song, bereft of most of its territories, with its refugee capital situated at Lin'an (the later Hangzhou). The emperors and government of Southern Song had few resources on which they could call, to face the continuing threat of military engagement with the north.

THE LATER EMPIRES

It was left to non-Chinese leaders, of yet a different ethnic origin, to resolve this situation and to impose a unified authority over China once again. By the thirteenth century the Mongols had grown to be a powerful force, whose armed strength had been felt across Europe

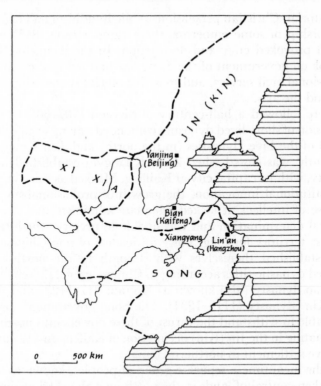

10. Southern Song, Jin (Kin) and Xi Xia, c. 1200 (after Wada)

and Asia, leaving a trail of bloodshed and destruction in its wake .
More thorough than the incursions into China that any of their
predecessors from other parts of Central Asia or further east had
achieved, the Mongol take-over proceeded by stages. By 1233 they
had seized Kaifeng. After a period of quarrels regarding the
succession, in 1260 Kublai Khan won acknowledgement as leader of
the Mongol groups, and in 1271 he inaugurated his own Chinese
dynasty, adopting the title of Yuan at the suggestion of Chinese
advisers.

Considerable violence and displacement of the population
attended the Mongol occupation of the north, but the new masters
of China eventually won their control of the south (1279) far more
easily and with considerably less cruelty than that practised, or said
to have been practised, in the north. It was the first time that an
alien dynasty, based in the north, had penetrated beyond the Yangzi
River. In reaching as far as the modern Vietnam the Mongols were
operating in a terrain with which they were quite unfamiliar. Their
campaign had involved a long siege (1268–73) of the twin cities of

TABLE 4

THE SONG DYNASTY AND THE ALIEN EMPIRES OF THE NORTH

916	Khitan kingdom founded in the north (Mongolia and Manchuria).
947	Khitan adoption of dynastic title Liao; based on five capital cities (in the modern province of Liaoning and adjoining areas).
960	Foundation of the Song empire.
986	Khitan victory over the Song empire.
1004	Peace of Shanyuan; humiliating terms imposed on Song by the Liao empire.
1038	Tangut occupation of north-west; foundation of the Xi Xia empire.
1044	Peace treaty between Song and Xi Xia.
1115	Jin (Kin) empire founded in the north-east by Jürchen peoples; capital established at Yanjing (modern Beijing).
1125	End of the Liao empire.
1127	Flight of the Song house to the south in face of Jin (Kin) pressure; establishment of the Southern Song dynasty, with capital at Lin'an (modern Hangzhou).
1162	Song defeat of Jin (Kin) forces at the battle of Caishi.
c. 1200	Rise of Genghis Khan as leader of the Mongols.
1227	End of the Xi Xia empire. Death of Genghis Khan.
1234	End of the Jin (Kin) empire in face of Mongol pressure.
1236–39, 1253–9	Mongol advance to Sichuan, Yunnan and Vietnam.
1245–7	Visit to China by the Franciscan friar John Piano de Carpini.
1253–4	Visit by William of Rubruck to Karakorum (near Ulan Bator), seat of Mongol power.
1257	Mongol occupation of Hanoi.
1260	Accession of Kublai Khan as emperor of China.
1264	Mongol capital moved from Karakorum to Khanbalik (modern Beijing; also called Dadu).
1268–73	Mongol siege of Xiangyang.
1271	Dynastic title Yuan adopted.
1272–9	Effective Mongol occupation of south China.
1274, 1281	Unsuccessful Mongol campaigns against Japan.
1276	Mongol capture of Lin'an.
1276–92	Marco Polo's visit to Lin'an.
1279	Suicide of the last Song emperor.
1281	Acknowledgement of Mongol suzerainty by Vietnam.
1292	Mongol expedition to Java.
1294	Death of Kublai Khan.
1335–45	Visit to China by Ibn Battuta.
1340–50	Breakdown of Yuan authority amid widespread revolts.

Xiangyang and Fancheng (on the Han River), in which gunpowder was used for the first time in the east for military purposes. Subsequent attempts to invade Japan were unsuccessful.

The Mongol dispensation unavoidably showed discrimination against the exercise of authority by native Chinese. Nevertheless the emperors were ready to listen to the advice of some Chinese advisers, or to that of some of their more realistic countrymen. It was they who pointed out that, if China was worth holding, it must be governed in a traditional manner that would allow the practice of agriculture to flourish in a controlled way. In administrative terms, the Yuan dynasty left its successors a number of gifts. For the first time the control of the entire empire, north and south, had been centred in the north-east. This was at the city known as Dadu (also Khanbalik or Cambaluc), on the site of present-day Beijing, which was destined to be chosen as China's capital city for most of the following seven centuries. Secondly, the territorial divisions of the provinces of the Yuan empire may still be seen on an administrative map of the People's Republic. In addition, in the postal service which they introduced the Mongols bequeathed a framework for China's internal communications that would last until the twentieth century.

In the face of dynastic weakness, growing unrest and local uprisings the Mongols withdrew to their homelands in the north. As they had not suffered defeat in battle, their forces were largely intact, and could constitute a potential threat to their successors, of the Ming dynasty. This dynasty was founded in 1386 by Zhu Yuanzhang, who had at one time served in a Buddhist monastery and had been engaged in subversive ventures against the Yuan authorities from 1350. In contrast with all other long-lasting dynasties, that of Ming was founded in the south, whence it extended its sway over the north; and for the first time a capital city for the whole empire was for a time situated in the south, at Nanjing. Reorganization and consolidation marked the early decades of the new regime, as may be seen in the establishment of a large number of local schools, the introduction of a new system of examinations and the preparation in new forms of a count of the population and a survey of the land. From this time onwards, emperors came to be known not by their posthumous titles, but usually by the single regnal title that was introduced for enumerating years at the start of their reigns and lasted until their conclusion, for example the Hongwu (1368–98), Yongle (1403–24) and Wanli (1573–1619) emperors.

In consolidating his position, the Hongwu emperor took the drastic step of abolishing the senior posts of the government and taking personal control of the many decisions that had hitherto devolved on the highest levels of the administration. But such an arrangement

TABLE 5

THE RISE AND FALL OF THE MING DYNASTY

1368	Foundation of the Ming dynasty by Zhu Yuanzhang; capital at Nanjing.
1368–98	The Hongwu period.
1403–24	The Yongle period.
1403–35, 1470–80	Defence lines built in the north.
1405–33	Sponsored maritime expeditions to India, Africa and South-east Asia.
1406–27	Ming occupation of Vietnam.
1421	Capital city established at Beijing.
1449	Chinese armies defeated by Mongols under Esen.
1540–55	Japanese pirates active on the Chinese coast.
1550	Beijing besieged by Mongol forces for seven days.
1570–1620	Renewed fortifications in the north, resulting in the surviving 'Great Wall'.
1573–1619	The Wanli period.
1583	Rise of the Jürchen leader Nurhaci (b. 1559); growth of Manchu strength.
1583	Arrival of the Jesuit father Matteo Ricci in south China.
1593	Chinese victory over the Japanese in Korea.
1615–27	Conflict in the Chinese court between the eunuchs and the Donglin group.
1616	Nurhaci's break with the Ming court.
1621	Manchus take Mukden.
1624	Dutch established on Taiwan (Formosa).
1626	Death of Nurhaci.
1635	Term 'Qing' adopted by the Jürchen.
1644	Suicide of the last Ming emperor; the rebel leader Li Zicheng enters Beijing.

was all too easily open to dangers and weaknesses, particularly if a successor emperor lacked the determination of the founder or his willingness to shoulder so great a burden of work. In the absence of strong ministers of state, there was no means of preventing one of the first emperor's sons from staging a *coup d'état* in 1403, ousting the duly enthroned emperor and establishing himself in his place; he is known under the title of the Yongle emperor.

It was at this juncture that Beijing replaced Nanjing as the capital city. This was in any case better suited for the co-ordination of defences against a threat that might come from the north, or for directing military operations against the Eleuths of the north-west or the Tatas (or Tartars) of the north-east. One conspicuous feature of the reign of the Yongle emperor and his successor was the series of seven seaborne voyages undertaken with the support of the government between 1405 and 1433. These were led by Zheng He, eunuch and Muslim, who acted as admiral of the fleets that made their way, at considerable expense and effort, to the ports of India and the Persian Gulf. Some Chinese may have made a pilgrimage to Mecca at the time. In addition, the voyages served to promote trading ventures that led outside the usual Chinese ambit.

In 1583 Father Matteo Ricci, first of the Jesuit priests intent on gaining Chinese converts to Christianity, set foot in the south and began to organize his long-term mission. By now the Ming dynasty had lost its momentum. The Wanli emperor and his officials were at odds with one another, and various elements were able to exploit the power vacuum to their own advantage. In its final decades the court lay open to intrigue and manipulation, and the growing strength of the eunuchs provoked somewhat unavailing protests from a number of brave traditionalists, known as the Donglin group.

No dynasty could preserve itself intact in such circumstances. When the last emperor hanged himself on the artificial mound that lay behind the palace (1644), Chinese rebels, led by Li Zicheng, were occupying Beijing; but the end of the dynasty came with the irruption of the Manchus from the north-east. These were a people of Jürchen origin, moulded into a firmly knit unit by Nurhaci (*c.* 1559–1626). The newly founded dynasty took the term Qing ('Pure') as its title. At its zenith it controlled a wider extent of territory than any earlier regime established in China. The degree of government was more intense than that of any earlier dynasty; and under Qing there occurred the greatest degree yet seen of an integration of Chinese and non-Chinese peoples under a single imperial dispensation.

The Manchu occupation of China was effected perhaps by cruelty and violence in the north, but more easily in the south. Surviving pockets of resistance, pretenders to the Ming throne and powerful rebel leaders determined to dispute the conquest delayed the completion of the Manchu victory until 1681. The island known today as Taiwan, and formerly as Formosa, afforded one anti-Manchu leader named Zheng Chenggong (also known under the form of Coxinga) opportunity to maintain hostilities against the new regime; and the island was occupied by the Manchus only as late as 1683.

TABLE 6

THE EXPANSION OF THE QING DYNASTY AND ITS RELATIONS WITH THE WESTERN POWERS

1644	Establishment of the Qing (Manchu) dynasty.
1645–1742	The 'Rites' controversy concerning the practice of Christianity; ended by the papal refusal to allow converts to maintain traditional ceremonies.
1646–50	Manchu occupation of Sichuan (1646), Zhejiang and Fujian (1650).
1661	Accession of the Kangxi emperor (reigned until 1722).
1662–1722	The Kangxi period.
1673–81	Rebellion of the San fan ('Three Satraps') and its eventual suppression.
1680	Manchu occupation of Guangdong and the south.
1683	Incorporation of Taiwan in the Qing empire.
1689	Russo–Chinese treaty of Nerchinsk and regulation of boundaries.
1696	Outer Mongolia and Hami under Qing control.
1723–35	The Yongzheng period.
1727	Treaty of Kiakhta with Russia; boundary agreement.
1736	Accession of the Qianlong emperor; abdicated 1795.
1736–95	The Qianlong period.
1750	Tibet incorporated in the Qing empire.
1755–7	Qing authority established in the Ili River valley.
1758–9	Muslim rising suppressed; Qing control extended to the Pamir massif.
1766–70	Qing campaign in Burma.
1781–4	Muslim revolt in Gansu.
1788–9	Qing campaign in Vietnam.
1790–2	Qing campaign in Nepal.
1793	British mission to Qing court led by the Earl of Macartney.
1796–1820	The Jiaqing period.
1820	Marked increase in Chinese imports of opium.
1839–42	Opium War with the British; Chinese defeat; by treaty of Nanking, treaty ports opened for western trade; Hong Kong ceded to Great Britiain.
1851–64	Taiping and Nian rebellions; suppressed with help of foreign intervention.
1856	Muslim rebellion in Yunnan.
1856–60	The Arrow War, ended by treaties of Tientsin (1858) and Peking (1860).
1858	Treaty of Aigun; regulation of border problems with Russia.
1860	Summer palace (west of Beijing) sacked by European forces.

1861	Chinese ministry of foreign affairs established.
1861–2	Muslim rising in Shaanxi and Gansu.
1873–8	Muslim rising in Xinjiang.
1883–5	Sino–French war; Chinese defeat and recognition of French presence in Vietnam.
1894–5	Sino–Japanese war; Chinese defeat; Taiwan taken over by Japan.
1898	The abortive 'Hundred Days' Reform'.
1900	Boxer uprising; suppressed with European intervention.
1908	Death of empress dowager Cixi.
1912	Abdication of the last emperor of the Qing dynasty.

Two emperors and one empress dowager stand out as personalities who affected the course of this dynasty's destiny. Possessed of a powerful character and an inexhaustible supply of energy, the Kangxi emperor (reigned 1661–1722) was responsible for taking much of the initiative in reducing all challengers to power and extending his authority over the Eleuths and Khalkas of Central Asia. In this way imperial territory was greatly enlarged to the north and north-west, and from 1750 Tibet became incorporated in the Qing domains. A policy of expansion and consolidation of strength continued under his grandson the Qianlong emperor (reigned 1736–95). But weakness and decadence were setting in during the final decades of that reign; the aged emperor had passed far beyond his prime; individuals such as He Shen were ready to exploit the advantages of proximity to the throne to increase their own wealth. It was a woman who formed the dominant force in Beijing during the second half of the nineteenth century. Cixi, the empress dowager, known also as Laofo or 'Old Buddha' (died 1908), had been favourably placed as the consort and then the mother of emperors, and had acted as co-regent at a time of dynastic weakness. Of a highly conservative frame of mind, she is best known for her refusal to brook the demands for reform that could not fail to reach the court at that time.

For the nineteenth century had exposed China to new influences and new concepts which she could not fail to recognize. The expansion of European and American interests in East Asia had led to commercial exchanges, and to an insistence that foreign traders should be allowed to transact business on Chinese soil. Several armed clashes had occurred, at times when imperial pride refused to accept western requests or demands. A number of incidents mark the progress of these developments. By the signature of an agreement with the Russian Tsar in 1689 (the treaty of Nerchinsk) a Chinese court found itself allowing some accommodation. Lord Macartney's

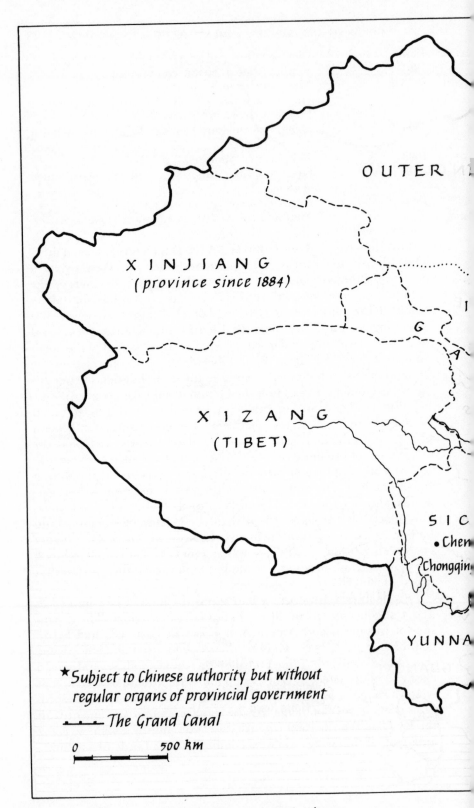

OUTER

XINJIANG
(province since 1884)

I

G

A

XIZANG

(TIBET)

SIC

•Chen

Chongqin

YUNNA

★Subject to Chinese authority but without
regular organs of provincial government

▪▪▪▪ The Grand Canal

0   500 km

11. The Qing empire at its close

mission of 1793 failed to gain the privileges that British companies sought by means of diplomacy. In the Opium War of 1839–42 and the Arrow War of 1856–60 the Manchu court was brought ineluctably face to face with the superiority of western weapons. Moreover, such a humiliation was accompanied by dangers of different types, to which the Chinese were well accustomed, in the form of the large-scale Taiping rebellion of 1851–64, and the Yellow River's change of course of 1855. The ceding of Hong Kong, followed by defeat by France (1883–5) and then Japan (1894–5), showed only too clearly that the days of the Qing's mandate were drawing towards their end.

*

There were other signs of the wind of change that was blowing through East Asia in the second half of the nineteenth century. Whether she liked it or not, China was obliged to enter into diplomatic relations with western powers according to western forms of protocol; movements for reform, based on new concepts, such as democracy and popular representation, were making themselves felt, albeit abortively. The Boxer uprising of 1900 forced the court to flee from Beijing and to accept humiliating terms from the western powers whose forces had brought about its suppression. The dynasty closed when Sun Yat-Sen proclaimed the inauguration of the Republic on 1 January 1912, to be followed shortly by the abdication of the infant emperor. But however high the hopes of new era might have run on that day, China was still to face nearly forty years of bitter dispute and social upheaval, of foreign invasion and civil warfare. It was left to Mao Zedong to make the final break with the imperial age, when the People's Republic was proclaimed on 1 October 1949.

III
DYNASTIC SUCCESSION AND ITS DIFFICULTIES

China's own traditional historians describe the rise and fall of successive dynasties as episodes that took their place within a well-known cycle. The strength needed to rise supreme above all contenders for power enabled the first emperors of a house to consolidate their positions. Within a few decades that strength began to ebb and the house started to lose its identity and sense of purpose; nor could it command the loyalty on which its integrity depended. In its final stages a dynastic house struggled to survive intact, until in time it was forced to make way for its successor. Key stages in the process are identified by historians in terms of the virtues and merits of the founding emperor and the disgraceful or criminal behaviour of the last one of the line.

Some measure of truth must attach to these somewhat simplistic and repetitive accounts of dynastic rise, decay and ruin. But the divisions between the dynasties were rarely as abrupt and the victories of one side were hardly ever as clear-cut as some of the official accounts would have us believe. New protagonists arose while the officials of an established but ageing dynasty could still command some service and obedience. The pretenders of a defunct dynasty might well maintain a large following and support in areas that lay beyond the reach of a new incumbent. Dynasties followed one another not in the manner of a family tree, where leadership of a line passes at death to an acknowledged heir; the process resembled more the movements of the tides of the ocean, sweeping in to overwhelm parts of the shore, but unable to submerge all the rocks, or leaving pools of lively activity along the beach as they recede beyond recall.

CONTINUITY OF RULE

Twenty-six 'Standard Histories', mainly devoted to a single dynastic period, are the fruit either of a few independent writers or of the corporate labours of the official history commissions, first established in the seventh century. The first of these works, the *Shiji*, takes in the history of man from his creation until *c*. 100 BC; the last handles the Qing dynasty of 1644–1911.

However, these centuries should in no sense be treated as a single period. New institutions were gradually but constantly being evolved; the intensity of a government's administration varied from time to time and place to place; and an ever-recurring cycle may be traced, of dynastic growth and decay, followed by the emergence of a new imperial house. Continuity is seen in the ever-surviving concept of single imperial rule; for this became the norm that could attract loyal service and to which contenders for power would aspire. But the succession of different houses (at times simultaneously), the varying degree of territorial control that they exercised and the diverse origins from which their families had sprung illustrate the difficulty of achieving that ideal in practice. Nevertheless, as compared with other major cultural centres such as Europe, China surprises us still with its repeated ability to survive incidents of turmoil or disruption and to re-establish its identity as a centrally governed unity.

In the full flush of military victory a successful and powerful leader would found his house and establish his comrades as his ministers. For some years, perhaps a few decades, they would control their empire with strength, and perhaps with some measure of ruthlessness or oppression. As the years passed, internal decay, loss of purpose or popular resentment against harsh taxation would develop; or contenders for power would seize a chance to promote their own interests at the expense of the imperial government. Other protagonists would then arise, secure perhaps in the local support of the outlying provinces whence they had originated. As they advanced their cause they would attract the loyalties of disaffected officials or an oppressed populace; by dint of fighting they could acquire prizes of territory, supplies or treasure; and in the final challenge to the existing house they could succeed in capturing a capital city and proclaiming themselves as new emperors. In such circumstances there could be relatively long periods when two or more imperial houses had been established; each leader had arrogated to himself the title of *Huangdi* and set up his palace and offices of state; none was able to command more than a part of China's land or people.

Long intervals when no regime could truthfully claim to be the sole existing authority give the lie to a belief that imperial unity persisted throughout the past two millennia, subject to some exceptional intervals of disruption. Indeed lengthy and disruptive intervals are most clearly apparent between the years 220 and 581, which saw a succession of regimes that coexisted in both the north and the south, but for the short-lived Western Jin (Tsin) empire. Similarly the Tang dynasty was followed by a division of the same type that lasted from 907 to 960; and when, in 1127, the Song house was forced to seek refuge in the south, the rule of China was effectively divided between three units, that of Southern Song itself along the Yangzi valley, that of Jin (Kin) in the north and north-east and that of Xi Xia, or Tangut, which had taken over the north-west.

On many of these occasions the houses that were established in the north had originated from non-Chinese stock in Central Asia. The first of such alien houses to succeed in extending its control to the southern and south-eastern seaboards was that of the Mongols, who adopted the Chinese term Yuan as their dynastic title in 1271. A second, longer-lasting and more effective example occurred in 1644 when the Manchu house from the north-east took the place of the native Ming house, adopting the title of Qing.

In many cases the alien conquerors found themselves obliged to rely on trained Chinese officials to administer the lands that they had won; for they themselves had had no experience of a settled agricultural life. As a result the foreign houses became more and more acclimatized to the Chinese way of life; some of their native hardiness and valour weakened as they became accustomed to the luxuries of the cities; and as the years passed, their administration came to adopt many of the institutions, such as taxation, that had been evolved and practised long since by the people whom they had conquered.

Following the establishment of a new house, few dynasties succeeded in maintaining the same degree of intensive control for long. Although the succession of emperors of a single line may have continued, in some cases, for upwards of 300 years, the latter days of a dynasty were often marked by notorious cases of administrative failure, dissidence or the loss of territories on the perimeter. Thus, although the Tang emperors remained enthroned until 907, from the middle of the eighth century onwards their governments had been severely weakened, their domains being often torn apart by revolt. Throughout the imperial age there were few periods of fifty years which were not marked by struggles for power, intrigue or factional plot designed to overthrow the dynasty, or the outbreak of violence. It may perhaps be estimated that out of a total of 2,000 years of the empires, effective centralized government was exercised for perhaps half of that time, and that the ruling houses of parts or even all of China came of alien origin for some 700 years.

Certain events are thus of far greater significance in China's political history than the flight or abdication of an emperor that set the final seal on an established dynasty. The rebellion of the Yellow

Turbans in 184 deprived the Han government of effective strength. The sack and capture of Luoyang and Chang'an cities, in 311 and 317, mark a further turning-point. The rebellion that broke out in 755 and was put down only with the help of foreign, Uighur, troops left the Tang dynasty permanently weakened. The Song emperors were forced to accept humiliating terms at the hands of non-Chinese in 1004 and 1044; their flight to the south in 1127 marked a turning-point in many respects of China's political and cultural history. In the Ming period, the year 1587 has been taken symbolically as 'a year of no significance' illustrating the low state to which the government of the empire had been reduced, thanks partly to decadence in the court and the failure of emperor and officials to co-operate. Finally the years 1851–64, which witnessed dramatic incidents in many quarters of the globe, saw China devastated by a major change in the course of the Yellow River; simultaneously much of south China was subject to the violence of the Taiping rebels, finally overcome in 1864.

ACHIEVEMENTS AND PROBLEMS

The adoption of different sites for the capital city mark the shifts of balance from north-west to north-east, and from north to south. Xianyang and Chang'an in the west served the Qin and the Han emperors, who at times would move to Luoyang, less well defended but blessed with better water supplies. Hitherto potential threats to security had come mainly from the north-west; and despite the growing movements and strength of non-Chinese leaders in the north-west, the Tang emperors likewise maintained their seat in Chang'an and Luoyang. An intermediate stage in the process is seen in the choice of Kaifeng by the Northern Song emperors (960–1127), subject as the city was to inundation from the Yellow River. The final move to the north-east is seen when Beijing or its predecessor cities acted as the capital for the Yuan, Ming and Qing dynasties. In the meantime the growing significance of the south and its importance in times of imperial disunity had been seen in the settlement of the palace at Jiankang (later Nanjing) in the fourth century, at Lin'an (later Hangzhou) in the twelfth century and at Nanjing by the first of the Ming emperors.

The names of Han, Tang, Song, Ming and Qing are usually cited as the titles of the more successful, long-lasting and significant of the empires, each capable of exerting a new measure of strength and intensity of government. Despite their weaknesses and failures, these houses certainly merit the praise that has been lavished upon them. They maintained the authority that they had founded sufficiently long to establish loyalties, to operate effective organs of government and to leave their mark on the traditional form of Chinese society.

It could however sometimes occur that experiments in administration or innovations in the economy were initiated by one of the lesser-known and shorter-lived regimes in a time of disunity. The next regime would then be able to take full advantage of its predecessor's experience, applying its new methods of administration on a wider scale. A pattern may perhaps be discerned of a short period of government, later pilloried for its ruthlessness, followed by what was perhaps a more stable and more relaxed rule of one of the major dynasties. Thus the Qin dynasty initiated imperial organs of central and provincial government, unseen hitherto, that were duly adopted by Han; and the new defence lines that had been built and manned in Qin formed the model for Han and some of its successors. The short period of Wang Mang's Xin dynasty (AD 9–23) saw the promotion of the ethical ideals and an appeal to the precedents of the 'glorious' Zhou dynasty; imperial pretensions of the Later Han period drew extensively on these principles. The Sui emperors introduced a new system of examinations as needed by the more advanced state of society, and built the first version of the Grand Canal; the emperors and officials of the Tang dynasty benefited significantly by the extensive application of these precedents.

An ironic paradox derives from the demands of official Chinese historiography. Although Qin, Xin and Sui each contributed enduring results to the future of imperial administration, they are precisely the regimes that have been most open to the virulent criticism of the very successors that battened on their achievements. Also, although Chinese writers have always tended to assume that a united empire has formed the ideal norm, it is at times of political disunity that some of China's most significant cultural initiatives have emerged. The simultaneous existence of several courts, with their established centres for the leisured life of scholar, littérateur or artist, has often encouraged the growth of local traditions, each with its own characteristic features. Ethnic admixture has brought enrichment.

Certain recurring problems which taxed the ingenuity of imperial officials often eluded satisfactory solution. The stability of the palace could all too easily be upset, because of the existence of several rival families of imperial consorts, each with its own ambitions. Individual statesmen were at times bent on founding their coteries and increasing their wealth; ideological differences could affect decisions of policy on which the fate of dynasties might depend. On many occasions these factors were inextricably woven together, giving rise to bitter disputes and bids to manipulate the imperial succession.

A further difficulty lay in delegating sufficiently strong independent military and civil authority to governors at the perimeter so as to ensure security of the realm, while at the same time imposing sufficient controls to obviate attempts at separatism. A careful balance was necessary, if governments were to survive, between the effort put into production from the fields, the call on human labour for defence or building projects and the freedom of choice left to individuals to order their own lives. Should these conflicting demands become unbalanced, resentment, banditry or rebellion could easily break out. In addition, those houses that had been founded by non-Chinese peoples from the steppe, such as the Liao, Jin (Kin), Yuan and Qing dynasties, faced their own problems, being obliged to integrate two types of population within a single regime. One of these was used to working the fields and accepting the demands of Chinese administration; the other had ridden in as conquerors, claiming the privileges due to their support of the new regime and hoping to retain their own hierarchies and power of exercising authority. It could perhaps take some time for the new masters of China to accommodate to their newly acquired gains.

Imperial China was by no means stagnant; each age drew on its predecessor as it worked out evolutionary changes of institution and practice. It is however possible to fasten on a few crucial stages in the process when a particular dynasty may be credited with moulding part of China's enduring heritage. In Former Han imperial government acquired the hallmark of respectability and would become the norm which leaders would aspire to establish; in economic terms a precedent was set for the state's assumption of sole control of certain activities such as the production of iron and salt. Marked as they were by political rivalries and dynastic intrigue, the years of Later Han saw the creation of an orthodox ideology and type of scholarship that characterized subsequent intellectual effort. Some of the Wei emperors left China a magnificent example of Buddhist monuments, thanks to their devotion to the faith. New organs of central government emerged and were operated during the Sui and Tang periods, and a complex system of examinations was introduced; during the Song dynasty the officials of the civil service acquired a new measure of prestige and privilege based on their literary and scholastic attainments. After a period of bitter civil warfare the new Ming government introduced a new system of examinations designed to extend the sources from which officials could be recruited; a new measure of autocracy could allow an emperor to take a more significant and personal part in government than hitherto. The Qing emperors could boast that they commanded a greater extent of territory than any of their predecessors, including much of Mongolia and, for the first time, Tibet and Taiwan.

SOME EMPERORS OF NOTE

With some exceptions little is recorded of the personal character of the emperors or the part that they played in shaping China's destiny. At times it is difficult to separate fact from fiction or allegation; for Chinese historians were obliged to depict the founding emperor of a line as being noble and gallant, whereas the last one would be shown off as a notorious example of evil conduct. Mythology praises the duke of Zhou who selflessly acted as regent to the young king of Zhou (that is, Cheng Wang: reigned, traditionally, 1115–1078 BC), and thereby left an example for others to follow. The first Qin emperor (Qin shi huangdi: 221–210 BC) was alleged to have practised ruthless oppression and arrogance. To Wudi, of Former Han (141–87 BC), there was credited a forceful personality which was responsible for mighty exploits. Han Mingdi (AD 58–75) is remembered for a dream in which he saw the arrival of the Buddhist faith; Taizong of Tang (627–49) for personal courage in confronting invading armies, almost at the walls of Chang'an. As last-but-one of the Northern Song emperors, Huizong (1101–25) goes down in history as a weak dilettante, whose character is betrayed in his handwriting. Zhu Yuanzhang, founder of the Ming house (that is, Taizu, emperor from 1368 to 1398, with the regnal title of Hongwu), had seen service in a Buddhist monastery; he had also been a member of a band of rebels. In the Qing period, historians describe the Kangxi emperor (1662–1722) as a forceful and robust ruler, courageously confronting a challenge to his throne, and riding across his provinces to demonstrate his imperial might. His grandson, known by his regnal title as the Qianlong emperor (1736–95), presided over a court and government in which personal motives and ambitions had eventually penetrated too far, thus ushering in the decadence of the nineteenth century.

In all the long saga of imperial succession it was sometimes the second emperor of a dynasty who left a more enduring mark than the founder; for the latter may well have come to prominence thanks to his military prowess, spending more time on saddleback or on the battlefield than in his palace. On many occasions infants were thrust on the throne, where they could be manipulated by their mothers or grandmothers, or forced to accord privileges to their relatives. Of a number of women who succeeded in ruling the empire or interfering with its government, three stand out: Lühou, empress of the first Han emperor (reigned under her own title 187–180 BC); Wu Zetian (sovereign empress 690–705); and Cixi, empress dowager and effective ruler at various times from 1860 until her death in 1908. History has dealt harshly with them all, blaming them for usurpation of power, arrogance and cruelty.

IV

MAN AND HIS NEIGHBOURS:
SOCIAL DISTINCTIONS

Throughout the centuries the pattern of Chinese society has been subject to change, and certain features have become recognizable as forming characteristics of China's own unique way of life. The names of certain families or groups recur in the pages of Chinese history in a variety of situations, exemplifying the attainment or loss of social distinction and the growth of hierarchies. Family connections or political affiliations, intellectual training or sources of wealth all played their own significant part in making or breaking an individual's fortunes. Distinctions of class or loyalties to a group emerged gradually and cumulatively; only rarely is it possible to define the moment when particular criteria grew to prominence, or to analyse the precise and relative importance of religious, political or economic motives in the development of social structure.

THE MAIN DISTINCTIONS

Distinct groups of men and women have arisen thanks to circumstances of birth, a command of material resources or the practice of an occupation. Usually these factors have been closely interwoven, sometimes arising spontaneously, sometimes being engendered deliberately, and at times being purposefully exploited by a government of the land. Religious belief, intellectual theory and political need have together formed the basis on which social structure has rested.

For some 2,000 years the Chinese have themselves stressed their distinction from other, less fortunate mortals. They have drawn attention to the nomadic way of life of those who live beyond the confines of the empire, as contrasted with their own settled agriculture and cities. In particular they have pointed to the harsh livelihood of the men of the steppe, their dependence on mobility to nurture their flocks and herds and their failure to evolve the disciplines of a civilized way of life. Cultural standards and achievements have formed an obvious hallmark for comparison, and the pride felt by Chinese at their own literacy and literature could be well justified in view of the failure of the steppe to produce its own forms of writing.

A further criterion could be seen in the presence or absence of established forms of government and ordered administration. The Chinese would accept as Chinese all those who expressed themselves willing to accept the authority of the emperor, to submit to the demands of his officials and to undertake the responsibilities that devolved on the emperor's subjects. Participation in the Chinese imperium and enjoyment of its cultural superiority could be accorded to a foreigner irrespective of his ethnic or territorial origin, provided that he would obey the magistrate, pay his taxes and serve in the labour force when called upon to do so.

Today's map of the ethnic categories which together make up China's population shows large areas as being populated by the Han race, and it is by the term Han that the Chinese often denote their own identity and origin. But the map also shows large areas which are populated by a majority that comes from other racial stock, be it Turkic, Mongolian or Tungusic in the north, Tibeto-Burman or Mon-Khmer in the west, or Tai in the south. Smaller pockets of lesser minorities, often speaking their own languages, lie enclosed within the autonomous region of Guangxi and the provinces of Yunnan and Guizhou. Such enclaves have come into existence partly because of the deliberate decision of an imperial government to isolate a group of alien peoples with their leaders, in such a way that they could be kept under control and potential dissidence could be contained. Simultaneously a great deal of intermarriage and racial admixture has taken place, with the result that Mongols or Manchus have become members of established Chinese families, and that Muslims, originally of western extraction, now take their place in Chinese society with their own recognizable physiognomy, wearing their white headbands and patronizing their own eating-houses in the land.

The great majority of the Chinese population has always been settled in the villages and on the farms rather than in the towns. Throughout historical times society has been marked by hierarchies, which have emerged for various reasons. Certain families have come to the fore either because they have provided the ruling house, or because they have assumed local leadership on a wide scale in the provinces. Such affiliations could bring the privileges attached to a nobility. Within the extended clan or family, members of a senior generation commanded the respect and obedience of their juniors, in a manner that followed strict rules of precedence and could not be gainsaid. Individuals could win a high place in public esteem if they had acquired professional qualifications and started on a career in public life; such a career was marked at all stages by the hope of advancement and the fear of degradation. Honours that were achieved or disgraces that were suffered in this way were there for all to see, in the rank that a man reached in the civil service, or the type of post to which he was appointed.

The chances of betterment, for example by marriage into a powerful family or promotion from a confined life in the provinces to the highest positions in the capital city, varied greatly from time to time. The foundation or restoration of a dynasty would clearly provide opportunity for the emergence of a new group of clans to prominence, as happened when the Later Han dynasty was established. Alternatively a newly arisen government might well take steps to recruit a new set of officials to the civil service; it could either call on the relatives of the new leaders, as happened with the Tang dynasty; or else, anxious to restore law and order after a period of civil warfare, it could attempt to train and recruit new members to staff its offices, chosen on a wide front throughout the provinces. Some measure of social mobility was brought about in this way at the start of the Ming dynasty.

THE FORMATION OF THE TRADITION

No direct evidence can be brought to bear on the social groupings or distinctions that characterize the prehistorical period. It must remain open to debate whether some of the earliest inhabitants of the land were subject to matriarchy, or at what point and in which communities this gave place to a patriarchic structure, thereby affecting the course of some of the neolithic cultures. It is perhaps a reasonable assumption that it would not have been possible for the neolithic revolution to have occurred – with its concentration on agriculture, its demand for corporate workings and its dependence on the collection of fuel for the kilns – without some form of leadership and control. The basis on which such authority rested and the extent to which it could be exerted can only remain subject to speculation. It may be supposed that a tribal form of leadership and organization may have formed the norm.

The advanced culture of the Shang kings called for social distinctions that must have been acknowledged at the time and whose traces are recognizable now; they arose from religious, political and economic reasons. Scribes served the kings by recording the accounts of their communications with the gods; seers or diviners were distinguished by virtue of their gifts or powers and the use to which they put them in the service of the community; and it is fair to assume that when the kings sallied forth for the hunt or war they possessed the necessary authority to control the activities of their supporters. Likewise they must have been able to call on obedience to ensure that the bronze weapons of war were distributed appropriately, and that men were stood to arms when it was necessary to protect the settlements from marauders.

There are signs that some measure of planning and some degree of social distinction must have preceded the construction of the Shang settlements. The work of building walls, by crushing layers of mud together within frames, of constructing the tombs of kings and of maintaining bronze foundries, depended on organized labour, and on the assignment to such men of food that had been grown or hunted by others. While the majority of the population were engaged in the work of the fields, including that of digging irrigation channels, special sites had been separated for craftsmen working in bone or wood, or fashioning the bronze vessels. Controlled labour gangs were needed to keep the kilns operative; authority of an unquestioned nature would be needed to designate victims for human sacrifice.

Major social distinctions which emerged during the long period of the kings of Zhou (traditionally 1122–256 BC) bore characteristics which have persisted ever since. In religious practice it was the king and only the king who was entitled to worship the supreme deity of Heaven (Tian). Those who stood possessed of estates or controlled village settlements worshipped at the local shrines dedicated to the spirits of the soil or of the grain. While participating in major festivals and regulating their activities so as to conform with seasonal religious prescriptions, the peasantry took no leading part in such ceremonial. Devotions paid to the souls or memories of ancestors concerned only those of the higher reaches of society.

Depending on the degree of kinship with the deceased person, hierarchies also arose in respect of mourning rites. In addition, later writers attributed a fundamental principle of Chinese society to these early stages, or indeed to the preceding ages. This prescribed a ban on marriage between those who bore the same surname and thus shared the same tribal origins. For the communities of the countryside marriages were often arranged by groups, with the young men of one village being paired in one set with the maidens of another.

Kings and officials, and those who are named among China's earliest philosophers of the Warring States period (481 or 403–221 BC), were requiring or formulating other distinctions. The relationship of the kings of Zhou to the leaders or rulers of the other estates and kingdoms was expressed in the ideal terms of a nobility, comprising four or five degrees. Confucius and his followers named ideal forms of precedence between, for example, father and son or friend and friend; they hoped by this means to ensure that respect was paid where it was due, and that a secure and stable fabric would preserve social order and discipline.

As the courts of the kings and their organs of administration grew in complexity, so there arose an increasing need for trained clerks or officials, to frame the documents that were needed in increasing volume and to ensure that obedience was rendered to the kings' commands. In this way there was founded the stress that China came to lay on professional ability and meritorious service. There arose too the concept of king and minister, each with his own virtues, and able to co-operate with each other for the general good of the realm. To attract loyal and successful service there was evolved a scheme of rewarding those who had acquired merit in this way by conferring upon them titles of rank, with attendant gifts of land and legal privileges.

Accompanying the economic changes of the Warring States period, material considerations and occupational functions were dividing man from his neighbour. Whatever the earliest systems of land tenure had been – and China's historical mythology harked back to one of corporate working – by the fourth century BC at least land was changing hands by means of sale and purchase. Some indeed remained under the control of a titled nobility and was transmitted on a hereditary basis, but acquisition by purchase enabled others to reach a new degree of prominence. The increasing use of iron had extended the acreage under the plough; the demand for weapons of war, equipment for transport and farming implements required the use of labour in the iron mines and in manufacture. Such goods were available for purchase, by means of a coinage that had started long since in the form of cowry shells and was now being minted in various shapes of bronze. The growing number of merchants who handled the exchange and distribution of articles of everyday use were sometimes operating over widely dispersed areas; they were acquiring a reputation for power, and were sometimes able to interfere in the destiny of kings.

THE IMPERIAL AGES

In the wake of Qin's unification of China and the establishment of the Han empire, dynastic, political and institutional considerations moulded the shape of Chinese society with increasingly great effect. Imperial governments were setting about the task of consolidating their leadership of the population and strengthening their means of administration. Sometimes an emperor would nominate his sons as kings, with the duty of governing large provincial territories, and in the hope that they would do so loyally. High-ranking officials, anxious to prolong the influence of their families, would contrive to marry one of their daughters to a member of the imperial family, best of all the declared heir apparent; in this way families of imperial consorts enjoyed great power and prestige, often engaging in conflict with their rivals in order to maintain their privileged position. At times groups of eunuchs rose to commanding places at court, sharing the trust of an emperor and able to thwart the ambitions of other contenders for power.

Formal distinctions, which could carry material privileges, marked the place reached in the scale of public life. A series of grades, sometimes as many as twenty, defined the hierarchies of the civil service. Duties, responsibilities and salaries corresponded with the grade; material symbols of the grade, such as the type of seal and sash to which an official was entitled, varied appropriately. As more and more officials were recruited and political life became more and more involved, factions would emerge, or cliques whose members were linked together by the bonds of patron and client. At times of political corruption a conflict could sometimes arise between the calls of conscience and service; for loyalty to an emperor or to the ideals of empire could sometimes run counter to support for a leader whose star was rising and who could promise the enjoyment of power at the top. To avoid embroilment in public life, there were times when some men of talent refused to accept appointments to office. They saw no way of avoiding compromise with their principles.

Orders of rank, instituted in the pre-imperial period as rewards for merit, carried privileges such as exemption from some of the obligations for service, or mitigation of punishment for certain crimes. Uniquely, the highest of the twenty orders was hereditary; holders were entitled to collect taxation over a specified part of the population, and they bore a title that is often rendered 'marquis'.

Writers of the pre-imperial age refer to four types of occupation, that is, those of man of letters, farmer, craftsman and tradesman. The catch-phrase used for this purpose, *shi nong gong shang*, ('scholar, farmer, artisan and merchant') has often been invoked as an expression of Chinese priorities, or to signify the relative prestige and importance ascribed to different types of individual. In particular it has been regarded as evidence of the low esteem placed on merchants and the high acclaim reserved for officials. While the importance of such priorities cannot be doubted, the distinction of society into four groups was in no way a formal designation with legal implications. Illustrating as it does the prestige enjoyed by men of letters, it also shows the high place accorded to the basic work of production of the fields and the silk-farms, as compared with the secondary occupations of manufacture and trade. The scorn of the merchants, as a class, recurs throughout much of Chinese writing, sometimes in inverse proportion to the prominent and valuable part that they played in Chinese life.

At least one writer of the pre-imperial age, the author of the *Mengzi* (probably fourth century BC), had realized that communal life depended on the co-operation of farmer, artisan and merchant. By about 100 BC large fortunes could be made, and with them a prominent place could be found in society, by those engaged in a whole variety of occupations. These included purveyors of alcoholic drinks or preserved foods; carriage builders and shipwrights; manufacturers of equipment in wood or bronze; stock-breeders or dealers in horses, cattle and sheep; hardware merchants, dealing in horn or lacquer; and those whose business lay in dried fish, choice fruits, rare furs, animal hides or fine cloth. The salt and iron magnates and the money-lenders likewise acquired great wealth. There was a growing disparity between the large landowners and an impoverished peasantry; at times a government would deliberately settle part of its population to work on sponsored farms, either so as to maintain the upkeep of imperial graves, or to provide the garrisons at the perimeter with their own supplies of food.

By the imperial age, convicts of both sexes were being set to work on hard labour; sometimes they were sent to serve in the armed garrisons of the frontier. A small proportion of the population, perhaps less than one per cent, consisted of slaves, either working at the behest of officials or made over for the use of individual owners in farm or home. Some of the cities included a special quarter, or lane, where groups of specialists practised their craft; for example, in the capital city of the Former Han empire one such lane housed experts in a variety of methods of seeking truth from occult sources. As professional prognosticators they gave advice to some of the greatest in the land; not being established officials, they earned the scorn of many who were in high places; some men of note were prepared to testify to their honesty and integrity.

A new degree of sophistication entered into Chinese society after the re-establishment of imperial unity by the houses of Sui and Tang. The new structured and competitive series of examinations, which regulated entry to the civil service, the requirement for larger numbers of officials and the growing disparity between the life of town and country served to enhance the prestige and privileges of the men of letters. From proven scholastic qualifications a man would attain appointment as a junior official; by dint of long service he would advance towards the senior ranks in the major offices of state; and if he survived the jealousies and intrigues of his contemporaries he might close his career as a statesman advising his emperor on decisive matters of policy. Above all, service in public life provided opportunity and incentive to promote and practise the arts. The Song period in particular is known as an age in which a large number of highly educated and distinguished officials enjoyed sufficient leisure from their duties to create masterpieces of literature, philosophy and painting that have long outlasted their public careers and ephemeral ambitions.

The civil service thus provided the sole profession that called on the resources of a training and merited the respect of the public. Its members were concerned with the organization of man and the administration of the land, and it included a complement of specialists in a number of technical attainments, such as religious observances, music, mathematics and medicine. Regulation of such matters and their application to daily life came within the scope of imperial government; practitioners were therefore enrolled as servants of the empire.

In the countryside the strength and cohesion of the extended families and the clans grew to new dimensions, particularly from the Song period. Their strength lay in their endurance beyond the transitory life of individual men and women. At their best they could provide an isolated family that was liable to official oppression or the misfortune of impoverishment with the benefits of an organization that it could trust, and with material benefits that would mitigate hardship. Settled on large estates, the clans founded charitable trusts designed to look after their members in times of need. The leaders of a clan would determine how the communal resources could best be spent, and whether the time was ripe to devote funds to the education of a promising lad who was growing up in the country and showed signs of possessing talent. For it would be the ambition of every family to boast that one of their kin held office serving their emperor; in time to come his glory would redound to the benefit of his ancestors and his village; and should he attain high office his power of patronage and protection could be of considerable material value in times of oppression. The short stories which were being written at this period often include a happy ending, whereby the hero is appointed to a high position of state, or marries the daughter of a senior official.

Conflicts could perhaps arise between the interests of a clan and its leaders, anxious to maintain the strength and solidarity of their flock, and the exacting demands presented by a provincial official in the course of his normal duties. In some cases it was to the advantage of all parties – the natural leaders of the villages, the clan member who faced the heat and burden of the day in the fields and the duly appointed officials of state – to reach a measure of co-operation. Villagers would pay tax with less resentment to the head whom they respected than to the provincial inspector whom they resented; and that inspector would more easily collect his dues by appealing to the help of the clan leaders than by arousing the antagonism of the crowd. Perhaps the most advantageous of all positions for a family, if it could be attained, was one that included the possession of extensive resources in the country with the support of one of their own members as a highly placed member of the central government.

During the Tang dynasty the hand of government had not yet penetrated to the south and the south-west with the same intensity as in the north. If an official was disgraced, his punishment might well take the form of a posting to an agency or minor charge in an area where climate, terrain or diet were strange, wild or execrable; or where the inhabitants were unassimilated to a Chinese way of life and spoke an unintelligible dialect. The 'exile' imposed on the Song littérateur Su Dongpo (1036–1101) to Hainan Island is one of the best-known examples of this type of punishment.

In a land where the great majority of the inhabitants were engaged in agriculture there was scope for major distinctions between large landowner, small holder, hireling and coolie. Able-bodied men rendered conscript service to local or provincial officials annually in the form that was required; they could be put to haul the bulky loads of staple goods from field to waterway and thence to the storehouses, or they could be ordered to maintain public roads and canals, or build public offices or an imperial mausoleum. In the eleventh century new ideas were being floated concerning the conversion of conscript service into tax with which hired labour could be paid.

Meanwhile wealthy merchant houses were developing on the banks of the Yangzi. To the consternation of the established officials a new class of *nouveaux riches*, whose wealth may have come from the tea trade, was asserting itself. Some members were able to penetrate into the ranks of the civil service; some espoused the call of learning, collecting books and antiquities and thereby becoming respectable patrons of scholarship. Shopkeepers, artisans and craftsmen of the towns were forming guilds with which to protect their professional standards and to maintain their independence. But a rise to social prominence in this way was subject to limitations. Loyalties were due, above all, to emperor and clan; and while there was no growth of municipal pride or independence comparable with that seen in

Europe, the ties that held a man to his forebears were of paramount importance. As it was habitual for property to be divided between all a rich man's sons rather than being left in its entirety to one, the strength and wealth of the great houses were relatively short-lived.

Buddhist monasteries had begun to grow to strength in the centuries before the Tang dynasty. By then they were receiving large landed estates which they were able to exploit to advantage, owing to their privileged position in respect of taxation. In addition, they could provide an asylum for the disaffected. Individuals who had tasted the delights of public life but become disenchanted with its compromises might well wish to end their days in the peace of the temple's courtyards, awaiting the bell's call to prayer or the abbot's summons to meditation. Set apart from the world, the monasteries came to harbour human talent as well as material wealth, and to some extent they could be said to be removing such resources from the greedy hands of the state. In the middle of the ninth century many were forcibly closed down and their inmates returned to lay life.

Moments of suffering or the endurance of acute oppression could lead to the emergence of social groupings of another type, known in general terms as the 'secret societies'. Vows of loyalty and acceptance of the obligations of brotherhood preceded admission and prevented members disclosing the arcane mysteries or the disruptive purposes of the group that they had joined. These groups had arisen from protest against an established order and its injustices, and the members were fired by a manic enthusiasm with which they hoped to initiate a new age, free from the suffering imposed by the state. By their very nature these societies were potentially subversive, and frequently enough they provided the springboard from which a rebellion could break out, such as the Boxer uprising of 1900.

Until some fifty years ago perceptive visitors to Beijing, capital city of the Ming and Qing dynasties, could recognize both symbolic and material signs of how Chinese society had developed in the later empires. Attended by courtiers, eunuchs and servants, the emperor sat enthroned at the centre of his domains, entrenched and protected by the innermost walls of his palace. Outer walls formed a series of concentric rectangles or courtyards; each one gave access to less favoured and less privileged mortals, in descending order of precedence; finally, beyond the confines of the external wall of the imperial city lay the habitations of the rest of humanity. These included some grand establishments of the mighty ones in the land, insulated in the same way from the realities, cares and dangers that beset the great multitude of the city's inhabitants. Trade was practised in specially designated markets or lanes; the houses and hovels of the poor jostled together alongside a variety of occupations; mighty walls formed a bastion of defence against intruders.

Entry to official life had become increasingly more competitive, as the rise in China's population had not been accompanied by a corresponding increase in the number of posts available in the civil service. In compliance with imperial commands some of the statesmen and scholars of the Ming and Qing emperors were responsible for voluminous works of literature and learning. To prevent the growth of local factional interests in the provinces, officials were appointed to serve in areas other than those of their own domicile. But on arrival to take up a post a man could easily find the local dialect unintelligible; he would perforce depend on the advice of the local henchmen and be open to the deception that they could practise in their own interests.

Family relationships and degrees of kinship were marked by strict hierarchies. A rich vocabulary provided for distinctions such as those between older, middle or younger brothers that are not usually expressed in other languages, and different forms of address designated the relationships between members of a family. Precise regulations governed the part played by kinsmen of different degrees in services of memorial that were conducted at the ancestral shrines. In town and country alike there existed a large underworld with its networks of beggars and criminals, sometimes bent on petty crime, or forming themselves into groups which harboured more dangerous ambitions.

*

Throughout the story of the growth of Chinese society there recurs the ideal of a well-structured, stable community in which each member knows and accepts his or her appointed place. This comprised obedience due to the emperor and his officials; compliance with the will of the family; and respect of neighbour for neighbour. There was no idea of the outcast who was banned on the grounds of ritual impurity, as in India and Japan; no hereditary tribe of a priesthood, as in the Jewish tradition; and despite the retention of some privileged groups, such as the Manchu 'Bannermen', there arose no professional military clique; nor was there an inalienable caste system, as pervaded the societies of India. Devotees of foreign religions, such as Buddhism, Islam and Christianity, were not banned from taking part in public life. In the formative centuries of the pre-imperial era some important or controlling positions may well have passed in hereditary fashion from father to son, as is seen in the survival of certain surnames, such as Sima ('Master of the Horse'); and the hereditary principle lay behind the succession of emperors and, at times, in the ranks of a nobility. In other walks of life, however, it was long the proud boast of the Chinese that the way to advancement lay by way of personal merit and attainment. That that ideal has all too often been thwarted by political ambitions or family rivalries need occasion little surprise.

Contrasts between the way of life of rich and poor are all too evident. In about 50 BC a critic was protesting against the abuses of the day and the imbalances that he saw around him in Chang'an city, capital of the Han empire. He described the highly embellished mansions of the counsellors of court and the hovels of roughly hewn timber of the many; the carriages drawn by well-fed horses in which the rich thronged the streets, and the crude carts laden with the city's daily needs and pulled by human hand. Silken fineries or rare furs of the affluent stood out against the rough hempen cloth that most of the inhabitants wore.

Similar contrasts are evident for later periods. Posted in 819 to govern Zhongzhou, in the upper Yangzi River valley, the poet Bo Juyi found that that part of China was inhabited by a strange unassimilated people; the faces of the women were strangely painted or tattooed; the farmers tilled their plots without plough or hoe; they spoke a language that he could not understand; their food and clothing were of the coarsest. For about the same time short stories tell again of Chang'an, now the capital of the Tang emperors; closed gates sealed the residences of the rich in the city's wards; female slaves with their characteristic 'double bun' head-dress served their mistresses; rival teams of undertakers competed with one another in spectacle of song in the market-places.

In about 1100 an artist named Zhang Zeduan painted a picture of scenes in the capital city of Kaifeng (see Chapter XIII). He shows the inhabitants of the city engaged in a variety of occupations, ranging from those of official on horseback to salesman proffering his stock-in-trade, from scholar intent on his books to boatman with his pole. Vivid impressions of the people of China are also forthcoming in the journal kept by the Earl of Macartney, during the course of his embassy to the court in 1793–4. He attended the theatre, with its repertoire of tragedy and comedy, of pantomime and acrobatics. He suffered from the demands of the formality imposed at court, and stood to see the Qianlong emperor carried by in his sedan. He noted how the streets of the capital city (Beijing) were closed at night by barricades, while guards maintained their patrols; and while he appreciated the lavish entertainment that his hosts provided, he was shocked by accounts of deprivation in the countryside, where a shortage of clothing in winter could spell death from cold.

In his journey on the Grand Canal, Lord Macartney noted the efficient management of the sluices and the operation of the lockgates, manned by conscripted labour, and he observed how constantly the boatmen were engaged on their arduous work. The size of the cities and the turn-out of the armed guards impressed him, suspicious as he was that some of their equipment was make-believe – burnished leather or glittering pasteboard masquerading as steel helmets. At the capital city he had seen women whose feet had been bound and become misshapen since childhood, as a means of enhancing their attractions; in the countryside he saw women unencumbered by such disabilities, working side by side with their menfolk in the fields. Great areas of land lay under cultivation, and as he travelled south on his return journey, he noted that some members of the rural population had a 'boorish, rustic aspect'. Aside from courtiers and officials, towards the end of his journey Lord Macartney talked with large-scale merchants in the hope of promoting commercial exchanges; and he contrasted the sly ways or ostentatious demeanour of some with the frank manners and modesty of others.

V

THE SPOKEN AND THE
WRITTEN WORD

China stands alone in East Asia as the progenitor of a native script. In its initial stages Japanese literature was written exclusively in Chinese characters; abbreviated forms of a select number of these were then adopted to act as a syllabary with which to convey the sounds of the elements of Japanese words. In Korea, Chinese characters were used regularly, until the invention of a Korean alphabet in 1446. For the Vietnamese language, akin to Mon-Khmer, there evolved an ugly script based on elements that formed parts of Chinese characters, with results that are marred by imbalance, that lack aesthetic appeal and that fail to express originality. In the steppes of Central Asia, the writings of the Mongol and Manchu languages were rendered in phonetic signs which owed nothing to the Chinese script. These had been evolved by the Uighurs, a people who had been dominant in Central Asia in the eighth and ninth centuries.

With the adoption or adaptation of the Chinese system of writing, Japanese, Korean and Vietnamese incorporated large elements of Chinese vocabulary; an obvious comparison is the inclusion of large elements of Latin in the English language. Those non-Chinese leaders who succeeded in taking over parts of north China, or even the whole of the subcontinent, came from a background that had been far less dependent on the written word than had China. When their administration was established they relied on Chinese officials to draw up their documents, and these were usually written in Chinese. A Mongol, Manchu or sometimes Tibetan version was at times appended; in the same way some of the inscriptions cut during the Qing dynasty and still erected for display bear a bilingual or trilingual text.

The pervasive use of a single written language throughout the imperial period is one of the most significant and formative influences on the growth of Chinese culture. It affected the forms of literature, both prose and poetry; it gave rise to the characteristic art form of calligraphy; and in its heritage there lay a framework within which many varieties of literary expression could develop and prosper.

THE SPOKEN DIALECTS

Chinese is classified within the Sino-Tibetan group of languages. The large number of dialects – well over twenty – that are spoken today fall into some seven major groups. One of these, which is named Han, is centred in the north; the six other groups predominate in the south. Differences depend on pronunciation, choice of vocabulary and grammatical forms, in a manner that is in some ways analogous to the differences between the Romance languages of the west.

Of the many dialects, three stand out by virtue of their widespread frequency and usage. Modern Standard Chinese, of the Han group, is closely descended from the form of speech of Beijing (that is, Pekinese), and is closely affiliated to forms known under various titles such as Mandarin, Guanhua and Putonghua. It carries the prestige of official use in the past. Cantonese, from the deep south, and Fukienese, from the south-eastern seaboard, are the two other forms which are encountered most frequently, both in the southern parts of China itself and among the immigrants who have settled in Southeast Asia, Europe and America. These two dialects incorporate their own idioms. With their markedly more musical intonation, they form a livelier medium than the principal dialect of the north, being well suited to the volatile way of life of the southerners. In addition, they retain features of an earlier pronunciation, from which all the modern dialects (including that of Modern Standard Chinese) have sprung, with greater integrity than the speech of the north. Due allowance must also be made for the less frequently spoken dialects which survive as enclaves in isolated communities in various parts of the land.

Chinese language is built up with a succession of units, and the tendency to use some of these singly has sometimes led to the mistaken description of the language as monosyllabic. In some dialects, principally of the north, some of the original distinctions of pronunciation have been eliminated, with the result that the language consists of a large number of homophones. However, these are not as numerous as might appear at first sight, since enunciation includes as an integral element a quality of tone. Thus, whereas the syllable *fa* may be used in English to represent the sound of a Chinese word, it requires completion by an indication of which one of several tones governs the way in which the word is enunciated. Allowance must be made for four distinct tones in the north and up to eight in the south, and it is difficult to find distinctions in English that are exactly equivalent. Some idea may be gained from the different ways of enunciating the word 'go', depending on its different grammatical functions, that is, as in (a) 'Tomorrow I go to London', (b) 'Go!' (as a command) and (c) 'Go?' (as a question).

The rise of different dialects and their pronunciations is intimately concerned with the origin and development of the written language. In European practice a limited number of signs are used in combination to record and indicate the sound of a word; Chinese writing consists of a very large number of separate units which convey a meaning but do not necessarily or certainly include an indication of how the unit should be voiced. Recent scholarship has succeeded in reconstructing earlier pronunciations (dating from as early as 600 BC) from which those of all the modern dialects were derived. The situation is rather as if, given the modern forms *due*, *deux*, *two* and *zwei*, it had been necessary to trace the existence of an original *duo*, which had long been forgotten, and never recorded, except in the form of II.

THE EVOLUTION OF CHINESE CHARACTERS

Single units of writing, or characters, first appear in recognizable forms as a medium for conveying language in the inscriptions made for oracular purposes on the shells and bones of the Shang-Yin kings. The earliest of these pieces date from perhaps 1700 BC, but they have been known to scholars from about 1900 only. The total of some 200,000 pieces were inscribed over a period of several centuries, and the handiwork of different scribes can sometimes be identified with some confidence. In the earliest parts of this archive the system of writing was relatively advanced and the ideas upon which it was based were somewhat sophisticated; it can only be assumed that it had been preceded by earlier stages, with the use of less durable substances, which have now perished.

Some of the characters seen in these inscriptions are close to, or even identical with, the forms used today. The meanings of many more and their relationship to the later forms have been the subject of painstaking and successful research; but many still defy attempts at interpretation. Of some 3,000 different characters which have been identified in these inscriptions, some 800 can be interpreted with a degree of certainty. It cannot now be known how they were pronounced in the Shang-Yin period.

From such beginnings it is possible to trace the evolution of the Chinese script over four millennia, and the stages of change correspond in part to changes in the media used for writing. Most of the inscriptions on the shells and bones were engraved with a sharp instrument, perhaps of bronze or of jade, and many of the strokes that were cut thereon were straight rather than curved. From perhaps 1000 BC characters appear as an integral part of the bronze ritual vessels, inscribed during the process of casting. Greater complexity has entered in, with some attempts at embellishment and considerable variety from place to place and time to time. The texts carried on this valuable and durable medium concerned a king's undertakings, a nobleman's title to land, a solemn compact between allies. As the centuries passed, a measure of standardization can be recognized, leading eventually to regularity and simplification. In time a form known as 'Greater Seal' gave way to 'Lesser Seal'. Although many of these inscriptions included characters whose use soon became obsolete, and were unknown to posterity, the great majority can be traced in the later forms that are in use today.

Possibly some of the oracle bones and shells once bore inscriptions made with a brush and pigments that have long since disappeared. A major change came about when a brush with ink became the regular means of writing, being used on materials such as wood or bamboo, and the more flexible silk and paper. The change coincided with three developments: the growth of recorded literature in the Spring and Autumn period (722–481 BC); the emerging need for official documents in the kingdoms of the Warring States (481 or 403–221 BC); and the enlargement of the Chinese vocabulary that philosophers and others needed to express their new ideas. Speedier writing, with the use of easier tools, had become both necessary and possible.

Bamboo and wood, easy to use and cheap to obtain, became the normal stationery of government office and man of letters; silken rolls were chosen for select literary texts, to be followed by paper when this came to be evolved. This occurred c. AD 100, but fragments of 'proto-paper' of an earlier stage date from some three centuries previously. With these changes, the curves and sweeps of the brush were taking the place of the sharp, angular lines made by the engraver's tool; the decorative forms of the 'Lesser Seal' were being replaced by forms of character suited to the narrow strips into which bamboo or wood could be cut.

The new forms of characters and media of writing (except for paper) were in regular use by about 200 BC, if not earlier. The following centuries saw the evolution of yet more characters so as to respond to new refinements of language, and by c. AD 100 a total of some 10,000 were being used for literary works and administrative documents. The same form of writing appeared on the epitaphs for famous men that were now being cut on tablets of stone; these also carried a few deliberately archaic forms at the head, by way of embellishment.

In this way there developed the forms of Chinese characters that have served to transmit China's literary heritage until recent times. A dictionary which was compiled at imperial orders in the seventeenth century included no less than 49,000 items, listing scholastic variants and idiosyncratic variations as these occurred in the large extent of Chinese literature at the time. Each item fulfilled the function of a word in a European language. For access to most works of Chinese writing, other than those specifically concerned with a technical topic, an educated person would need familiarity with perhaps 5,000 characters. On several occasions since 1911 a Chinese government has introduced measures to reform or simplify the script; those started since 1950 have been particularly effective.

Chinese characters are discrete, independent units of the written language which convey the meaning of a material object, a state of activity or a concept of the mind. Some characters possess an inbuilt indication of how they are pronounced when voiced, but such indications are by no means complete. For many or even most characters pronunciation, including the tone, must simply be learned from an informer, in the same way as a child learning to read English must be informed how to voice the sounds indicated by, for example, the letters A, E, I, O and U, or R, S and T.

The simplest characters are written with a single stroke of the brush; at the other extreme some require over thirty strokes. Some take the form of simple pictograms, such as those which denote 'tree' or 'horse', where the modern form is recognizably a stylized illustration. Others take the form of ideograms, for example where two parallel lines convey the meaning of 'two'. More complex characters were evolved by combining two or more simple characters of the type mentioned into a single unit, and it is these which form the majority of those in use.

Traditional Chinese scholarship explains the principles involved in such methods of combination, fastening on two which account for the greatest number. Many characters are explained as a direct association of two concepts or objects which together express a more complex idea; for example, juxtaposition of the two simple characters for 'woman' and 'child' indicates 'good' (that is, pleasant or likeable). The characters in another large group are regarded as including two adjacent elements, of which one conveys the general idea of the subject, or the category of its meaning, while the second element is an indication of its pronunciation. This second function is achieved by the choice of an existing character with whose pronunciation the reader is already familiar, and which can thus be used for its phonetic

1. *Preceding Page:* Court life in the Shang kingdom; a reconstruction

2. *Above:* Wine vessel *(zun)*, in bronze, of the Shang period, in the form of an elephant, with details of bird, tiger, etc. and characteristic decorative background; lid now missing; height 26 cm

3. Wine vessel, with animal features, in stoneware; olive green, brown and grey; height 28 cm;
c. AD 300

4. Lamp in shape of actor or shaman grasping snakes; bronze, with head in silver; from a tomb in the kingdom of Zhongshan (Hebei province) *c.* 300 BC; height 66 cm

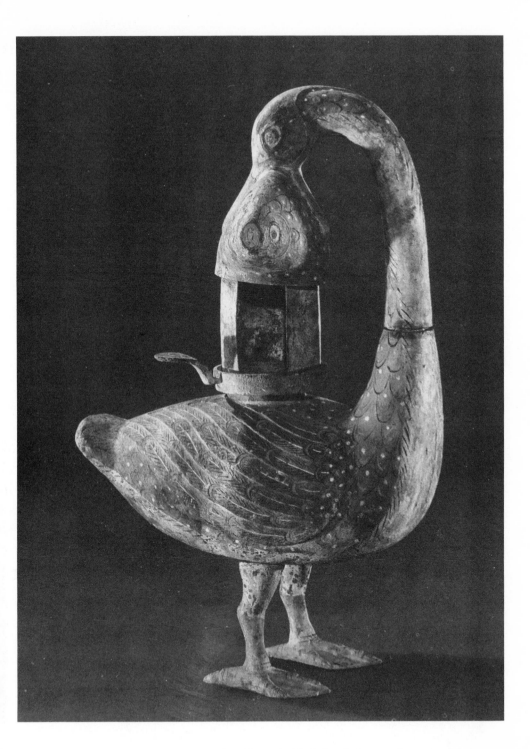

5. Lamp in shape of goose consuming a fish, with revolvable fitting, in bronze; from a tomb in Shaanxi province, *c.* 50 BC; 34 by 53 cm

6. The 'Seven Sages of the Bamboo Grove', engaged in literary, musical and artistic pursuits; low relief from a brick wall, in a tomb dated in East Jin (Tsin: 317–419); 88 by 120 cm

7. *Above:* Three of the twelve stoneware animals chosen to symbolize the divisions of time and to denote the years; Sui period; from a tomb in Hebei province; height 15–16 cm

8. *Below:* Screen of lacquered wood; in red, green and gold on black background, with a total of fifty-one animals, birds and reptiles (replica). From a site of the Chu culture, in Hebei province, Warring States period; 15 by 51 cm

9. *Below:* Bronze tiger, composing two halves, and used by Qin and Han emperors as a tally to convey authority to call out troops; height 5 cm

10. *Above:* Table of bronze with gold and silver inlay, with dragons, deer and phoenixes; from a tomb in the kingdom of Zhongshan (Hebei province) *c.* 300 BC; 47 by 47 cm; height 36 cm

11. *Below:* From a monthly return of stores and equipment held in one of the Han garrison forts AD 93–95; binding strings separated by 7 cm

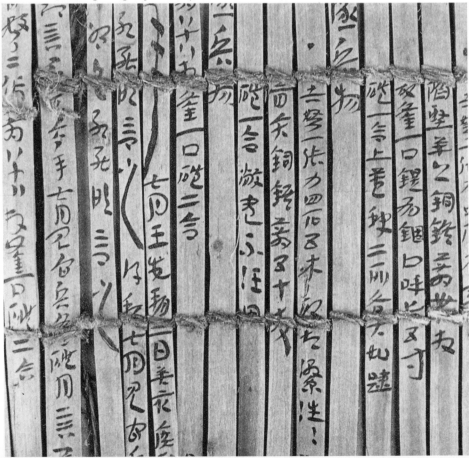

TABLE 7

CHINESE CHARACTERS AND THEIR VARIETIES

(a) The variation in the number of strokes required to write characters and in their complexity may be seen as follows:

一 *yi* one
保 *bao* to protect
靈 *ling* numinous

(b) Different types of character have been identified as follows:

pictograms: 木 *mu* wood   馬 *ma* horse
ideograms: 三 *san* three   中 *zhong* centre
juxtaposition 女 *nü* woman *plus*   子 *zi* child *combine as*   好 *hao* good
of ideas:
combination of elements for (i) general meaning (i.e. 'radical') and (ii) phonetic value:

         玉 *yu* jade *plus*   馬 *ma* horse *combine as*   瑪 *ma* agate

(c) In just the same way as the symbol I is pronounced differently as *uno* (Latin), *un, une* (French), *uno* (Italian) and *one* (English), so are Chinese characters pronounced differently in China's own dialects and in languages where these units have been incorporated; e.g.:

	Modern Standard Chinese	Cantonese	Sino-Japanese	Sino-Vietnamese	Sino-Korean	
I	yi	yat	ichi, itsu	nhất, nhú't	il	一
II	er	yi	ni, ji	nhị	i	二
III	san	saam	san	tam	sam	三
IV	si	sei	shi	tú'	sa	四
V	wu	ng	go	ngũ	o	五
VI	liu	luk	roku, riku	lục	yuk	六
VII	qi	chat	shichi, shitsu	thât	ch'il	七
VIII	ba	baat	hachi, hatsu	bát	p'al	八
IX	jiu	gau	ku, kyû	cú'u	ku	九
X	shi	sap	jû	thập	sip	十

value. In this way, for example, the character for 'agate' consists of two elements; one of these, being the simple character for 'jade', conveys the general meaning of a precious mineral; the second is the simple character for 'horse', pronounced as *ma*, and indicating how to pronounce the new complex character that has been evolved.

A number of anomalies appear if these principles are applied to the exclusion of other considerations. Some scholars have recently put forward the suggestion that the choice of some elements in the formation of characters depended on the association of ideas by way of metaphor; and that the metaphors in question call on concepts that play a similar role in the formation of other languages, harking back to mother earth and the creations of nature.

THE USES AND BEHAVIOUR OF CHARACTERS

China's system of writing is thus much more complex and demanding than the alphabets of Europe. There is no short cut to learning to recognize the basic meaning and pronunciation of each unit. In addition, with the natural development of language, characters came to express two or more ideas and to acquire two or more variants of pronunciation, and as a result the acquisition of literacy has become a much more arduous and time-consuming task in the east than it has been in the west. In the earliest texts, and in much of the literature dating up to the start of the present era, characters were used singly; gradually authors came to use two in combination (that is, binomes) as a means of imparting clarity or sharpening a definition.

Characters can play the part of noun, adjective or verb; there are no inflexions now which limit their grammatical function or modify their meaning in respect, for example, of number, tense or voice. Where such distinctions are essential they are specified by the use of another character chosen specifically for the purpose. A written sentence consists of a succession of characters whose sequence and relative position convey the grammatical form. The order of the words, whether spoken or written, is all important.

It is apparent that the quality or value of characters varies considerably, in so far as they fulfil different functions in the language. Traditionally Chinese scholars used to distinguish between 'full' and 'empty' characters; that is, between those used to specify a finite object or concept, and those which, whatever their origin may have been, had come to be used to indicate the relationships between 'full' characters, or to modify their meaning in the way that inflexions are used in other languages.

Chinese possesses a rich vocabulary which allows for precision and refinement with considerable economy of expression. Thus different words denote 'brother' or 'sister', depending on whether they are older or younger than the speaker; and long lists of characters denote particular types of bird, insect or plant. The expression of abstract ideas, however, may be somewhat more difficult as compared with some other languages, such as Greek. One device used to achieve this is the combination of a pair of opposites, for example *chang* ('long') and *duan* ('short') into *changduan*, to mean 'length'.

With the arrival of Buddhism in the first century of our era, Chinese writers were faced with the need to represent non-Chinese terms, especially Sanskrit names, and they solved the problem by using existing characters specifically for their phonetic value, irrespective of their meaning. Thus Śākyamuni was denoted by four characters whose pronunciation today is rendered as 'Shijiamouni'. At the time when this combination was adopted the pronunciation of the first unit was nearer 'Sak' or 'Sik', as it still is in some of the southern dialects. With the influx of words of European origin, in the nineteenth century, the Chinese found themselves facing the same problem, in a major way, and some of the suggestions or solutions of the time are immediately self-evident today. The galaxy of terms used in twentieth-century science also raised problems; these were solved either by forming combinations of two or more characters, or by evolving new characters; examples of the latter may be seen in the Chinese version of the table of atomic weights.

It is apparent that the task of learning to read demands far greater concentrated effort and time in the east than in the west; literacy is achieved by sheer learning by heart. While the written form of the language is marked by an economy of expression, the spoken forms are expansive. Economy of expression is seen to particular effect in poetry, where the written language lends itself to conveying matters of the heart with a terse juxtaposition of images, and a mastery of parallelism and contrast. By its very nature literature, whether prose or poetry, that is written in this way is the preserve of the man of letters, and it was far easier in China than elsewhere for an ever widening gulf to separate a literate and an illiterate population.

But even from early times some writings, such as short stories, were beginning to include elements of the language as it was spoken. With the new ideas of political and social equality, and the hope that the Chinese people would be able to share a common heritage of the written word, from whatever walk of life they sprang, early in the twentieth century there arose a determined effort or movement to compose literature in the vernacular. Official documents, learned treatises, articles in newspapers and the prose and poetry of today's authors are alike rendered in the language of everyday use, rather than in a traditional form that can be comprehended only by the few.

LANGUAGE AND ITS STUDY

Chinese men of letters may justly claim that they have laid the foundation of a heritage for all time. A long and sustained tradition has been concerned with both the production of literature and the promotion of scholarship. Literature has included both writings designed to please and those designed primarily to teach; scholarship has been directed to the comprehension of early texts and the application of their truths to contemporary conditions of life. In addition to a natural interest in language as such, the training of scholar civil servants and the provision of aids to the task of learning stimulated a study of the written form in which early literature was clothed. For the language of some of China's earliest and most highly respected texts (for example, the *Shijing* or *Book of Songs*, the *Yijing* or *Book of Changes*, the *Shujing* or *Book of Documents* and the *Chuci* or *Songs of the South*) is very different from that of later times, and by the start of the present era many of the terms and expressions used there had already come to elude understanding. Such difficulties gave rise to the production of commentaries, compiled after deep study and intended to clarify these early texts.

The philosophical essays, historical records or political tracts of the Warring States and early empires were written in language that was far easier to understand than that of earlier works, but which could still call for elucidation from as early as the second century AD. In the succeeding centuries some men of letters were composing with an eye more to form than to content; studied embellishment and artificiality were tending to take the place of clear, trenchant use of language; and written Chinese was lending itself to complex expressions that were often dependent on allusion. In time, a reaction in favour of simple and direct prose and verse set in, and for the last thousand years China has produced a full measure of literature marked now by simplicity, now by striving for effect. The greater the length and continuity of the tradition, the greater has been the temptation for, or sometimes the need of, a writer to allude to his predecessors' work. Perhaps the most difficult of all Chinese writings are those of some of the Qing (1644–1911) scholars, constrained by professional pride to demonstrate the depth of their erudition by the merest hint that the choice of a few characters could convey.

But by no means all the work of Qing scholars sacrifices clarity for effect; and some of their noblest achievements, which are a model of concise, clear statement, draw on a concern for explaining the complexities of Chinese language that was already several centuries old. The earliest of China's dictionaries, the *Shuo wen*, which set out to list the various forms of written characters with their meanings, had been compiled by Xu Shen in AD 121. In the sixth century another scholar had first formulated the distinctions between the tones; by the Tang period scholars were compiling lists of characters and choice expressions, mainly to assist candidates for the official examinations; and in those lists the entries were arranged according to rhyme. The men of letters of the Song age compiled some of China's clearest and most beautiful writings; they also devoted time and energy to collecting the evidence of China's use of language in the past.

In 1716 the Kangxi emperor ordered the compilation of a new dictionary, which has been reprinted subsequently on many occasions. The work was the second lexicon to be compiled where characters were listed according to the 'radical' system, which has remained in use in a number of standard dictionaries ever since, despite the evolution of several other methods. The radical system provides for the distribution of all characters in the language among 214 groups, in such a manner that, to all characters placed in one of the groups, there belongs one component element, or 'radical', in common. Thus, in the group that may be numbered 75, there are placed characters which include the element or radical 木 (*mu*, wood), as in 柏 (*bo* or *bai*, cypress), 梅 (*mei*, plum tree), 梓 (*zi*, catalpa) and 森 (*sen*, forest). The simplest of the 214 radicals consist of a single stroke of the brush, the most complex of seventeen strokes. The number of characters assigned to a group also varies considerably, reaching over a thousand in some cases. In each of the 214 groups, the characters are arranged according to the number of strokes of the brush needed to complete writing them in their entirety.

When the Jesuits first brought Chinese writing and literature to the attention of the learned world of Europe they adopted Latinized forms for some of the more prominent names; it is in this way that Kong fuzi, or Master Kong, has become known outside East Asia as 'Confucius'. Different ways of romanizing Chinese names made their appearance in the publications of the missionaries and diplomats who were working in China during the nineteenth century, and it was the system evolved by Sir Thomas Wade (1818–95) and Herbert Giles (1845–1935) that was for long used most frequently, appearing in many of the works of European and American sinologists. The Wade–Giles system partly reflects the pronunciation current in the lower part of the Yangzi River valley, with which the two scholars were primarily familiar, and which is marked by some obvious differences with the official 'Mandarin' pronunciation of the north. However, the system takes account of some phonetic distinctions which had died out in the north, while being retained in the central or southern provinces. Along with the Wade–Giles system there persisted certain other, less regular means of romanization.

Despite this pioneer work, no method of romanization has yet been devised that is capable of rendering the units of the Chinese language unambiguously. In 1953 the government of China introduced a completely new system, known as Pinyin, and this has taken the place of Wade–Giles in official documents and a great deal of western publications on Chinese subjects. The differences may be illustrated in respect of the names of a few well-known cities:

Common and incorrect usage	Wade–Giles	Pinyin
Peking	Pei-ching	Beijing 北京
Tientsin	T'ien-chin	Tianjin 天津
Chungking	Ch'ung-ch'ing	Chongqing 重慶

*

Evolution, continuity and creativity mark the development of China's written word. The shapes of characters have changed progressively in response to the growing sophistication of language and the needs for documentation. In the last 2,000 years different styles of calligraphy have developed, whether to serve the needs of an official, or to allow poet or artist to exploit the brush and its strokes as a means of expressing emotion recollected in tranquillity.

In addition, the use of different media for writing evokes the richness and variety of China's literary tradition. Our first records are those of acts of divination engraved on turtles' shells or animals' bones. There follow the texts of solemn oaths, a *monumentum aere perennius*, to be seen on the vessels that are on display in many museums today. Stone tablets bear the brush strokes of eulogies designed to commemorate respected officials. Bamboo and wood served the purposes of imperial official, historian and philosopher; in time their works would appear as scrolls, codexes and foliated books made of paper. For exceptionally choice purposes and rare occasions tablets or narrow strips of jade were cut with exquisite care and reverence to bear the text of an emperor's communications due for presentation to the highest of the gods at the summit of Mount Tai.

VI

BELIEFS, HOPES AND FEARS

As with other peoples, so with China artistic creations, a literary
heritage and religious practice drew on a rich store of human experience of which some traces, but by no means all, have survived. Much
was brought about in response to the hazards of nature and by way
of a search for a means of survival. Much that was believed or
practised harked back to a mythology that took shape from earliest
times. Compelling beliefs demanded symbolic actions and representation, as well as ceremonial mime and rite. Emperors and
noblemen, officials and clansmen all played their appropriate parts
in the practices that attracted public acclaim both in town and
country. In addition, individuals chose their own paths to explore the
mysteries of eternal truth, and in so doing contributed significantly to
the extensive and varied cultural heritage which now marks so many
features of China's achievement.

Rich and varied as that heritage is, its features do not respond to
a systematic classification in a manner that has become possible in
the west. From time to time officials of government made studied
attempts to impose an orthodoxy or to eliminate certain customs as
being crude or unworthy of a civilized way of life. But in many cases
the folklore, religious rites, music, dance or artistic motif on which
a central government has frowned survived unchecked in the remote
countryside. The mythology, beliefs and practices of the past have
both stimulated and inhibited the expression of human genius.

MYTHOLOGY AND ITS THEMES

In Chinese eyes the universe was seen as a whole. Mythology
explained its shape, its mode of operation and the awesome changes
that alter its face with recurring regularity. Mythology accounted
for man's place in the universe, providing him with an identity and
convincing him of the part that he plays, the necessity for his existence
and the survival of his efforts. Mythology fastened on the eternal
rhythms of the world and showed how human actions correspond
with those of other realms.

It was believed that cycles of change govern the operation of the universe, whether seen in the movements of the stars of the heavens, in the return of the seasons each year or in the daily succession of light and dark. To keep that cycle in perpetual motion regular meetings occur between partners, in the same way that man and woman meet and mate regularly, thereby ensuring the continuity of the human race. Such a meeting takes place once a year in the heavens, when the two constellations of the Weaver (in Vega) and the Oxherd (or River's Drum, in Altair) come together. For, long ago they were separated as punishment for their disobedience, and apart from this annual event they lie on either side of the Milky Way, reunited only exceptionally, so as to generate the force that keeps the cycle turning.

Creation and the emergence of mankind had come about as a result of struggle and conquest. From a primeval, formless mass a split separated the heavens from the earth. Between the two there lay a figure, named Pangu, portrayed in mortal guise, from whose members there arose the features of the physical world; his eyes were transformed into the sun and the moon, his blood into the waters of the rivers, his teeth and bones into the metals and stones of the earth. A further account concerns the relationship of the earth to the heavens. A mighty battle was fought between two heroes; in its course one of the supports that linked heaven and earth was struck and severed; thereafter they faced different directions. In this way the heavenly bodies struck out their course to the west and the earth lay tilted towards the south-east, where all its waters run.

Mankind was seen to be but a part of the single, organic universe, which was not necessarily distinct from the animal world. In the tradition that was fostered in educated and sophisticated circles, proud of their distinction from other mortals, some of the tribes of the south and south-west were said to have come into being through the union of animal with woman. Thus, a king of one of the southern tribes promised his daughter in marriage to anyone who could bring him the head of one of his enemies. The reward was duly claimed by Panhu, his pet dog, and from that union there arose a group of the Man peoples, in the lands of the present province of Hunan. Such an origin accounted for the failure of those peoples to assimilate to a more cultured way of life.

Orthodox tradition of a later age also sought to establish a direct association between the kings and emperors of history and their forebears of mythology. Some of these had conquered their rivals before proceeding to establish and preside over an ordered way of life on earth; some had practised an ideal form of conduct whereby man could be governed in justice and the fruits of his individual labours could be shared throughout the community. Some of these early monarchs were grouped together, in terms of the Three Sovereigns, sometimes said to be those of Heaven, Earth and Man, or the Five Monarchs, variously named, but usually including Huangdi (the Yellow Emperor), and Yao and Shun the Blessed.

Mythology also showed how man had been able to survive the hazards of nature. Originally there had been ten suns to take their place in the skies, following one another in succession, but the danger of exposure to excessive heat could be great. Only when Yi the Archer had shot down nine was the human race relieved of this hazard. As in other traditions, such as those of Israel and Greece, so in that of China, the waters had once covered the face of the earth. Following an unsuccessful attempt by his father, Yu the Great was able to reduce the floods and enable man to prosper. Other heroes of myth enabled man to set about the occupations of a civilized way of life. Thanks to Shennong, father of agriculture, man learned how to till the soil and raise a harvest; others showed the way to work metals. To Nügua and her brother Fuxi belonged the credit for teaching a number of crafts, as may be seen in the symbolic compasses and set square that they always carry, when portrayed by an artist. In this example mythology once again stresses the value and achievements of a partnership.

BELIEFS AND PRACTICES

Both magic, where actions or mime are thought to be capable of controlling phenomena, and religion, which depends on intercession with identified spirits or gods, feature in China's ritual observances, and distinction between the two is by no means always possible. Both of these approaches to the unknown affected the conduct of official cults and the practices that have continued on a popular level.

Writings of the Warring States period (481 or 403–221 BC) and the early empires tell of beliefs in a host of spirits or gods whose jurisdiction was limited to a specified region. There were the gods of certain mountains or rivers; there were those who controlled some of nature's forces, such as rain or wind, and could direct them to act either as a blessing, or as a curse, for humanity. As man's activities grew to be more complex and specialized, special spirits were conceived as presiding over skills, crafts and occupations, whether of the villager's hearth, the artisan's bench or the clock-maker's guild.

These were the *shen*, capable of affecting mankind for either good or evil. They were to be encountered in isolated spots, often on the mountain sides. Some inhabited the form of known animals; others were hybrid by nature, with head, limbs or tail drawn from diverse creatures, such as a carp with chicken's claws, or a dog with a human face. Contact could be beneficial or dangerous, either for the individual who observed these creatures or for the whole of his community. Identification between man and *shen*, brought about by consuming the latter's flesh or wearing its fur, could bring a blessing, or, in some cases, a curse.

Man communicated with the gods by prayer, or sacrifice, or through the services of an intermediary. The gift of human or animal victims could appease the anger or win the help of a powerful deity, such as the lord of the Yellow River or the Yangzi; eventually, according to the myth, these dangerous gods could be brought to heel thanks to human or semi-human heroism. Other devices, belonging perhaps more to magic than to religion, included invocation or mime; for example, a dance entitled the 'Steps of Yu' could exorcize evil or cure disease. A different type of dance, in which youths or old men played the part of dragons, was intended to ensure sufficient rainfall; for, according to the myth, by mounting the clouds the dragon would induce the rain to fall, and the act was played out, with great verve and elaboration, to show the dragons performing their part. Imprecations of a more deadly and sombre type (*gu*), such as enclosing specimens of different types of insect, maggot or serpent in a vessel and awaiting the moment when one had devoured the others, could, it was hoped, bring about the destruction of an enemy.

From the multiplicity of beliefs and practices some measure of formalization came about, with the grouping of certain deities together. Five special, renowned mountains and four special waterways were isolated as being worthy of particular service in view of the power that their gods could exert. The prayers that individual farmers might make for the blessing of their soil or their crops came to be presented in unison by the overlord of the land at a single shrine, the *she* for the soil, the *ji* for the grain. There also came about the concept of four deities, or *di*, whose powers operated over each of the four quarters of the globe; with later intellectual developments this concept was extended by the addition of one *di* for the centre. In the Former Han period (206 BC to AD 9) the five *di* formed the focus of cults in which the emperor himself sometimes took part.

From much earlier times, however, there had emerged the concept of a single, omnipotent god, supreme over all others and over the world of man. Worship to this deity was strictly limited to the ruler of mankind, whose kingship may well have owed as much to his religious functions as to his powers of coercion. The kings of Shang

had worshipped and sought the blessing of Di, or Shangdi, to whose
realm they believed the souls of their deceased ancestors had repaired;
the kings of Zhou worshipped Tian, or Heaven, as supreme arbiter
of the world, capable of disposing human destinies, and set apart in
a realm in which human beings or their souls did not participate.
Tian and Shangdi were perhaps conceived in anthropomorphic
guise. From about the beginning of the present era and until 1911
Chinese emperors rendered service on behalf of their people to Tian
as supreme arbiter of their destiny. But there was no insistence on
the exclusion of other gods, as in western monotheism. At times
Chinese emperors worshipped other deities, such as Hou tu, sovereign
of the soil, or Tai yi, Grand Unity.

Direct contact with the deity at times formed the aim and object
of these religious occasions. Invocations were pronounced to persuade
the god to descend so that man or woman could meet him face to
face. On the rare occasions when an emperor succeeded in climbing
to the summit of Mount Tai his duty lay in reporting to Tian on the
state of his realm.

Quite apart from the imperial cults, the majority of the Chinese
people were concerned with beliefs and practices at a popular level.
By offerings, prayers or invocations they sought the gift of rain.
Should the local deity refuse such blandishments and withhold his
blessing, he could in turn provoke the curses of his worshippers; and
if sorely tried by his rejection of their appeal they would banish him
from their land or smash the idols that stood for his presence. Or else
men and women would pray to other gods with heart and soul for
the gift of a son to ensure that the family's line would not be cut off,
and that religious links with the past would be maintained.

Shamans and shamanesses (*wu*) featured in early poetry such as
the *Songs of the South* and played a leading part in some of these rites.
By their trances, dances and invocations they could induce a god to
appear, cure diseases, promise a pregnant woman an easy delivery
or bring down the rain from the skies. But should their efforts to
fulfil such a promise fail, they could themselves be subjected to direct
exposure to the sun that was scorching the earth and ruining the
crops. By suffering in this way it was hoped that they would redouble
their efforts to stop a drought; perhaps they had themselves taken
on the role of a human sacrifice designed to appease a cruel master.
Some of the shamans' activities could provoke criticism, if they were
thought to be abusing their powers and imposing on a gullible public
which lay open to deception and the appeal of vulgar persuasion.

Fears that have assailed mankind in most cultures have left their
mark no less conspicuously in China than elsewhere. Evil spirits bent
on harm were known to be capable of wreaking havoc with human

TABLE 8

INDIGENOUS BELIEFS, RELIGIOUS PRACTICES AND DAOIST CULTS

c. 1700 BC	Divination by oracle bones.
	Worship by Shang kings of Di and Shangdi as the supreme authority.
1000	Worship of Tian (Heaven) by the kings of Zhou.
c. 800	Divination by yarrow stalks and hexagrams.
c. 700	Growth of worship at local shrines of the soil and the grain, and to a multiplicity of other deities.
221	State worship of the four *di* adopted for the Qin empire.
219	Ascent of Mount Tai by the first Qin emperor for religious purposes. Search for immortality from the Isles of the East (Penglai).
205	Adoption of worship of the five *di* for the Han empire. Divination with the use of instruments.
from 200	Poems of the *Chuci*, with shamanist content and invocations. Cult of immortality of the Paradise of the East.
c. 130	Han Wudi's trust in intermediaries to procure immortality.
114, 113	Inauguration of the imperial cults to Hou tu (Lord of the Earth) and Tai yi (Grand Unity) at sites distant from Chang'an.
110	Wudi's ascent of Mount Tai.
c. 31	Inauguration of the imperial cult of Tian (Heaven), at sites near Chang'an.
3 BC	Soteriological cult of the Queen Mother of the West sweeps northern China.
AD 56	Guangwudi, first emperor of the Later Han, worships Tian on Mount Tai.
first century	Cult of immortality of the Paradise of the West.
166	Imperial sacrifices to Laozi in association with the Buddha.
184	Yellow Turbans' revolt signals the strength of popular Daoist movements.
317	Ge Hong's production of the *Baopuzi* (treatise on Daoist techniques).
fifth century	Imperial reaction against the excesses of Daoist cults.
442	Patronage of Daoist cults by the Northern Wei court.
536	Death of Tao Hongjing, codifier of Daoist doctrine.
573–8	Imperial (Northern Zhou) proscription of Daoist and Buddhist establishments.
eleventh century	Magnetic compass fixed to divination boards; growth of geomancy as now practised.
1420	Parts of the existing Temple of Heaven built in Beijing.
1850	Rise of Hong Xiuquan (1813–64), leader of Taiping rebel movements, with messianic claims.

fortunes and they must needs be exorcized by the recitation of spells or confrontation with material symbols, or perhaps with the intermediacy of the shaman. Strange forms of worship, which could include sacrifice or debauched practices, took place in the more remote parts of the countryside, to the dismay and shock of officials removed from the shelter of a cultured and sophisticated town to take up an appointment there. But demons must be chased away, either by those means or by others that were thought fit. Such was the function of the apotropaic figures perched on the roof of a Chinese building to keep guard, and of the fire-crackers, ignited with great excitement and joy, and serving as a means of releasing the pent-up emotion of a community.

THE DESTINY OF MAN AND THE HOPE OF THE WORLD TO COME

Concepts of a life hereafter took a number of different forms in China, depending partly on the view of man and the nature of his soul and on the belief that all living creatures possessed certain properties. According to one set of ideas, man's bodily frame is informed with two spiritual elements; one of these, the *po*, is the force that keeps the body alive and enables its limbs to operate; the other, the *hun*, provides human beings with intellectual power and the capacity for spiritual experience.

Death severs the identification that these elements must share with the body if life is to continue. Once that link is ruptured certain precautions are necessary to ensure that the two spiritual parts will receive the treatment that is their due and to prevent them wreaking harm on earth. This could occur if, dissatisfied with the services rendered after death, one of the spiritual elements chose to inhabit another living body, returning to earth for the express purpose of so doing. There was no doubt that such a course of action would be possible; for it was believed that living bodies of many types were capable of transferring their being into the bodies of other creatures. Transformations of this type were well known to anyone familiar with the life cycle of the silkworm; in folk-tales and other writings they appear as changes between frogs and quails, or sparrows and clams.

There would thus be no difficulty in believing that one of the spiritual elements of man could return to earth in a new type of incarnation. Should it do so it would be termed a *gui* or demon or 'hungry ghost', determined to seek redress for sufferings received during an earthly existence, or to demand more diligent service or more regular offerings at its shrine. These then were other types of spirit, whom the unwary might encounter, and appeasement of their anger demanded care and attention. For a victim of murder could return to earth either to punish those who had slain him or to upbraid his own family for failing to bring the guilty party to justice.

The ever-present belief in the power of the dead, together with a sincere respect for their demands and needs, is manifest in a number of practices. From Shang times at least great care has been lavished on arrangements for burial; the dead person must be treated in a manner that corresponds with the status attained on earth and with the style of living to which he had become accustomed. For this reason treasures, articles of equipment and consumable stores of food and clothing were buried in a grave, to provide for the needs of the *po* in the next world. Regularly the next of kin would lay their offerings at the graveside or in shrines erected for the purpose; at set periods of the year, including the spring festival of Qingming, members of a family would forgather and repair the damages inflicted on a tomb by gale or flood. Epitaph inscriptions, engraved on stone with careful attention to calligraphy, recorded for all time the achievements of the dead. In specially constructed shrines an array of wooden tablets proclaimed to the worshipper the names, relationship and dates of a family's members. As one generation succeeded its predecessor, new tablets would be introduced and those of the oldest members reverently removed, to make way for the newcomers.

Observances of this type are sometimes described under the general heading of 'ancestor worship', but the term can be misleading. Fundamentally there was no concept that the soul of the deceased person was present to receive worship in the memorial shrine. The respect and obedience due to fathers in their lifetime was due no less to forefathers after death, and in this way the continuity and identity of a clan would be assured. At the highest level, shrines devoted to the memory of the founding emperor of a dynasty were sometimes built at the capital city and throughout the provinces. In other cases a famous teacher could inspire the same treatment, and it was in this way that temples were erected in honour of Confucius, and that 'Confucianism' has sometimes and inaccurately been described primarily as a religion.

Other beliefs concerned man's destiny at death, should all efforts of the shaman, the intermediary who could form a bridge between different worlds, fail to lure back the souls of those who had just died. According to some ideas one element of the soul, the *hun*, could be led to an upper realm, of paradise, to live in the company of eternal beings such as the sun and the moon. The road to this goal lay by way of the east, possibly by journeying to Penglai, one of the Isles of the Blessed, there to undergo preparation. Alternatively some believed that paradise lay in the realm over which Xiwangmu, 'Queen Mother of the West', presided, enthroned on a mountain fortress that lay to the west. Just as sun and moon, enduring members of the universe, took their place in the Paradise of the East, so in the Paradise of the West there was a link with the continuity of the cosmos; for the Queen Mother also possessed the secret of how to renew the cycles of universal being each year.

Tales of the Queen Mother's occasional but regular meetings with a partner take their place in China's mythology in various forms. Sometimes the partner is named as 'King Father of the East'. In earlier versions the Queen's partner is a known sovereign of the earth, bent on seeking the drug or elixir that the Queen preserves and which can ensure immortality of a different type. This would amount to the eternal continuation of life on earth, and the possibility of obtaining this drug obtrudes in many ideas that concern death and the hereafter. Some concepts, however, provide for the corporate life of the dead in a somewhat gloomy realm below the earth, sometimes termed the Huangquan or 'Yellow Springs'. It is for this purpose that articles of utility were buried in a grave, to enable the dead person to avert danger, to live a comfortable life or to enjoy pleasures and amusements. Yet a different concept envisaged a realm inhabited by spiritual beings of diverse shapes and sizes, more ethereal than this-worldly. As on earth, so in the Yellow Springs and elsewhere, existence was tempered by social hierarchies and could be subject to the supervision of authorities, conceived as members of an imperial dispensation.

ORACLES, OMENS AND DIVINATION

Without the systematic corpus of information that is available in an age of scientific enquiry, the Chinese looked to occult sources for guidance, information and a means of solving the problems of every-day life. Some of the means of so doing had been evolved by the time of the kings of Shang, and both these and the methods of later ages have coloured many aspects of Chinese culture, giving rise to intellectual enquiry, iconographic symbols or, alternatively, the abuses of charlatans. Guidance has been sought in the ever-present signs of the world of nature or by deliberate attempts to induce such signs to appear. Ineluctable warnings have been discerned in the form of strange and fearful phenomena which cannot elude observation.

Occult powers, it has been believed, may make it possible to choose an auspicious timing for an action, a suitable heir for adoption, or a wife for marriage. In imperial times a general might owe his commission to their guidance. These sources of wisdom and knowledge could foretell the chances of success in battle or in the hunt, or the prospects that would attend appointment to office.

Signs of future events could be seen in the normal workings of the world of nature. The shapes of the clouds could inform the observer of an enemy's activities or intentions. A careful inspection of the winds could reveal the presence of violence in specific parts of the empire, provided that attention was paid to the quarter from which they arose, the time when they started to blow and their degree of force. Observation of the winds at certain key dates in the calendar, such as New Year's Day, could inform an emperor of the prospects for the harvest of the incoming year.

Nature could also present man with signs of a different type, which arose from irregular or abnormal events, such as eclipses of the sun or the moon; unseasonable changes of climate; the burgeoning of trees or flowers in winter; the birth of a freak; the outbreak of fire in an emperor's palace; or sounds whose place of origin could not be traced. Such strange phenomena could be nothing but terrifying, for they were seen to be an upset in the harmony of the world that could threaten the survival of the human race. In time they were explained as the deliberate and inescapable messages conveyed by higher authority to man. They were thought to require an immediate response from the emperor, who had by this means been warned that he must adjust his rule so as to achieve a more just type of government. Such was the power of omens.

From Shang times at least it was believed that certain objects stood possessed of a store of accumulated wisdom and that they could be induced to reveal recognizable signs of this to man, if he would but take the correct steps to seek their purpose. Principal among these were the shells of the turtle; for turtles were accredited with living for several thousand years and thus acquiring a treasury of unforgettable knowledge. In the vegetable world a plant that is usually identified as the yarrow was believed to possess similar properties; for this too lived to a great age, and the multiplicity of its stalks displayed the extent of its capacities. The earliest attempts at divination were designed to produce visible signs from these sources of occult wisdom.

It was for this reason that the kings of Shang, and possibly some individuals before their time, had manipulated the turtles' shells or the shoulder bones of animals, in what is China's first known method of divination; and it is to this practice that we owe our knowledge of China's earliest writings. The shells and bones were exposed to fire, and the resulting cracks, which seemingly appeared at random, were then shown to a specialist or seer for interpretation of the question that had been raised. Fortunately for posterity, at the end of the procedure a scribe engraved the text of that question together with a note of the answer that had been vouchsafed, and such inscriptions constitute the earliest royal archive that is available in Chinese history. Interpretation depended, presumably, on the number, shape or position of the cracks on the plastron or scapula. But by the beginning of the present era a number of manuals had been compiled to explain how these mysterious signs could be understood. By that time some form of instruction was evidently necessary for the completion of the procedure. The seer, with his visionary gift, was apparently not always available for consultation; divination had come to depend on prescriptions that could be read by all.

By perhaps 800 BC yarrow stalks were being used for divination, possibly by means of methods other than those that had been adopted by the start of the present era and are still in use today. According to the method that has now become traditional, a number of stalks were drawn from a bunch at random and divided into small groups of four. Depending on the number of stalks remaining in the hand at different stages of the long and complex process, so did one of the operators inscribe a line of writing, either as a whole or split into two parts. Altogether six lines of writing were constructed in this way, in obedience to the accepted and respected prescriptions for the rite, with the result that the emerging pattern of a hexagram was one of a total of sixty-four possible combinations. Depending on the make-up of that hexagram, that is, its arrangement of whole or split lines, so would the seer be able to pronounce the answer to the question put to this occult source of wisdom.

From earliest times interpretation of the hexagrams was clothed in mystery, and the original writings on the subject that survive are couched in the terms of formulas with a technical meaning that has eluded full comprehension by the uninitiated for at least two thousand years. Divination by this means was open to men and women of all ranks of society; it has been practised widely throughout communities which share a Chinese culture; and it has given rise to considerable philosophical speculation and scholastic commentary.

The principle of another method, known not so widely to the west, resembles that of the Ouija board. An instrument is suspended in a frame, which is held in place by two men; as it swings in space its lower point traces marks in the sand that lies beneath, thus forming written characters; the ensuing enigmatic message lies revealed for all including the questioner to await and to see how the destiny of the future bears out the accuracy of the forecast. There were also many other ways of ascertaining whether the moment chosen for a project would be auspicious. Some of these depended on ensuring that the relevant moments of an individual's life cycle corresponded with the appropriate phases in the major cycles of sun, moon and earth. Misfortune could easily follow if a time was chosen at which those cycles were not in conformity and balance with one another. For easy consultation almanacs were compiled which were suited to the particular circumstances of a man or woman, such as the time and place of birth, and which would advise whether or not to embark on a project such as a marriage, a journey or the erection of a house.

The search for auspicious circumstances in which to initiate a project could determine a choice of place no less than of time. The early belief that certain sites on earth, such as mountains, were possessed of holiness was accompanied by a faith that others were blessed by virtues or marred by blemishes that could render them either suitable or unsuitable for human habitation or other activities. From this there arose the cult of *fengshui* or geomancy, which depended on the power of a seer to comprehend the qualities that informed a specified locality. Those qualities depended in part on territorial configurations; if auspicious, they could admit or even invite the flow of life-giving energies (*qi*); if inauspicious they would fail to block intrusion by injurious forces (*sha*). This belief has affected the choice of a site for residence of a household or burial of a parent; in modern times it can dictate the situation of business premises or even require interference with the landscape, to the point of slicing off the summit of an overlooking hillside thought to stand in the way of *qi*.

THE MYSTIC'S PATH (*DAO*)

The centuries of the Warring States (481 or 403–221 BC) witnessed some of the most formative advances in moulding China's religious and intellectual traditions. Major steps marked the formulation of thought; with the growth of kingdoms there arose specialists in framing documents; organs of government were designed to co-ordinate and control human effort. These developments could hardly fail to constrain individual initiative and to call for conformity with the values of the emerging body politic. But there were those who chose to react against these pressures; they saw through the subjective nature of those values; they rejected a call for conventional behaviour; they were bent on seeking the truths of ultimate reality.

In contrast with both those who saw individual man as forming the centre of the universe and those who believed in the paramount need to organize man and to control his activities, there were some who pursued a lonely path to find the *dao*, that inherent order that pervades the universe and all being, regulating its cycles and maintaining its balances. In this view of a nature-centred universe, with no rigid distinction between sacred and profane, man is but one of the myriad creations, whose powers and qualities are of no greater value than those of his neighbours. Human destiny and happiness or success are bound up neither with obedience to conventional rules of morality nor with the search for fortune; they are subject to an adjustment of human behaviour such that it will conform with the eternal *dao* and avoid despoiling nature's gifts for personal, material gain.

Dao is present in all aspects of nature, but it is not necessarily to be perceived in material form. As the opening sentence of the *Daode jing* (*The Way and its Power*) reminds us, *dao* is not to be described in words; for man-made language can only be limited in scope and origin, unable to express a concept that lies beyond. The path to the unknown and the mysterious leads to the gate of *dao*, which can never be found by a purposeful search conducted on human terms; and the immensity of *dao* is perhaps to be understood in terms of allegory. The splendid imagery of the opening chapter of the *Zhuangzi*, a text of perhaps the fourth century BC, takes the reader to a realm where human ideas of time and space are brought into question, and human aspirations reduced to size. Pursuit of the *dao* may lead to a vision of the infinite, detached from human ideas of goodness, beauty and truth; it may leave the seeker content with the isolated life of a hermit in the mountains, nurtured on a diet of pine-needles. As pilgrims among the hills, so may men and women be best placed to accommodate with the eternal mysteries of the universe.

THE DAOIST AND THE BUDDHIST CHURCHES

Daoist religious movements arose at a time of political and social instability, during the last decades of the Han empire. A few popular leaders were able to attract a following, principally from the poor, the deprived and the disaffected, by promising immediate rewards in return for obedience and the contribution of goods and chattels. The rewards that were held out could include relief from bodily pain, the cure of illness, the elimination of curses or exorcism of evil spirits. Above all the faithful might hope to acquire a draught of the elixir of immortality which would guarantee everlasting life in this world.

Soteriological cults were by no means new to China at this time; they had included one that swept through north China from east to west in 3 BC. But a new measure of leadership and organization was now becoming apparent. The movements of the second century AD prospered owing to the hope that they held out for relief from immediate suffering in a world subject to turmoil and oppression. Enrolled as members of a community, devotees were prepared to undergo disciplines and to perform exercises of both a physical and a spiritual nature; these included the practice of rhythmic breathing and subjection to periods of meditation; they affected diet, in the form of abstinence from certain foods such as salt or cereals, and they could involve the adoption of certain sexual techniques.

In so far as they collected and prepared herbs for curative purposes, compounded drugs for the elixir or experimented in turning base metals into gold, some of the Daoist establishments stimulated a practical study of aspects of physics and chemistry, and provided a base for the conduct of experiments in alchemy. Set in remote parts of the countryside, Daoist temples (*guan*) could provide an asylum from a turbulent world; they could also give scope for a leader to exert undue influence on his charges or abuse his position to his own advantage. As in other Chinese organizations, so in Daoist communities, hierarchies came to the fore, to the point of giving rise to a supreme head of the Daoist church, sometimes termed a 'Daoist Pope'. As the movements developed, their leaders sought to strengthen their authority by claiming affinity with certain earlier teachers or mystics whose search for truth had led to writings on the mysteries of *dao*. The leaders could also support their hold on their communities by the threat of punishments for disobedience; or, for those who had not merited the gift of the elixir, by that of relegation to a terrifying hell. Daoist religion included scope both for the worship of frightening deities and for the fear of exacting demons. On the credit side it prompted the compilation and preservation of a large corpus of literature, known now as the *Dao zang* or 'Daoist Canon'. Not surprisingly Daoist communities earned the distrust of established authority. Born of discontent, they could easily give rise to dissension or harbour secret groups bent on challenging the authority of an official.

Daoist establishments had borrowed some of their features from Buddhism, which had made its way into China during the first century AD. The faith had been brought by pilgrims who had trodden the Silk Roads from north India through Central Asia, and it was their destiny or honour to introduce a number of ideas that had not yet been seen in China.

TABLE 9

THE BUDDHIST PRESENCE

65	First official reference to Buddhism; establishment of a Buddhist group at Pengcheng.
148	Translation of Buddhist scriptures into Chinese by An Shigao.
166	Imperial sacrifices to the Buddha in association with Lao Zi.
286	Translation into Chinese of the *Lotus sūtra*.
from 300	Promotion of the Buddhist 'Pure Land' sect by Hui Yuan.
366	Construction and decoration of the first of the 'Thousand Buddha' caves at Dunhuang.
c. 400	Kumārajīva's introduction of new Buddhist doctrines and translation of texts.
413	Fa Xian's travels to Buddhist centres in Central Asia, Sri Lanka and Indonesia; his return with religious texts to Jiankang (Nanjing).
446	Northern Wei proscription of Buddhism.
from 489	Construction of Buddhist monuments, temples and outsize statues at Yungang (489) and Longmen (495).
502–9	Liang Wudi's patronage of Buddhism in the south.
546	Arrival of Paramārtha on south China coast with Sanskrit documents and teaching of *yoga* practice.
573–8	Imperial (Northern Zhou) proscription of Daoist and Buddhist establishments.
574	Establishment of the Tiantai sect of Buddhism. Anti-Buddhist measures of the court of Zhou.
626	Tang Taizong's patronage of Buddhism.
629–45	Xuan Zang's visit to northern India, followed by his translations of Yogācāra scriptures.
eighth century	Growth of Chan (Zen) Buddhism, traced to Bodhidharma (sixth century).
819	Han Yu's attack on Buddhism.
845	Proscription of Buddhist establishments.
c. 1036	Buddhist caves at Dunhuang sealed.

According to the teaching of Gautama Buddha (sixth to fifth centuries BC), salvation from suffering lies by way of spiritual practice, leading to a change in the mode of consciousness. Buddhism provides a cure for evils, in much the same way as medicaments bring about recovery from disease, or a rescuer releases a captive from prison. Its teaching centres round the Four Noble Truths: for ordinary mortals, suffering is inevitable; there is a cause for such suffering; that cause can be eliminated; and the way to eliminate it lies by way of the Eightfold Path. By such means all desires and the sufferings that go with them are expelled, and it is possible to escape from the inexorable turn of the wheel which conveys an individual from one stage of existence to the next, each marked by its own measure of hurt.

Two principal forms of Buddhism developed. In Theravāda, the older form, which spread to Thailand, Burma and Sri Lanka, the individual may seek his own salvation by means of certain disciplines, but he is not able to 'save' others. Mahāyāna, or the 'Great Vehicle', which is the name for the other form, implies that the way forward lies open to all sentient beings. For all partake of the Buddha nature; and whereas in Theravāda salvation is open only to those who practise its disciplines, Mahāyāna thought provides for the existence of the Bodhisattva. This is a saviour figure, whose vast store of merit can be transferred to weaker and more ignorant sentient beings. The Bodhisattva has renounced his own salvation in order to save others, and thereby represents a dimension of compassion as well as wisdom.

It was the Mahāyāna which came to China, with its message of compassion for all humanity, and there it diversified into a number of schools. These included that of Tiantai, whose adherents gave great veneration to the *Lotus sūtra*; they held that the ultimate truths expressed in that text formed a most potent vehicle that would lead to salvation. Another school envisaged rebirth in the Pure Land, a paradise free of all evil. The path thereto lies principally by the exercise of faith and devotion to Amitābha, the Buddha who presides over that paradise. Perhaps it was in Chan (or Zen) Buddhism that Chinese characteristics were most noticeable. Chan incorporates a regimen of spiritual disciplines and meditation that leads to the uncovering of the perfect Buddha nature. This lies latent within each individual, usually being obscured by greed, hatred and delusion; it is only when such passions have been dispelled that the disciple experiences a sudden and intuitive enlightenment and the Buddha nature is revealed without blemish.

Mahāyāna Buddhism came to Luoyang, capital of the Later Han dynasty, in the first century AD and settled in town and country during the following centuries. By about 150 the first real attempts were being made to translate the scriptures of the new faith from Sanskrit into Chinese – a daunting task that demanded much of the Chinese language and left its imprint thereon. In the seventh century this work was continued in a major way, when a Chinese scholar and pilgrim, called Xuan Zang, embarked on the long road to north India to collect new texts, for translation on his return to Chang'an. Meanwhile the faith had left other marks on the land. Temples had been built in a new form of architecture designed to house the relics of the faith and to provide for its services; monasteries had been founded and, thanks to the valuable gifts and privileges that they had received, they had become large landowners, sometimes granted exemption from taxation. At times the faith had enjoyed the patronage of an emperor; at other times it had suffered criticism. Temples were adorned with a rich panoply of images dressed in gold leaf and vestments of the finest silks; a few large-scale sites of worship, such as that of Yungang, had been built with an array of gigantic statues that symbolized the ideals of the faith, at the cost of many hours of work by China's sculptors and craftsmen.

The recent discovery (1985) of relics at a Buddhist temple close to the Tang city of Chang'an confirms in a dramatic way the historians' account of an emperor's devout service to the faith. The finds included several miniature shrines, whose inscriptions record that they contained relics of the Buddha's bones. Historical documents for their part relate occasions when a Tang emperor took a personal part in the adoration of such relics, and the recent finds add a touch of realism to the contemporary protests that were levelled at imperial patronage of these ceremonies. Such strictures stemmed from staunch Chinese traditionalists, who saw nothing but harm in the indulgence of these exercises, in view of the misapprehensions to which they could give rise. Han Yu's critical essay of 819 survives as a well-known piece of literature whose bitter, if ill-argued, criticism cost the author a chance of advancement in his career.

By the ninth century the wealth and strength of China's Buddhist establishments were attracting visitors from Japan, anxious to receive instruction and refreshment for their own spiritual resources. But tolerance of the faith was beginning to wane. Chinese officials of a conservative frame of mind were pointing out ways in which the Buddhist ideal conflicted with those of an organized society; for example, it weakened the stress that China had long laid on the duties of kinsmen to one another, in accordance with their relationship. At the same time the wealth of the monasteries was leading to envy, particularly at a time when the imperial exchequer was in some disarray. In 845 the suppression of a large number of monasteries struck a severe blow from which some aspects of the faith could

TABLE 10

RELIGIONS OF WESTERN ORIGIN

635	Nestorian monks arrive in Chang'an.
694	Manichaeism recognized and tolerated.
eighth century	Introduction of Islam.
781	Nestorian Tablet erected in Chang'an.
843	Suppression of Manichaeism.
from 1245	Visits by Christian emissaries: the Franciscan Friar John Piano de Carpini (1245–7); William of Rubruck (1253–4); Marco Polo (1275–91).
1289	Islamic academy founded in Beijing.
1583	Arrival of the Jesuit missionary Matteo Ricci in south China.
1645–1742	The 'Rites' controversy concerning the practice of Christianity; ends with papal refusal to allow converts to maintain traditional ceremonies.
nineteenth century	Growth of Protestant and Nonconformist missionary activity.

hardly recover. Later, in the twelfth century, a reassessment of Chinese ideas of state, society and individual sought to reconcile Buddhist principles with those of a sophisticated empire.

*

Mythology, worship of the gods, hopes of a future life and a search for guidance from occult sources reflect some of China's basic responses to the permanent problems that beset humanity. In the course of the long centuries major changes can be charted. Beliefs, practices and rites began from origins that were in no way rational; with growing sophistication and a sharpening of the mind new elements entered in, and reliance on magical devices or religious beliefs became subject to intellectual features; stylization and regularity were taking the place of spontaneity. Rites intended to produce the rain, which had been based on the myth of the dragon, were transformed into a structured and artificial set of procedures that were redolent of cosmological theory; manuals of instruction took the place of the immediate response of the seer to the linear patterns produced on shell or by hexagram. As established political authority developed its intensity, it came to rely on convention rather than on initiative; local cults and shamanist practices were castigated as being improper, and regular prescriptions for worship were taking their place. By the Han period many of these changes had already taken shape.

Meanwhile these ancient and major themes had left features that may still to be recognized in their integrity in much of Chinese practice. Artists have adopted the symbol of the goat's head as a talisman for good fortune. Paintings that display a three-legged bird within the sun, or a hare within the moon, reach back to themes of early myth. The festival of the dragon-boats, or the dance of the dragons that is enacted on the stage, evokes the compulsive need to induce the rain to fall and to pray for fertility. In many Chinese cities today the specialist in hexagrams stands in the street to offer his services to the wayfarer, whose eyes will note the geomancer's compass that is on sale in the shops. Xuan Zang's journey to the west in search of Buddhist scriptures formed a theme for one of China's few long novels, the *Xiyouji* or *Journey to the West*; tales of the supernatural and of the intervention of ghosts characterize short story and dramatic theme. Perhaps the most striking monument to be seen in Beijing today reminds the visitor of the religious mission of China's emperors. Few who see it will forget the park and set of buildings constructed for the Ming and Qing emperors, there to render their dues and their prayers and to repeat their solemn vows to Heaven on behalf of mankind.

VII

THE INTELLECT AND ITS POWER

Intellectual activity owed its origins first and foremost to the emergence of named teachers. Some of these felt called to identify a system that lay behind the operation of the universe; others were moved to formulate a means of sustaining the corporate life of a community, kingdom or empire. Some responded to the direct need to support the rule of a government, to demonstrate its duty of maintaining law and order or to show reason why its officials were entitled to demand obedience or to exact punishment. The development of a tradition with which to uphold family and empire, the hope of raising moral standards and a response to the problems of living all contributed to the growth of philosophical exercises and scientific innovations.

As Chinese societies grew, so also did the power of the intellect; early practices, born of human instinct or dependent on blind faith, became subject to explanations that would satisfy the questions and the concepts of the mind. Progress in the form of the diffusion of knowledge was nurtured by the early evolution and practice of printing, from the eleventh century; initiative was at times constrained by the need to conform with the orthodoxies of the tradition.

MOTIVES AND CONSTRAINTS

As compared with Europe, China was reluctant and perhaps tardy in facing the problem of defining terms and abstract ideas, possibly for two reasons. No tradition of rhetoric grew up in China, as it had in Greece; there was no call to convince the assembled inhabitants of a city, in public, of the advantages of a plan of action; there was no custom of pleading a cause or weighing up evidence in a manner that would demonstrate proof of guilt or satisfy a jury. Secondly, there are few records of metaphysical disputation or statement at the early stages of Chinese thought that are comparable with, for example, the Platonic dialogues or the treatises of Aristotle. The habit of argument and the formulation of principles of logic were late to arrive. In their place there obtruded an emphasis on the practical application of the intellect to the problems of daily life.

Discussion concerned the behaviour of man to man and the organization of his government, rather than the framework within which concepts should be defined.

As in mythology and religion, so in the exercise of the mind, a search for permanence characterized much of China's contribution to the humanities. In a way of life that is highly volatile and beset by natural danger, philosophers sought to establish schemes of being which would relate a particular moment of time to eternity and which would explain sudden or temporary change within a context of the major cycles of being. There was a call to understand the operation of the world, and to explain how an integrated system brought about the movements seen in the heavens and on earth. In place of a blind obedience to an inexplicable, and perhaps inconsistent, set of beliefs and practices, there was room for the growth of reasoned argument based on observation and experiment. If astronomers could satisfactorily explain the movements of the stars and apparent aberrations of the planets, they could dispel the fears of those who could regard such changes only as omens of disaster.

Kings and emperors who wished to establish a permanent regime that their sons and grandsons would inherit relied on intellectual support to demonstrate that their call for obedience and exercise of temporal power were legitimate. Theories of empire and statecraft must provide an acceptable explanation of how a monarch had received his charge to rule; they must justify the complex institutions that were being adopted to organize and control mankind; they must show that the hierarchies of authority were reliable and worthy, such that they would command respect and attract loyalties. From such motives were to spring essays on the theory and practice of rulership, and historical accounts designed to provide intellectual support for a kingdom or an imperial dynasty.

From the Warring States period (481 or 403–221 BC) onwards other motives were making themselves felt. It was becoming desirable, or even necessary, to place the requirements of an ordered, civilized society within the framework of the single, organic universe and to prescribe ideal forms of conduct that would distinguish the Chinese from those less fortunate mortals who lived beyond the pale. Kings, emperors and their advisers sought to mould individual behaviour so that it would conform with patterns that were suitable to the whole of the community and which would reflect the hierarchies of its structure. Some teachers concentrated on the need to establish a respect for ethical conduct and morality or to uphold the dignity of man. The resulting norms of behaviour, known as *li*, came to take pride of place in the upbringing of children and in the education of the schools; and they formed an integral part of that rule of life which has come to be known as the 'Confucian ethic'. But the force of these early teachings was such that, once they had become accepted as a norm, intellectual initiative could perhaps be inhibited by the need for conformity. Often enough a shock was necessary for ideas to take shape, before it could be accepted that old values had become outmoded.

Intellectual vigour lay behind the training of the scholar official. The leisure that the civil servants of the Song age enjoyed led to the production of some of China's most profound philosophy and some of her finest literature. These were men who had been nurtured on the established canon of classical writings. Their training and the examinations which they faced had been largely based on familiarity with ancient texts and their approved interpretation. Much of their scholastic effort was directed to further clarification of the teachings and lessons of the past. But despite the profound influence that it exerted in raising China's cultural standards, the system of examinations could tend to stifle the growth of new thinking and to limit the scope of individual initiative. Criticism on this score has sometimes tended to reduce the proper appreciation that is due to the system.

The Chinese love of classification could likewise lead to contradictory results. It could stimulate the collection of literature and the formation of catalogues of writings; but the need to identify different types of book or different philosophies could lead to an excessive trust in the categories that were being thus formed. As a result, from about the beginning of the present era there arose rigid and somewhat strained divisions between different schools of thought; or the teachers whose books had been neatly arranged on the shelves of the imperial library must needs be assigned to a particular and exclusive group. A compulsive need to maintain such categories has persevered in much of China's literary history and has served to blunt some of the more refined distinctions that China's philosophy deserves.

Along with the encouragement of the palace and government office, the needs of daily life provoked intellectual challenge and led to new departures and experiment. Science and technology indeed owed much to a king or an emperor's orders to observe and record the phenomena observed in the heavens; but astronomy and mathematics drew alike on the farmer's concern with the seasons. The demands of living in the straitened conditions of an uncertain existence stimulated landowners to devise new methods of agriculture and irrigation with which to increase the produce of their fields. Similarly provincial officials were encouraged to think out improved means of solving the practical problems of everyday life, such as those of the transport and distribution of staple goods or the relief of distress.

THE FIRST FLOWERING

As has been observed by other writers, the centuries that hinge on 500 BC witnessed major advances in religious, intellectual and cultural activities in many lands. Such results are seen in the later prophets of Israel, the discussions of Greek philosophers, the expression of the Buddha's teaching and the appearance of Zoroaster. The same centuries saw the growth of significant movements in China.

Systematic writings that can sustain an argument first appear in the Spring and Autumn (722–481 BC) and Warring States (481 or 403–221 BC) periods, and it is these, particularly those of the latter period, that tell of the growth of China's intellectual movements. Some such movements were localized within the kingdoms of the day; some owed their force to political circumstances or the ambitions of those who sought political power. As yet there could be no attempt to impose a uniformity or an orthodoxy of a type that would be witnessed in later ages, for example from the first century AD.

Some of the kings of the Warring States period set a precedent that was due to be followed in later centuries, culminating in the last years of the Qing empire. By royal command men of learning were assembled at the palace, there to discuss contemporary issues of state, and to receive emoluments for their services. Perhaps the most famous of these academies was that of Jixia, which flourished in the kingdom of Qi (in Shandong province) during the second half of the fourth century BC; and, if some of the records are to be believed, scholars answered the call by the hundred. But such patronage of learning did not necessarily bring to immediate notice some of the most prominent names of China's earliest teachers. The reputation of some is due in no small part to the pious work of their pupils, who set themselves to perpetuate the teaching that they had received.

Kong Qiu (also known as Kongzi, or Confucius: 551–479 BC) was a native of the small state of Lu, in the Shandong peninsula, and it is owing to the growth of his teachings and the maintenance of his work by disciples there that a particular branch of scholarship and philosophical thought has been known as that of the school of Lu. Its results are best known in two surviving documents, the *Lunyu*, or *Analects of Confucius*, and the *Mengzi*, or *Sayings of Mencius*, which derived from a teacher named Meng Ke (*c.* 371–289 BC). Compiled

TABLE 11

LEADING FIGURES IN CHINESE THOUGHT

The Pre-Imperial Period

The Confucian school	The Jixia Academy	*c.* 357–300 BC
	Kong Qiu (Kongfuzi or Confucius)	551–479
	Meng Ke (Mencius)	*c.* 371–289
	Xun Qing	between 335 and 238
Daoist thought	Laozi	?sixth, ?fourth century
	Zhuang Zhou	between 399 and 295
	Lie Yukou (Liezi)	?450–?375
Legalist schools	Shang Yang	?390–338
	Han Fei	?280–233
Mohist school	Mo Di	*fl.* 479–438
Yin yang, wu xing	Zou Yan	?305–?240
Hedonist	Yang Zhu	prior to Meng Ke

The Early Empires and the Age of Disunity

Lu Jia	Confucian moralist	*c.* 228–*c.* 140 BC
Jia Yi	Confucian moralist	201–169
Chao Cuo	Realist	d. 154
Contributors to the *Huainanzi*	Daoist	before 139
Dong Zhongshu	Han Confucianist	*c.* 179–*c.* 104
Liu Xiang	Traditional Scholastic	79–8
Yang Xiong	Rationalist	53 BC to AD 18
Wang Chong	Rationalist	27–*c.* 100
Wang Bi	Metaphysical interpreter of *Yijing*	226–49
Ge Hong	Master of Daoist techniques	*c.* 282–343
Guo Xiang	Commentator to *Zhuangzi*	d. 312

The Medieval and Later Empires

Han Yu	Confucian protagonist	768–824
Li Ao	Precursor of Neo-Confucianism	*fl.* 798
Shao Yong	⎫	1011–77
Zhou Dunyi	⎪	1017–73
Zhang Zai	⎬ Masters of the	1020–77
Cheng Hao	⎪ Neo-Confucian	1032–85
Cheng Yi	⎬ schools	1033–1107
Zhu Xi	⎪	1130–1200
Wang Yangming (or Shouren)	⎭	1472–1529
Huang Zongxi	⎫ Reassessment	1610–95
Gu Yanwu	⎬ and	1613–82
Wang Fuzhi	⎭ criticism	1619–92

by the disciples of these masters, these books are set partly in dialogue form, and partly in the form of aphorisms prompted by a political event, such as a king's decision to embark on war. The theme is that of the betterment of man, who must be taught to sublimate some of the crude practices of his ancestors. Under the influence of a more humane form of conduct as was being preached, habits such as those of human sacrifice would be eliminated.

These teachings were designed to uphold the dignity of man and to establish the ideal social relationships which would ensure such a result. Two principal qualities on which this code of ethics was based were named as *ren* and *yi*; *ren* was the need to treat human beings as such and with the respect that is their due; *yi* was the recognition of moral principles that outlaw certain actions as being unjust. These ideals, together with the acceptance of the rules and conventions of behaviour that would encourage their practice, formed cardinal elements of the 'Confucian ethic'.

This style of thought is man-centred. Deriving from the personal teachings of Kongzi, it is to be distinguished from various modes of 'Confucianism' which arose in later times and incorporated much of Kongzi's ethical teaching as part of a more general philosophy. Nor did Confucius and his followers hold a monopoly for enunciating teachings that were designed to improve human conduct. Those of Mo Di (*fl.* 479–438 BC), who is not classified as a 'Confucian', stressed the universal brotherhood of man and reacted somewhat against the ideas of social hierarchy that soon became fixed in Confucius' own teachings. The *Mengzi*'s insistence on moral conduct concerned both relations between man and man and the decisions of those who ruled the kingdoms; its teaching reflects some of the instability and cruelties attendant on the wars of Meng Ke's age. A characteristic mark of the *Analects* and the *Mengzi* is the reverence for the memories, precedents and institutions ascribed to the kings of Zhou. Such traditionalism was to survive as a feature of much of Chinese philosophy throughout the imperial age.

In formulating their rules of conduct and guiding their followers along the paths of benevolence and righteousness, as *ren* and *yi* are often termed, the school of Lu laid the foundations of the Confucian ethic by means of precept and example rather than by defining principles. As examples of *ren* and *yi* they would cite the decisions of a king, and explain how these related to the canons of ideal conduct; or they would fasten on the niceties of their behaviour and expose the nobility of their underlying motives. By way of warning, they would likewise cite examples of evil conduct by wicked rulers and leave their reader to ponder their subsequent fate.

Meanwhile political changes and military events were taking

place, largely in western China, that were to lead to the establishment of the Qin empire in 221 BC. The kings, chancellors and generals of Qin aimed to increase the strength and wealth of the kingdom at the expense of its neighbours. To achieve such results they depended on the obedience of the population and the willing support of those who could take the lead, in either a civil or a military capacity. That such support was forthcoming was due in part to a few thinkers or writers, such as Shang Yang (?390–338 BC) and Han Fei (?280–233 BC), whose views may be described as 'state-centred' or 'legalist' as compared with the 'man-centred' ideals of Confucius. Their writings concerned the basis and place of royal authority; the relation of a ruler towards his officials and the means of exercising his authority; or the universal application of his commands, irrespective of favouritism, religion or respect for the individual.

Some chapters of their books (that is, the *Shangjun shu* and the *Hanfeizi*) fastened on the material needs of a kingdom, such as the production of grain, the maintenance of effective defences and the imposition of discipline. Other chapters include tracts that seek to list the strengths and weaknesses of human government, or the ways whereby a ruler depends on his laws, his methods and his position in order to impose his will on his subjects. The themes are illustrated both by ordered essay and by anecdotal or historical homily; they draw on the success or failings of earlier kingdoms and the reasons for their success or ruin, their victories or defeats.

In later ages Chinese writers have stressed the contrast between the stark realism of these views and the idealism of Kongzi and his followers. But the gulf that is said to separate the two types of thought is perhaps not so wide as has been made out. Both were concerned with the corporate work of man and the organization of his societies; there was a far greater difference between a 'Confucian' and a 'legalist' view, on the one hand, and that of a mystic in search of the *dao*, on the other. Opinion has sometimes varied between classifying Xun Qing (between 335 and 238 BC) somewhat anachronistically in a 'Confucian' or a 'legalist' school of thought; there could never be any question of grouping him with Zhuang Zhou, whose Daoist writings are of the fourth century BC.

Other minds were bent on different matters at this time. By the Warring States period there had grown up a view of the three estates of heaven, earth and man that collectively constituted the universe. The three were interdependent parts of a single system, co-ordinated in such a way that the activities and events of one estate could bring about a corresponding response in the others; the force of this theory was affecting the interpretation that was being put on omens and the warnings that they were believed to express. The philosophers' problem lay in explaining the nature of change, whether regular or violent, as observed in any one of the three estates; change must be shown to be part of an eternal order, of which man, his undertakings and his destiny formed but a part; only in this way would human beings be reconciled with their fate.

Change was explained as the unavoidable function of a major recurrent cycle, which was conceived in two distinct ways. According to one set of ideas, the complementary forces of *yin* and *yang*, female and male, dark and light, destructive and creative, were seen to supplant one another in sequence through a series of five phases. Of these, two saw the process of birth and growth; a third moved towards decay, which was itself fulfilled in the fourth and fifth phases. Such a cycle accounted eternally for the birth, death and rebirth of all things; it could be witnessed in the growth and decay of the trees of the forest and the plants of the fields; it was manifest in the annual return of the seasons and the journeyings of the heavenly bodies in the skies; and it regulated the lives and deaths of animal and human beings.

The theory was based on the combination of two basic ideas, that of *yin yang*, and that of the Five Forces, known sometimes as the Five Elements, or Five Agents or Five Phases (*wu xing*). In time it was applied in an indiscriminate manner to many types of human activity, in the belief that the choice of, for example, sowing, reaping or tree felling would be suited to a particular phase of the cycle, and that it would be disastrous to undertake such work at other phases and thus provoke a conflict with the cycle's rhythms.

This mode of thought could be taken to extreme lengths, such that, for example, it could dictate the choice of colours of ceremonial robes; for to each phase there belonged its own proper colour or taste, the direction where it reigned supreme, and the season when its power was at its zenith. There arose a tendency to list all manner of creation in groups such that they included five members, with the result that, for example, smells, emotions, types of field crop or musical modes were classified in this way. Sometimes it was necessary to manipulate the natural order so that a fifth member could be included within a group, with the result that not only the seasons of the year but also the directions of the compass were seen as being five in number. Of equal significance was the way in which the theory was applied to human institutions, seeing the rise and fall of kingdoms or empires as no more than a part of the eternal cycle that governed all things, and that allowed for the captains and the kings to reach the summit and then to depart, to make way for their successors.

The second cyclical scheme to be envisaged developed from the fruits of one of the methods of divination. The random cast of the yarrow stalks would produce one out of a total of sixty-four possible hexagrams, and it was the part of the seer to determine the meaning that was implied. When the process and its possibilities came under the scrutiny of philosophers, they saw the sixty-four patterns playing a different role. Arrayed in systematic order they formed the symbols of sixty-four cosmic situations which follow one another in time and space, allowing change to take place gradually and imperceptibly, but also ineluctably. One cosmic situation could change into the next as easily as an unbroken line in one of the hexagrams could be split, or the two halves of a bisected line could be united. When they had first been created as the results of a method of divination, the hexagrams had been judged to be indications of actions that were right and proper for a specified moment of time; in intellectual terms, the symbols formed members of an ever-recurrent cycle of cosmic phases, within whose scope major changes of the universe were born and brought to conclusion. Much later, the scheme occupied a central place in some of the metaphysical concepts of the Song period.

Along with the sixty-four hexagrams there arose the concept of the eight trigrams (*ba gua*). Traditionally it has been thought that these were the original symbols from which the hexagrams had been formed. However, as has been observed, the hexagrams had emerged as patterns formed in a process of divination; the eight trigrams feature in intellectual speculation rather than in mantic exercises and are thus of significance in concepts of later rather than earlier periods. The trigrams came to be seen as the symbols of fundamental forces whose interaction or combination underlies the sixty-four cosmic situations of the universal cycle. Sometimes the eight are represented in terms of material entities or forces, that is, heaven, lake, thunder, flame, earth, mountain, wind and water. Considerable attention has been paid in Chinese thought to the part played by these eight forces in generating matter and controlling the lives of humanity; metaphysical discussion has ranged over the logical order in which these eight symbols should be arrayed in order to represent an integrated and balanced universe. Partly as a result of these speculations, in much of China's philosophical writing there lurks a preoccupation with numerology – a need to reconcile conflicting rhythms and patterns within a single scheme of being.

THE GROWTH OF IDEAS IN THE IMPERIAL AGE

The formation of the first empire in 221 BC set a new scene in intellectual, no less than in political, social and economic, terms. Some of the modes of thought inherited from earlier days had already pointed the way to the introduction or even imposition of a uniform orthodoxy; already some measure of standardization could be noticed at the expense of spontaneity. In 213 BC a notorious incident is alleged to have occurred, which is known as the 'burning of the books'. The first Qin emperor is said to have tried to suppress traditional learning and a love of the ideals of the past in order to concentrate attention on the prevalent and realistic needs of the government of man. But the effects of this incident and a proscription of scholars that was alleged to have accompanied it have probably been overstated. Whatever had taken place, the intellectual developments of the Han period and the succeeding centuries were of sufficient force to mould the pattern for much of the future.

A number of texts that survived in various forms from the pre-imperial age soon became subject to different interpretations. As a means of recruiting literate and educated men to fill the many new offices of state, the Han government called for the recommendation of men familiar with some of these texts and their lessons. In this way a canon of classical literature was first formed (136 BC), comprising the *Book of Songs* (*Shijing*), the *Book of Changes* (*Yijing*), the *Book of Documents* (*Shujing*), one of the treatises on conventional behaviour (*li*) and the *Spring and Autumn Annals* (*Chunqiu*). A few select scholars were appointed to be academicians of state, with responsibility for explaining these texts in such a way that they could be applied to the needs of the times. The same scholars were also responsible for instructing candidates for office in an orthodox mode of thought.

A highly significant tradition had now been established. Imperial governments would henceforth insist that approved texts and suitable interpretations would be used for this purpose and that teaching would be conducted along recognized lines. Compiled up to five centuries previously, much of this writing referred to social and political conditions that had long been obsolete, and it was the task of the academicians and other scholars to read them in such a way that they would fit their own contemporary world. The *Book of Songs*, the *Book of Changes* and the *Book of Documents* must be shown to include the patterns that were suitable for imperial government. As a result, concepts that were formulated in imperial times came to be applied anachronistically to much earlier stages of intellectual development. In this way those who controlled public affairs in the imperial age could call on ancient wisdom to support their policies and their authority.

The centuries of the Han dynasty (206 BC to AD 220) saw the formulation of what is known as 'Han Confucianism'. Attributed to the initiative of Dong Zhongshu (c. 179–c. 104 BC), this syncretic mode of thought combined a number of elements already seen with some of its own making. It included the ethical teachings of Confucius the man and elevated his status to one that was worthy of respect, almost as of an immortal being. Han Confucianism defined the context for imperial rule, seeing it as an essential element within the unitary universe of heaven, earth and man. The system provided for a direct relationship between the supreme authority of Heaven and the exercise of temporal rule by an emperor; and it explained the occurrence of ominous events as Heaven's way of communicating with man. A clear definition of the concept of Heaven and its powers was conspicuously absent.

A search for balance and harmony appears in many aspects of Chinese thought of these early times. These qualities were seen as the natural characteristics of a universe that had not been subject to violence, and of human societies that are not subject to excessive greed or ambition. The theme had been seen in the complementary rise and fall of *yin* and *yang* and in the succession of the Five Phases; in the same way symmetry came to underlie the concepts of the sixty-four hexagrams and the eight trigrams. It was the aim of the Confucian moralists to achieve a society whose internal harmonies would preclude the outbreak of discord. The theme is also seen in the work of certain scholars assembled at the court of the king of Huainan towards the middle of the second century BC. They portrayed a harmonious, balanced world as an ideal which had been despoiled by man, intent on his own enrichment and oblivious of the inbuilt order and essential balances of nature.

Other intellects were turning their attention to the shape of the universe and conceiving of three ways whereby the earth took its place within a cosmic system. Some saw the heavens as forming a dome which was perpetually in motion, carrying with it the sun, moon and other celestial bodies. Others envisaged the earth as being surrounded on all sides by the heavens; in yet another view the celestial bodies were free to move at will in infinite space. Such theories were being entertained during the Han period, when new and more advanced astronomical theories were being put forward, thanks to the evolution of more refined instruments, observations of greater accuracy and the maintenance of more complete records. The heavens were conceived in twelve divisions and the path of the sun traced along a zodiac of twenty-eight parts.

Several motives lay behind the attention paid to astronomy. There was a desire to chart the movements of the earth and to link such movements with those of other elements of the universe. There was also a compelling need to regulate the division of time, both in order to correspond with the sequence of the cycle of five or sixty-four, and also to order human activities of the fields so that they would accord with their correct seasons. In such endeavours, and in the preparation of the calendar, there arose the problem of how to reconcile the different cycles and rhythms that were believed to inform the universe. These included those of five and sixty-four, as has been seen; the twelve divisions of time; the twenty-eight 'lodges' which marked the sun's path along the zodiac; and the three hundred and sixty five and a quarter degrees of the circle.

Technical manuals which concerned these problems stood on the shelves of the imperial library at the beginning of the present era. Such scrolls were accompanied by works on other subjects, such as mathematics, medicine or agriculture. Special sections of the collection concerned *yin yang*, the Five Phases and a whole variety of mantic methods; others dealt with military matters.

Meanwhile there were those who were reacting against the trend of the times and the blind faith placed in unproven or inconsistent practices. In particular Wang Chong (AD 27–c. 100) was adopting a rationalist stance in protesting that the rules laid down by the almanacs of the day, to determine an individual's choice of action, rested on no reliable or consistent basis. He likewise rejected the force of divination, and tried to dispel the fear of death that captivated many of his contemporaries. He asked for proof to support Dong Zhongshu's theory that Heaven took a part in shaping human destiny; he sought reason to suppose that the paragon rulers of old, enshrined in China's mythology, had necessarily presided over an age of bliss; and he saw the creation of matter as deriving from accident rather than the design of Heaven. Flawed as many of his arguments may be, Wang Chong blazed a trail in showing the value of argument dependent on observation and experiment, and calling on analogy.

The renewed unification of China under the Sui and the Tang dynasties witnessed marked attention by the imperial government to the training of an educated class of officials, the promotion of scholarship and comments on the classical canon. The age is known for its remarkable literary productions, and for a new emphasis on the exploitation of intellectual initiative on behalf of the state. While the tradition of the men of letters was nurtured and reinforced, the clarity and trenchant style of some of the prose writings of the Tang period stand in sharp contrast with the artificialities that some littérateurs had been practising in the preceding centuries. But, with some notable exceptions, conformity with the established intellectual achievements and attention to the faith of the Buddha seem to have occupied a predominant place, to the exclusion of new philosophical ideas.

A somewhat different picture prevails in the Song period, weak as it was in dynastic and military terms, but no less than brilliant in those of intellectual attainment and technical initiative. The practice of printing on an ever-wider scale during the Song and the Ming dynasties provided a greater impetus for philosophical speculation and a new means of promoting the acquisition of knowledge. In place of the few manuscript copies of works which were, indeed, voluminous, woodcut prints were now circulating of books such as the *Taiping yulan*, an encyclopaedia compiled in 1,000 chapters in 983, or the *Bencao gangmu*, a compendium of botanical knowledge or pharmacopoeia that was completed in 1596. The application of the intellect to problems of daily life is seen in the evolution of new tools and methods used in agriculture, the textile industry or the production of ceramics, to name but a few occupations. Their results support the view that the Song age was the culmination of a period in which China's science and technology outstripped those of Europe; but by the middle of the Ming period the balance was changing beyond recognition. The major advance in metaphysical speculation that took place in the Song period will be discussed below.

MOMENTS OF CRISIS AND ASSESSMENT

Imperial government rested on a trust in the Confucian ethic and the value of the canon of classical writings as a fount of wisdom. From such a base there had evolved social hierarchies and official institutions. Emperors sought therefrom the support that they needed for the exercise of their authority; officials were proud to serve and staff the organs of government to which it had given rise; and by this means men and women of China had become accustomed to distinguish themselves from other peoples and to obey the demands of the heads of their families, their local officials or their emperor.

But on a number of occasions of imperial history these principles were seen to fail. The ideal of honesty had perhaps given way to corruption, or oppression by officials had taken the place of imperial bounties as a conspicuous feature of public life. Even worse, there were times when rude barbarians, unaccustomed to China's cultured ways of life, had been able to invade and occupy the land. At such moments a loss of self-confidence and the failure of established authority prompted reactions in both metaphysics and political theory.

An early example of such self-questioning arose in the second half of the second century AD. At the time pious injunctions based on ethical precept had been unable to restrain excessive or unjust behaviour in the palace or in the offices of the government. Some of those who tried to improve the standard of public morality were tempted to withdraw from public life; or they called for the imposition of a stern discipline with which to stamp out evil practices and to reassert law and order. With the fall of the Han dynasty (220) and the emergence of the Three Kingdoms (220–280), service in office carried even less appeal to some; but the escapist ideas that were associated with the Daoist mystics and that lay at the root of both Daoist and Buddhist communities were unsatisfactory in intellectual terms. A few philosophers, such as Wang Bi (226–49), reacted by applying themselves to exercises in metaphysics, discussing the nature of the universe in terms of *wu*, a state of non-existence, and *you*, a state of existence. These were regarded as two aspects of a single whole, whose complementary nature accounted for movement and change. It also included a proper place for human emotion; and it provided for the establishment of order among mankind.

Between the Han and the Tang dynasties authority to rule China had been divided between several houses and there had been a series of short-lived dynasties in both the north and the south. A similar situation had occurred in the fifty years that separated the Tang and the Song dynasties in the tenth century, thereby raising the basic question of the right whereby an imperial house could claim to exercise its rule; reason must be shown why it had been legitimate either to seize power by force or to accept the abdication of a predecessor. Historians and statesmen of the eleventh century and later who faced this problem wavered between insisting on a pre-ordained right to rule, conveyed by Heaven, and accepting the practical and realistic arguments of the success of a particular house's endeavours to establish an empire.

Perhaps the most radical reassessment of Chinese thought and institutions, which is termed the Neo-Confucian movement, occurred in the twelfth century, although some of its principles had already been discussed and considerable scholastic advances achieved in the Tang period. Crisis and failure had been seen only too readily in the split of China between the three regimes of Song, Liao (or Jin) and Xi Xia, and in the flight of the Song court to the south in 1127. Faith in traditional institutions and ideals had been undermined partly by the persistence of Daoist principles and Buddhist practice, despite the eclipse of the latter's communities in the ninth century.

To reconcile the strengths of these varied and partly conflicting modes of thought, a set of completely new interpretations was provided for the classical canon. In an almost new departure of the Chinese intellect, metaphysicians were distinguishing between two aspects of matter: *li*, which lent form and determined the function of created objects, separating, for example, one species of animal from another; and *qi*, which formed the substance of created matter and the energy whereby objects are motivated. Creation itself took place thanks to the alternate pressures of *yin* and *yang*, in terms of a binary system that drew on the permutations of the sixty-four symbols or hexagrams. Another significant concept that was formulated and discussed at this time was that of the Supreme Ultimate, or Taiji, which transcends time and space, allowing for the creation of the whole order of systematic being.

Neo-Confucianism is perhaps the best-known and the most influential of a number of formative stages in the continual process of adapting the messages of traditional thought to the contemporary needs of a changing situation. The differing approaches of a Confucian, Daoist and Buddhist way of life had alike failed to provide a satisfactory answer to a number of problems that were making themselves felt with increasing intensity.

In their professional capacity, scholar officials of the thirteenth century were required to look to the solution of problems of this world; but thanks to the new intellectual advances and insight into spiritual dimensions, as individuals they were seeking a deeper and a wider comprehension of the mysterious aspects of the universe; a broad gulf was separating attention to the immediate and reflections on the ideal. None of the three great traditions had shown how a suitable balance could be maintained between these different calls; none had shown how the needs of the inner self could be reconciled with those of the community, or how the organization of mankind could be maintained with adequate justice and stability. In intellectual and psychological terms there was a manifest contrast between the claims of a dry scholasticism and a dedicated search for enlightenment.

Zhu Xi (1130–1200) stands out as one of the most significant figures who contributed to Chinese thought. He started by enunciating the metaphysical ideas to which reference has been made above. He hoped to combine elements of the existing traditions and to uphold the ethical standards of the past with a view to the general betterment of all mankind, rather than the individual members of humanity. He saw a need to avoid the extremes to which some forms of academic activity and religious practice had both led, and he called for the immediate application of learning and Confucius' rules of life towards eliminating the dangers and sufferings that beset the community. For both Buddhist idealism and Confucian statecraft had been only too prone to compromise and corruption. Zhu Xi saw the true aim of learning as that of widening the scope of education in order to achieve a moral uplift that would serve the whole of mankind.

Zhu Xi expressed ideas whereby the individual could achieve ennoblement in a way that Chan Buddhism could not provide. Certainly the disciplinary steps that he had in mind had something in common with those of the Buddhist's Eightfold Path, or even with Chan's meditative methods. But he also sought to clarify self-knowledge and to relate this to the phenomena of the external world. It was here that he propounded the principle of *ge wu*, the exhaustive enquiry into the nature of all that may be perceived and that thereby forms the context of an individual's own nature. By self-knowledge and a comprehension of universals, the individual's character would be formed on the basis of both intellectual and moral norms.

It was Zhu Xi who composed the new commentaries on the classical texts that were to enjoy official sponsorship until the seventeenth or eighteenth century. He drew particular attention to four of these texts (the *Lunyu* or *Analects of Confucius*; the *Mengzi*, or *Sayings of Mencius*; the *Daxue* or *Great Learning*; and the *Zhongyong*, or *Doctrine of the Mean*) which became known as the 'Four Books' (*Si shu*) and for long remained the basic reading matter in China's schools.

By the fifteenth century Neo-Confucian thought was being directed in a somewhat different way, thanks largely to the influence of Wang Yangming, also known as Wang Shouren (1472–1529). Wang tried different means of achieving Zhu Xi's objective of relating belief directly to action, and ensuring that practice did not diverge from ideas, and his emphasis was somewhat different. He believed that introspective or meditative methods formed a more certain way of attaining self-knowledge than concentration on a wide scheme of learning. Such views would draw criticism in the future, when they were alleged to have been responsible for the loss of imperial strength and the decline of standards in public life.

The fall of the Ming dynasty in 1644 and the occupation of China by ill-educated masters from the north-east shocked the complacency of Chinese officials. Once again a proud Confucian establishment had been unable to withstand the impact of force; traditional institutions, ways of thought and training had been of no avail to save the empire from ruin. A strong reaction followed. In the first place some judged that it was because of their faith in meditation as a means towards enlightenment that officials had become effete and debilitated.

Secondly, Zhu Xi's commentaries to the classical books were judged to be imbued with Buddhist or Daoist thought. As a result, a new brand of scholarship, known as Han learning (*Han xue*) came into being. This sought to provide a more valid insight into the meaning of those books, by returning to interpretations that were already some 1,500 years old. Being nearer in time to the compilation of the works in question, they were judged to be more in line with their original intent. In a different type of development, some men of learning who were averse from taking part in public life embarked on a systematic search for factual information, over a wide range of interests. These included subjects such as historical geography, problems of provincial administration, linguistics and bibliography. By such means they hoped to collect substantive arguments to bring to bear on contemporary issues of state.

The events of 1644 also prompted a review of the place of the emperor and his relation to his subjects. Essays on political theory discussed the rights of an emperor, the duties of his officials or the obligations of his subjects; some were concerned with the nature of law as against the adoption of temporary expedient. In addition, an underlying problem of loyalty beset some senior officials at this time, as a choice lay between two calls of duty, one to the defunct dynasty that they had served, and the other to the ideals on which they had been nurtured. Incapable of rule as the survivors of the Ming dynasty were, they could still claim the allegiance of their own duly appointed officials. However, in the general interests of mankind the Confucian ethic required service to a *de facto* ruler who could provide stable government. Once again there had arisen the problem of authority; did legitimacy depend on inheritance or on the power of the sword?

Finally, the nineteenth century saw a further call for reassessment. A Chinese empire had again been defeated and humiliated by foreigners, this time from Europe; new political ideas and terms were being introduced from the west, together with the concept of a comity of nations; to the east, Japan was rising to new strength by way of modernization. It was in such circumstances that the Chinese mind lay open to the impact of Darwinian evolution and Marxist philosophy.

*

Themes of Chinese thought stand revealed in the symbols adopted by an artist, in literary allusion and in the norms of behaviour. The strength of the Confucian ethic is seen in the persistence of *xiao*, that inbuilt duty of children to care for their parents that has been inculcated for two thousand years and more. The opening sentence of a famous novel of the fifteenth century, the *Sanguozhi yan'i* (*Romance of the Three Kingdoms*), reminds the reader of the ineluctable cycle that prescribes the fall, as well as the rise, of an empire, 'In general, the world must unite when it has long been divided and it must be divided when it has long been united.' Charts of the heavens, depicting the stars and the Milky Way, were painted on the vaults of tombs, to place the deceased person in the cosmic context of heaven, earth and man.

The heavily laden shelves of a Chinese library testify to the fruits of scholastic labour spent on interpreting the texts and sayings of the old masters. Nor need we be unduly surprised that in the continual tale of violence, deceit and the pursuit of ambition that marks Chinese politics there stands out a steady stress on promoting the ideals of the Confucian ethic. If human achievements were in any way to retain their value, it could only be done by tempering political endeavour with the qualities of *ren* and *yi*.

On a practical level, a manual of algebra that was compiled at the start of the present era includes examples based on problems that an official could expect to meet, such as the measurement of land or the calculation of tax. The four devices of dragon, tiger, phoenix and tortoise-cum-serpent that symbolize four of the Five Phases appear in their appropriate positions on bronze mirrors; elsewhere the intertwined semicircles of light and dark remind the observer of the rule of *yin* and *yang*; and, perhaps alongside, the eight trigrams draw attention to the forces that underlie the unity of the universe.

VIII

IMPERIAL SOVEREIGNTY

The first creative stages of Chinese thought, of the Warring States Period (481 or 403–221 BC), saw the growth of three major ways of looking at the world and evaluating man's part in the created universe. Those who believed that the workings and rhythms of nature were of primary interest and importance stood somewhat apart both from those who concentrated on human values and the need to order human conduct, and from those whose objective lay in organizing mankind with a view to expanding the wealth and strength of a kingdom.

These three ways of thought were by no means as separate or exclusive as those who have propagated the Chinese tradition over the centuries would have us believe. There were many who could devote their working effort, in their public life, towards the improvement of human relations or the growth of a government's power, while seeking, in their private life, a deep understanding of universal truth in terms of the *dao*. Within such a framework there was gradually evolved the concept or ambition of organizing mankind, of controlling human effort in the major interests of the whole community and calling on loyal obedience to serve the recognized authority of a single political establishment. Such ideas were put into practice in 221 BC and have lasted for over 2,000 years as an ideal and inspiration that all contenders for power have had in mind. That the ideal has by no means always been achieved is hardly surprising, in view of the great diversities which underlie China's land and people; that it has none the less retained its force through imperial, republican, Maoist and post-Maoist eras is all the more remarkable, when this is contrasted with the absence of similar endeavours in Europe.

The achievement has rested on the concept of emperor and subject, or governor and governed, rather than on that of state and citizen. It has resulted from a search for religious and intellectual support, and from an appeal to mythology; social hierarchies have been moulded in its interests; its aims have been expressed by modes of behaviour and material symbols. Religious associations were soon found to be necessary, if only to eliminate challenges from contenders to power, and as a means of maintaining continuity from one gen-

116

eration to the next. Intellectual effort placed the concept of imperial sovereignty firmly within the scheme of the universe; it demonstrated the essential need for the existence of an emperor who would rule over man, and validated his right to require service from his subjects. Solemn ceremonies, grand buildings and uniquely prized treasures exhibited the dignity and majesty of the throne and distinguished the Chinese emperor both from the leaders of the Asian confederacies and from the tribal leaders of the unassimilated groups of the south.

THE EMPEROR'S RIGHT TO REIGN

The establishment of the Qin empire in 221 BC was the result of active, and partly deceptive, diplomatic negotiation, and the ruthless application of military strength. Weak-minded kings allowed themselves to fall victims to the persuasive powers of a visiting envoy, or were obliged to cede territory in response to Qin's demands. By 221 the newly established emperor and his supporters had eliminated all claims that others might make to royal title or landed estate, resting as these might on long-standing hereditary rights. However strongly traditional scholarship might press the case that it was only the kings of Zhou who possessed a moral claim to rule mankind, their words would fall only on deaf ears at the court; for, like other rulers, the kings of Zhou had already been dispossessed of all their lands; power rested with the *de facto* masters of China.

According to the historical record, compiled some century or so subsequently, the first of the Qin emperors had boasted with some pride that he was founding a house that would endure for ten thousand generations. In the event such hopes were doomed to be but dupes, as his dynasty collapsed within fifteen years. The failure of a mighty empire, whose values lay expressly in the exercise of force, to survive what were at first the uncoordinated attacks of local rebels soon called for comment. Those who had spent ten years of hard fighting to establish the Han dynasty realized that military might was not enough to sustain an empire successfully for long. It was the lasting achievement of the Han emperors and their statesmen to leave to China a heritage: they showed how sovereignty, if it was to be successful, must depend on other considerations than those of force.

The four centuries of the Han dynasty were punctuated by a number of incidents in which it was brought to the point of collapse; there was a crucial interruption for a dozen years or so by another house; and a number of its emperors were too young or perhaps unfitted to discharge their responsibilities. But despite such difficulties and the failings of many imperial regimes in the succeeding two millennia, the compromise that was reached by the Han emperors and their advisers endured as an ideal throughout the imperial period. The stark needs of a government to face its problems realistically were tempered by a respect for other values; this respect outlasted the manifest failure of several regimes to live up to the ideals that they had inherited.

The measure of this early achievement may be seen by comparing the terms of two declarations, the one originating at the outset of the Qin empire and the second forming the final episode of Han's dominion. Immediately after his conquest of the last of the independent kingdoms (221 BC) the king of Qin determined to adopt a title that would be commensurate with his new power and that would draw a sharp distinction from those of all his predecessors. He reminded his followers of how he had accepted the surrender of six other kings together with their cession of territory, only to find them ready to break their word and stage an open revolt. Without hesitation he had punished them with brute force, thereby achieving their final submission and settling the state of the world. It was in such circumstances that the new ruler of mankind sought a title that would demonstrate his paramount position. He chose the term *Huangdi* ('Emperor' or literally 'August Power'). Hitherto these two epithets had each been used by various monarchs in isolation; combination of the two was an assertion of unparalleled supremacy. This proclamation of a power that rested on might may be contrasted with the instrument of abdication of the last of the Han emperors, which will be considered below. The term *Huangdi* remained in use until 1911.

Whatever the justification for the Qin emperor's choice may have been, within a few decades of its fall the Qin dynasty had acquired an unsavoury reputation for unjust government that had depended on oppression and severity. If a successor whose regime was in many cases similar to that of Qin wished to acquire sufficient support for survival, he must needs provide imperial sovereignty with a measure of respect; to do so, Han emperors, statesmen and philosophers invoked both the force of the tradition and the power of the intellect.

Tian, or Heaven, had been the godhead whom the kings of Zhou had worshipped; it was the kings of Zhou who had been praised by Confucius and his followers as monarchs who had presided over a just dispensation amid popular content. To some it followed inescapably that a newly established dynasty could be shown to be virtuous and to deserve loyal respect if it shared in the ways of Zhou; such a result could be achieved and shown to have been achieved by overt action of a symbolic and a religious nature.

Some centuries before the imperial period had dawned, the kings of Zhou had been proud to term themselves *Tianzi*, or sons of Heaven; and by calling on that expression they had voiced the hope or the belief that they owed their kingship to Heaven's own gift. This was the *Tian ming*, or 'Mandate of Heaven', specifically conferred on a recipient who was blessed with the requisite moral qualities and character to render him worthy to assume so sacred and onerous a charge. During the Spring and Autumn and the Warring States periods a number of leaders who had exercised power in various parts of China had styled themselves 'king' (*wang*); but none had dared to claim that his situation was comparable with that of the kings of Zhou or that he merited use of the same term, *Tianzi*; nor had the first emperor of Qin, whose aims were specifically opposed to all that Zhou represented, wished to do so. Eventually the Han emperors resuscitated the link with that highly praised tradition; and by so doing they tried to assume the respectability accorded to the practices of a hallowed past.

By dedicating their cults of state to the worship of Heaven (*c.* 30 BC) the Han emperors set a long-lasting precedent and instituted ceremonies that demanded conformity until the end of the imperial period; and once more the term *Tianzi* came into use, to remain in force until 1911. The altar and temple that were duly built to the south of Chang'an city for the conduct of the state's rites were in time followed by similar edifices erected at other cities that served as imperial capitals. On the south side of Beijing there stand today the altar and shrine built for this purpose and visited regularly by the Ming and Qing emperors, there to acknowledge with all awe the debt that they owed to Heaven for the gift of their charge.

Some imperial regimes sought to strengthen their link with the kings of Zhou by adopting the titles of offices and institutions that had supposedly existed under their dispensation. Such symbolic steps carried intellectual implications of two types. If indeed they had ever existed, the offices and institutions whose names were deliberately incorporated in imperial administration would have been devised for social, economic and political conditions of the pre-imperial age; these however had been outmoded for several centuries. Secondly, in the tradition that the empires sought to foster these offices were deliberately associated with the explanation of the universe in terms of the Five Phases. Their adoption was intended to link specific aspects of government with the sponsorship of that one of the Five Phases whose protection was deemed to be appropriate. However, a basic anachronism could have vitiated this attempt. At the time when the titles of those offices were assumed to have been in existence, that is, the earlier centuries of the kingdom of Zhou, the theory of the Five Phases had hardly been formulated, let alone applied to institutions devised for the government of mankind.

LINKS WITH THE FIVE PHASES

The office of official of 'Spring' (*Chun guan*) is an example of a title which was designed both to evoke the traditions of the past and to link a dynasty's administrative arrangements with the universal cycle of the Five Phases. The title is said to have been adopted in the first instance by one of the rulers of mythology, the 'Yellow Emperor', along with those of the offices of Summer, Autumn, Winter and a central season. An idealized account of the offices of the kings of Zhou includes the same series, and they are identified by a commentator of the second century AD as the 'controllers of wood, fire, metal, water and earth' respectively. In AD 684 the Empress Wu took the title for a dignitary in her own short-lived dynasty for which, significantly enough, she had actually given the title of Zhou. A 'Spring' official recurred in the institutions of the Ming period.

Of greater and more conspicuous significance were the measures taken to link the very existence and destiny of a dynastic house with the universal cycle of the Five. Special proclamations would announce that the imperial house saw itself under the sponsorship and protection of one of the material elements. The one so chosen symbolized the phase with which the dynasty wished to be associated, be it the one of steady growth or of achieved fruition. Should a dynastic house wish to demonstrate a change in its purposes or its ambition it could proclaim that the source of patronage had moved, for example, from the phase of spring (or wood) to that of summer (or fire). Just such a change occurred in 104 BC, when the Han dynasty announced that its allegiance was now made over to earth (or height of summer) in place of water (winter); it now saw itself under the protection of the central stage of ultimate fruition rather than the initial stage of growth.

These changes were of major symbolic significance, at least in the earlier dynasties. By its choice of patron element or phase an imperial house not only claimed a place in the eternal cycle of being; it also displayed its relationship with and its attitude towards its predecessor. For the choice indicated whether a dynasty had acquired its place by conquest or by way of natural succession; it could show whether or not it viewed its immediate predecessor as an illegitimate interloper; or it could assert a direct affinity with a glorious house or ruler of the past. Thus, just after the restoration of the Han dynasty, in AD 26, the new emperor declared that his house lived under the protection of fire, symbol of the second phase in the cycle. In doing so he showed that he discounted his immediate predecessor, founder of the Xin dynasty, as lacking legitimacy; he also laid claim by means of a line of descent to be the legitimate successor to the rule of Yao, most blessed of the rulers of the remote, mythical past.

Nearly all Chinese dynasties arose after rebellion against duly constituted authority or through the exercise of force. In the last resort a claim to rule under the aegis of the mandate of Heaven could rest only on a *fait accompli* and the failure of a rival to dispute a conqueror's pretensions. Throughout the centuries there thus persisted the need to demonstrate that a house possessed a legitimate right to the throne that was based on grounds other than those of mere force. The problem was solved by compounding make-believe with mythology; and the solution was successful enough because it suited the ambitions of those who took a part in a new regime and enjoyed its privileges.

Reliance on a claim to be Heaven's son and to preside over a regime set in an eternal cycle of being could be reinforced by citing strange phenomena, or omens, as signs of Heaven's blessing. Edicts refer to the fall of honey-dew, or the appearance of golden dragons as messages sent by Heaven to show its pleasure and its promise of success. Alternatively abnormal events could be explained as warnings to an incompetent ruler, too easily open to cajolery or flattery of the wicked, to mend his ways. A rising champion who was contending for power or who had just succeeded in establishing his house could point to the disasters that his predecessor had suffered as a clear sign that Heaven had transferred its mandate elsewhere.

In this way officials or statesmen described how a change of dynasty had been backed by the sanction of the highest of all powers. In time historians and theorists were writing of the *zhengtong* or 'Legitimate succession', whereby a change-over from one house to another could be seen to be approved and justified. But at times such a theory could be sustained only through arbitrary choice; for there were occasions when it became necessary for an historian to determine to which one of several coexisting regimes the succession legitimately belonged. Treatment of the regimes of the North and South Dynasties (386–589) or of the Five Dynasties (907–59) posed acute problems of this sort. Some of the clear-minded writers of the Song period, such as Ouyang Xiu (1007–72) realized the inherent weakness of the theory of the *zhengtong* and set out to dispel the misapprehensions to which it gave rise.

In 221 BC the first Qin emperor proudly asserted that he had successfully united all that lay beneath the skies; that both the members of the former nobility and the common people enjoyed peace and contentment; and that he had adopted the title of *Huangdi*, or 'Emperor'. The statement, with its overtone of strength through conquest, was repeated many times, being cast on the sets of standard weights and measures that the new government distributed. When the last of the Han emperors abdicated, in AD 220, many of the ideas that had arisen in the meantime had become accepted as the norm. Acknowledging that the newly arisen authority of the King of Wei had won overwhelming popular support, Han Xiandi summoned his senior officials to hear and accept his solemn declaration. The scene took place in the shrine dedicated to the memory of the founding emperor of the Han house, and it was in that sacred spot that Xiandi ordered his imperial counsellor to render up the imperial seal and its sash for commitment to his successor. Xiandi's declaration drew on mythology, recalling precedents whereby the blessed sovereigns Yao and Shun had each abdicated in favour of the successor whom they had chosen. It was of some importance that he also asserted that, so far from resting permanently in the same family, the charge of Heaven found its rightful place only with one whose qualities could satisfy the mandate's needs.

The last of the Han emperors recalled the misfortunes and disasters that had befallen his house and the highly successful way in which the new ruler to be, self-styled at present as king of Wei, had repaired the state of the realm, picking up the threads of the past and restoring the heritage of the most famous of the kings of Zhou. It was to him that the cycle of Heaven's destiny had now turned; it was for him to take it upon himself to accept the charge. The account then records that the king of Wei ascended a newly constructed altar and took his rightful place, there to preside over prayer and sacrifice, in the company of his officials. One of his first acts as emperor was to proclaim a general amnesty.

THE QUALITIES AND FUNCTION OF THE EMPEROR

China's twenty-six Standard Histories recount the story of the dynasties from 221 BC until 1911. These voluminous works were framed in such a way that, no matter what the subject might be, it was the statements and actions of the emperors which took pride of place and precedence. The names, titles and genealogical descent of the emperors are recorded meticulously with full recognition of the respect that was their due as leaders of mankind. Certain chapters of these works, and of other documents, describe minutiae of their life-style, whether this concerned the robes that they wore, the carriages in which they rode or the style of burial to which they were entitled.

But despite this wealth of information, it is only in exceptional cases that we learn anything of value about the man himself who merited these honours. Only rarely are there any suggestions of his character or personality, or of the motives for his actions. Indeed, if there are such hints, they must be accepted with due caution; for they may simply be serving the political purposes of those for whom the records were being compiled, and they may be cloaked in suitable cliché, with its inbuilt allusion or innuendo.

There were many occasions when the imperial throne passed to an infant, or was occupied by a man who was in his dotage; and from such occurrences it is likewise apparent that the institution of monarchy was usually of greater importance and value than the part that an individual monarch might be able to play in practice. For, both in symbolic and in religious terms, and in respect of the continuity of China's unity, the existence of an emperor, be he heroic leader of his country or puppet dominated by his court, was nothing short of essential. It was he alone who was entitled to conduct certain forms of worship and thus perpetuate the link with Heaven, and it was he who stood at the highest point of the social hierarchy; in no Confucian scheme of man could a society survive without its duly acknowledged head.

It was from the emperor as head of state that all political and administrative authority devolved. He acted as a visible figurehead, recognized at all levels; his approval was essential if edicts and commands were to be promulgated; without his nomination, no appointments of senior officials would be valid. He was the final arbiter of justice, and the source of bounties, punishments and amnesties. His word apparently reigned supreme; and so indeed it did in strictly constitutional terms.

But limitations were all too apparent. An infant who succeeded to the throne could all too often be weak, pliable and subject to the will of the ministers whom he had inherited. On occasion his mother, or later one of his consorts and their kinsfolk, could exercise a dominating influence (for example, Zhongzong and Ruizong, Tang emperors between 684 and 690, reigned under the shadow of the woman later known as the Empress Wu). Or else, sheltered from the realities of the outside world, an emperor could well come to depend on the flatterers who filled his court or the eunuchs who could dominate his audiences (for example, in his last years the Qianlong emperor of Qing, who reigned from 1736 to 1795, was unduly influenced by He Shen). In such ways important decisions of state and policy could lie in any hands but those of an emperor, and there was rarely an absence of ambitious statesmen, quick to take advantage of such weaknesses. But in the last resort the validity of a document rested on imperial signature. The incumbent may well have lost his independence; the throne upon which he sat retained its essential function.

Exceptionally, and usually at the outset of a dynasty, an emperor took an active part in public life (for example, Gaodi, first emperor of Han, who reigned as such from 202 to 195 BC; Taizong, second emperor of Tang, 626–49; or the second emperor of Qing, known as Kangxi, 1662–1722). As a successful military leader he had shown his mettle and could impose his authority on his supporters. Exceptionally, as in some of the non-Chinese houses of Liao, Jin (Kin) or Yuan, a few emperors could exert their personalities with considerable force; some could make a point of evading the shackles of the position that they had inherited, and were able to select their own senior ministers. But however strong or weak the man may have been, the virtues and responsibilities that were ascribed to him as a figurehead were clear and beyond dispute, drawing from the principles of the Confucian ethic.

As an article of faith, or of make-believe, Heaven was thought to confer its mandate only on those whose qualities and character could support the responsibilities of the charge. An emperor's behaviour must therefore call for respect, as an exemplar of moral conduct, whose very actions should be taken as a precept for all ranks of society to follow. As a source of ethical teaching he must instruct his subjects in the principles of just living. Just as Heaven extends its beneficence to the world, so must his son confer bounties on deserving humanity, relieving their sufferings and saving them from material distress; for he is the father and mother of his people, who, if treated with respect and generosity, will turn to him in loyalty, as certainly and naturally as the waters will flow to the lowest part of the earth.

Other concepts on which the ideal of sovereignty drew had emerged at an early stage from either a Daoist or a Confucian frame of mind. A passive acceptance of both the blessings and the disasters of the world of nature could rid mankind of values and emotions that were vain and transitory, and lead to freedom from distress. For this reason Daoist contemplation extolled the virtues of *wuwei*, the conscious decision to avoid positive and determined action. So too could it be asserted that the ruler of man should refrain from active interference in the problems and affairs of empire. He should be content to preside as the intermediary of Heaven, remote from the turbulence of the world and its disputes, exerting his authority passively and unconsciously thanks to his detachment.

But *wuwei* could not by itself control an empire, and for this task the true sovereign relied on his assistants or ministers. The best of these were to be found only rarely, combining as they did two principal qualities or virtues that were for ever being praised in Confucian writings. They must be men of integrity who unquestionably put the cause of their sovereign first; and they must be men of sufficient wisdom, intellect and courage to propose successful measures of government and to reprimand an emperor if he was bent on injustice. These ideal qualities of the minister of state were denoted as *xian*; and they complemented the ideal characteristic of *sheng*, the holy sage, that was demanded of the best of monarchs.

Together the holy king and the wise minister formed a partnership; the one aloof, responsible for his stewardship to Heaven; the other deeply involved in the problems of man and in duty bound to solve them. Ideal, and perhaps impractical, as the partnership might be, it suited only too well the ambitions of those men who sought political power; for they would hope to convince their sovereign to detach himself from the realities of the world and to leave authority to regulate mankind in their own hands.

Chinese society and its stability rested on *li*, the acceptance of forms of behaviour that were appropriate to the station in life to which a man or woman had been called. At the summit of the social scale the emperor must choose a style of living and practise a type of deportment which corresponded with his position. The dignity and majesty of his court must, thanks to *li*, provide an example of civilized behaviour. It must expose the contrast with the untutored and uncultivated ways of a general's headquarters, or the mobile habits of a leader from the steppes of Asia.

Nor were the visible and material signs of imperial majesty to be forgotten. All officials validated their documents with the use of a seal; so too did the emperor's approval of a decree require the imprint of his own seal, fashioned with particularly splendid craftsmanship, and denoted by a special term reserved for the purpose. In framing documents, officials used a special terminology to record an emperor's actions, thus distinguishing them from those of other mortals. When mentioning an emperor's title, they arranged their text so as to bring that honoured expression up to the heads of the columns, as a means of showing the respect that was his due.

From Han times onwards, imperial palaces were designed with careful attention to their symmetry, their orientation and their layout. They must be set in line with the four directions of heaven and earth; and when the emperor sat within his audience hall he would face due south, there to meet the gaze of Heaven's own power and glory, in the light of the sun at noon. Around his courts the buildings set on the east side matched those on the west, thus symbolizing the balanced harmony that he sought to establish within his realm. Secluded in the innermost chambers of the whole ensemble, his presence lay removed from the lower ranks of society, securely protected by the walls of a 'Forbidden city'.

Within those walls a number of devices signified the supreme nature of the emperor's position, the respect that was his due and the dignity that must attend his person. He wore robes and jewellery of distinctive patterns and symbols; his audiences were conducted according to strict rules of precedence and deportment. Each of the attendants who stood in their serried ranks within the courtyards, be he priest or eunuch, chamberlain or guardsman, was charged with his own function and duty; each carried material symbols which, to the knowing eye, conveyed at once the rank that he enjoyed; each contributed to the pageantry of the imperial palace.

The ideals of imperial sovereignty rested alike on religious sanctions, some of which were manifest in the ceremonies of accession. First, an incumbent must stage a show of modesty, refusing the awe-inspiring responsibilities of the office; only after repeated requests and appeals from his attendant officials could he agree, with reluctance, to submit himself to the charge. Already he may have consulted the shells of the turtle or cast the yarrow stalks to ascertain whether he should accept. Once the decision was taken, he took part in two ceremonies; in the one, as has been seen in the case of the king of Wei (AD 220), an altar was constructed and a pyre of wood was laid; and when the blaze had died down, the smoke which ascended to Heaven signalled his assumption of his charge. Of equal importance was the visit that the new emperor paid to the shrines that commemorated his ancestors, principally the founder of the house of which he was now the head; and there he made a solemn declaration, assuring them of the continuity of their line and the services that he would pay to his heritage.

*

Sovereignty rested on compromise. The Confucian ethic combined service to the empire with respect for the individual; in stark contrast, the methods associated with the Qin dynasty and pejoratively described as 'Legalist' fastened on the ruthless need to instil order and maintain discipline by way of obedience. Neither of these extremes was sufficient by itself to sustain an empire and retain loyalties, without religious and intellectual support. By the start of Europe's Christian era most of the ideas which have been described above had been formulated and their value had been acknowledged;

and those ideas survived, with some development, until the end of the imperial age.

At a time when several contenders for power were striving to wrest control of China by force, Ban Biao (AD 3–54) composed his famous essay on the 'Destiny of Kings', stressing that sovereignty lay in the gift of Heaven, and that only an incumbent with suitable qualities was fitted for the task. At a later stage, Wei Zheng (580–643) saw fit to remind Taizong, second of the Tang emperors (reigned 626–49), that the ruler of mankind bears the weight of a sacred mission. He pointed out that many of Taizong's predecessors had made a fine enough beginning, but no more than a few had seen their task through to a successful conclusion. For, easy as it may be to win control of the world, retention is a different matter. Wei Zheng solemnly advised the emperor of his duties; of the need to keep faith with his subjects, to recognize the danger of excess; and of the value of restraint and moderation.

Some thousand years later China was once more under the firm control of a strong dynasty, but with a difference. The Tang emperors had been of Chinese stock; in the seventeenth century the Qing emperors had driven in from the north-east to found a foreign house. Huang Zongxi (1610–95) came of a family whose members had served the Ming dynasty, and it would have seemed that he was destined for office in the same cause. The disaster that overcame the Ming dynasty in 1644 left his loyalties unimpaired, despite the corrupt state that had prevailed in the early decades of the seventeenth century, and his father's death in a vain protest against injustice. Choosing to take no part in official life under China's new masters, Huang Zongxi devoted himself to the cause of learning, compiling a set of essays that concerned several aspects of political theory and practice. He remarked on the unselfish nature of the true monarch, who puts the interests of the world before his own, and resists the temptation to exploit his position for the sake of his family. Ideally the prince acts as a guest, recognizing that his people are his host; and he devotes himself to attending to his host's needs. But too many emperors failed to reach the standard, regarding the empire not as a trust within their keeping but as a personal possession with which to enrich their families.

At much the same time the second of the Qing emperors, usually known as Kangxi (reigned 1662–1722), was formulating a set of maxims that were to exert a wide influence. His 'Sacred edict' (*Shengyu*) of 1670 included no more than sixteen pithy sentences, to be promulgated for the instruction and edification of his subjects. His injunctions were designed to sustain some of those very ideas on which kingship had come to rest; the stability of social relationships

and the elimination of discord; respect for scholarship and the orthodox doctrines that it expounded; and dependence on *li* as a means
of regulating human conduct. For if the well-being of the nation
depended on such premises, so too did the successful practice of
imperial sovereignty; whether a dynasty arose from Chinese or other
origins, its survival and justification depended alike on China's
religious and intellectual traditions.

IX

THE ORGANS OF GOVERNMENT

China's deep respect for her traditions stamped its indelible mark on the institutions of government of the imperial period. But the framework comprised sufficient scope for evolutionary change that could meet the demands of an ever-advancing way of life and provide for an increasingly intensive control of the land and its population.

Those who staffed the institutions were members of a profession who were both anxious to retain their superiority over other groups and ever conscious of the place that their own walk of life enjoyed in the social hierarchy. Obliged, and even willing, to maintain that they were operating systems inherited from the holy rulers of the golden past, they were well aware that practice could not invariably conform with the myth, and that the ideals of the past were by no means necessarily perfect for all time.

Tension and conflict could hardly be avoided. Officials were ever mindful of the road to advancement and their need to secure patronage; but with no clear distinction between their legislative, administrative and judicial functions, personal affiliation as well as moral principle could at times affect the conduct of public business. The continual need for a supply of trained administrators and loyal servants led to the creation of an educated class of individuals, greatly privileged as compared with others. They held their offices by virtue of personal appointment and not on a hereditary basis. They had won their place thanks to success in the public examinations, with all their strengths and weaknesses; and the prestige of the high rank that they had attained could lead just as well to arrogance and oppression as to a determination to carry out their duties with justice. At times it could be asked which of the two was of greater importance: the institution and its purposes or the individual incumbent and his judgements.

The need to discipline the population and to render it responsive to both the punishments and the bounties of emperor and official could at times conflict with the ideals of the Confucian ethic, which had formed the basis of all officials' training. Imperial government could be operated successfully only by reconciling a respect for human, individual values and a determination to impose the will of a master on an obedient community. Official and imperial pro-

129

nouncements continually stressed that loyal support and service must be won, and could not be extracted by forced demand; at the same time officials recognized that certain measures were essential so as to collect revenue, conscript servicemen and control crime. Compromise was necessary between the two attitudes to life described as 'Confucian' and 'legalist'; between an assumption that *li*, conformity with the golden rules of civilized society, would prevail, and the imposition of authoritarian orders backed by penal sanctions.

THE CENTRAL GOVERNMENT

Whether it was situated in Chang'an (now known as Xi'an), Luoyang, Kaifeng, Lin'an (now known as Hangzhou), Nanjing or Beijing, the imperial capital housed a variety of offices each one of which took its appropriate place within a strictly defined system. Authority devolved from the emperor, proceeding along strict lines to lower and lower levels of the administration. In this way decisions passed from a single voice at the apex of a pyramid until they reached the multitude of humble clerks at the base, busily engaged in preparing, copying and circulating documents in order to implement the orders that they had received.

There soon emerged a pattern or structure. A small number of senior statesmen were in direct communication with the emperor, acting as his immediate consultants. At the next level were placed those officials who were not of quite such high consequence, but who carried heavy responsibilities of a more specialist nature. These were in turn served in their departmental duties by deputies, assistants and clerks, enjoying stipends and status which corresponded with their degrees of seniority. Changes wrought in this general pattern may be seen in respect of the Han, Tang, Ming and Qing dynasties.

Two, and at first three, senior statesmen served the Han emperors, their status being distinguished by the type of seal and sash which they were entitled to carry and the stipend that was their due. The Chancellor, we are told, bore the general duty of being 'responsible for assisting the Son of Heaven to regulate all the myriad matters that were subject to decision'. The Imperial Secretary, who was his immediate deputy, was specifically in charge of documents and archives. He and his staff received submissions sent in from lower levels; they supervised the work of some of the provincial officials and performed certain judicial functions. The third member of this most senior triumvirate bore responsibility for military matters, but this post was by no means permanently established.

The nine ministers of state at the next level could exercise considerable power by controlling the departments over which they presided. Some of their duties seem to have been more suited to the smaller regimes of the pre-imperial age than to the structure of the Qin or Han empires. They were severally responsible for maintaining the religious cults of state; security of parts of the palace and of the emperor's person; other guard duties in the palace; arrangements for imperial transport; the conduct of legal processes; the receipt of foreign dignitaries; precedence and order within the imperial family; receipts to and payments from the imperial treasury and the finances and household of the emperor.

Within these departments subordinate officials bore responsibilities of a specialist nature. They attended to the requirements of state ceremonies, such as musical performances, the recitation of prayers or the conduct of divination. They cared for the imperial stables, and provided interpreters who could communicate with non-Chinese leaders from the steppes of the north or the fastnesses of the south. They looked after the maintenance of granaries, waterways or the sponsored farming colonies. They arranged for artists and craftsmen to exercise their skills in providing embellishments and jewellery for the imperial palace.

Besides the nine ministers of state there were other senior officials who were responsible for specialist tasks, such as the court architect. In addition, there were officials deputed to supervise the households of the empress and the heir apparent, and to act as tutors to the latter.

Disunity prevailed in China during the four centuries that followed the Han empire. The short-lived and localized regimes drew on the precedents set by earlier governments or perhaps introduced new departures, so as to provide for a ruling house and its supporters who were not of Chinese extraction. As accepted masters of the land the Sui (589–618) and then the Tang (618–907) emperors once more established a strong government that constituted China's sole recognized authority. The new pattern which emerged drew partly on the Han model and partly on the experiments of its successors.

Below the emperor, supreme authority rested with three bodies, the Department of State Affairs (*Shangshu sheng*), the Secretariat (*Zhongzhu sheng*) and the Chancellery (*Menxia sheng*). It was the intention that these three very senior organs should exist on terms of parity and that their powers should interlock in such a way that they would restrict opportunities for corruption and prevent the advancement of personal ambitions at the expense of public interests. The Secretariat was responsible for drafting imperial edicts and promulgating orders; but its drafts came under the scrutiny of the

Chancellery; that body was also in receipt of documents which emanated from the lower levels of the administration.

The third senior organ, the Department of State Affairs, was responsible for the implementation of decrees and the conduct of the normal and regular tasks of government. For this purpose it controlled the work of six specialist boards (the *liu bu*), in charge of staffing the offices of state (*li bu*: the board of civil office); revenue and taxation (*hu bu*: the board of finance); ceremonies and protocol of state (*li bu*: the board of rites); military matters (*bing bu*: the board of war); judicial procedures (*xing bu*: the board of punishments); and public buildings (*gong bu*: the board of works). This division of responsibilities persisted until the Qing dynasty.

A further concept which emerged in the Tang period showed the way towards a new departure that was to come to fruition at a much later period. The second emperor (Taizong; reigned 626–49) arranged for regular meetings to take place with his most senior and highly respected advisers; these were intended to be held daily for the discussion of important matters of state. Five or six senior officials or statesmen, including the heads of the three departments and others who had been nominated for the purpose, formed this élite group, or consultative cabinet. These were the 'chief ministers' (*zaixiang*); attendance at the meetings was of a consultative nature, and involved no new or special administrative duties.

In this way there was formed a precedent which the Ming and Qing dynasties were to follow. The Ming dynasty had been founded after a particularly bitter period of unrest and fighting; as a native house it followed a century or so of rule by an alien family of Mongols, who had none the less attracted some measure of loyal support from Chinese officials. The Ming victory of 1368 provided both the opportunity and the need for initiative, and in the first instance it was the emperor himself who exploited the position by exerting his authority, and taking direct control of the senior ministries. In this way he could prevent his most senior statesmen from acquiring great powers, at the cost of assuming arduous duties himself. But by no means all his successors were willing or able to follow his example, and control of state affairs came largely into the hands of an organ named the Grand Secretariat (*Neige*), which included some of the most distinguished men of the day. From early in the fifteenth century imperial government was largely characterized by the rise and fall of both this body and a further group, known as the Council of State (*Junjichu*), which was established in 1730; below these there operated, as hitherto, six subordinate boards, each with their specialist responsibilities. The last two imperial dynasties could provide an emperor with far greater opportunities for autocratic rule than his predecessors had enjoyed; they also saw the growth of consultation as a formative element in taking decisions of state.

Hierarchies marked the civil service; its conduct of business could be cumbersome, slow and illsuited to face an emergency. But there were few decades in dynastic history when it was not necessary to take speedy and forceful action to save the empire from disruption. At such moments emperors would look in vain to their senior ministers if they wished to bypass the normal procedures, or if they hoped to find a confidant with whom they could share informal discussion.

The void was filled partly by the eunuchs, introduced into Chinese palaces from before the days of the empires, and present in varying degrees of strength until their close. From the pages of the official histories readers gain an impression that the eunuchs were invariably schemers, intent on furthering their own ambitions and placing their own interests above those of the emperors in whose courts they walked. Many officials who had risen to prominence thanks to the arduous training of the examinations or who had successfully formed their own factions regarded the eunuchs as objects of enmity and envy; for they enjoyed a proximity to the throne to which they themselves could not aspire.

It was the officials, and very often senior ones at that, who were responsible for framing the histories; it is therefore hardly surprising that the eunuchs are often portrayed as being intent on the seizure of power at the expense of the civil service or as manipulating the organs of government so as to secure their own following or to amass their own fortune. Such a picture needs modification. Certainly there were times, during the Han, Tang, Ming and Qing dynasties, when certain eunuchs wielded great authority and may well have misused it. But there were also occasions when the survival of a dynasty depended on the support that the eunuchs could give their emperor in face of the intrigue that lurked in the corridors of power. In addition to those conspicuous cases where eunuchs practised corruption, there were those when a beleaguered emperor could find help only from the loyal eunuchs who stood around him.

PROVINCIAL AND LOCAL ADMINISTRATION

From the outset of the imperial period two conflicting principles determined the exercise of control over the provinces. From the old tradition, associated with the kings of Zhou, there survived the belief or hope that kinship with a king or emperor would necessarily carry with it loyalties to his regime; and that if territories were entrusted to the care of his sons, to be held in possession on a hereditary basis, thoughts of separatism or dissidence would not be strong enough to quench the natural love and support owed to the ancestral house. But to some of those who were acquainted with China's pre-imperial history such hopes could appear to be no more than illusory. For it could be seen how with the passage of generations such links and loyalties would become ever more tenuous; there was no certainty that they would preclude the temptation to promote personal ambition by way of dissidence.

As against such arrangements, which have often and not altogether correctly been termed 'feudal', the kings of Qin had entrusted the control of some of their newly won territories to individual officials whose performance and strength of character had been marked with ability, and who had demonstrated that trust in their powers would not be misplaced. Appointments of such provincial governors, especially at the borders of their kingdom, were made on a personal basis, without the possibility of transmission to a son; they were rewarded by suitable emoluments.

The histories include an account of a debate on these issues of principle which was said to have been held in the presence of the first Qin emperor, shortly after the conquest of the six kingdoms and the unification (221 BC). By deliberately adopting a provincial system the emperor signalled the start of a new regime, in which all claims or pretensions to hereditary titles and lands of the past were to be surrendered, and nostalgic loyalties that might be attached to houses other than his own were to be eliminated. At the outset of the imperial age the land was thus divided into thirty-six units, whose governors were appointed by the centre and were subject to dismissal in case of dereliction of duty, failure to administer or suspicion of crime.

With the succeeding dynasties the ruthless decision of the first Qin emperor was modified by the realization that strongly affirmed family ties could serve to strengthen the fabric of the empire. There may also have been ideological reasons, based on the Confucian ethic, behind arrangements that allowed an emperor opportunity to display his respect for the social solidarity and stability on which his empire rested. As a result, at varying times throughout imperial history areas of territory were designated as hereditary princedoms, dukedoms or other types of estate, over which a scion of the imperial house presided.

There were obvious advantages in such arrangements; they served to strengthen administrative control of the realm; they could enable a newly acceded emperor to reward those members of his family who had supported him but yet sought to exercise their own power; and at times when trained and loyal administrators were in short supply, the appointment of favourite and trustworthy sons as kings over large areas could solve some of the problems of government. But inherent dangers persisted. It could easily occur that an ambitious man who succeeded to a kingdom would stand possessed of large provincial resources with which he could stage a revolt against the imperial court only too easily.

Against such a background it is possible to trace the growing intensity and sophistication of provincial and local government; and again these developments may be observed at three formative periods. At the outset of his rule in 202 BC, the new Han emperor had made over half of his domains in the form of some ten comparatively large kingdoms. By AD 1–2 when imperial government had been practised for over two centuries, these had been so greatly reduced in size and strength as to be barely recognizable. They survived as twenty small enclaves, nestling among the eighty-three administrative units, known as commanderies (*jun*), that had been placed under the direct control of governors. These governors were senior civil servants with full military and civil resources at their disposal. Their commanderies were themselves divided into a number of counties (*xian*), in one of which they established their seat of authority. Each county, perhaps the size of an English shire, included a walled city and a large area of agricultural land; the county magistrate was responsible for controlling the population, calling up its members for service, dispensing justice and collecting taxation.

The counties were themselves divided into districts (*xiang*); below them were the hamlets (*li*), and it was with the local officials of those units, such as the overseer, that the great majority of the population would be confronted, when the hard and heavy hand of the imperial administration was brought to bear. Considerable differences occurred in the degree of intensity with which its will was implemented. In the lower reaches of the Yellow River, and south of the Shandong peninsula, the population was relatively dense; the land had been subject to continuous cultivation, and the commanderies were comparatively small. The inhabitants of those regions were thus more likely to be open to an official's demands than those of other areas such as those at the perimeter of the empire. For here the administrative units were much larger and the impact of the official would be felt less severely.

In some of the border regions it was necessary to adopt special measures; for these lay midway between China and the steppe. A roving population, of mixed ethnic stock, practised a nomadic way of life, and the type of administration that had evolved for the farmlands of China's home provinces was not suitable for such conditions. In addition, these lands were frequently subject to incursion by potentially hostile bands, and therefore required defensive installations that were not needed elsewhere. As a result imperial authority could hardly be maintained to the same degree or in the same way as was possible in the counties of the south. The situation required arrangements that were more flexible and which allowed some of the unassimilated peoples of the north comparatively more freedom of movement than was usual in the settled farmlands or cities of the home provinces. Han governments solved the problem by establishing 'dependent states' over which a Chinese official presided, in tacit recognition that actual authority often lay in the hands of some of the local leaders, who were not of Chinese stock.

At the height of their powers the Tang emperors ruled over an area whose size was roughly equivalent to that of their predecessors of Han. But provincial government had by now attained a greater degree of intensity. In AD 2, 1,577 counties were subordinated to the 103 commanderies and kingdoms of the empire; under Tang, approximately the same number of counties were grouped in some 300 to 400 prefectures. At the height of Tang power and at its greatest extent of territory, this number had risen to 856. In order to increase its control over the provinces, in 106 BC the Han government had established a series of inspectors, with orders to proceed within a prescribed area of several commanderies and to report back directly to the centre should they find anything amiss with the administration. The Tang governments followed this precedent, by dividing the empire into fifteen circuits within which their inspectors operated. Neither then, nor indeed formerly, did such arrangements constitute large administrative units to which the governors of Han or the prefects of Tang were subordinated.

To consolidate their hold on the outlying areas of the borders, the Tang governments appointed a series of military governors (*jiedushi*), who came to dispose full military and civil powers and to command large military forces. In the middle of the eighth century the imperial house paid the price of its failure to control some of these satraps, and faced a crisis in the form of a major rebellion that was launched by An Lushan. Of mixed Sogdian and Turkish blood, An Lushan was a man of considerable ability who had much to offer the Tang administration by way of skilful generalship. Appointed concurrently to several military governorships, he had in effect become master of the north-eastern part of the empire; his rebellion (755–63) jeopardized the survival of the dynasty and weakened its structure beyond repair.

The Yuan dynasty (1260–1368) introduced a new departure, in

12. Reliquary, in the form of a miniature Buddhist shrine, and embellished with precious metals and jewels; from a set of 10; from Famen si, Shaanxi province; height 53cm

13. Śākyamuni; figure in brick, included in the Bao'en si, Nanjing (completed 1431); 43 by 35 cm

成申
端午戲寫
高其佩

17. Zhong Kui, a spirit
who appeared in a
dream to Tang Taizong
(reigned 626–49),
curing him of illness;
painting by Gao Qipei
(1672–1734), dated
1728; 149 by 67 cm

15. *Above:* Tang wrestler, ceramic; Tang Dynasty; height 23 cm

16. *Opposite:* Seated Apsaras ('Heavenly musician') in limestone; late sixth century; height 53 cm

14. Pavilion, in courtyard of the Confucian Temple (Ming Dynasty), Xianyang; now enclosing a statue of Śākyamuni

8. Bodhidharma's visit
to China; rubbing from
a stone engraving
based on a painting by
a monk (Ming period).
Bodhidharma reached
the Liang court in 520
and discussed Buddhist
doctrine with the
emperor. He is shown
on his passage across
the Yangzi river to
Northern Wei; 142 by
62 cm

19. Host bidding farewell to his guest; painting by Zhou Chen (late Ming period) on a theme from a poem by Du Fu (712–70)

the creation of new units of a far greater size than any that had been seen so far. Existing divisions were retained, and subordinated to the *sheng* or provinces, of which ten and later thirteen were formed. In some cases the governor or governor-general of a province was responsible for an area equal to that of a country of twentieth-century Europe; by 1600, under the Ming dynasty, the number had risen to fifteen; the Qing empire comprised eighteen, and then twenty provinces. Some of the territorial divisions that were adopted at this time have persisted until the present day with little or no change, as may be seen in the case of Shandong or Zhejiang.

At the lowest level the counties (*xian*) remained much as they had been from the outset of the imperial age, numbering some 1,500. It was the county magistrates (*zhixian*) who in effect exercised supreme control over the majority of the inhabitants of China. Between them and the awe-inspiring governors of the provinces lay the prefectures (*fu*); and in some cases yet another intermediate level was formed by grouping prefectures together to form circuits (*dao*). The existence of these hierarchies could play a decisive part in determining the conduct of the state examinations, the course of justice and litigation and an official's success in seeking advancement in his career.

THE MEANS OF SURVEILLANCE

The Chinese empires covered large areas that comprised different types of terrain, that supported different types of people and gave rise to different types of occupation. But officials whose loyalties were no less certain than their administrative skills were often in short supply, and opportunities for self-seekers were not hard to find. It was in recognition of these dangers that certain features, perhaps peculiar to China, had emerged in both central and provincial government. To prevent personal intervention and to check malpractices, established procedures ensured that matters of public business would proceed in a regular manner up and down the levels of administration. To preclude obvious opportunities for corruption, from time to time regulations forbade officials from serving in organs of local government that operated in their own native places of origin. Despite such measures there remained the constant danger that officials would be open to corruption or ready to practise oppression; from early days attempts had been made to solve the problem.

The short-lived Qin empire had included provision for inspecting the performance of officials or checking their degree of loyalty. Later, the thirteen regional inspectors who were first appointed in 106 BC were responsible for travelling up and down the commanderies and kingdoms that were specified as being within their jurisdiction. They were to watch for cases of inefficiency on the part of officials; to observe how open they were to corruption; to satisfy themselves that the populace was not subject to oppression or extortion and that those accused of crime would receive a fair and just hearing. These inspectors were controlled entirely by the central government, to whose officers they reported directly and independently.

The principle of surveillance was taken to greater lengths during the Tang empire, when inspectors were appointed to examine many different aspects of the administration. A single censorate was established for this purpose in 713, with powers of operation both in the centre and in the provinces. But it was in the Ming and Qing dynasties that this aspect of government received most marked attention. The Ming government included a headquarters staff of censors and 110 officials who were posted to carry out these duties as was desirable. But in times of despotic rule considerable courage was required if a censor were to risk offending the great ones in the land by rendering an honest account of the misdeeds that he witnessed. There were times when censors were brave enough to face the consequences of arousing political animosity; on some occasions censors would themselves constitute no more than another element in the in-fighting of the court. In the Qing dynasty the censorate was retained as a highly honoured organ of government.

THE ARMED FORCES

According to the Confucian ethic, emperors had no need to call on force; the strength of their example and the precepts which they both preached and practised would be sufficient to ensure the willing submission of all peoples of the earth to their beneficent dispensation. It followed that the overwhelming stress in Chinese institutions was on those organs which were devoted to cultural pursuits (*wen*) rather than to the practice of military arts (*wu*). Dynasties might well depend on the courage and tactical qualities of those who led troops in battle, whether to establish a regime, to put down rebels or to engage the armies of enemy confederacies; but while local protagonists, fighting like Robin Hood to protect the weak from oppression, would earn praise for their exploits, successful generals would not merit the reputation of heroes, in a manner comparable with Alexander, Hector or Lysander.

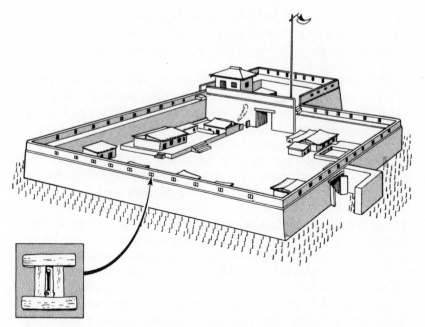

2. Company headquarters: fort with signalling pole, revolving aiming devices attached to the walls and defensive barrier of upturned stakes, approximately 40m by 40m, with northerly extension 20m by 20m; in service from c. 100 BC. Reconstruction on the basis of finds near Juyan (Gansu province)

There was a reluctance to set up, or at least to admit to setting up, a permanent framework which would acknowledge the need to deploy force. The central government would include provision for a few general officers, who were probably independent of the other organs. In addition to these few posts, the imperial government would appoint individuals as commanders of task forces, for a limited period of time and with a specific objective in view. They too might carry the title of general (*jiang* or *jiangjun*), which they would relinquish once their campaign had been brought to a conclusion. On a lower scale some independent commanders might be given the more junior title of 'colonel'. On some occasions military failure or defeat could follow from a lack of the necessary co-ordination or the pressure of personal jealousies; of several commanders who were campaigning in the field not one would carry the authority of a designated commander-in-chief.

Practice differed somewhat under the emperors of those dynasties which had arisen from alien stock and which were willing to recognize the value of armed might. In the process of foundation, members of the future imperial house had themselves shown their mettle on the field of battle; their commanding position at the head of their newly established empire could rest on an acknowledgement of their personal courage.

The ranks of China's armed forces were filled for the most part by conscript soldiers, dutifully fulfilling their statutory obligations. Reluctance to establish professional regular armies, and in their place to rely on short-time service, could effectively limit the resolution with which a campaign could be maintained. Exceptionally, static defence lines were built in the long walls of the north and the north-west, but provision of troops to man the watch-towers could not always be achieved with ease. Unused to the saddle themselves, the Chinese were at times glad to recruit the help of the men of the steppe as cavalry. Special privileged bodies of troops were sometimes formed, of those who had personally fought to enthrone the emperor of a new or a restored dynasty; in the case of the Qing dynasty such units enjoyed a highly favourable position, as the 'Banners' on whom the empire depended. Governors of the provinces usually carried full responsibility for both military and civil activities, being sometimes supported by a special official whose concern lay with the recruitment of servicemen and the maintenance of defence against marauders.

*

A division of responsibilities, in the hope of precluding the growth of excessive power in a single official's hands, marks the organs of central and provincial government, and the control of the armed forces. There were times when two men were concurrently appointed to the highest post of Chancellor, one of the left and one of the right, or when a Chinese and a Manchu held offices that were exactly on a par. The same principle prevailed in the establishment of two financial organs of state, as seen in the Board of Finance and the Salt Commission of the later years of the Tang dynasty; it also appears in the retention of a general of the right and a general of the left by the Han emperors. If possible it was contrived that the senior departments of state would be interdependent and incapable of taking unilateral actions of a decisive nature. But as always there remained the question of *quis custodiet ipsos custodes*, and there was no shortage of historical examples to prove the point. The first Ming emperor had entrusted considerable military forces to some of his sons, partly in the hope that they would form a bastion against threats from the north. But it was with the help of just such resources that one of them could launch a successful bid for the throne and establish himself as the Yongle emperor (reigned 1403–24). At a lower level, should the regional inspectors choose to exploit their advantages to promote dissidence, they might find none to block their way; nor could the system of censors guarantee that protest against an entrenched establishment could be launched effectively.

Service in the central government formed the principal aim of the civil servant. In the capital city he lived at China's cultural centre, whose company was enriched at times by the presence of visitors from other lands who could tell tales of different forms of civilization. Enjoying the deep respect due to an imperial official, he would see around him no lack of opportunity to pursue the arts. Engaged as he was in an ambitious struggle for advancement in his career, he need not lack for congenial company with whom he could exchange literary compositions or forge a lifelong friendship. But the higher an official rose in his profession, the more prone he would become to the hazards of political strife. Senior counsellor of state one day, on the next he could find himself the target of a rival's hatred, disgraced and appointed to a minor post in the deep recesses of the south or south-west, bereft of the refinements and luxuries to which he had been accustomed in the capital city.

Senior officials of the central government stood aloof from the day-to-day implementation of their orders; they based their decisions on reports submitted from the lower levels and eventually from the countryside. If it could be claimed that their judgements were thereby likely to be objective, it must also be admitted that they could also be excessively theoretical. For the highly cultured scholar official of the Song, Ming or Qing periods needed to possess no direct knowledge of the soil and working conditions of a remote area for which he was prescribing a system of taxation or land tenure. Direct administration of China's men, women and children, the settlement of disputes and the provision of relief at a time of famine devolved on the local official of the provinces. But recognition of his services to the realm rarely measured up to the extent of his contributions, as compared with the prestige that was attached to his colleagues at the centre.

X

OFFICIALS AND THEIR DUTIES

Respect for hallowed tradition no less than response to emergent difficulties tempered the growth of China's organs of government. Their strength lay in their indissoluble link with imperial sovereignty and in their interaction with the social distinctions of the nation. Their weaknesses were due as much to the size of the task laid upon them as to immaturity of political theory. Their successful operation depended on the balance between a retention of form and an indulgence of initiative.

References have already been made to some of the outstanding problems of governing a mighty empire; to that of delegating power in the outlying provinces while ensuring that it would be used to support the throne with loyalty rather than to split the empire by dissidence. Effective government involved the administration of different types of people who had attained varying standards of culture and who practised diverse types of occupation; and it required a constant supply of that somewhat rare individual, whose talents were matched by his integrity. Long distances, arduous terrain and rugged mountain ranges separated the capital city from some of the provinces, and there could be no certainty that reports and orders would reach their destination in time to remedy a problem or stave off a crisis.

Such difficulties were daunting. At times they could spell catastrophe; that imperial government could nevertheless be conducted at times with considerable efficiency calls for no small degree of admiration. However grave a situation might be, only the bravest of local officials would dare to embark on heavy expenditure or to initiate military action without express approval from his superiors. But despite the profusion of documents that couriers conveyed across the provinces, there could be no certainty that those senior officials who framed major decisions of policy had necessarily been supplied with all the intelligence that they needed to form a calm and objective judgement. Similarly the normal tasks of the government could also be hampered by a lack of the necessary information. For example, regulations for registering the population and accounting for tax that had been rendered had existed from the earliest days of the empires and had been implemented with meticulous care; but many centuries had to pass before a Song statesman could begin to think in terms of estimating revenue and expenditure and thus preparing a budget.

THE OFFICIAL AND HIS TRAINING

Documents of state repeatedly stress both the need to recruit officials who possessed the right qualities, and the duty of such persons to place their talents at the disposal of their emperor. The resultant systems of recruitment, examinations, grading, stipends and privileges were of such importance that they characterized many of China's social distinctions, moulded China's cultural continuities and coloured the conduct of government. For by these means there came about the identity of scholar, civil servant and statesman.

Many of the masters of the land in the pre-imperial period claimed titles that are often rendered 'marquis', 'duke' or 'king'; and they appointed their own kinsmen or henchmen to supervise the work of the fields and control their men in battle. Some of these responsibilities passed from father to son within the same family, meriting the gift of estates and the right to their produce. With the growth of larger units and the need for more sophisticated types of administration, a new type of leader came to the fore. A few men of high ability sought to found their fortunes by migrating from their place of domicile and placing their services and advice at the disposal of the kings of the Warring States period (481 or 403–221 BC). At the same time those kings needed the help of men of intellect and literary training to provide them with counsel and to undertake specialist and technical tasks such as recording observations of the heavens, regulating the calendar, collecting tax or implementing decrees. In appointing their advisers, rather than trusting solely to the claims of heredity, some of the kings began to look more purposefully for intellectual merit and ability to serve. Privileges and emoluments accompanied the authority that was now conveyed to officials to control the population and punish criminals.

By the start of the imperial period the all-important principle that ability was of greater importance than birth or favouritism had been acknowledged; but it was by no means translated into fact on a universal scale. The early emperors of the Han dynasty named the qualities and characteristics that they wished to see in candidates proposed for office; these included moral integrity, intellectual ability, conformity with the code of good manners and courage to speak their minds. Preference was expressed for those who were conversant with literary works that stemmed from the Confucian school of ethics, rather than with those works which concentrated attention on the practicalities of organizing a state.

Provincial governors were soon required to present a specified number of candidates of this type to the centre; here they would be subjected to some forms of test and graded accordingly; and they would then be posted to hold offices that were commensurate with their performance. Unfortunately little is known of the type of questioning that was customary at this stage; possibly the standard history of the Han dynasty may include some examples of replies made by successful candidates, in the form of essays that touched on questions of ethics, politics or man's place in the universe. A surviving fragment of Han law, whose interpretation is by no means complete, stipulated that students aged at least seventeen should be subjected to tests; they would be required to show familiarity with a large number of characters or, according to a different interpretation, with a comparably large piece of literature; and they should be able to handle different styles of writing, or possibly undergo some period of probationary experience in an office. Once appointed to a post they must show proficiency at drafting and presenting documents of state.

Much more is known about the system introduced and operated by the Sui and Tang governments, which could draw on the experience of several centuries, and make provision for the more complex organs of government and duties that had emerged. There were now several series of examinations: one which secured the basic qualification needed to serve in office; one to determine the type and grade of office to which a candidate was fit for posting. In a third series, known as the Palace Examinations, it was the emperor himself who supposedly framed the questions that were set.

Of all the many types of qualification that could be won by these means, it was the degree of advanced learning (jinshi) which candidates sought most avidly. For it brought with it a reputation for literary distinction and the entrée to some of the most valuable posts in an official career. The tests that were involved were almost exclusively of a literary nature; candidates must show a thorough familiarity with the classical texts associated with the great Confucius and his tradition, to the point of recognizing a short quotation at sight, and completing the remainder of the passage from which it was derived. They must also show themselves able to compose in prose and poetry in a variety of styles, some of them of a highly artificial nature; and in some tests they were required to frame judgements on matters of public concern.

In all these procedures the road was hard and the competition was severe. Chinese fiction of the Tang period tells of heroes engaged in arduous study for years on end before eventually seeing their efforts crowned with glory, and hearing their names called in the list of successful candidates. But even greater perseverance was needed in the Ming and Qing periods, when the system was yet more complex and the degree of competition yet more acute.

The newly established Ming dynasty was well aware of the need to restore order and stability to Chinese society after the century of Mongol rule and the afflictions and disturbances of civil warfare. To provide for the nation's needs, radical steps were taken to improve the means of training; no less than 1,200 local schools were established in the prefectures and counties, at the expense of the central government and with officially appointed teachers. This original number, which dated from 1398, had risen to 1,810 by 1886. At the same time a new system provided for examinations at the three levels of locality, province and capital city, on a regular basis. As the size of China's population grew during these centuries, so too did the number of successful candidates who emerged at the lower levels; but as the quota of successful candidates at the highest level, who would thereby be qualified for office, remained little changed, the chances of success grew markedly less as the decades passed from 1400 to 1600.

'Read your text a hundred times and the meaning will become apparent of itself.' So said Dong Yu, of the third century. He was a man who was wont to take his texts with him however menial the work on which he was engaged; and he never lost an opportunity of dipping into those texts, to the great amusement of his brother. In time he rose to serve as superintendent of agriculture, but before then he had compiled his annotations to two famous works, one of philosophy (the *Laozi*) and one of history (the *Zuo zhuan*). But Dong Yu refused to give any teaching, firmly telling his would-be pupils to read their texts for themselves. His dictum is symbolic of the style of instruction as this developed in China, be it directed to an understanding of literature, a mastery of calligraphic skills or the exercise of remedial callisthenics (*taiji quan*). Teachers showed their pupils what they should practise, and enjoined them to do so continuously, without seeking an understanding of what they were doing. Only after sustained practice and exercise would there come a sudden but basic realization of the inherent meaning of the text, an ability to write effortlessly with artistic skill or the attainment of a harmonious balance of mind and body.

It was the proud boast of imperial scholars that the system of examinations provided a just and fair means of recruiting men of the best quality to the service and that the profession lay open for all those who were sufficiently talented. But the claim must be treated with some reserve; other routes to office and advancement, such as direct nomination, paved the way for the exercise of favouritism so as to strengthen a family's position or to build up a political faction. Nor could there be certainty that the examinations themselves would be conducted with scrupulous impartiality. Preparation for the examinations demanded an arduous training; but by no means all families of the land, particularly in the more remote provinces, could find suitable teachers for a potential candidate or the necessary resources to exempt him from his share of work in the fields; here again there could be considerable bias in favour of a family of highly placed officials, whose privileges included the entrée for their sons to schools reserved for the élite. Once locked inside the examinations' cells, candidates faced demanding tests that called no less for physical endurance than for intellectual brilliance.

Criticism of the examinations was voiced intermittently by Chinese statesmen and writers from the Tang period onwards and it has been elaborated by western historians. The training, syllabus and tests provided, as it may be claimed, a general education of a strictly limited type, without reference to contemporary realities or the need to prepare a civil servant to handle the actual problems that he would face. The system could also encourage artificiality of composition, if it obliged Tang candidates to confine their poems within the straight-jacket of rigid rules of rhyme; or if budding scholars of the Ming and Qing periods were obliged to frame their essays within the preconceived form of the 'eight-legged essay'. Excessive concentration on the precepts and practices of an obsolete past could engender a false respect for the golden ages of long ago, irrespective of their faults and errors; and it could end by stifling intellectual initiative. For the syllabus depended unduly on learning by rote and on a dogmatic acceptance of the orthodox interpretations of text; despite the existence of some types of specialist examination, for example in law or mathematics, success in such tests carried little prestige as compared with that attached to the degrees of advanced learning (*jinshi*), or familiarity with the classical texts (*mingjing*). In general the system is charged with encouraging undue adherence to bureaucratic procedures, exclusive and inward-looking attitudes of established officials and a lack of specialized training.

Such strictures have at times been overstated, but they cannot be dismissed entirely; nor can the fundamental virtues of the system be ignored. Concentration on the ways of a cultured life (*wen*) rather than on the specialized needs of the service or of training could lead only to a more intimate familiarity with that bedrock on which Chinese civilization rested. Acquaintance with pre-imperial history and the rise and fall of dynasties, whatever the bias with which such subjects were presented, could serve only to enrich the resources on which a civil servant depended for the exercise of his judgement. An intensive study of the writings associated with Confucius and his school must always bring to mind ethical values and social ideals which aimed at stability and encouraged service. The long training to which they had been subjected rendered civil servants accomplished men of letters, or practising calligraphers and painters, anxious to contribute to literature and the arts in the many hours when they were free of official duties. Their training had established a common standard of scholarship and education, without which China's single profession could easily have degenerated into the preserve of uncultured despots and oppressors.

One further consideration enabled some officials to repair the deficiencies of their training. In social terms they stood at the head of the scale; in terms of administrative practice they often found themselves obliged to seek help from others at a lower level, such as the leaders of the clans in the country and the guilds in the towns. Without the direct knowledge of actual conditions that these men had, and without their practical guidance, few civil servants would have been able to resolve local disputes or apply the central government's decrees. Sole reliance on the precepts of the *Mengzi* or the precedents of an earlier regime was not a sufficient basis with which to govern a mighty empire.

DOCUMENTS AND PROCEDURES

Much of the work of government derived from the reports that were submitted from officials at a low level, duly transmitted along the correct channels until they eventually arrived at the uppermost reaches of the central offices of state. Proposals that were forwarded in this way might well meet with rejection, but some of these reports would merit careful consideration, in which advantages were weighed against objections, and finally a proposal would be made either to accept or to reject the advice that had been proffered. Such submissions, in written form, are often termed 'memorials', and the Standard Histories of the dynasties include summaries of those that were of greatest importance. In framing these documents officials had taken considerable pains to use formulas and terms that were appropriate to the occasion and consistent with their rank in the service.

Some memorials could concern matters of ephemeral and local importance only; and in such cases they could be handled at an intermediate level of government, without the need for transmission to the capital city. Others constituted state documents of a high level and quality, recommending a change of policy, or initiating a discussion of major issues, such as the retention of outlying territories or withdrawal in the face of expense and hardship. Some memorialists presented their sovereign with a disquisition of a philosophical nature, arguing on the basis of historical precedent, citing the opinions of accepted masters and teachers or invoking the examples of the ages of the golden past.

All these documents were duly signed by the originating official and by those of the higher levels as they transmitted them to their final destination. As proof of validation, the official stamped his seal on to a clay mould which secured the cords whereby the document was fastened; baked hard in fire, the unbroken imprint informed the recipient immediately whence the document had come. At a later stage, officials' seals were affixed with red ink to the paper on which the document had been written. Examples of such seals are also seen on paintings to display the name of the collector.

If a memorialist's work reached the highest levels, it would merit a reply in the form of an imperial edict. Sometimes these would include orders for action on the lines that had been suggested. In such cases an edict could consist of no more than three characters, signifying 'We decree Our approval'. Edicts could also be promulgated on the initiative of a senior official or the emperor himself; these would not necessarily take the form of a response to a matter that had been put forward in a memorial. In this way orders could be given, for example, for an enquiry into the sufferings of the nation, or the causes of a series of catastrophes that had occurred. In some cases, so far from ordering new departures, edicts were in effect the recognition of a *fait accompli* that had been practised hitherto without approval. As in the drafts of memorials, so in edicts, use of the correct formulas and terminology was essential. In asking his ministers to explain the cause of disasters, the emperor must refer to his own inadequacies; the niceties of etiquette prescribed that on occasion orders would masquerade as the conveyance of 'Gracious Imperial permission'; there must always be a display of due deference to the status of the most senior advisers of the throne.

Officials were in duty bound to collect revenue and to call up able-bodied men for service. They would arbitrate in disputes; apply the penalties prescribed for failure to abide by regulations or for crime; and take whatever steps were necessary to protect the population from banditry and relieve them in time of want. Most of this work was carried out at the lowest levels of local government, whose recruiting officers, tax collectors and magistrates' lictors would personify the impact of imperial government for the majority of the population.

Officials of the county and province were required to submit regular returns of the number of registered inhabitants in their area, the extent of the land under their jurisdiction and the amount of tax rendered. Surviving fragments or summaries of just such documents provide an insight into the intensity and care with which the administration was operated. The figures that feature therein for the size of the population should, however, not always be taken as a true census; they were more in the nature of counts of taxable households or individuals, and there would be every reason for a man or woman to evade the official's eye and thus avoid obligation for the statutory duties. In addition, there were conflicting reasons why these returns might be subject to falsification. An increase in the population, if duly reported, might be interpreted as a sign of successful provincial administration and earn an official promotion; on the other hand, responsibility for delivery of tax or for call-up of individuals in direct proportion to the number of inhabitants registered might induce some officials to conceal the true size of their flock, in the hope of reducing their payments to the centre proportionately.

The earliest figures that result from a survey of the land date from AD 1–2 and are somewhat difficult to interpret. They included provision for land that was actually under the plough; land that was potentially arable; and land made over for roads or other purposes and not usable for crops. An early textbook of mathematics, dating from the start of the first century BC, includes guidance in the form of algebraical problems, for officials who faced the need to calculate the area of land of different and somewhat odd shapes. At the much more sophisticated stage of imperial government in the Ming dynasty, officials were ordered to draw up regularly two types of return. There was the 'Yellow Register' of households and their landholdings, with maps, which was prepared in four copies; the name of this document derived from the provision that the copy which was destined for the board of finance (*hu bu*) was made on yellow paper. The second document, the 'Fish Scale Register', took its name from the maps or diagrams which accompanied the text; this gave details of the area and shape of landholdings, with the names of the owners and notes on the type or quality of the land, whether flat or hilly, salty or uncultivated.

Tax was collected in kind (either grain, or textiles made from the hemp or silk grown on the land), in cash or in the form of service. Kings of the pre-imperial states had established the principle that they were entitled to conscript men to serve in public labour gangs or in the armed forces; and by mounting extravagant expeditions or undertaking demanding projects they had received stern criticism, on the grounds that manpower should be left to produce grain from the fields as far as possible. The principle of conscript labour was upheld in the imperial ages, and able-bodied men were put to work on the upkeep of communications, building and repairing bridges or keeping the transport or irrigation canals in working order. In some cases they carted China's staple goods from field to granary or from granary to city, carefully steering their heavily laden craft along the waterways. And however strong the force of criticism may have been, there were times when these men were obliged to leave the seasonal and essential work of the farms, and to serve as conscripts building the palaces and mausoleums that stand today as a witness of imperial grandeur.

Whatever malpractices and corruption may have taken place, meticulous accountancy was seen to accompany the collection and delivery of tax, whether this was rendered in kind or in money. Already in the fourth century BC, Shang Yang, the statesman who is credited with measures that had given Qin strength to conquer its rivals, had introduced a standard set of weights and measures for use in the kingdom. With the formation of the first empire (221 BC) the new government enforced the use of its standard sets, and subsequent imperial authorities continued to do so. Specifications for length, volume and weight rested in the final instance on the average size of grains of cereal, when taken in the bulk, and thus varying but little and assuring reasonable accuracy and uniformity. These official scales were used for transactions where tax was concerned, and accounts were duly forwarded to a superior authority; on a popular level it was sometimes customary for a different set of weights and measures to predominate.

Officials were also concerned with regulating and promulgating the approved calendar. Like other cultures, China depended on a luni-solar calendar, which took account of the cycles of both the moon and the earth. Such a system involved both advantages and disadvantages. If poor weather precluded accurate observation of the phases of the moon, mistakes could be rectified very quickly; but it was also necessary to reconcile the moon's cycle with that of earth and sun. To achieve such a result, it must first be determined which of the months would be counted as long (with 30 days) and which short (with 29 days), with the result that the normal year of twelve months would amount to 354 days.

Quite frequently, however, it was necessary to introduce an extra, or intercalary, month into the year, in order to reconcile such years, of 354 days, with the cycle of $365\frac{1}{4}$ days of the earth's orbit round the sun. According to the Metonic cycle, 19 such solar years amount to 235 lunar months; to bring the luni-solar year of 354 days into register, it was necessary to insert approximately four such extra months in every ten years. It was therefore also necessary, in regulating the calendar, to determine at what point due count should be made of these additions. There was also room for further choice, in specifying the point at which a new year was deemed to start; the terminology of months that is in use in Europe today serves as a reminder that such a matter cannot be taken for granted.

Traditionally it had been the privilege of kings to prescribe the calendar for the incoming year. In particular the kings of Zhou had exercised their prerogative in this respect, and adoption of their calendar by other leaders had signified acknowledgement of their superior status. In imperial times, the government continued to issue the official calendar, adjusting it when necessary; new types of instrument enabled observations to be made with greater accuracy; with more advanced skills the astronomer-mathematicians of the day could claim to be capable of more precise calculations.

In regulating the manner in which years were to be designated, imperial governments could make use of a propagandist device. After considerable thought an expression was chosen to name the start of a regnal period, and years were numbered in sequence from such a start. The terms that were adopted for the purpose were intended to allude to the achievements of which the dynasty could be proud, or the character to which it wished to lay claim or the hopes that it entertained for its dispensation. Thus, the years 28–25 BC were designated as years 1 to 4 of the period Heping, 'Pacification of the River', to commemorate or advertise the government's achievements in bringing the Yellow River under control. The Khitan emperors referred to the years 1055–64 as years 1 to 10 of Qingning, 'Pure Tranquillity'; the term Qianlong, 'Continuous Glory', was used to name the sixty years from 1736 to 1795.

Conformity with the calendar that had been prescribed by the central government and circulated in multiple copies to all offices of state served two purposes. In ideological terms it was hoped that it would prevent the emperor's subjects from embarking on activities that were not suited to a particular phase of time, and which would thereby conflict with the cycles of the universe (for example, in cosmic terms, trees should not be felled in the spring; conformity with the imperial calendar would ensure respect for this principle). In practical terms use of the same, officially sponsored calendar would prevent mistiming for the seasonal work of the fields.

Possession of the imperial calendar was essential for the conduct of official business; for example, a local official required this document in order to supervise work schedules in his village or county.

Copies were made not only to show the arrangement of the months in the year and the days of each month; they also carried the notation of certain cycles of an esoteric rather than a practical nature, which reached back into other, and perhaps irrational, attitudes to time and its passage. Such notations, which were already used on almanacs of the third century BC, take their place today on the calendars that adorn the walls of banks and offices in Hong Kong, Taiwan and Japan.

As always, efficient communication was the *sine qua non* of effective government. From the Han period onwards a service of official couriers had been established. For normal purposes these men would proceed on foot by means of relay; when express speed was necessary, they were mounted on horseback. Schedules prescribed the time to be taken on such journeys, and the despatch notes recorded the date and hours of departure and arrival. To maintain this service a system of post-stations gave facilities for a change of horses and a night's lodging for the emperor's messenger. Other travellers could be admitted, provided that they could prove their identification. This could be achieved by showing an inspecting official a passport, duly issued by authority, and made in the early days as a rectangular wooden board measuring six by one inches (Han measurements; that is, 13.8 by 2.3 cm). This was indented, or notched, so that it would be matched with another copy; it carried the date for its validity, and bore a number and perhaps a list of names of the holder and his family.

Fragments of administrative records reveal that in the Han period despatch riders on military business covered a distance of 160 kilometres in nine days; in times of emergency, a series of express cavalrymen could deliver a despatch over a distance of 575 kilometres in twenty-four hours. The Yuan dynasty (1260–1368) left China the heritage of a highly efficient postal service which formed a framework for the future, with the result that at the close of the imperial period approved schedules were as follows:

		Days (normal service)	Days (express service)
from Beijing to	Chengdu	48	24
	Guangzhou	56	32
	Lanzhou	41	17–18
	Nanjing	23	13–14

STATUTORY RULES, AND PUNISHMENTS FOR CRIME

Some of the Standard Histories of the dynasties include a treatise which is specifically concerned with legal matters and the conduct of trials for crime. Nevertheless, documentation for this major aspect of government is by no means as complete as it is for certain other institutions. Knowledge of the provisions of the kingdom of Qin and of the Qin and Han empires derives from fragments of manuscripts, many of which have been found only recently, and from citations in later literary sources. A revised form of the Tang code, first compiled in 653, dates from 737; and the Qing code of 1740 is based on a document of the Ming empire, of 1397. In many cases there is a tendency both in these and in other codifications to repeat the provisions or clauses of their predecessors. To these there would be added *ad hoc* decisions based on case law, and such accretions could well lead to inconsistencies. It could sometimes be difficult for an official to chart a straight course through the extensive documentation and to reach decisions or interpretations of a judicial nature that could not be challenged.

Traditional China did not produce a concept of law as an agreed instrument with which to restrain the arbitrary use of power, whether by a monarch or an official. Nor were the legal provisions the principal means of maintaining social stability and order. The statutes and ordinances of the emperors were influenced by the Confucian ethic, authoritarian methods of government and concepts of cosmic being such as that of the Five Phases. Many of the provisions were framed as sanctions in case of dereliction of duty, or as penalties to be imposed for certain crimes. There was no equivalent to the oath whereby English sovereigns are obliged to swear to govern in accordance with the laws of the land, or the undertaking that a President of the United States of America gives to abide by the constitution. For the laws were an instrument of the rulers, and they were open to abuse. Writing as a Ming loyalist, whose views on sovereignty have already been mentioned, Huang Zongxi (1610–95) drew a distinction between the proper function of laws and their misuse by despotic emperors in order to safeguard their own powers and interests.

The statutes (*lü*), ordinances (*ling*) and supplementary provisions (*li*) that the central government promulgated were expressions of that government's will; they were not a statement of rights, obligations and privileges attendant on an individual. Some of the provisions included an attempt to regulate human conduct so that it would not conflict with a view of the universe and its rhythms; others specified minutiae of practice, showing how a government would interfere or oversee activities of daily life, such as sowing, tillage and harvesting; many laid down the penalties for stated crimes, such as theft, bribery and murder.

Accusation of crime, investigation of a case and pronouncement of punishment were subject to careful procedures, which were described in technical language. Arrest of a suspect was followed by interrogation and the collection of supporting evidence. Confession, extracted if necessary under torture, was required before a charge could be proved. Conduct of a case at these stages usually devolved on the county magistrate and his minions, who were charged with the task of finding their way to the truth.

The magistrate was in fact responsible for processes and decisions which are separately assigned in some parts of the west to detective, jury and judge. At the close of an investigation or trial it was the magistrate's duty to determine what penalties should be enforced. Some cases might well be of so grave a nature that they would pass beyond his powers of jurisdiction, and these would be conveyed to the levels of the province, or the offices of central government. In extreme cases the papers would be sent for final decision to the emperor himself; and here there was some guard against undue despotism, as he was not entitled to impose penalties that lay beyond the accepted provisions of state. If they were fortunate, criminals would profit by the declaration of an act of amnesty, extended by an emperor's will throughout his domains and freeing those who awaited punishment for their deserts.

Throughout the tradition punishments had been harsh, at times including mutilation and castration. In the early empires possession of some degrees of social status served to exempt a criminal from punishment or perhaps to mitigate its severities. Some of the earliest documents that are available, of the Qin kingdom, provide for payment of fines in respect of certain misdemeanours. Later, in some circumstances, redemption from punishment could be obtained by monetary payments. In customary Chinese fashion, by the Qing period five grades of punishment had been drawn up in hierarchies, ranging from flogging to penal servitude, to life exile, to military exile to the frontier and finally to the death sentence. The latter type included three principal degrees, of strangulation, decapitation and death by slicing. Imprisonment was not a punishment as such; it amounted to no more than detention pending trial.

Chinese tradition did not include scope for a professional pleader whose duty lay in defending a man or woman standing trial; nor were there safeguards that would ensure that evidence was proven or that its implications were not subject to abuse. A criminal trial necessarily ended in punishment: either of the accused person or, if the charge was not proved, of the accuser, thereby shown to be guilty of perjury.

THE WALLS AND THEIR GUARDIANS

There has been no single 'Great Wall of China'; succeeding regimes have erected defence lines, and these have been manned from time to time when imperial strength has been adequate to do so. In the pre-imperial days of the Warring States, some of the kingdoms had erected defence lines against their immediate neighbours, situated as these were in the interior of China. Able to call on larger forces of conscript servicemen than any of his predecessors, the first of the Qin emperors (reigned 221–210 BC) established a set of defence lines on his northern borders, which was designed as a protection against the potentially hostile confederacies of the Xiongnu. This was the first of China's 'Great Walls' (*chang cheng*); it had been built under the supervision of a famous general named Meng Tian, and the extravagant expenditure of manpower on the project has often been cited by way of criticism against the regime of Qin.

Severe as such protests may have been, they failed to dissuade many of the first emperor's successors from embarking on comparable projects, until the days of the Ming dynasty. As the hold on territories changed hands and tactical considerations were altered, the walls that successive dynasties erected took differing routes, but they were all intended as a protection against an enemy from the north. In some periods, such as that of the Yuan dynasty, there was no call to build defence lines for such a purpose; and no dynasty was able to keep the walls fully manned for more than short periods. Reluctant as Chinese governments were to maintain standing regular armies, they perforce relied mainly on conscripts to man the watch-towers of the north; in its turn, the existence of a garrison gave rise to problems of supply and communications, which could tax the slender resources of an imperial government yet further.

The Han emperors inherited from Qin both the potential enmity of the northern peoples and a precedent for solving the problem. In time they succeeded in restoring the earlier defences and extending the lines deep into Central Asia, ending at the outposts of Dunhuang. By now the walls had come to serve several purposes. Not only were they designed as a protection from an intruding marauder; they also formed an armed and protected causeway along which trading caravans or officials on diplomatic missions could travel in safety. The walls also enabled the provincial authorities to check passage in and out of China, and thereby prevent deserters or criminals from evading their statutory dues or escaping from the harsh hand of justice. In addition, the walls separated two groups of peoples who might threaten Chinese security; for had the Xiongnu of the north and the Qiang, or proto-Tibetan tribes, of the west been able to act in concert, Han security would have been under grave threat.

Built partly by means of the traditional stamped-earth or *terre pisé* method, and partly of brick, the walls connected a series of square watch-towers, which acted as signalling stations and command posts, housing orderly rooms and garrison quarters. Units of the garrison were under the command of provincial officials, with no hard-and-fast distinction between a civil and a military organization. Officials posted to these stations maintained, as always, written records and reports, and it is from fragments of such documents that details are revealed of the working life of the servicemen and their officers, between *c.* 100 BC and AD 100.

Senior officials of the commanderies, called commandants, were responsible for maintaining the service and the defences. Their troops were divided into units corresponding with companies, platoons and finally the sections, which comprised an officer and some two to four servicemen. Surviving fragments of lists of Han units and their complements make it possible to reconstruct an order of battle, and to learn how the men were disciplined and employed. When manning the watch-towers they were responsible for the observation of enemy movements. They must be familiar with the code of signals, so that they could recognize the adjoining units' warnings and convey them further up or down the line. Servicemen were sometimes sent out on patrol duties; or they would be set to control points of access, inspecting the documents of travellers and watching for goods whose export was banned. From time to time commanding officers tested their men in archery and the use of weapons, and inspected the equipment with which they had been issued. They also inspected the sites and buildings which the men had constructed, looking for badly laid signal piles or misuse and wastage of stores.

Some of the Han conscripts were posted to work on the official farms that had been established where natural supplies of water permitted. Their purpose was to supply the troops with locally grown grain; and their records, sometimes kept in duplicate, included all receipts of grain in the official granaries, all issues of grain and salt to servicemen and their families and all issues of clothing or other equipment. In addition, the clerks of the service recorded sums paid to officers as stipends and the names and descriptive details of travellers whose passage had been allowed through military lines.

The surviving parts of the Great Wall which are visible today date from the Ming period. They formed an essential part of the strategy to maintain a strong Chinese presence in the face of potential enemies, and the years 1570–1620 saw the most energetic attempts of the Ming governments to complete this project. These walls were built of large bricks; raised causeways connected the signalling stations, of which it was hoped to erect no less than 3,000, each one being manned by fifty men. On the northern side a parapet and set of battlements afforded protection to the defending troops; transverse channels drained the water away from the causeway itself. Remnants of the Ming wall that may be traced today run for perhaps 3,440 kilometres.

*

Magistrates and clerks, censors and ministers of state all played their part in governing the empires and implementing their rules. Distinctions of the robes that they wore, the badges affixed to their hats and the seals with which they stamped their reports signified their degree of seniority. The statutes of Qin obliged them to supervise matters of considerable detail, such as the volume of seed-corn to be sown, or the care with which horse or oxen were put to work in the fields. The dossier of Kou En, a civilian who faced a charge of the misuse or embezzlement of public stores in AD 28, is but a short example of the documentation to which such cases gave rise, with a statement of the charge and its rebuttal, and repetition of all such matters for reference to a senior official for decision.

Occasionally we hear of a woman who performed the duties of a senior official. In about 320 the governor of Jinning zhou (Yunnan province) died in office, and the local inhabitants prevailed upon his daughter to assume his duties. It was she who had walls erected around the town, now disappeared without trace; local tradition has it that a statue was carved in her likeness and that she was treated as an object of worship.

Fang Xuanling (578–648) had achieved the degree of advanced learning at the early age of seventeen. In time he rose to serve the second of the Tang emperors as chief minister; his duties, and indeed his privilege, included supervision of the compilation of the Standard History for the Jin (Tsin) dynasty. A century and a half later Bo Juyi (772–846) was alluding in poem or letter to his experiences as a junior official at the capital city: as an assessor re-marking some of the examination papers over which questions had been raised; or to his life and duties when holding a post in the Yangzi valley. Other literary references sometimes shed light on the work of more junior officers. Thus, in describing the hardships brought about by taxation, Bo's contemporary Liu Zongyuan (773–819) once wrote in vivid terms of the descent of officials on a village, there to hector its inhabitants and harry them into more and more intensive work in the fields.

In the eleventh century a senior official named Wang Anshi (1021–86) tried to introduce a series of reforms to stabilize the prices of staple commodities, to provide loans for indigent farmers and to replace the call for corvée labour by direct taxation. He also hoped to establish militia units for defence and to provide them with a steady supply of horses; in the syllabus for the examinations he wished to see less emphasis laid on literary merit and more on practical ability.

Repeated injunctions urged officials to speak their minds fearlessly, but considerable courage was needed if this was to be done. A career official must be ready to undertake any task, as may be seen in the case of an official who was serving in a city under siege in 1207, and found himself saddled with responsibility for medical care and victualling of troops, albeit with no training or prior experience of such matters.

But the service was too large to exclude all opportunities for malpractice. The system of 'customary fees' (lougui) that prevailed in the local or provincial offices of the Qing dispensation allowed scope to clerks, runners and officials of all ranks to engage in corruption and to practise oppression. There was also scope for strong leadership and powerful minds to influence the destiny of the nation. In the closing decades of the Qing empire major dynastic decisions lay largely in the hands of Prince Gong, subject as he was at times to the anger of the empress dowager or the criticism of the censors. The Manchu house of which he was a member had recently suffered defeat and humiliation at the hands of foreigners from the west; it was largely due to his stature and wisdom that China emerged from such a situation with dignity, eventually to earn the respect of European statesmen and to find a place in the comity of nations.

XI

LITERATURE AND SCHOLARSHIP

By its richness and its variety, its extent and its contrasts, literature
is one of China's most enduring gifts to mankind. Its creations arise
from the palace downwards, being the product alike of scholar official
and individual mystic; its characteristics derive from motives that
may sometimes conform and sometimes conflict with other calls.
Pupils of a teacher wrote in order to perpetuate their master's
precepts. Scholars wrote to serve the established authority of the day
with the hope of instilling an orthodox frame of mind in the leaders
of the community. Historians compiled their accounts to bring the
lessons of the past to bear upon the problems of their own time, or
to marshal intellectual support for dynastic masters. Poets wielded
their brushes to recapture moments of intensity and to invest them
with permanence. Essayists wrote to entertain or to amuse, to escape
from the constraints of official life or to portray a contemporary
problem in terms of allegory. Some wrote to describe the beauties of
the mountains and the lakes that lay around them and to relate them
to human achievements and failings. Philosophical enquiries and
attempts to explain the truths of ultimate reality stemmed alike from
the training of the scholar, the doubts and meditation of the mystic
and the critic's protests against religious practices of the day.

Chinese prose includes elements that are didactic or lyrical, moralist or esoteric. Sayings of the early masters, couched as precept or
moral aphorism, developed into ordered and systematic essays. If
China has produced no equivalent of the epic of the west, Europe
has rarely contrived an economy of expression such as that of the
jueju poems; at its best, China's historical prose is worthy to be ranked
with that of Thucydides or Gibbon.

THE CLASSICAL CANON

For 2,000 years China's education, examinations and scholastic effort
have been subject to the overwhelming influence of a few select texts,
parts of which were of even earlier origin. All men of letters have
been required to gain complete familiarity with these works, so that

they can recognize allusions in what they read and cite apposite quotations in their own writing. These were the texts of the classics which concerned nearly all aspects of the Chinese tradition, be they of a religious, philosophical, literary or historical nature.

These texts were singled out for special respect and treatment by a deliberate act of imperial government; and they were in all cases intimately associated with the examples of the kings of Zhou, the teachings of Confucius and his school and the principles of moral behaviour and an ordered society that formed the mainstay of the Confucian ethic. In 136 BC the Han government established posts for five academicians, who were charged with the duty of studying and teaching five works: the *Book of Songs* (*Shijing*), the *Book of Documents* (*Shujing* or *Shangshu*), the *Book of Changes* (*Yijing*), the treatise on conventional behaviour (*li*) and the *Spring and Autumn Annals* (*Chunqiu*). A dozen years later a further step was taken in the establishment of the Imperial Academy (*Taixue*), to be attended, at first, by fifty students. This number soon grew, and if the sources of information are to be believed, by the middle of the second century AD it had risen to 30,000. Of equal importance to the number of attendants was the precedent that was hereby set for the imperial promotion of scholarship and learning, and the provision of official institutes for that purpose.

A sixth work concerned music; this may well have elicited equal respect at one time, but it soon disappeared, and attention was concentrated on elucidating the meaning of the other five texts. As parts of these were up to six or seven centuries old when the imperial academicians were appointed, they both demanded expert interpretation and laid themselves open to special pleading. The *Book of Songs* was said to comprise poems which had been collected by Confucius himself. Its lyrics, inescapably linked with music, include passages that may be said to match the Psalms in beauty and dignity, as well as some that are of an erotic nature; and their content draws on folklore and religious practices of a bygone age. But when used as the basis for a scholar's training, these poems became subject to a special type of application. They were accredited with moral injunctions and lessons that can hardly have been formulated in or been appropriate to the age when some of them were written; the purpose in doing so was to lend force to the homilies of a teacher or statesman of the imperial age. Unfortunately the violence done to the beauties of the poems in this process often succeeded in masking their original significance.

The solemn declarations of the *Book of Documents* evoke the moral powers of the kings of Zhou and the authority with which they conveyed charge of the land to others, or expected service, loyalty

TABLE 12

THE CLASSICAL CANON

Successive dynasties and scholars adopted different selections and arrangements of certain texts, which were to be treated with special respect as a
classical canon, and which were to form the basis of the systems of examination and education. These works were grouped together first as the Five,
then the Nine and finally the Thirteen Classics, and they were subject to
continual study and reassessment, so that the approved interpretations
would conform with intellectual, religious and social developments. The
received versions of today can be traced to China's earliest surviving prints, of
the Song period, but in many cases their relationship with the original texts,
of up to two thousand years previously, must remain subject to question.

(i) *Basic Works*

The *Shijing* or *Book of Songs*	Three hundred poems allegedly collected by Confucius (551–479 BC); earliest parts from perhaps 1000 BC; latest from perhaps the sixth century BC.
The *Shujing* (*Shangshu*) or *Book of Documents*	Earliest parts from perhaps 700 BC; some half of the extant work dates from the fourth century AD.
The *Yijing* or *Book of Changes*	Earliest parts (the *Zhou yi* or *Changes of Zhou*) from the ninth century BC; later parts (the 'Ten Wings' , explanatory essays on the *Zhou yi*) third or second century BC.
The *Yili, Liji* and *Zhou li*, compendia on *li*	Extant works, reputedly based on earlier writings, dating probably from the Warring States period (481 or 403–221 BC) or later.
The *Chunqiu* or *Spring and Autumn Annals*	Reputedly compiled by Confucius.
The *Yueshu* or *Book of Music*	Lost by Han times.

(ii) *Ancillary Works, Closely Associated with the Foregoing*

The *Gongyang zhuan* and *Guliangzhuan*	Exegetical comments on the *Chunqiu*; from the Warring States period.
The *Zuo zhuan*	Chronicle of events, compiled perhaps 350 BC, and linked with the *Chunqiu*.

(iii) *Other Works*

The *Lunyu* or *Analects of Confucius*	Compiled by Confucius' disciples
The *Mengzi* or *Sayings of Mencius*	Compiled by Mencius' followers.
The *Xiao jing* or *Classic of Filial Piety*	Warring States period.
The *Erya*, an interpretative glossary	Warring States period.

and homage. Some portions of the present text claim to go back to the kings of Shang, but already from the third century AD the work had been subject to interpolation, and careful discrimination is necessary to distinguish its genuine parts and its later additions. Some of the documents may perhaps be dated at 700 BC, and the archaic language in which they are couched is by no means always to be understood; interpretation is sometimes helped by comparison with the inscriptions made on bronze vessels in these early centuries.

Of equal antiquity at least are the earliest parts of the *Book of Changes*, strictly known as 'The Changes of Zhou' (*Zhou yi*). These short statements are written in formulaic and even repetitive style; they are concerned directly with acts of divination performed with the yarrow stalks, and they provide guidance for the meaning attached to each line of the hexagram that was formed, and to the hexagram itself and its behaviour. This part of the work is highly esoteric, and by perhaps 200 BC, if not earlier, much of its meaning had been forgotten. There then arose a series of attempts to interpret the text, relating its terse statements to the philosophical theories that were then in vogue, but which had not appeared at the time when the original formulae had been written down. These accretions, which are usually printed along with *The Changes of Zhou*, are known under the general title of the 'Ten Wings'; and while the earliest parts of the *Book of Changes* derived from mantic activity, these later additions are the product of the intellect, almost taking the form of an exposé of philosophical theory.

There are several extant compendia or treatises which include rules or guidance for human behaviour (*li*). They may regulate procedures for a royal, social or religious occasion, prescribing the conduct that is suitable at a service of prayer or sacrifice, at an audience granted by a monarch, at weddings or at the ceremonies when youths attained their majority. These works instruct men and women how to behave so as to preserve the niceties of *li*; their importance lies in the support that they may give to maintaining the stable relationships of society. For, by keeping the duly prescribed rules of *li*, so will a community or kingdom live in a state of security and freedom from strife. The books on *li* lay down the correct relationships between senior and junior, whether at court or within the family, with the intention of ensuring an orderly conduct of affairs and the imposition of authority. It is not certain which, if any, of the surviving treatises were identical with the one which was entrusted to the special academician who was appointed to look after this subject in 136 BC.

The *Spring and Autumn Annals* (*Chunqiu*) is the title of a chronicle of the state of Lu, said to have been compiled by its most distinguished denizen, known as Kongzi, or Kongfuzi. With an inbuilt respect for the royal house of Zhou, it records in strict chronological order events of significance that took place between 722 and 481 BC, be they sacrifices of state, visits paid by princes or notable dignitaries, alliances that were sealed by solemn oaths or natural phenomena that were treated as omens. The record is written in a terse style, ever praised for its direct simplicity and clarity, and forming a model for those who wrote the histories of the imperial dynasties. But the style was so terse and the text so pregnant with meaning that the work soon gave rise to explanatory commentaries. Since the beginning of the Christian era the *Chunqiu* has always been read in association with a separate historical record which treats some of the same events, providing detail by way of exposition. This is the chronicle known as the *Zuo zhuan*, compiled probably *c.* 350 BC, and regarded, like the *Chunqiu*, as a model piece of composition in prose.

By the Song period the canon of classical writings had been extended so that it comprised thirteen works. These included the three principal compendia on *li* and the three principal commentaries or amplifications of the *Spring and Autumn Annals*. In addition, three other works which were specifically associated with the teachings of Kongzi and the Confucian ethic now took their place in this select body of literature. One of these, the *Classic of Filial Piety* (*Xiao jing*), circulated widely as a textbook for teaching moral principles. The other two (the *Analects of Confucius* or *Lunyu* and the *Sayings of Mencius* or *Mengzi*) were destined to receive the greatest degree of respect accorded to any pieces of Chinese writing. Together with two small chapters entitled the 'Great Learning' (*Daxue*) and the 'Doctrine of the Mean' (*Zhongyong*) that had formed parts of the compendia on *li*, they were selected for special study and came to be known as the 'Four Books' (*Si shu*). Since the twelfth century generations of Chinese schoolchildren have learned their letters and acquired their first acquaintance with Chinese thought from these works.

TABLE 13

THE GROWTH OF CLASSICAL LEARNING

213 BC	Qin edict for the suppression of traditional learning; order for the Burning of the Books.
191	Repeal of edict of 213; followed by various finds of copies of texts, in either contemporary (*jinwen*) or archaic script (*guwen*).
136	Appointment of academicians to specialize on five basic classical works.

124	Establishment of the *Taixue* (Imperial Academy) with fifty students.
51	Official conference, in the Pavilion of the Stone Canal on authenticity and interpretation of various texts.
8 BC	Three thousand students reported as attending the Academy.
9–23 AD	Appearance of apocryphal literature (possibly earlier); promotion of ancient traditions and texts; compilation of a catalogue of extant literature by Liu Xiang (79–8 BC) and Liu Xin (died AD 23).
79	Official conference, in the White Tiger Hall, on interpretation of the classics; extant written account compiled as the *Bohu tong*.
c. 140	Thirty thousand students reported as attending the Academy.
second century	Intensive study of problems of authenticity and interpretation; rival claims by the New Text and Old Text schools; leading contributions by Ma Rong (79–166), Zheng Xuan (127–200) and He Xiu (129–82).
175	Precedent set by first engraving of approved texts on stone tablets; repeated in 240–8.
226–49	Wang Bi's metaphysical interpretation of the *Yijing*.
574–648	Kong Yingda, commentator to the classics.
653	Promulgation of state-sponsored commentaries on the Five Classics; emergence of the concept of the Nine Classics.
830	Project initiated for engraving nine classical texts, eventually to include thirteen works on 228 surfaces (the so called Kaicheng classics).
from 932	Production of the first printed edition of the Nine Classics.
1177–89	Zhu Xi's (1130–1200) comments on the *Analects*, *Mencius* and two chapters ('The Great Learning' and 'The Doctrine of the Mean') from works on *li*; prominence of these texts as the 'Four books'.
1313–1906	The Four Books adopted as the basis for state examinations.
seventeenth and eighteenth centuries	Formation of the school of empirical research (*kao zheng*), sometimes known as the school of Han learning, led by Gu Yanwu (1613–82), Huang Zongxi (1610–95), Dai Zhen (1724–77) and others; a reaction against the Neo-Confucian interpretations of the Song and Ming scholars, criticized for their inclusion of Daoist and Buddhist ideas.
1745	Publication of Yan Ruoju's (1636–1704) doubts on authenticity of parts of the *Book of Documents*.
1816	Publication of the collected commentaries to the Thirteen Classics, in 416 chapters, by Ruan Yuan (1764–1849).

nineteenth
century

Continuation of comment, and re-emergence of the New Text and Old Text controversy, by notable scholars such as Sun Yizang (1848–1908), Kang Youwei (1858–1927) and Wang Guowei (1877–1927).

The training of scholars and civil servants rested on an intimate acquaintance with the classics; the interpretations which they received from their mentors needed necessarily to accord with the contemporary state of empire and society. As the centuries passed, these interpretations came to reflect scholastic developments and to satisfy the growing sophistication of the intellect. Before the establishment of the academicians in 136 BC the books had had a somewhat mixed history, as the masters of the Qin empire had attempted to eradicate the influence that they already exerted and the appeal that they made to a glorious past. Unsuccessful as such attempts were, they may well have hampered circulation of the texts at a crucial stage, and China owes a great debt to the Han emperors and their advisers for the steps taken to ensure their survival. Different versions of some of these texts had come to light at this time, thus provoking scholastic dispute that concerned both the authenticity of the various copies and the style of interpretation. Ideological issues soon became intertwined with scholastic questions; early imperial governments took it upon themselves to sponsor particular interpretations and to determine which of several versions of the text were correct; and to ensure that the approved texts would be available, beyond doubt, to scholar and student alike, they were engraved in permanent form on tablets of stone.

This project was started in AD 175 following some two centuries of scholastic disputation regarding the accuracy and basic meaning of these works. But while the sponsorship of imperial government did much to enhance the value of the classical texts, it also contrived to reduce the scope for independent evaluation by scholars who were not aligned to a particular political cause. Imperial government required the existence of a single version, and an interpretation that lay beyond challenge; attempts to impose uniformity could threaten the growth of individual criticism.

In 175 the Han government set a precedent for engraving these texts on stone that was to have wide implications. Seven centuries later the Tang government followed the earlier precedents, in a somewhat grand manner. It took seven years to complete the project, which had been initiated in 830, and at later times certain other works than those that had been originally planned for inclusion were added. Altogether the texts of thirteen books were engraved, in columns of ten characters, on the surfaces of 114 stone slabs. Despite the damage wrought by earthquake in 1556, these inscribed tablets are still almost entirely intact, and they are open for inspection in Xi'an. To acquire possession of their own copies of the approved versions of these works, some scholars had formed the habit of making rubbings, or ink-squeezes, directly from the stones. Such habits were one of the formative factors behind the evolution of printing.

The new system of examinations, of the Sui and Tang periods, enhanced the interest in the classical works and the need to produce orthodox interpretations; these were duly forthcoming in the hope of moulding the classical tradition to fit the conditions of the medieval empires. As happened so often in respect of other matters of intellectual moment, it was in the Song period that radical change made itself felt. It had been Zhu Xi (1130–1200) who had selected the 'Four Books' for special treatment, and it was largely due to his influence that a new set of commentaries received official approval. Zhu Xi was trying to restore the reputation of the Confucian ethic after some years in which it had suffered an eclipse. He saw the need to close the gap that had come to exist between precept and practice, and he hoped to show the essential unity between thought and action. His new set of commentaries to the classical works tried to achieve such results and to relate the texts to some of the universal problems that face mankind.

In place of the philological explanations of the past, Zhu Xi tried to demonstrate the philosophical content and significance of these early writings. His exercises in metaphysics and his contribution to classical learning outlasted him by many generations. But a further change came with the high point reached by Chinese scholasticism in the seventeenth and eighteenth centuries. Academics of the Qing period were reacting against much that had followed from Zhu Xi's ways of thought, and they were seeking to revert to an interpretation of the classical works that they believed to be of older origins and less subject to adulteration by later ideas.

THE WRITINGS OF THE HISTORIANS

Great prestige attached to the work of compiling the twenty-six Standard Histories (*zhengshi*, sometimes termed 'Dynastic Histories'), whose scope extends for the whole of the imperial period (221 BC to 1911). The first of these works, the *Shiji* (*Historical Records*), begins its story with the first traces of human organization and ends at a point of time close to the death of Sima Qian, the principal compiler (shortly after 100 BC). By its arrangement and form it set the pattern for subsequent works, which are usually confined to a single dynastic period. As the time span of such periods varied greatly, so too did the length of their histories, ranging from 36 chapters for the Chen dynasty (557–89) to 496 chapters for the Song period (960–1279). Compilation of the last of the series, as a draft for the Qing dynasty (1644–1911) in 534 chapters, was started in 1914 and completed by 1927, and an annotated edition of part of the work was published in Taipei in 1986. Successive regimes have commissioned the publication of comprehensive prints of this majestic series of works. The last set was initiated in Beijing in 1959.

These histories were prepared as documents of state that vindicated a dynasty's right to rule. In one set of chapters attention focuses on the words and deeds of the emperors and on activities in which they were concerned. Chapters of treatises, or disquisitions, take select topics such as imperial protocol, institutions of government, laws, calendar, waterways or economic practice as their subject. Tables set out lists of princes, noblemen or ministers of state, showing how hereditary titles passed from one generation to the next, or how careers were advanced by merit or favouritism, or terminated by death or disgrace. By far the greater proportion of the Standard Histories was taken up with biographies of prominent men and women, thereby complementing the somewhat stark account of events in other chapters.

The earliest examples of the Standard Histories were the result of individual initiative, but from 629 onwards responsibility for these works lay with an established office of state, called the History Commission. Officials assigned to this work could supposedly call on documents of state as their main source, and their final compilation was preceded by a number of preliminary diaries and drafts. From the *Shiji* onwards, comments and appreciations at the close of a chapter allowed some scope for criticism or appraisal; but readers will look in vain in these magnificent works for reference to the personal characteristics of the principal actors, or for direct attention to causation.

China's preoccupation with the past led to a paradox. While it was important for historians to remind readers of the golden ages of long ago, it was equally necessary to vilify the immediately preceding regime. Such demands could not fail to affect the manner in which the histories were written. Individual statesmen or protagonists tend to be classified, almost in cliché fashion, as good or bad, depending on the success that they achieved, or the outcome of political incidents in which they were involved. In choosing subjects for the biographies the members of the History Commission held it in their power to hold a man's example up for praise or to leave his name to be for

TABLE 14

HISTORICAL WRITING AND CRITICISM

c. 86 BC	The *Shiji*, by Sima Tan (d. 110) and Sima Qian (c. 145–c. 86 BC); the first example of the Standard History form (annals, tables, biographies and treatises).
AD 92	The *Han shu*, by Ban Gu (32–92) and others.
200	The *Han ji*, by Xun Yue (148–209); a record of events of the Han period in strict chronological sequence.
fourth century	The *Huayang guozhi*, by Chang Qu; first of the local histories.
629	Tang establishment of the state agency responsible for the compilation of the Standard Histories.
710	Completion of the *Shitong* (*Generalities of History*) by Liu Zhiji; a critical appreciation of historical writing.
1061	Compilation of the *Xin Tang shu* (*New Tang History*) by Ouyang Xiu.
1084	Completion of the *Zizhi tongjian* (*Comprehensive Mirror for Aid in Government*) by Sima Guang (1019–86); an historical account, in strict chronological sequence, for the period 403 BC to AD 959.
1172	Completion of the *Tongjian gangmu* by Zhu Xi (1130–1200) as an abridgement of the *Zizhi tongjian*, with moralist overtones.
sixteenth century	Publication of two editions of twenty-one Standard Histories, sponsored by the Ming government.
1739	Project started by the Qing government for official publication of editions of twenty-four Standard Histories, with critical annotation (*kaozheng*).
eighteenth century	Zhang Xuecheng's (1758–1801) new views on historiography.
1914	Draft Standard History of the Qing period (*Qing shi gao*) started.
1959–74	Government-sponsored publication of punctuated editions of twenty-four Standard Histories.

ever forgotten, with no place in the records. Treatment of a dynasty's rise and fall or of a champion's bid to seize power followed contemporary dynastic demands; for these histories were written with a purpose, that of supporting the cause of an imperial house.

The Standard Histories form the mainstay of historical writing; they are voluminous and comprehensive, and they include some of China's finest prose, marked by clear and crisp writing. There are however a number of weaknesses seen principally in their inbuilt bias. In addition, their content mainly concerns the uppermost ranks of society and tends to leave activities at other levels out of consideration. Only rarely is it possible to call on external sources to provide material by way of control or to counteract the prejudices of the compilers; but some other sources of information, which depended on other motives, could be forthcoming from China itself. A scholar's fascination with China's past, an official's reliance on written records to provide guidance and the local loyalties of a family or a province gave rise to other types of historical writing. From the Tang period onwards authors were drawing up compendia which were intended to describe the growth of imperial institutions and their operation throughout the ages. With such a vade-mecum beside him a puzzled civil servant could ascertain how his predecessors had solved an administrative problem that confronted him. Local gazetteers were also being produced, to praise the famous men of a town or county, to describe the natural features of hill or river or to record the cults of worship paid to a local deity.

The early examples of both the compendia on institutions and the local histories drew on existing material, sometimes from the Standard Histories themselves. But from the Song period onwards records of these types were becoming ever richer, calling on documents of state that had otherwise been neglected, or papers that had been lovingly preserved in the fastnesses of a family or shrine. Local histories are of particular value in their accounts of folklore and folk religion, whose existence may well escape notice in the Standard Histories; for those noble, officially inspired works would not wish to elaborate on practices that would invite the disapproval of the central government.

The beginnings of a critical attitude to history may be seen at least as early as the writings of Wang Chong (AD 27-c. 100), who had seen reason to doubt the reputation ascribed to the kings of earlier ages. In the Song period some scholars were voicing their doubts regarding the validity and value of parts of the *Book of Documents*. But it was Sima Guang (1019–86) who left the principal monument to the growth of historical research at this time. He was well aware of the motives that had prompted the compilation of the Standard Histories and he recognized the inherent weakness of taking dynastic periods as the sole criterion for chronological treatment, and forcing history to fit such a framework. He also realized that there were inconsistencies in the Standard Histories and that it was necessary to seek corroboration and further evidence from other sources. In recasting much of the material of the Standard Histories in his own work, Sima Guang cut through the inhibitions of dynastic change and arranged his material strictly in chronological order. The title of his work, the *Comprehensive Mirror for Aid in Government (Zizhi tongjian*), betrays some of his motives.

In their hours of leisure, other famous littérateurs of the Song age were bending their attention to history, looking back to crucial issues of the past, famous incidents that had made or broken a dynasty, or key figures whose reputation called for reassessment. It was in this way that Ouyang Xiu (1007–72) wrote on factionalism and the legitimate succession of dynastic rule; and Su Dongpo (1036–1101) produced his appraisals of Shang Yang (*c.* 390–338 BC), of the pre-imperial kingdom of Qin, and of Jia Yi (201–169 BC) and Chao Cuo (died 154 BC), two statesmen of Former Han. Such essays are uninhibited by the need to write for official purposes; they reflect the mature judgement of some of China's best-educated and most sophisticated minds.

The contributions of later scholars, particularly of the Qing period, are no less significant. As in their treatment of classical writings, so in respect of the histories, they were anxious to explain the texts of their heritage in terms of their original context rather than in response to contemporary modes of thought. Schooled in some of the most advanced academies yet founded in China, the Qing scholars set themselves to prepare critical notes to the Standard Histories, comparing different accounts of the same incident in the hope of eliminating inconsistencies; and they produced an annotation (*kaozheng*) which set a new standard of professional achievement. In the nineteenth century these scholars were responsible for a series of reference works or aids designed to solve a reader's problems; the historical atlas of Yang Shoujing (1839–1915), which shows the administrative shape of China dynasty by dynasty, may be quoted as but one example. At the same time others had been maintaining the practice of writing critical essays that assessed the achievements or decisions of the past. Examples may be seen in Gu Yanwu's (1613–82) account of the defensive walls erected by various dynasties; and in Huang Zongxi's (1610–95) analysis of the relative advantages of the different cities chosen as the imperial capital.

THE MASTERS OF PROSE

Surviving literature cannot fully represent the full muster of the many thinkers and teachers who visited the courts of the kings of the pre-imperial period; for a high proportion of their writings and of accounts of their teaching have been lost. Some of the books which survive are the work of their pupils, dutifully and lovingly recording their masters' sayings. Others derived from the habit of some of the leaders of the land of assembling notable men of learning at their courts, there to discuss ethical or other problems and to formulate their agreed views. There resulted two types of writing; some works which are attached to the name of an individual teacher, such as Han Fei (280–?233 BC), are marked by a reasonable degree of consistency. Others, which derived from corporate work, such as the *Lüshi chunqiu* (*Spring and Autumn Records of Mr Lü*), may be somewhat eclectic in content and may even include statements of conflicting views.

Official steps to promote the study of the classical works and to use them as a vehicle of education were partly intended to emphasize those modes of thought or expressions of view that suited the imposition of imperial authority. In addition, in edicts of 140 BC and a little later, the Han governments tried to direct attention to approved moralist teaching, and to discourage the study of books which advocated concentration on the growth of power at the expense of ethical principle. In doing so they set precedents for the future.

Attention will be paid below (see Chapter XII) to the steps taken to collect copies of writings at the beginning of the Christian era. Such measures, when combined with the Chinese love of exact classification, led to a neat and over-simplified distinction between a number of schools of thought and their texts, of which a few have been treated with special and somewhat exaggerated prominence. These included the category of *rujia* or scholastics, with the moral aphorisms of Confucius and his followers; the mystical writings of the *daojia*; and essays on the means of organizing human effort, grouped as *fajia*, often termed 'legalists'.

Accompanying these three major ways of thought there were other writings of the pre-imperial age which stressed different aspects of thought or behaviour. These included the Mohists who wished to extend charity in human dealings to the exclusion of undue stress on ritual; the sophists who indulged in problems of language and definition; and specialists in theories of *yin yang*, or the Five Phases and their place in the universe. Examples of these and many other schools of thought lay on the shelves of the Han imperial library, together with a large number of writings of a more technical nature, on, for example, agriculture, medical practice, the occult arts, astro-calendrical science, military strategy or diplomacy and its expedients.

During the Han period essayists were composing systematic works of criticism or expositions of their modes of thought. Some men of letters were evolving contrived and artificial styles of prose, depending on balance within a sentence and juxtaposition of content in a form of parallelism. At the same time a new genre of literature, the *fu*, had been emerging. *Fu* took the form of rhymed prose, with no limitation on length; as contrasted with the memorial, in which an official expressed his views to his superior, the *fu* enabled him to write in a more personal way that need not be so didactic. Ban Gu (32–92), principal compiler of the Standard History of the Former Han dynasty, wrote two *fu* describing the capital cities of Chang'an and Luoyang; others described the extravagances of court, palace or imperial pleasure grounds; Zhang Heng (78–139) used the form to express his yearnings for the mysterious. Composed with an extravagant choice of language, the *fu* enabled a man of letters to write in a non-official way, perhaps to give vent to criticism or perhaps specifically to please or amuse a reader. *Fu* continued to be written after the Han period; composition in this form was included in the requirements for examinations during the Tang dynasty.

Strict attention to realities lay behind many of the creations and achievements of the Tang age. A reaction took place against the artificialities of some of the prose writings of the previous centuries, with their fixation on form rather than content; in a deliberate attempt to emulate the styles of the Han age and earlier, authors sought to write with clarity and immediate effect, rather than to rely on allusion. Prose pieces of the Tang and Song ages included descriptions of natural scenery and the lessons that the townsman might learn from the country. Allegories drew on mythology in order to comment on the failings of the contemporary world; some prose writers concentrated on the discussion of historical themes. Matching the paintings of the day, some of the essays of the Song period take as their theme the place of man in nature; other writers of both this age and later were reaching a new degree of refinement in their philosophical discourses.

It had become customary for men of letters to write on a personal level in the letters that they exchanged with their colleagues, where they might express their personal reactions to public events or offer sympathy at a setback that had marred an official career. In due course they would compose epitaph inscriptions for their friends, tracing their ancestry and praising their achievements. One of the greatest compliments that a scholar could pay to a friend or colleague would take the form of a preface written to introduce his poems or other writings to a wider public; and here the author would need to display his erudition, often puzzling a later reader with the complexity of his allusions. Sometimes these various types of composition would include an exposé of a writer's theory of literature or his evaluation of its different forms. There were also those who entrusted their private musings to 'jottings' (*biji*), the equivalent of a westerner's diary or commonplace book. These notes, such as those of Gu Yanwu (1613–82), reflected an observer's thoughts on witnessing

TABLE 15

PROSE STYLES AND THE DEVELOPMENT OF LITERARY CRITICISM

c. 320	The *Soushenji* (*Tales of a Search for the Supernatural*), by Gan Bao.
fifth century	Emergence of *pianwen* style, marked by parallelisms.
c. 430	The *Shishuo xinyu* (*New Account of Tales of the World*), an anthology of anecdotes.
441–513	Shen Yue, poet and formulator of rules of euphony.
c. 500	The *Wenxin diaolong* (*The Literary Mind and the Carving of Dragons*), a treatise on literary criticism.
early fifth century	The *Wenxuan*; an anthology of prose, *fu* and poems, compiled by Xiao Tong (501–31).
Tang, Song period	Eight recognized masters, of whom the first two are known as protagonists of old-style prose (*guwen*), with concentration on clarity rather than ornament: Han Yu (Tuizhi), 768–824; Liu Zongyuan, 773–819; Ouyang Xiu, 1007–72; Su Xun, 1009–66; Zeng Gong, 1019–83; Wang Anshi, 1021–86; Su Shi (Dongpo), 1037–1101; Su Che, 1039–1112.
Tang period	Growth of short stories.
Song period	Emergence of *huaben* (short stories in the vernacular).
987–1009	Compilation of the *Wenyuan yinghua* anthology of literature.
1387–1906	Composition of essays in 'eight-legged' form required in official examinations.
1939	Publication of the *Weishu tongkao*, a critical examination of the authenticity of early works of literature.

The Principal Novels	
thirteenth century	*Shuihu zhuan* (*Water Margin*).
1494–1522	Sanguozhi yanyi (*Romance of the Three Kingdoms*).
c. 1570	*Xiyouji* (*Journey to the West*).
c. 1617	*Jinpingmei* (*The Plum in the Golden Vase*).
c. 1745	*Rulin waishi* (*Unofficial Lives of the Scholars*).
1791	*Hongloumeng* (*Dream of the Red Chamber*).

local customs in a strange area, or learning of problems of administration and popular suffering; others, such as those of the famous official and scholar Ji Yun (1724–1805), recorded legend or tale heard in the inns, or stories of the occult whose claim to truth could not easily be denied.

Short stories and long novels likewise take their place in China's prose literature. The professional storyteller would make his living reciting his tales to an entranced crowd, as is sometimes depicted in a painting; and thereafter these would be set down in writing. Their themes both included aspects of the mysterious and evoked scenes of life in the upper reaches of society. They told of ghosts that had made their presence felt, of crimes detected thanks to a traveller's skill or of strange experiences that defied explanation. Some of the tales might present an allegorical account of human organization; others gave an insight into the seamy side of a capital city's life, with its underworld of beggars, tricksters and thieves; some concluded with a happy ending, when a life spent in distress and suffering was followed by the privileges and indulgences of a career devoted to public service.

China's few long novels, which have fascinated readers of the west no less than the east, fasten on different themes. Those who liked a tale of Robin Hood type fighting, or the stratagems of opposing generals, would read the *Romance of the Three Kingdoms* (*Sanguozhi yanyi*), set in the third century AD. *Water Margin* (*Shuihu zhuan*), with its account of brigands and heroes of the thirteenth and fourteenth centuries, tells of the salvation of the oppressed from suffering and the cry of ordinary folk against the heavy hand of the official. Those romantically inclined might favour *Unofficial Lives of the Scholars* (*Rulin waishi*), or the *Dream of the Red Chamber* (*Hongloumeng*), where they could read either with scorn or with envy of the gulf that separated official life from the real world, or of the thick walls that sheltered aristocratic society from the struggle for existence without. *The Plum in the Golden Vase* (*Jinpingmei*) would satisfy a taste for eroticism or debauchery; but the *Journey to the West* (*Xiyouji*) was framed as a religious allegory. This was based on historical truth, of the search undertaken by pilgrims in the seventh century to bring a new supply of Buddhist scriptures back to China; the novel tells of their adventures and their hardiness, and of the temptations and dangers to which they lay open.

THE GIFT OF POETRY

The earliest examples of Chinese poems are those of the *Book of Songs*. Enshrined in the classical canon, they received special treatment and regard. They became part of officially sponsored literature which was used as an instrument of instruction; and however spontaneous their origin had been, much of their lyrical qualities had been lost to the reading public in the process. By the beginning of the imperial era they were being studied in various recensions, each of which strove to interpret the obsolete language of their lines. As with 'set book' material in other examinations, they required a different approach from that which welcomes the expression of emotion recollected in tranquillity.

But a different type of poetry was taking shape during the centuries that preceded the imperial era, from an entirely different background; and it was destined to acquire a different type of appeal. The *Songs of the South* (*Chu ci*) originated from the Yangzi River valley; they were imbued with a romantic approach to the world and its inhabitants; they called on the mythology of the mountains and the forests, and they accompanied religious rites and shamanist practice that had no place in the staid ceremonials that the masters of the north were establishing in line with Confucian ideals. While the *Book of Songs* came to be used as a means of restricting human conduct and relating it to accepted norms of behaviour, the *Songs of the South* gave vent to emotional fervour. They spoke of meetings between human and divine figures, or they told of intermediary shamans performing their role as a bridge between different worlds. Some of the poems reflect the pilgrim's lone search for eternal truth, unhampered by the values and burdens of the world of the flesh; some allude to the abounding mysteries of the universe and the answers that myth provides to reassure man of his proper place therein; yet others voice a plea to the human soul to return to the body that it has just abandoned, rather than face a voyage into the uncharted perils of another realm.

Other forms and styles of poetry arose during the imperial era, based on various types of metre and schemes of rhymes. In general terms, old-style (*gu shi*) poems were free; the poet could choose whether his poem would consist of short lines of five or long lines of seven characters. The number of lines was not restricted, and a different rhyme was introduced for each couplet. Poetry in regulated style (*lüshi*), however, was subject to far greater restrictions; the poems must include eight lines only, and within each pair characters must be so arranged that they balanced one another throughout; in addition, the poet must choose his characters in such a way that the tones, which are an inherent part of their pronunciation, would be set in alternation and balance, thus adding a new quality to the resulting parallelism of the whole. The examination syllabus of the Tang period required candidates to master this particular art of composition. Outside those restrictions, poets were free to express themselves in 'stop-shorts' (*jueju*), or poems of four lines only that were subject to the same rules. Some of the most enduring and poignant of all Chinese poetry was expressed in this medium.

TABLE 16

POETRY AND THE POETS

Of necessity it is possible to mention no more than a few of the large number of Chinese poets and their compositions. The names which have been selected for inclusion here should be taken as being no more than representative of the many different types of poet and poetry that arose from Chinese civilization.

third century BC	Qu Yuan; died *c.* 277 BC.
Han period	The *Chu ci*, including some poems of the Warring States period.
201–169	Jia Yi; composer of *fu*.
179–117	Sima Xiangru; composer of *fu*.
c. 114–	Existence of the Bureau of Music (*Yuefu*), founded to
c. 7 BC	collect poems and to arrange musical performances of state.
Later Han	The *Nineteen Old Poems*.
192–232	Cao Zhi.
223–62	Xi Kang.
third century	The 'Seven Sages of the Bamboo Grove'; poets of a Daoist frame of mind and unworldly outlook.
365–427	Tao Qian (Yuanming).
385–433	Xie Lingyun.
Tang period	Development of regulated poetry (*lüshi*), the 'stop-short' (*jueju*) and lyrics (*ci*).
699–721	Wang Wei.
701–62	Li Bo (Bai).
712–70	Du Fu.
772–846	Bo Juyi (Letian).
ninth century	Development of *xin yuefu* (new-style ballads).
1125–1210	Lu You.
Yuan, Ming	Development of *qu* (arias, or lyrical verse).
1703	Publication of collected poetry of the Tang period (*Quan Tang shi*).
1716–98	Yuan Mei.

Other forms were also evolved, such as ballads, known under the term *yuefu*. The Standard History for the Former Han dynasty includes the text of nineteen hymns that were sung at the imperial religious cults, invoking the god to appear. In another form, a series of *Nineteen Old Poems*, again of the Han dynasty, treats of themes of human sadness known for all time, such as the sorrow felt at leaving a family for departure to the wars. The succeeding centuries saw the creation of an extensive corpus of love poetry of a particular type.

But it is to the Tang period that there is ascribed the title of China's golden age of poetry. Many candidates were practising the art as part of their preparation for the examinations; social occasions would be enriched when friends would play the competitive game of exchanging verses with one another. Nostalgia for home, the peace of the moonlight, the growth of children or the loss of dear ones all take their place as subjects in the rich variety that China's poets produced at this time, setting a pattern for emulation in succeeding ages. New styles of lyrics (*ci*) emerged in the Song, and arias (*qu*) in the Yuan and Ming periods. Nor need it be forgotten that Mao Zedong composed some poetry in classical styles.

*

Throughout the imperial age the classical texts of the Chinese tradition exerted a formative influence on the upbringing of Chinese officials. In some cases the language in which they were written or the institutions and way of life that they treated had become outmoded; and their importance lay more in their educational value or scholastic interests than in their literary merits. In their finest passages historians composed trenchant prose, shorn of stylistic embellishment, and describing in vivid terms a poignant event that sealed the fate of a dynasty; in their more tedious moments they recounted the sordid details of political intrigue; and by omitting mention of matters that were of little importance in their own eyes, they may leave today's historians frustrated or bewildered.

China's written language lends itself easily to economic use. It can express a depth of meaning in a few words; it can likewise convey refined distinctions and nuance with subtlety. In the hands of those who wrote technical treatises, it served to set out the intricate mechanism of clockwork or other types of instrument; by their skilful use of the same medium, poets, essayists and philosophers could relate transient emotions or sufferings to their universal context; and in doing so they left a heritage for humanity. If literature ranks as one of the most enduring of China's gifts, it must go hand in hand with two other art forms in which the men of letters so often excelled, those of painting and calligraphy.

XII

THE CREATION AND CIRCULATION OF BOOKS

The continuity of China's contribution to the humanities is nowhere more conspicuous than in the products of her men of letters, the patronage of scholarship, the foundation of libraries, the evolution and practice of printing and the dissemination of literature. Along with an intense respect for tradition there ran a readiness to experiment with new literary genres and new techniques for the production of books. Books took their place as the instruments of training; the preservation of rare copies as scholastic treasures marked the distinguished place that a family or a man had attained in society, earning respect and admiration. An invitation to take part in producing a new edition of a famous or choice text, whether by writing a preface or inscribing the title with mannered calligraphy on the titlepage, was regarded as a compliment due to the ranks of the most learned. An imperial command to compile and submit a work for official publication could enhance a civil servant's prestige and earn him both glory and envy. The compilation of catalogues or the assembly of rare works with a view to reprinting them in a large encyclopaedic series exemplifies the Chinese penchant for classification and for setting all manner of created things in hierarchical array.

MANUSCRIPTS, RUBBINGS AND PRINT

The earliest examples of Chinese writing appear on the shells and bones used for oracular purposes during the Shang-Yin period. Somewhat more complex types of script, used to convey more sophisticated texts, appeared on the bronzes of the following centuries; and the simplification of the script that was brought about in the third century BC accompanied the more extensive use of other materials. Wooden and bamboo strips had been in use for some time and were now doing duty for the more prolific documentation required by officials of the recently established empire; less mundane projects, perhaps as ordered by the palace, called for the use of the more precious material of silk; and shortly the throne was to receive notification of a new invention that was to lead directly to the use of paper.

178

The use of bamboo or wood was by no means as clumsy as might appear, nor did it involve all the difficulties that might be imagined. Trained scribes could lay out a complicated text on the narrow strips, neatly planed and cut to even size, and bound together with tapes. They might even choose to exploit some of the features of this medium, using the tapes as a means of regulating their spacing or setting out their text as a table; and if the strips had been fastened together with due skill, they could be used to carry a diagram. Variation was also possible in the size of characters used in drawing up a document, so that bold entries could be seen as standing out against the insertion of detailed information in smaller size. Should a scribe make an error, he had but to draw the knife that hung at his waist and peel the surface clean for correction. Nor need books made in this way necessarily be short. Two copies were made of the *Shiji* (*Historical Records*), the first of China's Standard Histories, which was completed shortly after 100 BC in 130 chapters; they were written on wood or bamboo.

Nevertheless copies of texts were still rare and expensive; to obviate the difficulty, one philosopher at least, Wang Chong (AD 27–*c.* 100), took to visiting the bookshops in the capital city of Luoyang, there to browse among the stacks free of charge. One disadvantage lay in the bulk and weight of large documents written on wood or bamboo and the difficulty of safe transport. In addition, in the received versions of early texts today there are sometimes signs of where a column of writing has been omitted, or transposed, or where a few columns have been left out. Such errors could be brought about only too easily if a bundle of strips was dropped and some of them were broken. Above all, books written on wood were singularly liable to destruction by fire.

Silk was expensive; and it was open to similar hazards of fire. It could however lend itself to framing documents of any shape or size, and to the inclusion of illustrations with greater finesse than was possible on wood. A very small number of paintings which were made on silk survive from the pre-imperial period; the earliest surviving text written on silk, in perhaps *c.* 350 BC, shows how a scribe could use the material, writing his columns of characters in different directions, adorning his text with figures of gods or shamans and using several colours by way of embellishment. Other early examples of the use of silk, which date from shortly before 168 BC, include parts of a copy of the *Book of Changes*, some local maps of central China and a set of diagrams of callisthenic exercises or postures.

But a major change which affected the production of the Chinese books was taking shape. In AD 105 an official who was employed in the imperial agency for arts and crafts submitted to the throne his invention for the use of the bark of trees, rags or hempen textiles to make a new substance that could be used for writing, but which would be far less expensive to make than silk. In this way Cai Lun introduced the use of proto-paper publicly. Probably the process which he described had been evolved for some time, and it is possible that certain fragments of this material may date from the first century BC. By the third or fourth century AD proto-paper was coming into more general use and dislodging wood as the usual medium for writing. In time it would itself be replaced by paper proper, manufactured over the centuries with great skill and attention to beauty.

Yet another type of medium was used for carrying types of writings. In the hope that they would long survive the dangers attendant on wood, silk or paper, certain texts were engraved on tablets of stone; and it was believed, with some justice, that careful preservation would protect them with a greater degree of permanency than would be possible otherwise. Such treatment was given to approved versions of the classical texts, which formed a fundamental element in the training of imperial officials. By engraving them on stone, the government left no doubt as to which versions were to be used and treated as orthodox; and there need then be no reason why scholars or students could plead ignorance, or claim that they had access only to versions which lacked approval. For the tablets were set up for public inspection and use, and it was open to any observer to make his own copy, by a process known – and still practised – as taking a 'rubbing' or an 'ink squeeze'. Possibly this habit arose during the second century, with the use of the newly evolved paper; for the first set of 'stone classics' had been cut in AD 175 on almost fifty tablets, each measuring about 175 cm by 90 cm by 12 cm; several large, and many small, pieces of these stones survive.

In this way the Han government set a precedent that some of its successors would be glad to follow, in order to display their zeal in promoting orthodox Confucian scholarship. They also created one of the first of the component elements that were to give rise to printing. Other such elements included the seals with which an official authenticated his document, carved either in relief or in intaglio, and with the characters in reverse; for, unlike the stone classics which were intended to be read by observers, officials' seals were used to stamp an impression on clay, silk or paper, and therefore required engraving in mirror fashion. Buddhist icons likewise played a part in the evolution of printing. The faith had been gaining ground since the third century, and with it there followed the need to reproduce in large numbers the symbols or icons of the Buddha which would satisfy the longings of the devout or inspire the faith of a potential convert.

TABLE 17

THE DEVELOPMENT OF BOOKS AND PRINTING

Shang-Yin period	Inscribed shells and bones.
Zhou period	Inscriptions of bronzes in 'Greater Seal' script.
fourth and third centuries BC	Development of 'Lesser Seal' script.
c. third century	Use of brush with silk, wood and bamboo.
Former Han dynasty	Development of officials' use of *lishu* (formal script) for official documents, and of seals for auth-entification.
AD 105	Official recognition of 'proto-paper'.
Later Han dynasty	Memorial stelae with inscriptions on stone.
175	Engraving of classical texts on stone; copies made by rubbings or ink squeezes.
279 or 281	Discovery of wooden and bamboo manuscripts some 500 years old.
fourth century	Wang Xizhi the calligrapher (d. 365 or 379).
fifth century	Increasing demand for Buddhist icons.
868	Date of earliest surviving printed scroll.
from 932	First print of the classical texts.
Song period	Active development of block printing.
971–83	Buddhist canon printed.
c. 1036	Caves and bookstores of Dunhuang sealed.
1041–8	Evolution of movable type.
?Yuan period	Evolution of polychrome printing.
1407	Production in manuscript of the *Yongle dadian*.
1445	Earliest surviving print of the Daoist canon.
c. 1500	Active development in China of movable type printing.
1573–1619	High productive period for printing.
1584	Matteo Ricci's map of the world printed.
1728	*Gujin tushu jicheng* printed in 10,000 chapters.
from c. 1900	Discovery of oracle bones (Shang-Yin period); wooden and bamboo manuscripts (Han and later) at Dunhuang; manuscripts and prints from the age of disunity onwards.

It cannot be known exactly when the major breakthrough occurred whereby the techniques that lay behind these practices were combined together and extended so as to bring about block printing. Complete long texts were now engraved, in reverse; and copies were rolled off with the use of ink and paper. According to an account of one of the earliest experiments of which there is a record, wood was chosen for engraving the text for reasons of economy; but whatever the reasons may have been, smaller and lighter blocks of wood, which could be cut to any convenient size, were much easier to handle than heavy blocks of stone.

So, the calligraphers inscribed the text that was to be reproduced, and this was pasted in reverse on the series of wooden blocks that had been prepared. Craftsmen then set to work to carve the text, in exact conformity with the strokes and flourishes of the scribe's brush. If, as in some Buddhist *sūtras* or an old Chinese text such as the *Classic of the Mountains and the Lakes*, illustrations were necessary, these too could be subjected to the carver's skilful knife; and when these had completed their work, copies could be made in any number that might be desired, given sufficient supplies of ink and paper. One of the earliest and best-known examples of early Chinese block printing is the text of the *Diamond sūtra*, printed as an act of piety in 868, and measuring nearly five metres in length. In all probability this was preceded by printing a large number of copies of shorter texts, as may be suggested by practice in Japan. Here, as early as *c.* 770, the empress Shōtoku had ordered the production of a very large number of copies of short sacred texts designed for retention in the base of miniature pagodas; many examples still survive.

Probably the initial promotion of block printing owed much to the sponsorship of a small authority which ruled part of western China at a time of imperial disunity in the tenth century. The initiative taken on this occasion forms an excellent example of how a small-scale experiment of a localized regime can be maintained or extended by a successor dynasty whose sway proves to be firmer and longer-lasting. For the Song period is sometimes described as the golden age of Chinese block printing. Masters of the craft paid great attention to the clarity of their products, to the use of good-quality paper and to a generous provision of margins; their formats were drawn up with wide spacing, and room for annotation, to be included in two narrow columns, between the columns of the main text. The Song printers used their skills for the production of the large literary projects that were taking shape at that time, thus preserving the texts of some of China's most important philosophical and historical writing, and publishing for all time the clear prose and poetry of their contemporaries.

In the meantime a further development was taking place, in the evolution of printing with movable type. We owe a description of the early technique to the brush of Shen Gua (1031–95), an observer who noted some of the remarkable features of his age. He wrote how, in about 1045, a man named Bi Sheng was using types of clay, baked hard, ready for insertion within the squares of an iron grid; this was set upon an iron plate which had been coated with a glutinous substance; once the type had been firmly and evenly set in its position, printing could start, in a manner that could be very speedy and well suited to the production of a large number of copies of a document or book. Bi Sheng used two sets of plates and grids, in alternation, so that while the one was actually in use the second would be being prepared; and he had taken the precaution of engraving a large number of types for characters that occur frequently. Once printing had been completed, the type was dislodged from the iron plate and stored in frames; arranged by rhyme, the characters would be found easily enough by the compositor for his next job.

Bi Sheng's experiment was followed by others, who used type made of wood. Early in the fifteenth century the kings of Korea were promoting the use of movable type, which lent itself well to the newly evolved alphabetic script of the Korean language. At the end of that century movable type came to be used much more generally than hitherto in China, largely thanks to the work of the Hua and An houses, and their use of copper in place of clay or wood.

During the Ming and Qing dynasties printing enjoyed the patronage of the palace, merchants and antiquarian collectors; production of official editions of the classics and the Standard Histories provided work for the presses of all sorts; collectors who were anxious to display the beauty of their jades or bronzes could order illustrated catalogues to be printed, with reproductions of their choice treasures appearing in woodcut. By early in the seventeenth century printing was being practised in up to five colours; and as compared with the earliest woodcuts, known at least from the ninth century, printing houses were now turning out products with far greater finesse and attention to detail, as may be seen in some of the compendia on botany, or the map of the world that Father Ricci had drawn, to show his hosts some aspects of lands of which they had no concept. The great volume of printed work that was produced in the Qing period depended on both traditional methods and new techniques; and it served the needs alike of teacher and pupil, of antiquarian and bibliophile, ever ready to appreciate the beauty of the printer's art and his choice of paper of first-rate quality.

LIBRARIES, CATALOGUES AND BIBLIOGRAPHY

From the Han period onwards imperial governments prided themselves on the measures that they took to preserve traditional literature. It was recalled that the first Qin emperor had adopted precisely an opposite policy, hoping that by the proscription or destruction of the written records of past precedent he would eliminate any surviving nostalgia for or loyalty to the kingdoms that had given place to his own united regime. Probably the allegation of his misdeeds had been grossly exaggerated, but it served to excite some enthusiasm for the work of the later dynasties in collecting rare literary items, establishing imperial libraries and compiling descriptive catalogues of their contents.

Copies of books thought to have been lost came to light on several occasions during the second and first centuries BC, and their discovery provoked academic discussion of their value and authenticity. For various reasons, including a desire to settle some of the issues that had been raised, deliberate steps were taken in 26 BC to institute an empire-wide search for copies of texts; duplicate or incomplete versions were to be compared, and accurate copies were to be made for approval and retention in the imperial library. Two famous scholars, Liu Xiang (79–8 BC) and his son Liu Xin (died AD 23), were entrusted with the work, and in the course of collating the books which had been delivered to the palace they wrote up detailed accounts of precisely what material they had received and how it had been handled. Fortunately some of their accounts survive, such as that of the work ascribed to the statesman Guan Zhong of the seventh century BC; from a total of 564 bundles of wooden strips at their disposal, the scholars had selected no more than 86 to form a standard text, rewritten on strips of seasoned wood; the remaining bundles were discarded.

In this way there began China's science of bibliography. The survival, albeit in abbreviated form, of the record that had been made gives a clear indication of the extent of the library that was being formed at this time. The system used for classifying the works affected the habits of Chinese librarians until the twentieth century; and whereas this made for a certain degree of regularity and order, it also imposed a set of traditional categories whereby some books became liable to an excessively rigid identification within certain schools of thought; such dangers tended to preclude the growth of an analytical view of Chinese philosophy.

No less than 677 items appear on the surviving list of books that lay on the shelves of the imperial library at the start of the Christian era; but of these 77 per cent are no longer extant, save for fragments which are preserved in the citations of later writings. Throughout imperial history there is a sad tale of the destruction of imperial and other collections, as cities fell victim to looting by insurgents, to the hazards of fire or to the dangers attendant on removal. Considerable destruction accompanied the sack of Chang'an, where the imperial library was housed, at the hands of the Red Eyebrow bands of rebels in AD 26; nevertheless, when shortly afterwards, the seat of

TABLE 18

BIBLIOGRAPHY COLLECTIONS AND TEXTUAL HISTORY

By AD 23	Collation of texts and compilation of the catalogue of the imperial library by Liu Xiang (79–8 BC) and Liu Xin (d. AD 23); summary of these lists incorporated in the *Han shu*.
26	Destruction of collections in Chang'an.
190	Destruction of literary collections in Luoyang.
374	Catalogue made of Chinese translations of Buddhist works.
622	Major losses of the Sui imperial library in the Yellow River.
656	Catalogue of the imperial library.
1034–8	Catalogue of the Song imperial collection.
1127	Major losses in the Song imperial library.
1774–89	Suppression of certain types of literature in the literary inquisition of Qianlong.
1782	Completion of the officially sponsored collection of literature in four classes (the *Si ku* project).
1803–4	Catalogue of the Tianyige library by Ruan Yuan (1764–1849).
eighteenth and nineteenth centuries	Collections made by Qing bibliophiles and critics, such as Huang Peilie (1763–1825), Mo Youzhi (1811–71) and Ye Dehui (1864–1927).

government was moved to Luoyang, conveyance of the books and documents of state to their new depository required, as we are told, the use of 2,000 waggons. But incidents of further violence and destruction were all too frequent, as may be seen from a few examples; they occurred when the capital was re-established at Chang'an in 191; when both cities were sacked in 311; and when the bulk of the imperial library of the Sui dynasty sank to the depths of the Yellow River in 622.

The emperors of Han had set a precedent for the establishment of palace libraries; the hazards of civil warfare and natural disaster showed the recurring need to ensure preservation and to retain ordered lists of the items retained in the collections. A number of the Standard Histories, from that of Former Han onwards, include such catalogues, which, together with the scholastic annotation that may be appended, make it possible to trace the textual history of a particular work through many centuries. With the greater attention that was being paid to literature, private scholars of the Song, Ming and Qing periods became deeply interested in such bibliographical studies. In the prefaces that they wrote for new editions that the printers were turning out, or in their private correspondence, they would record their joy at lighting on a copy of a rare print, and ordering its reproduction; such notes savour both of the collector's temperament and of the instincts of the scholar.

It was in the eighteenth century that Chinese interest in books and their history reached one of its most advanced points and resulted in one of its finest products. This followed from the inauguration in 1773 of a major project for publication, known as the *Si ku quan shu* (*Complete Collection of the Four Treasuries of Literature*), which will be described below. As part of the project some of the most distinguished scholars of the day compiled a set of introductory notes to the texts collected for publication, setting forth details of authorship, discussing problems of authenticity and informing readers of the editions that were already available. The 'four treasuries' were those of classics, history, philosophy and literature, both prose and poetry. By their decisions how the vast corpus of works should be arranged the editors accepted some of the traditional schemes of classification that had already been accepted, and set a pattern for the future; their work remains a monument of erudition.

Meanwhile other libraries had been growing up and other catalogues were being prepared. These derived from the desire of certain rich merchants to demonstrate that their appreciation of cultural achievements was in no way inferior to that of the members of the official classes. With wealth at their disposal they were able to promote the collection of rare books and the printing and publication of new editions. Some of the collections that they built up formed the nucleus of libraries which existed in the provinces until recently.

WORKS OF REFERENCE AND THE GRAND COLLECTIONS

In traditional style, Chinese books were made ready for distribution in small paper-bound fascicules, each divided into chapters. Large works required several fascicules and these were placed together and protected by wooden boards or a cardboard case, usually coloured dark blue; it is in such a form that China's literature has rested on the shelves of an imperial, official or private library. Of conspicuous note on such shelves, and without parallel in Europe, are the sets of works produced in uniform manner and sometimes filling hundreds of these cases; they include lexicons or other works of reference, encyclopaedias, anthologies and, above all, the *congshu*. These latter are collections of complete works that are sometimes extensive and voluminous enough to constitute a library in themselves.

By their very concept, major literary projects and giant publications of these types call for admiration; by their size they call for awe. They arose from motives of which some have been encountered already, such as a determination to prevent the further loss of rare literature and a love of a hierarchical classification. Some arose in response to the needs of candidates for the examinations; some were designed to assemble material needed to explain the revered scriptures of the past; or to present a reader with a compendium of information on a given subject; or to solve problems of a practical nature. Their growth and popularity owed much to the early emergence and practice of printing.

The *Erya*, parts of which may date from the third century BC, is probably the earliest Chinese work of reference to survive. Being a collection of glosses, or explanations, that seek to clarify the meaning of expressions seen in earlier texts, the work is sometimes, but erroneously, described as a dictionary. In so far as it assisted an understanding of classical works by the Tang period it had itself been included in the august company of such texts and commanded respect accordingly. But it was the *Shuo wen*, compiled by AD 121, that may be regarded as China's first dictionary proper. The work assembles characters according to its own system of distinguishing their component elements; by giving an indication of both the pronunciation of the character and its meanings, the book is an exercise in philology; and by including among its items the somewhat strange forms of characters that might be seen on old inscriptions but which were obsolete by the second century, the *Shuo wen* contrived to serve the needs of the scholar traveller as he roamed the countryside and his eyes rested on the monuments of a bygone age. The book long exercised a strong influence on scholastic work and on the training of officials. Being compiled at a time when the Han governments were anxious to promote the precepts of the Confucian ethic and to uphold its social ideals, it is at times marred by anachronism; there are occasions when it forces upon a passage or word of old literature an interpretation that could only apply to the contemporary conditions of the Han empire.

In western practice, which starts from the *Encyclopaedia Britannica* of 1768, encyclopaedias include specially written entries or articles that summarize the state of knowledge for a given topic. In Chinese practice large voluminous works set out to reproduce either the complete text or parts of existing writings that bore on a given subject. The compilers were able to draw on a wide variety of sources.

Such works started from different motives, beginning from the

TABLE 19

DICTIONARIES AND ENCYCLOPAEDIAS

c. AD 121	The *Shuo wen* dictionary, including 9,353 items.
seventh century	Production of the *Beitang shu chao*, *Chu xue ji* and *Yiwenleiju* (collections for educational purposes).
eighth century	The *Yilin*, by Ma Zong; extracts from philosophical works.
c. 800	The *Tongdian*, by Tu You; institutional records and precedents.
983	The *Taiping yulan*, in 1,000 chapters; categorized information on all subjects.
1013	The *Cefu yuangui*, in 1,000 chapters; documents concerning imperial administrations.
1252	The *Yuhai*, by Wang Yinglin; general encyclopaedia.
1317	The *Wenxian tongkao*, by Ma Duanlin (1254–1325); collection of administrative precedents.
1607–9	The *Sancai tuhui*; illustrated general encyclopaedia.
1711	The *Peiwen yunfu*; dictionary of phrases for aid in composition.
1716	The *Kangxi zidian*; officially sponsored dictionary of the language, including 47,035 characters.
1728	The *Gujin tushu jicheng*; general encyclopaedia in 10,000 chapters.

seventh century. The *Chu xue ji* (*Manual for First Steps in Learning*) set out to convey information in a systematic way over a whole range of subjects, such as the phenomena of the heavens, the animal and plant world, the physical features of the world about us, the institutions devised by man for his own government, and his religious beliefs and practices. At much the same time acknowledged masters of literature were drawing up lists of choice expressions with which a composer of prose or poetry could embellish his product, possibly with a view to impressing his examiners with his deep familiarity with earlier writings and their information on a select subject. Such motives had inspired the production of the *Beitang shuchao* (*Transcription of the Northern Hall*) by the statesman Yu Shinan (558–638) in 160 chapters; others were prepared by famous men of letters such as Ouyang Xun (557–641), also known for his calligraphic skill, or Bo Juyi the poet (772–846), who drew on his own experience as a candidate for office and then as a junior official to find the means to ease the path for his contemporaries.

There were other types of collected works from which the fully formed Chinese encyclopaedias arose. Some had been made to present a reader with salient parts of an argument in a philosophical tract, or to display its originality. From the sixth century there were appearing collections or sets of essays, or of poems in their entirety; these would make it possible to compare works by different authors on similar themes, for example, *fu* (or prose-poems) on China's capital cities, memorials presented to the throne by leading statesmen or epitaphs composed for inscription on memorial stelae. At a somewhat later date the collected works of a famous author were assembled together for publication, again in their entirety.

The first work that may properly be termed an encyclopaedia was the *Taiping yulan*, whose scope was greatly in advance of any of its predecessors. It was compiled by Li Fang (925–96) for presentation to the emperor of the new Song dynasty, and the author cast his net widely, to gather information and extracts of writings from 2,000 different texts. The work handled some 5,000 items, which were arranged under fifty-five sections; it extended to 1,000 chapters.

Many other examples of this type of work followed, until the climax was reached in the eighteenth century. The *Gujin tushu jicheng* (*Collection of Texts and Illustrations Old and New*) owed its origin to the private initiative of Chen Menglei (born 1651), who came from the south-east seaboard of Fujian province. While he was still young it had been alleged that he was involved in a plot of treason against the Manchu dynasty, and he had been sent in exile to the cold climate of Mukden. Restored to imperial favour, he conceived the idea of his project for compiling a new encyclopaedia, on a grand scale hitherto unseen. Thereafter, the gift of favouritism and favour changed and changed about along with changes in dynastic fortunes. Chen Menglei's initiative was subjected alternately to the friendly support or the vindictive anger of different members of the imperial family.

The first draft of Chen Menglei's project was completed by 1706, and it is remarkable that despite its size and complexity, and the incidence of the emperor's wrath, the whole work was published in 1728. By then it had been entrusted for 'revision' to Jiang Tingxi (1669–1732), a famous statesman who enjoyed the favour of the new Yongzheng emperor, but whose duties and activities were such that he can hardly have taken much part in the work.

The *Gujin tushu jicheng* stands alone as a monument to Chinese book production. A quarter of a million copper characters had been specially cut for printing its 10,000 chapters, whose five hundred cardboard cases weigh heavily on a librarian's shelves. The work arrayed its information in the six major categories of phenomena of the heavens, geography, human relationships, arts and sciences, literature, and political economy and organization; these were subdivided into a total of thirty-two sections. The chapters included illustrations from earlier publications where these were appropriate; some of these had derived from the learning of the Jesuit fathers who had been preaching their faith in China since 1583. Textual matter, long or short, was culled from a wide variety of sources; there are statements of historical fact, expositions of general ideas, literary compositions, biographies of those intimately concerned with a subject and anecdotes. Inclusion of information of an unofficial nature or source which may not be readily available elsewhere is of particular value for the study of subjects upon which Chinese authorities frowned or practices which they tried to conceal from the prying eyes of a foreign investigator. Less than 100 copies of this work were printed in the first instance; 1,500 copies of a second edition, of lesser quality and in smaller format, were produced towards the end of the nineteenth century; and a facsimile edition of the original print was made with the use of lithography between 1895 and 1898.

As distinct from the encyclopaedias, the *congshu* were collections of works which were reprinted in their entirety. They date mainly from the Ming and Qing periods, and arose at the wish of certain bibliophiles to rescue rare works from obscurity and to circulate them to their colleagues or the general public in easily available and readable form. Works for which a single copy only, whether in manuscript or print, existed were chosen for the purpose; or a *congshu* might reproduce a rare print of a well-known book, if the unique features of that edition were worthy of study. Together with such works a *congshu* usually included other texts which were related to these rare items, by virtue of either authorship or their contents. As a result, some of the *congshu* are very extensive. Their value lies in their preservation of rare material, of variant readings of texts or of scholastic comments found hitherto only in a remote library but now saved from oblivion.

One of the most famous of these collections was entitled the *Si ku quan shu* or *Complete Collection of the Four Treasuries of Literature*, already mentioned above in connection with bibliographical studies. An edict of 1773 gave orders for the assembly of rare works from all parts of the empire; texts of rarities were to be examined; duplicate copies of some of the items were to be compared; and an accurate transcription of the approved text that followed from such scrutiny was to be made by hand. Altogether seven sets of this enormous project were made; each one consisted of 36,000 volumes, comprising the 79,000 chapters of 3,400 works. These had been classified under the four headings of classical works (bound in green), histories (in red), philosophical texts (in blue) and literature (in grey). A fifth part of the project consisted of bibliographical notes and assessments; this part was bound in yellow. The first set of the *Si ku* was completed by 1782; but of the seven sets that were made three only survived in their entirety after 1860. A facsimile reprint has recently been produced in Taiwan.

It must be added that a motive other than the pure love of learning lay behind this great concept. By collecting rare material, including some that had been carefully shielded from the prying eyes of officials, the Qing government found the means to confiscate or suppress documents whose message was hostile to its own authority. In this sense part of the exercise has been described as the literary inquisition of the Qianlong emperor, which was conducted with considerable success between 1774 and 1789. It is estimated that, out of a total of 2,320 titles marked for total elimination and 345 for partial suppression, less than 18 per cent survived. This was by no means the only occasion when a Chinese government has taken inhibitory steps of this nature; it had been ordered by the first of the Qin emperors, shortly after 221 BC; it was effected with ruthlessness and violence during the Cultural Revolution of recent years (1966–76).

Of equal and in some respects greater importance than the *Si ku quan shu*, was one *congshu* that had been compiled for completely different motives with an array of material of which much was at distinct variance from that favoured by the officials of imperial government. This work, which was known as the *Dao zang* or *Daoist Canon*, included a number of esoteric works and teachings; many of these sprang from the religious practices, medical treatment and alchemical experiments that had sheltered behind the walls of a Daoist temple. The 5,000 fascicles of the *Dao zang* were first printed in uniform style in 1445; but much of the material reached back over the centuries, appearing in somewhat rare prints that had been made in the meantime.

The tradition of compiling *congshu* has lived on to take full advantage of the more modern methods of printing of the twentieth century. Of a number of series that have been published, attention may focus on two that were first produced and bound in traditional style. The *Si bu cong kan* reprints 468 titles by means of photolithography, thus presenting the reader with facsimile copies of early prints of the Song, Yuan or Ming periods that are otherwise available only in a few libraries. In the *Si bu bei yao* students will find 351 titles printed uniformly with the use of type cut specially for the purpose, in Song calligraphic style. Each of these compendia includes the text of the Standard Histories, some of which run to several hundred chapters.

*

By the early manufacture of paper, the development of block printing and movable type, the classification of literature and the production of multi-volume works, China long led other civilizations in the publication and dissemination of the written word. In about AD 1000 the contents of a library had been entrusted, for safety, to the sealed caves of Dunhuang, at the extreme north-western tip of Chinese territory. Discovery of that cache at the start of the twentieth century revealed the wide extent of the collections that could be made during the Song period, even at settlements that were separated by long distances from the cultural centre of the empire. More recently archaeologists have unearthed manuscript texts, on wood or silk, that date from the second century BC or earlier. Some of these manuscripts carry unique material, unknown previously; others are copies of works which have been transmitted throughout the centuries, and they provide a remarkable testimony of the accuracy of that transmission. Meanwhile the diligent study of early texts and their editions had long been opening the eyes of scholars to the possibility that, ancient as some works were said to be, they might well include interpolations or fabrications of later dates; and they were recognizing the need to investigate questions of authorship or authenticity with critical caution.

Imperial patronage and professional pride contributed largely to these achievements. Despite the predilection for a scholarship that concentrated on the approved texts of the tradition, China's literature embraced a far wider field and a far greater variety of subjects than that of other cultures, which derived from the patronage of church or state in Europe. Other motives that operated in China produced a wealth of technical books, on agricultural methods, materia medica, botany or the intricate workings of machinery, often embellished with woodcuts of a high order of accuracy and beauty; and it was China's example that inspired enthusiasm and initiative in the neighbouring lands of Japan and Korea to develop their own characteristic styles and techniques for the production of books.

XIII

THE CAPITAL CITIES OF THE EMPIRES

Emperors, officials and men of letters have always taken pride in China's cities. They embodied achievements to which the confederacies of the steppe had not aspired; neighbours such as the Japanese had been ready to borrow their shape and some of their features from the mainland. Cities were a living reminder of the privileges and benefits that attended success, forming the home of perhaps no more than one tenth part of the total population of China. Those townsmen who were comparatively fortunate could shelter behind their city's walls to live the comfortable life of the official and to enjoy the material advantages of wealth. Those who were less fortunate passed their years as servants, beggars or criminals, confined perhaps to cramped living quarters or to the dreary and insalubrious life of the slums.

Writing from the remote fastnesses of exile, eminent Chinese writers could see their capital cities in two ways. In some moods they wrote of them as the centres of civilized life, where they yearned to advance their careers in the company of talented poets and painters, or of distinguished philosophers and historians. But there were times when a governor of a province would delight in his opportunities to explore the countryside that lay around the town where his office was established; and he would write perhaps with cynicism or with despair of the failure of the high and mighty denizens of the main cities to appreciate the real values of a life that was spared the ambitions, quarrels and corruption of the metropolis.

THE GROWTH OF CITIES

With the neolithic revolution there came the need for protection. Human settlements clustering together in villages could form a tempting prey to intrusive or hostile neighbours; domesticated and stock animals needed the shelter of cages or walls to save them from marauding beasts; and the supplies of grain, carefully garnered from the earth and stored in the new pots that the craftsmen were turning out, contained highly prized provisions against the hungry days that were to come. It may be presumed that the earliest types of defence were made of wooden palisades, the forerunners of those mighty walls which much later became a characteristic mark of many of China's cities of the historical period.

Possibly sites such as those of the neolithic (Yangshao stage) village of Banpo, near Xi'an, were guarded by defences of wood in this way. But the more advanced and sophisticated way of life of the Bronze Age demanded a more robust type of defence; for the settlements now included the presence of acknowledged kings and their advisers and a host of treasured vessels with which they rendered their services to Shangdi. The site of Erligang, in modern Zhengzhou, yielded traces of what may perhaps be termed a 'city', dating from the sixteenth century BC; a wall of stamped earth ran for some seven kilometres around the four sides of a square. Within the enclosure there were traces of habitations, with floors and doors; and the presence of an altar and burial pits for animals suggests that provision for certain ritual practices existed at the site.

The kings of Zhou and the leaders of the states or kingdoms that grew up during the five centuries before the first empire was formed (221 BC) could call on larger numbers of servicemen, more abundant supplies of materials and the application of greater skills than their predecessors; and their craftsmen and builders enjoyed the great advantage of using tools of iron. Major cities were now built with two sets of concentric walls as a protection against a besieging enemy; and should such forces lie encamped beyond the outer defences, the land between the two sets could be sown with grain, thereby providing the defence with a source of food in time of need. There is much talk of siege warfare in the records of the fighting in which these early kingdoms were engaged, and of the stratagems whereby an encircling army could reduce a city to surrender, perhaps by inundating it with water. In other cases we read how the defenders of a city could achieve relief by the dexterous use of spies to sow treachery among their enemies; or they could arrange for a quick-witted diplomat to escape from the siege and make his way to an ally to invoke help.

In the imperial era statesmen were frequently proclaiming the need to prevent the population from leaving the hard and penurious life of the farms in preference for engaging in the more lucrative crafts, or commerce, that centred on the cities. Such statements themselves tell of the way in which cities were developing, with the more organized way life of the empires and the greater call for the manufacture of equipment and the exchange of commodities. Cities grew up in larger numbers, often following the lines of the rivers, and sometimes taking root at an intersection of waterway or road.

Some towns arose as a result of the deliberate planning of governors or officials, others in a more haphazard manner. Official descriptions tend to concentrate on the formalism and order that shaped a city, and to ignore the responses therein to the pulsating needs of a community to maintain its crafts and its other activities efficiently, and to engage in merchandise with profit.

CHARACTERISTIC FEATURES OF THE CAPITALS

Considerations of military strength, ideological conformity and economic convenience governed the choice of the city that was to serve as an imperial capital, and the saga whereby the changes were rung between Chang'an, Luoyang, Kaifeng, Hangzhou, Nanjing and Beijing illustrates how China's masters could adjust to the changing pattern of dynastic strength and strategic need. In addition to those cities that housed the emperors and governments of the major dynasties, other towns, such as Chengdu, Taiyuan and Chongqing, served some of the short-lived minor houses, with their limited territorial authority; or they acted as a secondary capital whither the court could flee in times of danger. There were also summer retreats to which the emperor and his household could repair to avoid the extremes of heat, such as Ganquan, lying to the north-west of Chang'an, and loved by the Former Han emperors, or Rehe (that is, Jehol) north of Beijing. It was from Rehe, where they had taken pains to deck their palace in rich beauty, that the Qing emperors would set out on their hunts; for Rehe formed a symbol of their Manchu origins and a reminder of their ancestral strength. Practical reasons, such as the ease of water supplies, would sometimes persuade the Tang emperors to transfer from Chang'an to Luoyang, despite the great toll of human labour and energy that the removal of the court and government could involve.

While the names of capital cities lived on from one dynasty to another, they did not necessarily refer to precisely the same set of streets and buildings. A new dynasty could settle close to an earlier capital, build its own palaces and offices, and transfer the old name to the new site. If practical reasons affected the choice of situation, so also, it was claimed, did the pronouncements of the geomancer; late imperial woodcuts sometimes show these specialists operating their boards at the behest of one of the mythical rulers of the land, who wished to ascertain where he had best establish his seat. In addition, reasons of ideology could sometimes persuade the master of a ruling house where he had best place his centre. In imperial times a conscious desire to demonstrate that a regime was linked with the glorious kings of Zhou may well have induced some dynasties to choose Luoyang in preference to another city as their capital.

An idealized layout of streets and buildings in some of the cities followed an express desire to represent or reproduce the pattern of the cosmos; for in this way the emperor's realm would be seen to accord with the universal rhythms and shapes that lasted for eternity. Chang'an, Luoyang and Beijing were thus set with their walls facing the four quarters of the compass; the somewhat irregular shape of Chang'an's walls, as they were built shortly after 200 BC, is sometimes explained as a deliberate attempt to follow the patterns of two constellations, Ursa Major on the northern side and Sagittarius on the south. The regular rectangular shape of the Han city of Luoyang, of Tang's Chang'an and of the Ming and Qing city of Beijing was perhaps intended to symbolize the earth, surrounded as this was by the circle of the heavens.

In such plans it was sometimes possible so to place certain buildings that their function corresponded with the character of the area wherein they were situated. Thus according to the theory of the Five Phases (*wu xing*), punishments, including the execution of criminals, should be carried out in autumn or winter, but not in the spring or summer; autumn and winter corresponded with the west and the north, and it would therefore be appropriate to site the execution grounds on those sides of the city. By the same token the names given to some of the features of a city, such as to the gates of the walls or to the palace buildings, were sometimes those of the animals which symbolized four of the Five Phases; for example, the southern gates of the imperial palace of Luoyang, of Later Han, bore the name of the 'Vermilion Bird'; so also, some centuries later, did the southern gate of the imperial palace built in imitation of the Chinese models at Heijōkyō (near modern Nara), to house the emperors of Japan.

Accommodation for religious needs featured in the imperial cities. The Han emperors had at first conducted their cults of state at a variety of sites, often lying at a distance from their capital city; but when, in the closing decades of the first century BC, the worship of Heaven (Tian) replaced that of the Five Powers (*di*), new sites were established; altars and temples to Heaven were set up to the south of Chang'an, to be followed by similar buildings at the later capitals, as may be seen in Beijing today. As was appropriate, altars to earth were likewise set up on the north side of the cities; and recent excavations south of the Han city of Chang'an have revealed traces of a further edifice which may probably be identified as a ritual building, known as the Piyong. As reconstructed, this site was itself shaped as a microcosm, with the square shrine in the centre surrounded by the encompassing circle of the heavens.

From the Former Han dynasty onwards, capital cities have included shrines dedicated to the worship of the ancestors of the imperial house; as the years of a dynasty lengthened, so too did the number of those shrines and the extent of the services that were conducted therein increase. Other temples and monasteries, with their formal halls of worship and their provision for the preservation of relics, served the cult of either the saints of Daoist religion or the Buddha. Mosques, and later Christian churches, arose in Chinese streets or countryside from the Tang period onwards. Occasionally, as at Kaifeng, tablets record the existence of a synagogue. At a discrete distance from the main cities lay the sacred sites chosen with great care and attention to geomancy to be the burial places of emperors and their consorts.

For those who had eyes to see, other features displayed the correct place that the emperor occupied in the cosmos, where he could receive the homage that was his due from all those who lived beneath the skies. Integral elements of the city and palace, such as the walls and their majestic gateways, exemplified the strength and security of his dispensation, such as would attract the loyalty of the alien; alternatively, a visible display of material wealth would prompt the strangers from the steppes to seek the enjoyment of luxuries which were unknown in their own bleak lands of the northern climes. In addition to demonstrating the strength of imperial power, these features displayed the function of the emperor. He was clearly to be seen as the intermediary who represented the cause of man to Heaven, as the head of state who bestowed bounties on his deserving subjects or as the mighty lord of the earth who entertained his visitors with dramatic performances, games and spectacles. If the capital city had been orientated to face the four quarters of the compass, the palace was built in like manner. The emperor would sit enthroned in his principal audience chamber facing due south, and balancing the glory of Heaven's chief luminary as it rose to its full power at noon; the expression *Nan mian* ('Facing the south') was used regularly to denote the person of the reigning monarch.

Within the Ming and Qing city of Beijing provision was made for all principal members of the imperial family within the one palace. Hitherto it had been the practice in some dynasties to build several palaces to house different members of the family, such as an empress dowager or the heir apparent and their retinues. There might also be a series of detached palaces, standing aside from the hubbub of the city; alongside, a series of botanical or zoological gardens would house the strange plants or exotic beasts that had been presented as tribute to the throne; or a hunting park could provide somewhat

meagre facilities for the sport of kings. One of the detached palaces
built for the Han emperors saw the experimental growth of new
types of crop that had been introduced recently from the west. We
read that, in about 100 BC, the 'Son of Heaven ... had grapes
and lucerne planted in increasingly greater quantities alongside the
detached palaces and the lodges, as far as the eye could reach.'

The massive walls that stood four-square around a city had been
built by conscript labour. They protected the homes of the privileged
from the perils of the external world, and while acting as a means of
defence, they also served to control the more unruly members of the
population. The towers that flanked the gateways to the outer world
afforded a wide view of the approach to the town, so that watchmen
could give warning of imminent danger. At night would-be intruders
would leave their footprints, or their horses would drop their spoor,
on the carefully raked sandbanks that skirted the outer perimeter.
In the hours of daylight access was granted to those incoming or
outgoing travellers who presented their correct documents, and the
guardians of the gates could ensure that controlled or banned goods
would not evade detection.

Avenues and streets were laid out in parallel lines, running from
north to south or east to west to form a grid. Such a plan allowed
the division of the city into a large number of residential wards, each
one of which was enclosed by its own walls. Once the curfew had
rung to put an end to roaming and loafing in the streets, the gates
were firmly closed. Within the city's grid, some quarters were set
apart as market-places, whose transactions were conducted under
the beady eyes of supervisory officials; other sites housed the chief
ministries of the government. Special areas were often reserved to
accommodate those who came annually to the capital to render
homage; or for visiting foreign dignitaries; or, in later times, for a
resident foreign population. Housing was often in short supply and
high demand, and multi-storeyed buildings were sometimes erected
to make the most profitable use of the land. When candidates for the
metropolitan examinations came to the capital to try their luck, they
must needs find lodgings where they could, risking the dishonesty of
a landlord or the deceitful tricks of fellow competitors who shared
their billet.

The capital cities were the administrative centres of the empire;
they housed the emperor and his entourage and the offices of government; and their thick walls and garrison troops protected the symbols
of majesty such as the bronze vessels of state and the jade seals, whose
use was restricted to emperors and kings. The barracks in which the
garrisons were quartered were sometimes divided into two sections,
on the northern and southern sides of the town, thus precluding an

easy take-over of the city by a general who might otherwise command all the forces that were stationed there. Some cities boasted special towers where the drums or bells that could arouse the population were hung. Canals which ran around the outer walls eased the transport of the inhabitants' necessities of life. In the Han city of Luoyang a stone bridge had been built to allow the safe conveyance of heavy loads to the nearby storehouses. Ceramic pipes carried supplies of water beneath the city wall of Han Chang'an, and drains led away the sludge beyond the city's gates. In later years, Buddhist temples might give themselves over on a feast day to communal services, when the chanting of the *sūtras* filled the makeshift shelters erected against the sun, and a brisk business was conducted at the booths set up within the precincts.

CHANG'AN, LUOYANG, KAIFENG AND BEIJING

Mountain ranges to the east and the south protected the area wherein lay Chang'an, capital of Former Han and Tang, to name but two dynasties. The Han city was built on the south bank of the sluggish Wei River, and it included one of the palaces of the Qin empire. It took five years to build the walls which the second of the Han emperors ordered, between 195 and 188 BC, and on which a large force of conscript labour was employed. Somewhat eccentric in shape, they did not form a regular rectangle; from a base of over 16 metres in width, they rose to a height of 8 metres, being over 12 metres wide at the top. The three gateways on each of the four sides were divided into three lanes which gave access to the three lanes of the principal streets or avenues. The officials who registered the households of the city in AD 1–2 gave a count of some quarter of a million inhabitants; the total population may well have amounted to nearly twice that figure.

The city was built to face the four points of the compass. It included several palaces, each oriented in similar fashion, with their several courts, audience halls, quarters for the staff that attended the principal resident and stables for their use. There were perhaps as many as nine market-places in the city, and a near-contemporary relief depicts one of these under official supervision. Chang'an's ornamental parks and pleasure gardens included the famous Shang-lin complex that lay outside the western wall, and included, if the accounts are not exaggerated, 36 gardens, 12 palatial buildings and 25 halls. Within the city terraced edifices, towers and other buildings served the needs of religion and the observation of the heavens; there was an extensive armoury and a depository for books and documents. As stone was in short supply, most of these structures had been built in wood, and surviving traces are confined to the more solid foundations, or to fragments of the decorated tiles that sealed the ends of the roofing.

Some of the additional features that appeared during the reign of Wudi (141–87 BC) were designed to serve contemporary religious beliefs and ideas of cosmology. Within one of the ornamental lakes that were constructed at that time there appeared a model of Penglai, one of the Islands of the Blessed through which there ran the road to paradise. Elsewhere there stood statues of the Oxherd and the Weaving Maid; all who admired these works of art were familiar with the myth whereby the annual meeting of these two constellations is thought to be essential for the continued operation of the cosmic rhythms.

The site of Luoyang had been closely associated with the kings of Zhou. During Former Han it had been a centre for commercial activities; but when the first of the Later Han emperors decided to choose it for his capital (AD 25), it is likely that he was deliberately seeking to affirm a relationship between his own regime and that of the Zhou dynasty.

Luoyang lay to the north of the Luo River; as the site was liable to flooding, traces of the southern wall of the city have long been destroyed. Like Chang'an the city had been set to face the four quarters, with walls that ran for a length of some 3,800 metres from north to south and 2,500 metres from east to west. More massive than those of Chang'an, the walls of Luoyang enclosed over ten square kilometres of almost perfect rectangular shape. As at Chang'an, twelve gates, which were closed at night, controlled access to the city. With an estimated population of over 500,000 individuals, during the first and second centuries AD Luoyang was probably the largest city of the world; the figure may be compared with those of 350,000 for contemporary Rome and 24,000 for Byzantium. At least eight other Chinese cities are known to have been populated by between 200,000 and 381,000 inhabitants at this time. In terms of area, Luoyang was somewhat smaller than Chang'an.

Water supplies for this city came from the Luo River itself, being levered by means of a variety of mechanical devices. An elevated and covered way provided a safe passage for the emperor or others who wished to move between the two palaces, one of the north and one of the south. A large number of halls included some that were used for audiences, and others which housed the books and docu-

20. *Preceding Page:* The Temple and Altar of Heaven, Beijing; Ming and Qing periods

21., 22. *Above and Left:* The Juyongguan; fourteenth century defensive strongpoint north of Beijing, pre-dating the Ming wall, with low relief carvings of Buddhist motifs and inscription of a sacred text in six scripts

23., 24. *Above and Right:* The Great
Wall, of the Ming Dynasty, as recently
reconstructed; north of Beijing

25. Sundial of stone, with socket for insertion of a pole, sixty-nine graduations to mark the fall of its shadow, and linear markings. Former Han period, from Inner Mongolia; 27 by 27 cm

26. Astronomical tower, used to measure the sun's shadow with use of a 12-metre long gnomon; built for Guo Shoujing, *c.* 1276, reconstructed 1542. Reproduced by courtesy of Birkhäuser Verlag, Basel, from Chao Kang Chang and Werner Blaser, *China: Tao in der Architektur – Tao in Architecture (1987)*

27. *Above and Left:* Female textile workers, of aboriginal stock; from the lid of a bronze drum from a tomb in Yunnan province, *c.* 100 BC

28. Camel laden with silk bales, ceramic; from a tomb dated AD 559; height 29 cm

29. Paper currency note of the Jin (Kin) Dynasty, issued 1222; 24 by 14 cm

ments that had been transported to the new capital from Chang'an. One of the halls, named after the White tiger of the West, was the venue of a conference that was assembled in AD 79 for academic discussions that concerned the texts of the classics and their meaning; a written account of the proceedings which was made at the time still survives.

The city included a number of hostels built for the use of officials; they performed a double duty, acting both as the inns needed by travellers and as the court houses for certain judicial proceedings. As at other capital cities, the heads or corpses of executed criminals were at times suspended on the walls, by way of warning to the public. There were at least two prisons. Two shrines built to honour the memory of the founding emperors of the dynasty were used for the regular rituals of prayer and sacrifice, and for depositing statements of important dynastic events that an emperor wished to make to his ancestors. There were also altars dedicated to the worship of the spirits of the soil and the grain. A special field had been laid out where, once a year, the emperor performed his ritual act of ploughing, with a view to stimulating a prosperous season.

Outside the city's walls lay the altars to Heaven and Earth, supreme objects of worship in the imperial cults. The *Ling tai*, or 'Spiritual Terrace', housed the instruments used for astronomical studies, and the mechanism that Zhang Heng (78–139) had evolved in 132 for detecting the occurrence of earthquakes in different parts of the empire. In the same complex of buildings were the twelve specially made and carefully measured pipes whose purpose was to show how the two forces of *yin* and *yang* were inexorably advancing or retreating with the succession of the seasons. The Academy, which was also situated between the southern wall and the left bank of the Luo River, included a lecture hall and accommodated the stone tablets on which the approved versions of the classical texts had been engraved in AD 175. Elsewhere there were several markets, including one for the sale of horses; less privileged members of Luoyang's population lived in the dwellings of the suburbs, in a manner that must have been far removed from that of a few prominent favourites or statesmen. Some of these had built their own villas at pleasant spots beyond the walls; the descriptions of these mansions, of their luxurious style of life and the expense of their furnishings, are doubtless subject to the exaggeration of political rivals or the protests of those who were consumed by envy.

Attention to symbolism is revealed in the names that were accorded to Luoyang's buildings; many bore a title chosen to attract the joys, successes and blessings that any Son of Heaven might desire. The southern palace thus included halls for the attainment of good fortune or of perfection; other names were doubtless designed so as to attract qualities such as that of 'All-Embracing Virtue'. The 'Cloud Terrace' gave room to portraits of thirty-two generals and supporters of the founding emperor of Later Han; and to ensure that the imperial palace was placed in a felicitous cosmic context, the gates on its four sides were named after the animals that symbolized the four quarters, and whose presence, if placed correctly, would bring eternal blessing to its chief occupant. Beyond the western wall lay the 'Lodge of Tranquil Joy', used as a meeting point to greet incoming visitors or to escort those who were departing elsewhere. Statues of suitable creatures drawn from mythology gave the Lodge its blessing.

But Luoyang, proud capital of the Later Han emperors as it had been, was destined to be as one with Nineveh and Tyre. In 189 a powerful and brutal warlord, Dong Zhuo, set his troops to terrorize the city with rape and looting; in the following year he brought about the deliberate destruction of much that the Han emperors had set up as their memorial; palaces, temples and private houses were burnt; the contents of the imperial archives were made over for use as sacks or domestic furnishings; the bronze figures that had graced so many buildings were melted down to be used for baser purposes. For renovation and recovery the city must needs await the foundation of other dynasties.

In 960 the founder of the Song dynasty settled on Kaifeng, also known as Bianjing, as the seat of his empire. As elsewhere, many of the buildings were made of wood and the risk of fire was high. For the first time we hear of an attempt to counter this, by positioning firefighting stations or appliances at regular intervals in the streets. Fortunately we possess first-hand evidence of the rich and varied life of this city. For, shortly before the court and palace were forced to flee south (1127) to seek asylum in Lin'an (Hangzhou), Zhang Zeduan completed one of the masterpieces of Chinese painting. On a horizontal scroll measuring 5.25 metres in length he depicted a party returning to the centre of Kaifeng city from the countryside; it was the day of the spring festival and they had been cleansing their ancestors' graves after the ravages of winter.

The party passes through the neatly worked countryside, where the farmsteads sheltered behind the windbreaks of the trees, and the fields have been ploughed ready for sowing. Their route follows the river, which dominates much of the painting. Barges moored to bollards on the bank discharge their sacks of grain for a brisk sale; for the travellers have reached a settlement of shops and teahouses, where transport and carriage depend on coolie or mule. Clinker-built vessels with rudders controlled by rope lie alongside the mansions and streets of the suburbs, while men are straining on oar or hawser to manoeuvre or hold their craft in the fast-running waters of the stream. Across an arched bridge, aptly named after the rainbow, travellers pass from one bank to the other; some are carried in sedan chairs, while others prefer to loiter on foot. Tradesmen take their goods by mule, and coolies suspend their loads from the poles that lie across their shoulders. On each side of the bridge, booths are set out, with their stock-in-trade of ropes, knives, cakes or sweetmeats on view. Teahouses provide for those who wish to enjoy their refreshments at leisure; large coloured banners and lanterns proclaim the type of business or trade in which the houses are engaged.

In one of the streets, man and boy set to work to repair the light waggon that has evidently collapsed on the roadside; on the opposite side a crowd gathers around a kneeling raconteur. A lady returns to her sedan from her shopping; oxcarts, crowned with thatch or basketware to protect their contents from the elements, rumble through the streets; a fortune-teller sits squarely at his table, imparting to his client the news that he is seeking, or the destiny that he fears to hear. Further along the street the gates of a mansion have been swung open, and loungers sit around, hoping for commissions or largesse; hawkers cry the value of their goods, and a mother holds up her child to seek protection from the traffic; for a drover has been steering his pigs to market, and waggons follow one another nose to tail through the busy streets.

Bystanders hang over the balustrade of the flat bridge that crosses the last waterway before the eastern gate of Kaifeng city proper. A troop of laden Bactrian camels emerges from the imposing gatehouse on its way out of the city; for, holiday or not, the business of exporting silks, teas, porcelains and other Chinese products to the communities of Central Asia must go on. These merchantmen have left behind them one of Kaifeng's busiest streets, which houses a draper with his bales of cloth on show; next door a professional letter-writer has hung up examples of his best calligraphy, while he writes a message for his illiterate client. Barrels stand ready for sale in a cooper's shop, next to a more grandiose establishment where incense and perfume may be bought; all manner of goods are apparently on sale at the large shop next door.

There is evidently a similar row of shops on the opposite side of the street, as a lady who is carried in a sedan chair has lowered the shutters of the window to look at the frontage and its display. Aloof from the mundane activities of the city, a man sits at a table in one of the upper storeys of these houses, bent perhaps on his books. Down below in the fairway, porters, coolies and priests wander around to chat to one another and to pursue their business; they must take care to avoid the carts that are being pulled by a team of four mules, and urged to ever-greater speeds by their drovers. In his final scene, Zhang Zeduan paints a picture of activity and excitement tempered by dignity; a crowd hangs upon the words of a story-teller; robed priests stand around the streets in solemn conclave, while a travelling salesman cries his wares and strikes up his tune; a noble official follows on his grey palfrey, whip in hand, as his servants guide his mount and carry his umbrella. Should he glance to his left he would see a team of three men drawing supplies of water from a well; they are next to Mr Zhao's clinic, which stands open to view. Banners and posters advertise his skill at curing fevers or relieving alcoholic hangovers, and the fragrant pills that he makes up; and two ladies who have come for a consultation hold up a baby for examination.

Ornamental gardens, with their waterways, trees, rocks and pavilions, lay attached to the mansions of the more wealthy residents of a Song city. They had been designed both to satisfy the demands of proportion and to rely on nature's own beauties, but they do not appear in Zhang Zeduan's painting. Nor does this scroll depict the astronomical clock-tower that Su Song had designed and erected in the city by 1090. Its elaborate mechanism was operated by water; by a display of manikins or other devices and by ringing bells or gongs, the clock tolled the hours of day and night, striking every quarter; and the tower incorporated a celestial globe which displayed the observed situations of the celestial bodies. The masters of the Jin (Kin) dynasty who drove the Song house south in 1127 had this massive tower removed to their own capital city near Beijing, where the mechanism required adjustment to fit the latitude in which it then stood.

Traces of the Yuan dynastic capital of Dadu which have been excavated recently show that this city had been designed on a regular square plan, with its walls, its grid arrangement for the main thoroughfares and minor lanes, and a site for the palace on the southern side. But Beijing, immediately to the south of Dadu, reached a new height of grandeur and splendour under the Ming and Qing emperors. The double set of walls which girded the town were themselves a monument of imperial endeavour and a witness of the corporate work of Chinese labour; and the city now exemplified traditional features which were conceived in majestic form.

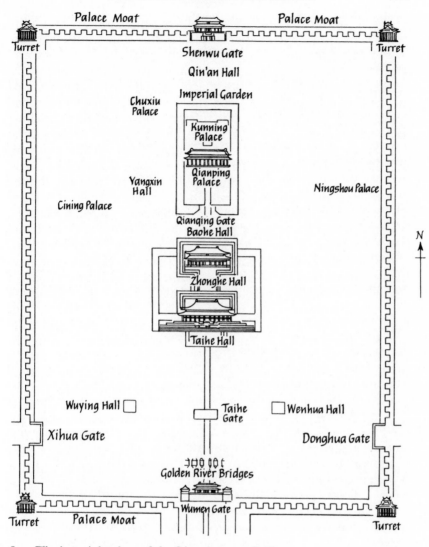

3. *The imperial palace of the Qing dynasty, Beijing*

Unhappily no more than isolated fragments now remain of the
two sets of walls and their massive gateways. They protected a city
formed of two nearly square parts, with the one set immediately to
the north of the other. The northern, or Tartar, city had like Dadu
been laid out with its regular streets and lanes in parallel, oriented
to the four quarters; and it included the palace itself, the offices of
government and, in the latter decades of the nineteenth century, the
legations of the foreign powers. The streets and narrow lanes (*hutong*)

of the adjoining section on the south, sometimes called the Chinese city, had grown up in anything but regular fashion, responding in haphazard way to the daily needs of the humbler elements of the population.

At the centre of the northern city lay the imperial palace, or 'Forbidden City'. Within the lofty and thick walls that severed contact with the world without there stretched a series of courtyards, paved in stone and surrounded by living quarters and offices. These housed not only the emperor and his family, but also the large number of eunuchs who controlled the domestic services and saw to it that the main occupants were maintained in the style of living that was their due. Placed in a position that was often unassailable, the eunuchs commanded paramount strength, being open to persuasion or graft to secure the appointment of a suppliant's kinsman or favourite, and controlling the procurement of the large consignment of consumable supplies that the Forbidden City needed.

In the layout of this complex structure, courtyard and building matched one another in symmetry; ornamental bridges crossed the rivulets that ran through the squares; richly carved stairways to the balustrades of the main audience chambers bore the devices of cloud and dragon that were the fit accompaniments of the Son of Heaven. Boldly written notice-boards proclaimed the title, character or function of the buildings, appearing sometimes in Manchu as well as in Chinese. Large timbers or perhaps complete tree-trunks, glazed tiles turned out in yellow by the thousand, vertical facings in green tiling and marble blocks transported from Yunnan province in the deep south-west were the raw materials on which the labourers, craftsmen and artists had set to work. From within his courts the Son of Heaven could catch a glimpse of towers that housed the bell or drum to which his people must needs respond, or of the glistening white stupa of the adjoining park with its call to serve the Buddha's ways.

At the south edge of the southern section of Beijing stands the site where emperors offered sacrifices and prayer to Heaven, in the fervent hope of securing an abundant harvest. Laid out with a consummate sense of space and proportion, the complex is redolent of those symbols which informed the Chinese idea of sovereign majesty; there is a complete absence of any reference to the faith of the Buddha. Structures designed solely for religious purposes are flanked by functional quarters, where vigil could be kept, or where the victims were slaughtered for sacrifice. Within the large park which encloses these buildings groves of trees grace the courtyards and serve as a reminder of the link between Heaven, the immediate object of worship, and earth, over whose rule the imperial worshipper presided.

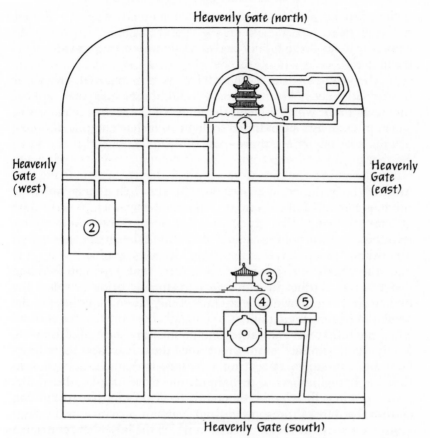

Heavenly Gate (north)

Heavenly Gate (west)

Heavenly Gate (east)

Heavenly Gate (south)

4. *The altar and temple of Heaven (Ming and Qing dynasties), Beijing. (1) Principal hall of worship, for the emperor's prayers for the incoming year. (2) Hall for the emperor's vigil and purification. (3) Hall of worship, surrounded by circular echoing wall. (4) Altar. (5) Quarters for preparation of sacrificial victims*

The park wherein the altar and temple of Heaven lie is set precisely to meet the four quarters of the compass. From the main entrance in the south, a long raised causeway leads directly north, first to the altar and thence to the two halls of worship. The altar itself consists of a raised platform, built up in layers, each with its marble railing; the delicate handling of the stonework is matched by careful attention to shaping the paving slabs, each cut to different dimensions and assembled with a keen eye to symmetry. The first of the halls of worship is surmounted by a dome, roofed in dark blue and gold, and surrounded by a wall, whose perfectly circular shape lends itself today to those who delight in the sound of an echo. Finally the causeway reaches the hall of prayer used for invoking the fortune of the incoming year; a dome formed of three layers – again of brilliant dark blue – crowns this noble edifice. Within, the rich sparkle of blues and greens, golds and reds, ever draws the eye to the apex of the vault. On the east side a covered veranda affords the departing worshipper or visitor shade and shelter in which to compose his mind before returning to face the turmoil of the outer world.

*

Most of the information concerning China's capital cities relates to the upper reaches of society; that the luxuries to which they were heirs did not come the way of all is evident in the protests of a few statesmen against the imbalances that they saw around them, or in a few Tang short stories which reveal something of the prevailing ugliness of the scene. For the cities housed both fine mansions and mean hovels, setting the scene for extravagant living or tolerating dire poverty. Squalor may have lurked behind an imposing façade, while the regular layout of the town and its wards was matched by a disarray of shacks and slums. Public market-places also did duty as execution grounds; ornamental waterways may well have acted as drains. The gaily painted archways (*pailou*) that marked the entry to Beijing's main streets until recently could be contrasted with the mean openings to some of the lanes where most of the city's population passed their lives. Meanwhile other anomalies and incongruities were hard to miss; the first of the summer palaces, which lay north-west of Beijing, had been built with the help of Jesuit advisers, in Italianate style, following the fashion of contemporary seventeenth-century Europe; but it was the forces of the European powers who destroyed the palace in 1860. The new summer palace which replaced it was built at the orders of Cixi, the empress dowager (1835–1908), with no expense spared to create its lakes, its bridge, its special theatre and its covered walkway in a style fit for kings; the funds to do so had been diverted from moneys intended to build a strong Chinese navy.

XIV

TOMBS AND THEIR TREASURES

Dramatic results have been forthcoming from the energetic work of Chinese archaeologists since 1950, and especially since 1976. By far the greater part of their efforts has been devoted to the excavation of tombs, which extend in time from the palaeolithic ages onwards. Such discoveries have been found in all parts of China, in addition to those that have come to light over the years in areas where China's cultural influences had left their mark, although Chinese administration had never been established on a permanent basis; such sites are found, for example, in the settlements of Korea. Chinese artefacts have also been found in graves dug for chieftains of other peoples, as at Noin Ula (in Mongolia); and examples of burials that follow Chinese styles may be found in Japan.

A high proportion of the tombs and graves that have been discovered date from the Han period, before the practice of cremation had become accepted on a regular basis, and while the habit of filling a grave with valuables was held in high esteem. Such a custom has enriched our appreciation of religious symbols and provided art historians with a fine supply of new evidence; and it has also served to supplement our knowledge of Chinese technology.

One of the principal motives for the burial of treasures and other goods in tombs lay in the desire to provide for the needs and comforts of the deceased person in the afterlife. Social status determined the style of burial and extent of the furnishings to which a man or a woman was entitled; the hope of impressing contemporaries with their devotion to their kinsfolk could tempt mourners to put on an ostentatious show of their wealth. Such displays, which could involve a family in crippling expenditure, and drew the criticism of an emperor or a philosopher; they also gave rise to the long-standing practice of grave-robbery.

209

BURIAL HABITS AND THE STYLE OF TOMBS

As might be expected, the styles of burial have differed considerably over the wide areas of time and space that are involved; they have been variously marked by the hope of satisfying different types of belief in the life hereafter and by the need to conform with changing social distinctions. The kings of Shang (around the fourteenth century BC) were buried at Anyang in deeply dug chambers, carefully constructed with steps, and with special pits below for the reception of the human victims who were immolated to accompany their lord. The same style was maintained in the succeeding centuries, when the practice of human sacrifice had given place to less cruel types of offering. Examples which have been found in the middle reaches of the Yangzi valley (for example, at Shazitang), where the pre-imperial kingdom of Chu was situated, included a large wooden structure made of outsize timbers that had been worked with skilful joinery. In the same area, at Mawangdui near Changsha, such tombs had been constructed (168 BC) to house the bodies of local leaders or their consorts, encapsulated in a series of three or more stout coffins, and surrounded by packages of funerary furnishings. Some of these precautions had been due to a desire to preserve the corpse from corruption; the faith placed in the efficacy of such measures has been dramatically vindicated in a few instances.

At other sites and times tombs have been cut into the living rock of a hillside, or a series of chambers have been fashioned with a symmetrical arrangement of rooms intended for ritual purposes, such as purification. The insulation of the corpse in a suit of jade, which has been witnessed in such tombs and elsewhere, was likewise intended as a preservative, but failed dismally to achieve its purpose. In yet a different manner, a few tombs of the Warring States period (481 or 403–221 BC) were surmounted by a large shrine wherein the requisite devotions could be maintained.

New styles developed during the Han period. From the second century BC there are example of tombs which were designed in the form of a residence, with entrance hall and gates, and corridors that surrounded the innermost chamber where the coffin was laid. The whole structure was made of wood; on the outside, a barricade formed of courses of horizontally laid timbers was set to form a rectangular bastion; and the whole was sealed by a coating of lime and an earthen canopy. The efficacy of this method of insulation is well illustrated in the case of the tomb of Dabaotai, south of Beijing; when archaeologists uncovered the site, a fragrance arose from the timbers, which were still yellow in colour, as if they had been hewn only recently.

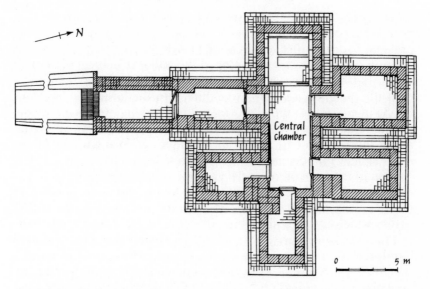

5.   Plan of tomb no. 1 Dahuting, Mixian (Henan province); multi-chambered, and decorated with stone carvings, as in Figures 8 and 10; c. AD 200

A large number of Han tombs were built of brick, at first in small dimensions but later in comparatively sizeable structures, and in cases crowned by a cupola or domed vault. Very often an impression was made in the clay before it was baked hard, perhaps as a symbol representing the circular heavens and the square earth, perhaps as an ornamental device or perhaps to remind an observer of the status of the deceased person or the wealth of his kinsfolk. In one example of perhaps 50 BC a frieze which carries symbols of the Five Phases separates the structure into two parts.

Many of these brick tombs were built to house but one occupant; in some it was possible to reopen the entrance and insert a second coffin, when the time had come for spouse to join spouse. The style was developed considerably in the centuries after the Han period, leading sometimes to the construction of a remarkable beehive type of vault. There are also a number of instances where groups of brick-built tombs were grouped together as it were in a cemetery, and it may be assumed that the site was chosen after due consultation with specialists in geomancy. One such site, which existed at Shaogou near Luoyang, was excavated in 1953; systematic investigation of its 225 tombs yielded considerable information, including chronological schemata, for distinguishing the sequences of different building designs, or of the types of articles buried there, be they made of pottery, bronze, iron, gold, jade or bone. It has subsequently become possible to correct or refine such schemes and to apply them to the problem of dating discoveries at other sites.

From these styles there developed the major structures of brick or stone that comprised several compartments. Some of these were carefully designed, as if by an architect, in the form of a residence for the living (for example, at Yinan, in Shandong province); or else, considerable attention was paid to achieving a symmetrical layout of all the component parts (for example, at Wangdu, in Hebei province). A number of such tombs provided ample scope for decoration in the form of low relief carvings or fresco paintings.

In a surprisingly large number of cases it has been possible to identify the person lying beneath a tomb, or to specify the period within which it was built. Clues for doing so are to be found in the seal that was often buried with an official's body, or in the occasional inscription that was painted on the walls, or scratched on narrow lead plaques. Some of these were intended as testimony that the deceased person or his family could establish a valid claim to the land where the grave lay, and in some cases it can be shown that they were made and deposited long after the burial itself had taken place.

The type and nature of the objects interred with the coffin may often provide a reasonable indication of the tomb's date, provided that undue attention is not paid to items that may have found their place of honour there as valued heirlooms. Depending on social status, precise details specified the entitlement of the deceased person to particular types of equipment; for example, the use of gold, silver or other metals for the wire with which to link the segments of a jade suit was variously prescribed for emperors, kings or noblemen; the presence of such materials may define the rank of a deceased person, who may then be identified as a king, queen or nobleman whose habitat lay within the area.

At the lowest level a few cemeteries have been identified as the burial sites of convicts. They were placed in pits dug to mean dimensions and laid out beside one another in rows, grid fashion. Such graves were given no funeral furnishings; roughly engraved inscriptions gave the name of the dead person and the type of punishment to which he had been subjected. They form a conspicuous contrast with the grand epitaphs, cut with particular attention to calligraphic quality on large memorial stelae, to record the meritorious service that an official rendered, together with details of his genealogy and the appointments that he held during his career. Such stelae are to be distinguished from the small structures set up as votive shrines, to perpetuate the services due to an ancestor, or to demonstrate the diligence whereby his successors were fulfilling their duties. The large slabs of stone of which these shrines were made afforded sculptors considerable scope for the depiction of figures known in mythology, scenes of an historical or pseudo-historical incident or vignettes of daily life.

THE SEPULCHRES OF KINGS AND EMPERORS

Of the countless tombs that have been revealed in recent years, it is those which were intended for kings, emperors and their consorts that have attracted most interest; for they are the most splendid of all examples, whose creators could call on large forces of manpower to handle great supplies of materials, and the most skilled of artists and builders to exercise their ingenuity. Examples may be studied throughout the pre-imperial and imperial ages.

In its later years the seat of the Shang kings was at Anyang, and it is at that site that eleven royal tombs have been identified. Their very size, which extended to a depth of some twelve metres, betrays that they were dug for no ordinary mortal. Their tapered walls led down to a wooden chamber, and had these tombs escaped the hands of robbers they would still have boasted the rich stores of ritual vessels, bronze equipment, military weapons and other precious commodities with which the occupant was sent off to the next world, along with a large number of human victims, sacrificed to be his companions. King Pan Geng was the nineteenth of his line, and he may be dated at perhaps 1400 BC; these enormous tombs may be identified with some certainty as the resting places of that king and most of the eleven successors who followed him. One tomb, which had evaded plunder, was that of Lady Hao (Fu Hao), principal consort of one of the Shang kings, and its discovery in 1975 with no less than 440 bronze vessels has been of immeasurable value in establishing type-sequences for these sacred objects.

Zhongshan was the name of one of the smaller of the kingdoms that arose during the Warring States period, some 100 kilometres to the south of Beijing. The area was probably subject to influence from non-Chinese peoples from the steppes of Asia, and historical accounts refer to its own special methods of hunting. The title 'king' was adopted by its leader only in 323 BC, and it is the tomb of King Cuo, who took this step, that has been excavated recently. It was one of a complex that had been designed but never executed, as is now known from a remarkable and unique find made at the site. This was nothing less than a builder's plan, on bronze, for the construction of a mausoleum that would include three major and

中山王嚳陵園全景想像圖之二   王堂三層.用飛陛叠上王堂面積較大

图一○　陵园全景想像图之二

6.   Mausoleum as planned (c. 300 BC) but never completed for a king of Zhongshan (Hebei province) and consorts; external dimensions 475 by 220 metres. Reconstruction based on finds, which included a builder's plan, in bronze, specifying names and measurements of different parts of the complex

two minor tombs; but before the work could be completed the kingdom fell victim to one of its acquisitive neighbours and was incorporated in its territory (296 BC).

In the meantime King Cuo and his principal consort died and were buried in the style that had been envisaged. For each one, a large memorial hall had been built to surmount the tomb, with a further separate chamber, presumably for the storage of equipment, at the rear. Thanks to the dimensions that are specified on the bronze plaque and the material evidence of the site it has been possible to reconstruct the plan of the buildings, surrounded by a set of double walls, and with a storeyed edifice arising over the tombs; the overall dimensions of the site ran to a width of 1,900 feet and a depth of 885 feet, corresponding to 475 and 220 metres.

King Cuo was buried at much the same time that King Mausolus of Lydia was laid to rest in Halicarnassus. With King Cuo there were buried a number of remarkable objects, some of types not seen elsewhere. Large symbols of majesty, made of bronze, were probably intended to emblazon the royal residence so conspicuously that none could fail to recognize the king's presence. A few bronze vessels carried some of the longest inscriptions known to have been made on that medium, and their text has supplemented the little that historical writings tell of the kingdom. Some choice lampstands (one anthropomorphic), bronze figurines of animals with gold and silver inlay, miniature jade figures and exquisite boards for playing the game of *liubo* were included in the treasures of the tombs of Zhongshan, whose metallurgists were clearly past masters of their art.

Perhaps the most spectacular of all the recent archaeological discoveries in China is that of the site of the tomb of the first Qin emperor, who died in 210 BC. The *Historical Records* (*Shiji*), whose account is biased against that emperor, tell of the careful plans that were laid to construct his tomb, regardless of expense, but with full precautions against robbery. The tomb was to include a representation of the universe, with the constellations of the heavens depicted on the vault, a plan of the emperor's domains on the floor, and the course of the rivers flowing in mercury.

The site of this tomb at Mount Li, near the Qin capital city of Xianyang, has been long known; excavation has been mainly confined to pits on the east side, and the hillock that surmounts the tomb itself awaits full examination. The avenue of the now famous 'terracotta army' lies buried on the east; it included at least 7,000 figures of officers and privates, cavalrymen, charioteers and horse, each executed individually. Details of harness and equipment are plain to see; the life-size realistic figures of the men portray different expressions and manners of deportment, showing that attention was paid to differences of age and rank. A different locality on the site included somewhat rare items, that is, two teams of horses and chariot fashioned in bronze, half life-size.

Although some of the tombs of the Han emperors have been identified, they still await excavation; in some cases they are known to have been surrounded by walls of carefully measured and dressed stone. Maoling, where Wudi (reigned 141–87 BC) lies buried, takes the form of a four-sided pyramid, with a perimeter at the base that measures 230 metres. The tumulus rises to a height of 46 metres, and each of the four sides of the level square at the summit measures 10 metres in length. The type of tomb that lies beneath this structure and the extent of its treasure are as yet unknown. More, however, can be said of some of the tombs of some of the kings who bore authority which the Han emperors recognized or conferred.

Liu Sheng, son of Jingdi, was created king of Zhongshan in 154 BC. His kingdom lay to the south of Beijing, in roughly the same area as that of the pre-imperial kingdom of that name over which King Cuo had presided until *c.* 300 BC. Liu Sheng died in 112 BC, to be followed by one of his consorts shortly afterwards, and they were buried in adjoining tombs that had been cut into the living rock of the hillside. In each one a short approach-way led to a series of chambers, crossed at right angles by a long corridor and its southern and northern wings. There was a wealth of furnishings, including a number of carriages and horses, as well as food containers of bronze and pottery; somewhat uniquely for this period, the tomb included examples of gold and silver needles that were used for medical purposes, possibly acupuncture. The chambers that housed the coffins were built with a wooden structure long since perished, apart from the tiles with which the roofing was made; and some provision was allowed for drainage.

These tombs were situated at Mancheng, and they have yielded some of the most beautiful examples of the metallurgist's art of the period. A few small animals of bronze, with gold inlay, are reminiscent of similar pieces found in nearby tombs of some two centuries previously, and it may be suggested that a tradition had grown up in the district for the production of masterpieces made of this medium. A lamp fashioned in the form of a slave-girl, with adjustable parts, is often hailed as evidence of this type of achievement; its aesthetic appeal and its value in the history of technology are paralleled by the importance of the inscriptions, which, along with those engraved on other items, make identification of the site certain.

Li – those all-important regulations which laid down the correct procedure for behaviour on all occasions – included detailed provisions that governed the style of burial to which an individual was entitled, depending largely on social status. The kings of the empire ranked close to the top of this hierarchy, and as a result both the king of Zhongshan and his consort were encased for burial in carefully measured suits, made of slender rectangles of jade. By commanding the use of this precious substance and maintaining the considerable expense and energy needed to make the suits correctly, the king and his kinsmen were inspired by the hope that its magical qualities would enable the deceased person to escape from bodily corruption. A number of other examples of encasement in a jade shroud are known, either from material evidence or from accounts in the histories. In many cases these were kings and queens, as the regulations specified. Occasionally an emperor bestowed the privilege of burial in jade on a favourite or a leading statesman, but such a gift was of questionable value. In no surviving instance has the jade's power of preservation been vindicated; in several cases the family whose member was honoured by this type of imperial bounty suffered the enmity, jealousy or active animosity of rival politicians.

In 109 BC the Han emperor confirmed the title of king of Dian to a non-Chinese ruler of lands and peoples in the modern province of Yunnan. When the site of the royal cemetery of this line of kings was excavated in 1959, it revealed evidence of a way of life that had mastered a number of skills, quite independently of the Chinese officials, colonists and traders who had been making their way to these distinct regions for perhaps two centuries. Characteristic of these tombs are a number of bronze drums, used as containers for the cowry shells that did duty as money. The lids of the drums carry a series of scenes in deep relief that portray human and animal figures in their various occupations. From such rich evidence it is clear that the inhabitants both practised agriculture and bred cattle; some of them lived as nomad pastoralists; others were attached to permanent habitations. They are shown at their ceremonies of worship and human sacrifice, enjoying music and the dance. Some of the drumheads depict armed warriors fighting their neighbours, distinguished by their own form of head-dress; sometimes a mounted commander of Dian directs the battle. The prominent appearance of the ox in the décor suggests that this animal formed a totem figure, and the snake may have fulfilled the same function.

Close to Xi'an there is spread a complex of seventeen monuments built as the last resting places of the Tang emperors, with their consorts and kinsfolk. The joint tomb of Gaozong (reigned 649–83) and the empress Wu (reigned 690–705) lies at the head of a stately avenue lined by statues of beasts and birds, including ostrich that were brought as tribute to the Tang court. Adjoining the tomb there stand rows of solemn statues of some of those who came to pay their respects from distant lands. In the tomb of the princess Yongtai (died 701) the polychrome frescoes of courtiers and attendants give a vivid impression of the processions that attended the court and of the splendid robes that graced such occasions.

Some of the emperors of the short-lived, minor dynasties have also left their memorials behind them. Wang Jian (died 918) had served the last of the Tang emperors, but on the demise of that dynasty (907) he had been able to establish his own regime, known under the name of Former Shu, in what is now Sichuan province; this was one of the Five Dynasties, which were singled out as the more important of the regimes that speedily followed one another before the house of Song was founded. Wang Jian's tomb, in Chengdu, consists of three principal chambers built as a unity, on a line running from south to north. The building is marked by its precise masonry, with a long barrel vault that is supported by a series of internal buttresses. Entry is by way of massive wooden doors; within the central chamber lies the stone plinth on which the coffin rested; around the base there run no less than twenty-four figures of female dancers and musicians, with their instruments at the ready. The borders of this magnificent structure are decorated with floral motifs, animal designs and a long device resembling the egg-and-dart pattern of the west. In the final chamber at the northern end of the

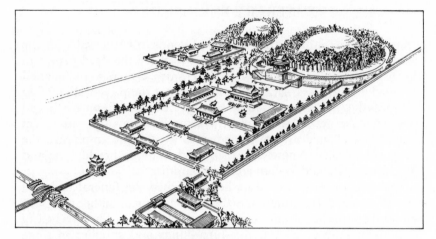

7.   Dingling: one of the imperial Ming tombs, north of Beijing, built for the Wanli emperor (reigned 1573–1619)

tomb a statue of Wang Jian rested upon a plinth. Of especial interest are the two sets of narrow jade tablets, each of fifty-three pieces. These were drilled at each end for the insertion of silver thread with which the whole set could be bound together. On the tablets were engraved the texts of two panegyrics extolling the virtues of the emperor and formally recording the title whereby he was posthumously honoured.

Few visitors to Beijing fail to visit the tombs of the thirteen emperors of the Ming dynasty who were buried north of the city. The site lies within a valley, chosen with great attention to its numinous qualities which even now transcend the intrusions of tourist motor coach and loudspeaker. Access lies by way of an avenue lined by stone figures of real or mythical animals, armed warriors and senior officials of state who waited upon the pleasure of the Son of Heaven. Throughout the site the eye follows vistas formed by free-standing marble columns, or pavilions which shelter a monumental stele. Large-scale memorial halls are approached by marble stairway or ramp, with balustrades of marble forming a frontage; an ornamental gateway (*pailou*) that is sometimes described as the most beautiful one ever to be built in China leads the way forward through its five arches. Throughout, a wealth of carving testifies to the quality and skill of the artists and craftsmen of the Ming period. Underground lie the tombs of the emperors, designed on a massive scale in the style that had become traditional, with corridors, main chambers and side apartments, each fulfilling their own functions in the ceremonies that marked the obsequies of the Son of Heaven.

FUNERARY FURNISHINGS

Various motives affected the choice of goods to be buried with the dead. Some objects acted as talismans, to place the dead person in the most advantageous position in the cosmos. Others were designed for religious purposes, such as purification, or the presentation of an offering; they had been used in this way during life on earth and they could be expected to fulfil the same functions thereafter. Yet other types of object were intended to identify or emphasize the status that the dead person had enjoyed in his or her lifetime and that he or she would look to enjoy in paradise.

Very often the next of kin who supervised the funeral included instruments of entertainment, articles of equipment, either real or as miniature replicas, or stores of consumable goods. The survival of written inventories of funerary furnishings and supplies in some tombs may be due to no more than accidental causes, deriving from the carelessness of the undertakers in leaving such lists behind them. Alternatively they may have been included purposefully, so that the dead could present the authorities of the next world with an impressive record of their worldly goods. To provide for all types of emergency, the dead were sometimes equipped with arms with which to fight an enemy, written medical manuals with which to cure diseases or instruments and almanacs with which to determine a time when a project would be most likely to have a successful outcome.

Of necessity it is from the tombs of the rich and the higher reaches of society that these objects derive. A few examples survive of paintings that were made on silk to portray the journey of the deceased person to the next world, there to enjoy the eternal company of sun and moon. Thanks to the principles of imitative magic it was hoped that the presence of such a painting would enable the deceased person himself or herself to embark on the same journey, and the same intention doubtless lay behind the frescoes of immortal beings that adorned the walls of a tomb, or the designs that were sometimes made in relief or on brick.

Similar results would, it was hoped, ensue from the burial of certain types of bronze mirror. These were skilfully fashioned so as to include the symbols of two different ways of explaining the cosmos and its workings, that is, those of the Five Phases and those of the twelve divisions of the heavens. A symmetrical design successfully reconciled these two sets with each other, and combined them with symbols of the life of the immortals, feeding off the choice fruit of the jujube tree and the springs of jade, after a journey which had taken them through the clouds. The correct juxtaposition of the symbols on these mirrors could act as a means of ensuring that the occupant of the tomb was situated in perfect balance with the elements of the universe and its interplay of forces.

In time the craftsmen who made these mirrors forgot what their original purpose had been. The all-important symbols were misplaced; or motifs that were purely decorative were given such prominence that by the Tang period these had assumed first place. In the meantime another type of talisman that appeared, sometimes on mirrors, sometimes impressed on brick, was likewise intended to direct the soul of the dead to paradise; but this was to the Paradise of the West, over which the Queen Mother presided. Sometimes, in the absence of a mirror with its cosmic blessing, or of a complete representation of the Queen Mother in a tableau, symbols of these or of other ways to paradise would appear on the walls of a tomb; or they might be cut into the stone coffins in which some persons were buried. In this way tombs and their furnishings may include medallions that enclose the three-legged bird and toad, which represent the sun and moon of the Eastern Paradise. Others portray the dragon and tiger of east and west, which are integral parts of the Five Phases' scheme of universal being. Or perhaps there might be seen an outline of that special crown whose use was reserved for the Queen Mother of the West; it was within her power both to control the rhythms of the universe, and to confer the gift of the elixir of immortality.

Some of the tomb's furniture derived from the faith that certain objects could expel evil influences; these included manikins made of peachwood, or wooden figures crowned with elongated antlers, with tongues protruding sometimes as far as the waist. Incense burners, exquisitely made by the bronzesmith, were presumably intended for purposes of purification. Some of the most beautiful and valuable of all jewels that were buried were the discs of jade, either whole or semicircular, plain or delicately carved, and conveying a promise of that felicity that this most precious of all minerals was believed to bring. The proportions of the patterns of these discs varied according to the rank of the occupant of the tomb.

Vessels of bronze, lacquer or pottery were included in the tomb for a variety of reasons, and the inscriptions that they bore formed another means of identifying or stressing the status of the dead person. Such vessels contained food or drink, often provided in generous supplies, and separated into the component courses of a banquet. These would be accompanied by the equipment needed on those occasions, such as sets of dishes, plates and goblets, often of the brilliant scarlet and sleek black that repeated coats of lacquer can achieve. Reliefs which showed a banquet in progress or the preparations of the kitchen could likewise suggest that the occupants of the next world could look forward to enjoying the delights of the table. Bales of silk, of first quality and coloured with the latest patterns that were in fashion, or ready-made clothes of the latest cut, were another type of consumable goods that was often provided.

Attention to other needs of daily life also featured in the goods interred with the dead. Carefully designed boxes of lacquer, containing within them smaller cases, sometimes accompanied a lady's coffin, providing her with the means of adjusting her toilet or make-up. Terracotta models of farmsteads and their animals, towered houses and their guardians, wells and their winding gear, boats and their oars, or granaries resting on stilts may all be found, dating mostly from the Han period and illustrating the occupations of the time. Models of kitchen stoves may carry in low relief the figures of the knives or ladles that the cooks used. Money was provided in the form of real cash or, occasionally, as imitation coins made of pottery.

Many of the tombs included models, paintings, or reliefs of horse and carriage, which served both as a means of speedy transport and as a sign of status and wealth; for possession of these valuable animals and their choice of harness or of a carriage with its exquisite finish showed that the occupant of the tomb was a person of high rank and considerable substance. The habit doubtless followed the earlier custom of burying real carriages and their teams with them, as is exemplified at Zhangjiapo (Shaanxi province, Western Zhou), Huixian (Henan province; Warring States period) and Dabaotai (south of Beijing, second to first century BC).

Burial of an official's seal of office likewise identified his status and entitlement; in some cases his coffin carried a copy of an imperial decree which had granted him special favours or privileges. Other texts, such as copies of the statutes and ordinances, or of one of the classical books, could be chosen as a mark of a man's professional skills or of his masterly scholarship. Paintings or models of the colleagues who had worked with an official or of the underlings who had served him were a vivid reminder of the powers that he had held and the life that he had spent at court. Frescoes from Wangdu (Hebei province) and Holingol (Inner Mongolia) show Han officials in solemn attendance on their superior, decked in their robes of office, or actively engaged in their duties in the provinces. For the Tang period, paintings in the tombs of two imperial princes, Li Xian (654–84) and Li Zhongrun (682–701), show an array of staid officials solemnly in attendance, standing or with their mounts, their weapons at the ready; or the scenes of the hunt bring to life the energy, speed and colour of these occasions; one tableau shows ladies of the court in the garden, admiring the trees or catching the crickets.

Nor did kinsmen neglect the need to provide their dead with the means of entertainment, and for this reason tombs would include models of jugglers or reliefs of acrobats. On rare occasions models of a complete orchestra may be found; more frequently, before a tomb was sealed, a set of bronze bells, stringed instruments or pipes would have been placed among the items for interment. Possible some of the texts that have been found were provided as a means of enabling an ancestor to while away the long hours of the next world, with the help and solace of philosophical or historical writings.

*

The extent of the archaeological discoveries of recent years has been bewildering, and it has been possible to concentrate attention on no more than a few of the thousands of tombs that have been excavated. Meanwhile not a month passes without the announcement of the discovery or identification of new sites. The oral tradition of a locality has at times suggested their position; at times a modern place-name has included a clue to where kings, emperors or their kinsfolk have been laid to rest. On a few occasions it is possible to relate such sites or their finds to references which appear in the Standard Histories or other writings.

Nevertheless, much material evidence has been destroyed in the past, either by robbers in search of loot or by those who have been bent on desecrating the remains of their dynastic rivals. An early example of this odious practice is recorded for the tomb of Han Shundi (died AD 144); in a particularly unpleasant incident of 1928 the tombs and remains of the Qianlong emperor (died 1799) and of the empress dowager Cixi (died 1908) were looted and their bodies dismembered. It was perhaps in recognition and fear of these dangers that a number of philosophers and emperors enjoined their followers to refrain from extravagant burials; for their expense could bring a household to ruin, and the treasures that were buried for this purpose could hardly fail to attract robbers.

In recent years archaeology has transformed a number of ideas. The rich stores of goods still left in tombs has vindicated accounts of burials that are found in the histories and which were prematurely judged to be exaggerated. While regional variations have yet to be fully analysed, the accumulated evidence of some localities suggests that certain areas made a speciality of some types of production. The new evidence serves to clarify received ideas of China's religion, to distinguish between the differing styles, themes and trends of China's artists and to promote research in the development of technology.

XV

THE ARTS

Of all China's achievements, it is those of her artists that have perhaps made the greatest impact on the western world. Few major museums fail to devote galleries to their display; European painters have been ready to borrow themes and styles that originated on the banks of the Yellow River or the Yangzi; less scrupulous imitators have not hesitated to adapt or abuse such themes, or to place them in incongruous contexts; and patterns of Chinese porcelain and textile have left a permanent imprint on some of the equipment seen in everyday life of the west.

Inspiration has derived from religious motives or the needs of government; patronage has been forthcoming from emperor on his throne or merchant in his counting house, and the themes or subjects that have been chosen have sprung from a variety of causes. Some artists have drawn on incidents enshrined in mythology; others have used their skills to exemplify the stern lessons of Confucian precept and their call to duty; and some have incorporated reminders of philosophical theory or of a defined attitude to life. Styles have varied from the formal to the unrestrained, from classical to romantic; subjects have been chosen to display the majesty of emperor and court, to satisfy the needs of Buddhist worship and its symbolism or to reveal the freedom enjoyed by the lone Daoist hermit. Many painters have sought to combine a Confucian and a Daoist view of the world, by deliberately cutting man down to size within the compass of his natural surroundings. If Buddhism was the main motivation of art in Tang, it was a search for human values that characterized the arts of the Song age.

The media include jade and bronze, known from long before the imperial age had dawned, and lacquered wood, which was developed in the few centuries before the Christian era, principally in the Yangzi River valley. Sculpture perhaps reached its finest point in the centuries after the Han dynasty; porcelains and textiles have carried fine decorative embellishment, particularly from the Tang period onwards. A few paintings may survive from that time, to be followed by the masterpieces of the Song, Ming and Qing dynasties. Meanwhile stately buildings arose to serve the needs of worshipper or courtier, whose design and decoration depended on the skills of China's many and varied craftsmen.

RELIGIOUS MOTIVES AND THE NEEDS OF RITUAL

Shrines and temples of many shapes and sizes were built to serve the memory of departed ancestors, to worship the omnipotent powers of the universe or to receive prayer and offering at the wayside in honour of local spirits. Imposing edifices with their courtyards enclosed sufficient space for the worship of Daoist deities and the colourful and dramatic rites that may be involved; some housed the large statues and the altars that accompany Buddhist ceremonial. Characteristic of Buddhist temples are the detached towers, or pagodas, erected to protect a holy relic, and acting as a prominent beacon to show the way to shrine or hall of meditation. These were built in China of wood, masonry or brick, being square, polygonal or circular. Some are of but a single storey; others comprise as many as fifteen layers. Outside Buddhism, and of especial interest, are the circular buildings of those temples in Beijing where the Ming and Qing emperors paid their dues to Heaven.

Within these temples and shrines were set the altars that bore the instruments used in the ceremonial, be it devoted to the gods of the land, the protecting figures of the Daoist church or the images of the Buddhist saints. The innate Chinese love of classification led to the adoption of different shapes of vessel for different occasions or rites, and each type was duly known by its own proper term. There were containers used to offer grain, meats or spirits, or the fruit and flowers that were suitable to some creeds; there were special vessels shaped with a lip, for pouring a libation, and dispensers of wine in slender or more bulbous forms. Practical considerations could affect the design, as in the case of the tripod or tetrapod vessels in which sacrificial foods were cooked. They were designed for use over a fire; and for this reason they were fashioned with a pair of loops wherein a stout pole could be inserted, to allow for safe removal from the source of the heat.

From the Shang period onwards these vessels were made in bronze, and the many examples that have been found, often in the tombs of the Shang kings, testify to the high degree of skill that was attained and the great effort that was put into their making. The earliest examples were made with the use of moulds, and it is only comparatively late, from perhaps the sixth or fifth century BC, that the lost wax process is evidenced. In many examples the artists made full use of all the surfaces that were available for ornamentation;

sometimes this was confined to discrete bands; but repetitive as the themes may appear at first sight to be, the effect is anything but monotonous. A meander type of pattern may sometimes set the background for head or body of animal or bird, or for the apotropaic figure of the *taotie*, or 'glutton's mask', that is seen so frequently, recognizable either in full-face or in profile. On rare occasions a human face is incorporated in the design.

As the centuries passed, the décor of these ritual vessels tended to become more and more elaborate, and by the end of the Zhou period it had become somewhat stylized. By then ritual vessels were being made in central China; but while following the shapes and designs of the existing long-standing tradition, artists were using lacquered wood instead of bronze, and their ornamentation suited that medium. Much later the same shapes were adopted for certain ceramic wares which were being made not for purposes of ritual but purely as decorative objects, wherein a craftsman could display his virtuosity.

Within the porticoes and outer pavilions of a temple, as well as in the innermost recesses of the main halls of worship, stood the statues that attuned the mind of those attending a service. Probably the Buddha was first represented in sculptured form at Gandhāra (north-west India), whose artistic styles combined features of both the Hellenistic and the Indian traditions; and it was from Gandhāra that such figures first came to China. The eye would gaze on figures of saints or devout worshippers; or perhaps on that of the Buddha, seated or reclining. There were statues of the many attendant Lohan, or Bodhisattva, imparting their blessings to the world; or of Maitreya, the Buddha to come; or of the gentle and comforting presence of Guanyin, goddess of mercy.

Statues of these types were placed in the Buddhist temples that arose in large numbers from the fourth century AD onwards. Outsize examples survive in the shrines and statues carved in the living rock of the cliff face, at Yungang (Shanxi) or Longmen (Henan) from around AD 500 onwards. So far from being intended as idols or objects of worship, they were designed to personify some of the ideals that characterized the faith, such as detachment and tranquillity, or freedom from desire. The heads of the holiest of the figures are framed within a mandala, and the hands are posed or the fingers are outstretched in symbolic attitudes; the drapery of the robes carries its own message of dignity, and the device of the lotus recurs on pedestal and column.

Many of the caves of Dunhuang, at the extreme north-western tip of Chinese territory, were furnished and decorated for Buddhist worship, and their frescoes carry similar figures. Some paintings

8.   *Design carved in stone from tomb no. 1 Dahuting (see Fig. 5) c. AD 200;*
1.8 by 1.1 metres, with symbols of four of the Five Phases (dragon, bird, tiger
and warrior), real and mythological animals and a cloud-scroll pattern; there
are no signs of Buddhist iconography

represent scenes such as the Buddha's birth, or the teaching of Amitābha, and such subjects also appear on carvings made in the round on the living rock, as at Maijishan (Ganzu province). At a few famous sites sculptors carved figures of the types described, in giant dimensions that were doubtless intended to dwarf the human beings who faced them and to remind them of their place in the scale of creation.

Imposing, majestic and often frightening figures greet the visitor to a Daoist temple; for if they were set up as warlike guardians whose duty lay in warding off evil-doers, they could equally well deter mortals who were intent on other pursuits. Some of these figures portrayed a particular spirit and his calling, or acted as a reminder of his powers. But the innermost sanctuaries could house the most important and highly respected of figures, the supreme lords of heaven and earth, or Laozi, the saintly teacher and mystic to whom the ideals of Daoist religion were ascribed. Flowers stand in vases on the altars of these shrines; dim lamps light up the recesses, which frame the statues of the holy ones, garlanded in banners of scarlet or gold.

Beliefs in different forms of immortality played a significant part in determining the provision of the funerary furnishings that were buried in a tomb. Demands for suitable items taxed the ingenuity of the artist and stimulated his imagination, in an attempt to evoke ancient myth and incorporate it in fresh designs. Fortunately a few examples survive of such work, including the painting that was made, on silk, as part of the means of wafting the soul of the countess of Dai to the next world, in about 168 BC. The painting shows the countess, or her soul, ascending through successive stages to attain immortality; she is seen passing through a vase, which represents the Island of the Vase (or Penglai), known to lie in the eastern seas as the gateway to eternal life. Formally clothed in her fineries, and attended by her acolytes, the countess finally passes through the gates with their stern guardians to the upper world of paradise; and the unnamed artist envisaged her casting off her mortal coil, as she embarks on her new phase of existence.

Other types of talisman helped to escort the dead to the paradise of the Queen Mother of the West. Reliefs or frescoes show the Queen escorted by her attending servants; the hare busily engaged in compounding the elixir of eternal life from the herbs that have been gathered; the three birds who wait upon the Queen to do her bidding; or the fox, proudly waving the nine tails that proclaim him to be an animal of good augury.

THE DEMANDS OF EMPEROR AND COURT

Palaces enabled emperors to display their majesty and wealth; they provided a venue for the most beautiful objects that the provinces could supply and the tribute that the leaders of unassimilated peoples would render. They must comprise a series of halls where audience could be granted to those paying homage, and they must impress such subordinate subjects with the grandeur of the imperial way of life. Large courtyards were necessary for the parades and colourful processions in which large numbers of officials, monks or attendants took part. In addition, the palace must be large enough to include living quarters for the imperial family and their retinues, as well as for the many eunuchs who supervised domestic arrangements and acted as trusted advisers to the emperor or his consort.

Imperial palaces were constructed on a symmetrical plan, with a strict alignment to the points of the compass. Courtiers, officials or priests who took part in civil or religious ceremonies could thus take up the position and face the direction duly specified for the occasion, while the Son of Heaven himself faced due south. The design of the palace contrived to set it apart from the world, to form its own self-contained unity; its external walls both protected the emperor from intrusion and acted as an impenetrable barrier from which he could not escape. For the buildings set him in his rightful place, at the centre of the cosmos, where his duty as the personified link with Heaven lay. Should that link be severed, his place must needs be elsewhere, and for this reason, when the last of the Ming emperors determined (1644) that suicide was his only option, he chose to leave his palace precincts, to make an end on the artificial hillock raised on the north side of the compound, no longer encapsulated in the sacred centre of the world.

Balustrades that are set below the audience chambers could carry symbols of the emperor's duty, such as a sundial that related his charge on earth to the presence of the heavens, or standard weights and measures whereby he imposed fair dealings among his peoples. Other beautiful and valuable objects that acted as symbols of dynastic authority derived from mythology or official practice. Originally it had been claimed that nine bronze tripods stood as the material symbols of the authority vested in Yu the Great, founder of the Xia dynasty; an artist's representation of such tripods at once called the myth to mind and suggested where true dynastic authority lay.

Chinese artists designed the seals of jade with which an emperor signified his approval of a document; possession of these 'sacred instruments' was essential to vindicate a claim to reign, fulfilling the same purpose as the crowns of Europe's kings. For other purposes emperors and others depended on the jade carvers' art to produce the sceptres that graced some of the ceremonies of court; artists who worked in other media designed the splendid golden robes used on imperial occasions, emblazoned with dragon or cloud, phoenix or mountain, as prescribed for an emperor's use.

Within the halls and living quarters of the palace only the choicest creations could be used as furnishings or for embellishment, whether they were of jade, lacquered wood or gilt bronze. From early imperial times special agencies had been appointed to collect the finest examples that they could find of paintings, statues or figures of birds and animals. Sometimes artists were required to express the needs, depict the possessions or vaunt the successful achievements of an emperor. Paintings of court favourites and imperial consorts were made to order during the Han dynasty; possibly an artist was once commissioned to represent the scene of victory that Han arms had won on a field of battle; others were ordered to prepare reliefs of horse and groom to adorn the tomb of Tang Taizong (reigned 626–49), as a reminder of the active part that he had taken in affairs of state and on campaign. Just as a prose-poem (fu) enabled a literary man to describe the glories of a court, so could a painting be used to show the majesty of an emperor graciously engaged in giving audience.

THE HUMANITIES AND THE PURSUIT OF BEAUTY

Painting and calligraphy were the art forms on which scholar officials would engage in their hours of pleasure. Along with poetry they were the accomplishments that were expected of educated courtiers and officials, and a few emperors who have been glad to exhibit their virtuosity have left examples of their handiwork behind them. For it was these arts which afforded opportunity for personal creativity and for the pursuit of beauty for beauty's sake; brush and silk or paper scroll enabled an official to turn away from the duties of administration and to explore a new outlook on the civilization of which he formed part.

It is in landscape painting that some of the characteristics of Chinese art appear most conspicuously. In the long vertical scrolls of the Song painters the eye proceeds on its journey up the mountain, through the woods or along the rivers until it reaches the apex; some painters unrolled long horizontal scrolls, with which to guide their viewers through a landscape and its details and the occupations of man that they frame. Human figures are placed in the context of their natural surroundings and reduced to their proper size and strength by the towering cliffs of the mountain, or the fast eddies of the stream. In the rugged landscapes that often evoke the Yangzi river and its gorges, the interplay of sky, land and water blends with the detail and delicacy of trees and flowers, animals and birds, to lend Chinese painting its distinctive characteristic as compared with the arts of other cultures.

As the strength of dynasties declined and the vigour of societies gave way to decadence, so too could the freshness of Chinese painting suffer eclipse. The art was practised on a large scale by a large number of artists, and it cannot be expected that all would be able to maintain the highest standards of the day. There arose a tendency to repeat themes, or a failure to treat them with originality. Blossoming trees, boats riding the lake, pavilions nestling in the hills could be juxtaposed without essential connection, to act as no more than decorative devices. None the less most artists retained their mastery of detail, partly thanks to the training which they had received. This had included work on copy books which gave examples of bamboo, or other leaf, peony or other blossom, with which the apprentice could master his technique and be ready to embellish his painting.

Portraiture took as its subjects the holy sages who had mastered the *dao*. Or perhaps figures of mythology were depicted to illustrate an ethical homily; and emperors are painted wearing their robes of state. In most of these figures it is the action or pose of the subject which is of greater importance that his personal features, and it is only in the later centuries, of the Ming and Qing periods, that painters began to exploit their medium and their skills to depict character. Some figures are shown idealized, as worshippers at a shrine; others as officials of state, attending to their business. Some of the more interesting examples of portraits came from the hand of Giuseppe Castiglione (1688–1766), who worked in both Chinese and western styles. Known as Lang Shining, this Italian Jesuit was one of the westerners who were commissioned to practise their art at the Qing court. In addition to his well-known scenes of horses, his paintings include portraits of the Qianlong emperor (who reigned 1736–95), seen in audience or in the company of his concubines, or on horseback with his troops, witnessing a hunt.

The characters of Chinese writing lend themselves to artistic treatment far more readily, and with a wider range of variation, than the letters of a western script, and fine calligraphy has long been acknowledged as a mark of distinction. Like painting, the art was dependent on a mastery of the brush; it was practised on silk and paper, or engraved on tablets of stone. Carefully written characters could form an integral part of a painting, where they explained details of the work or added a proud note of ownership or appreciation. Authors could pay a compliment to their patrons by inviting them to write the title pages of their books, in fine characters which would be reproduced through the medium of the block-print boards. Wooden notice-boards bearing characters in large scale were affixed for visitors to identify the name of a hall that they were entering in a palace or a temple; and special efforts were made to engrave the text of an epitaph stele, which applauded the deeds of the dead, with particular attention to the beauty of the script.

For certain purposes calligraphers reproduced a text in old-style characters, which had become obsolete by the start of the imperial age, and in so doing they were deliberately straining after the effect of archaism. But more usually they wrote the characters that had been evolved in the Han period and which remained in use until the simplifications of the script of the twentieth century. Five different genres or styles may be discriminated, ranging from those that are highly regular and formal to those that are cursive and decorative. The resulting wide spectrum, from the classical to the romantic, allowed for an interplay of the influences of *li* and *dao*. Texts written to convey the pronouncements of an official, or the texts of an approved classical work were best written in clear, bold characters whose formality matched the content. Notes inscribed in the same styles would accompany paintings which took as their theme an expression of the Confucian ideals. The flourishes and sinuous strokes of the cursive or 'grass' styles enabled poet or artist to express his personality and give vent to his individual reactions to his surroundings.

The combination of artistic and literary skills is seen in the illustrations made to accompany certain books, and reproduced therein by woodcut. Surviving examples from the Ming and Qing periods concern the flora and fauna to be observed in strange lands; odd creatures that take their place in mythology; paragons of behaviour who exemplify the moral values of Confucian teaching; scenes and personalities of the long novels; or mechanical devices used in the daily occupations of farm, waterway and workshop.

THE NEEDS OF DAILY LIFE

Sericulture, or the production of silk, depends on the long and skilled processes of planting orchards of mulberry, nurturing the silkworm (*Bombyx mori*) in the different phases of its life cycle and spinning its product, the longest thread made by nature, to form the most delicate of all textiles. Such processes demand considerable time and energy, and the product is therefore expensive; while the material used by most mortals for clothing derived from hemp (and later cotton), silk long featured almost as a symbol of luxurious extravagance, whose use was usually restricted to the higher reaches of society.

The origins of silk posed a mystery, which is reflected in mythology. According to some accounts it was one of the gifts of those culture heroes whose skills had moulded Chinese society and distinguished its way of life from that of the steppes. According to one legend, a strange incident resulted in the discovery of a particularly valuable type of silk. A lonely girl had promised her horse that she would wed him, if he could but bring back her father from the wars. When the horse succeeded in doing so, the girl went back on her word; her father slew the horse and left his hide to dry in the sun. But the hide took revenge for its late master, wrapping itself around the girl and whisking her off to the forest. Once settled in the branches of the trees, girl and hide were transformed into silkworms, whose threads were so infinitely superior to those of other breeds that the women of the neighbourhood deliberately collected them for farming.

Certainly silk was being produced in the Shang period, and it may well have originated at an earlier time. Technical advances were achieved in the Warring States period (481 or 403–221 BC), and the material evidence that has come to hand in recent decades testifies to the fine products of the Han period. A critic of the first century BC who was castigating the extravagance of the times pointed specifically to the fineries of the rich. Some of the silk (both in the bale and as made-up clothing) that has been found in Han tombs recently is in monochrome; some includes two or more bands of different colours; but the quality is seen to best advantage in the patterned weaves, with their cloud-like curls, or the interplay of lozenge and floreate decoration. Some patterns included sets of four written characters, repeated endlessly with a recurring message of felicity. The new types of loom that had been introduced at the time and which are depicted in a few stone reliefs were doubtless responsible for these fineries. In addition, silk formed a medium for the painter with his brush, or the embroiderer with her needle.

Silks of the Tang period sometimes carry the same style and details of decoration that appear on other media, such as bronze mirrors.

圖絲治

9. *Silk-reeling; woodcut illustration (1637) from a manual of crafts, occupations and technology by Song Yingxing (the* Tian gong kai wu*)*

A favourite device was the circular medallion, in which a pair of birds or animals confront one another, encircled by a border that symbolizes pearls. Some of the Tang looms turned out cloth patterned with birds or leaves that might have come from the hand of a painter, accompanied by floreate devices that fill the background. Rich colours and elaborate patterns characterize the silks of the later dynasties.

Emperors performed a ceremony in which they personally set their hands to the plough in order to encourage the pursuit of agriculture in the new season. In the same way empresses took part in a rite that symbolized their sponsorship of sericulture. Along with the growth of cereal crops, the production of silk was seen as one of China's basic and essential occupations, taking priority over the secondary work of manufacture and trade. Silk also featured in China's relations with the peoples of the steppe or even further afield. Silk bales formed the principal material with which it was possible to appease a potential enemy and deter him from raiding Chinese territory; and when, in about 100 BC, trading routes were extended from central China to the north-west, they allowed passage to caravans which carried bales of silk for sale, some of which were destined to reach the Mediterranean world.

Legends tell of the carriage west of the secrets of silk manufacture. According to one, which derived from China, a Chinese princess was once required, for political reasons, to remove to the western regions, there to wed a leader from the steppes. Determined not to be cut off from future supplies of clothing, she concealed silkworms in the tresses of her hair, with the intention of rearing them in her distant exile. Another account, this time from the Greek side (Procopius), tells of monks who, on their return to Europe, carried the precious creatures in the staffs which supported them as they trod their weary way. Justinian's attempt to impose a monopoly on silk production in 552 suggests that by then it had achieved a significant place in the economy of the Byzantine empire.

Ceramic wares feature in Chinese life from the neolithic periods onwards. They appear in the first instance as vessels to store foods and liquids, or for use in cooking; later they took the place of bronze wares for religious purposes, and in time they came into regular use as tableware and articles of furniture such as flower vases or stools.

Many of the neolithic sites of the west and north-west included large earthenware jars, somewhat bulbous in shape, and decorated with geometric patterns in black on a maroon background. Other sites produced somewhat characteristic wares of a different type, black and lustrous. By the Han period earthenware vessels were being coated with a green glaze that gave them a sheen; others, which had not been so treated, carried a band of painted decoration. A number of the types turned out at that time were shaped after bronze models of earlier periods; simultaneously the kilns were producing terracotta models of homestead and farm in miniature, to be buried in tombs for use in the next world. By the Tang period realistic models of horse and rider, or camel and his pack of merchants or musicians, were being designed with greater attention to detail, and with a lavish use of hard colours, such as green, yellow and dark brown; if the effect was vivid, at times it could also be garish.

The regularity and attention to form that were the keynote of much of the Song age are seen in its porcelains no less than in its attention to philosophy and its institutions. The age produced ceramic wares of classic shapes, whose effect rests on their proportions and their deeply satisfying slender forms. New techniques resulted in the production of glazed porcelains of higher quality, on which the skilful use of monochrome showed to full advantage, in place of the gaudy colours of the previous age. But with the introduction of cobalt blue in the fourteenth century a new chapter opened in the decorative arts. Kilns such as those of Jingdezhen (in the modern province of Jiangxi) were turning out new designs, resting on a bold use of dark blue on a white background, and for long this style was practised with a vigour and freshness, before giving way to monotonous repetition.

The eighteenth century saw the evolution of yet different techniques, in which enamelled wares were able to carry the details of bird, flower or tree in the same way as they were incorporated in paintings. So arose the different style of *famille verte, famille rose, famille noire* or *famille jaune*, so called after the dominant colour that formed the background. By now Chinese ceramic products were making their way to Europe, at times in great quantities; large services of tableware were exported to the Ottoman court at Constantinople; plates and dishes were being specially designed to meet the taste and needs of the western markets, sometimes incorporating coats of arms of some of Europe's noble houses.

Other artists and craftsmen were practising their skills in other media, as may be seen in lacquerwares and the precious metals. When applied as a paint to wood, lacquer – the sap drawn from the tree *Rhus vernicifera* – serves two purposes; it renders it waterproof and it provides a surface for decoration. Repeated coats are necessary to achieve the most beautiful results, marked by an evenness and a sparkle which shows the contrasting colours to best advantage. Fine examples of this art have been preserved from the Warring States period, largely from the Yangzi valley. Thanks to the efforts of the tomb-builders to seal their structures from moisture, lacquered plates, dishes, cups and toilet-boxes have often been kept in an excellent state of preservation for over two thousand years, still retaining their decorative patterns of brilliant scarlet and black. These often combine the curvilinear strokes of a brush with a geometric background in a manner that is both balanced and yet suggestive of the less restricted way of life of that region. From the Yuan period onwards lacquer was used in a somewhat different way; it formed a coating which enhanced the delicate patterns carved by master craftsmen on wooden boxes or other items of domestic furniture. The finest examples of this art date from the Ming period.

Possibly on account of the great value that was attached to jade and its properties, the products of the goldsmith and the silversmith feature more rarely in Chinese than in western collections of treasure; possibly the comparative shortage of gold and silver from the later dynasties is due to the practical use to which silver was put for coinage, or, in the case of gold, as the casing that covered a Buddhist statue. Exceptionally, recent finds have included a number of cups, bowls and jugs of the Tang dynasty, which may have been buried for safety when the great rebellion of An Lushan broke out in 755. The patterns include animals, or birds enclosed by a floral motif. In view of the cosmopolitan nature of society at Chang'an in the eighth century, it is hardly surprising that Sassanian and other influences from Central Asia have been detected in these beautiful pieces. More frequently the art of the metallurgists is seen in wares of *cloisonné* enamel. Known from the Yuan period, this medium was widely worked in the Ming and Qing dynasties; colours vary from bright yellow to a sombre blue, and the surfaces of vase or platter are interlaced with naturalistic or geometric patterns. Since the nineteenth century the medium has frequently been used to make the trinkets that are designed for European tastes and tourists' markets.

*

Precise periodization can hardly apply to the arts and their continually evolving changes, but it is possible to point to a few major influences that were brought to bear at specific times and which led to innovation or new themes. Jade is first seen in the form of material symbols thought to confer a spiritual blessing or to enhance the dignity of kings; eventually it came to serve the cause of decoration, and the stark purity of early designs in this medium gave way to the virtuosity of the carvers' skills. The growth of the bronze industry produced new styles of vessel used for religious purposes; Buddhism required or stimulated new forms of statuary and architecture. The traders who came to China from the west along the Silk Roads left their mark on Chinese taste; the discovery of new types of glaze, and

图一二 墓1北耳室西壁的宴饮图 (摹本)

10.   Banqueting scene; stone engraving from tomb no. 1 Dahuting (see Fig. 5)
c. AD 200; 1.5 by 1.1 metres

then of cobalt, transformed the creations of the potter.

A few conspicuous characteristics mark the contrast between the Chinese love of regularity and convention, and the yearning for individual expression. The delicate refinement and artistry of the Shang bronzes could tend to appear formal when compared with the exuberance of some of the figures from the Yangzi valley. Many of the models found in Han tombs derived from shopwork, and Han sculpture tended to adhere to well-worn themes; the sculptures of the succeeding centuries owed their individuality to Buddhist influence. The unrestrained use of bright colours in Tang ceramics contrasts with the purity of style and insistence on proportion in the wares of the Song period. Ming's contribution lay in the vigorous blue-and-white porcelains, to be followed by the repetitive decoration of the latter part of the Qing age.

Decadence may sometimes be observed; the refinement seen in the bronze vessels of the Shang period was followed in later centuries by crudities. The symbols that had been incorporated in their correct form on Han mirrors came to be abused as elements of decoration; jade had been prized as a medium that conferred spiritual, and then material, blessings, before it was cherished for purposes of ornament;

and those elements of the world of nature which a Song painter had used creatively took their place later as the stylized or lifeless fill-in of a background. It remains an open question how far individual talent was able to shake free of the conventions and needs of palace, office or temple, or to what extent a devotion to tradition stifled initiative.

XVI

THE ADVANCEMENT OF SCIENCE
AND ITS APPLICATIONS

In many respects China was the first of the great civilizations to exploit the gifts of nature effectively, to solve some of the basic problems of everyday life, and to devise mechanical aids to ease human labour; and some Chinese discoveries were of sufficient importance to alter the character of living fundamentally. Some of the fruits of this inventiveness have inescapably appeared already in an account of the Chinese achievement; for they resulted in the production of paper (from at least the first century AD), the printed book (ninth century), gunpowder (ninth century) and the magnetic compass (eleventh century). To these may be added the early appearance of cast iron (from the fourth century BC) and a conspicuous example of mechanical skills in Su Song's (1020–1101) water-driven clockwork, with its devices to display the hours of the day, its armillary sphere and its celestial globe. Chinese inventiveness and application also produced those finely finished ceramics and delicately woven textiles that soon became the envy of the rest of the world. In a number of cases other cultures have been glad to borrow such results and the processes whereby they came about, and thereby to enrich their own life-styles in a sudden and unexpected way.

Much of the story of the interchange of ideas and skills between east and west has been unfolded; much remains yet to unravel; and as such studies have developed they have given rise to a number of questions. A number of scholars have concluded that whereas up to perhaps 1500 China's understanding of nature, her appreciation of the heavens and her use of mechanical devices was considerably in advance of those of Europe, thereafter it was Europe which drew ahead. As has been observed, China enjoyed two contradictory but yet complementary advantages as compared with Europe; first, that of the political unity and imperial organization that she achieved from time to time; and secondly, that of the dispersal of intellectual effort and the local experimentation that occurred in the intervals of such unity and which could later be applied on an imperial scale. It may therefore be asked why China did not develop a study of the pure sciences spontaneously, without the stimulus brought from elsewhere in the nineteenth and twentieth centuries. If it is agreed that China's results derived largely from practical experiment rather than theoretical abstraction, the question arises of the particular intellectual trends or circumstances in which Chinese inventiveness thrived, and whether the traditional political and social fabric inhibited the growth of scientific thought. It need hardly be stressed that such questions are more easily raised than answered.

SOME BASIC ACHIEVEMENTS

The scope of Chinese scientific enquiry and the extent of its results are far too wide to permit more than allusion to a few examples which demonstrate the early progress that was made and the attention that was paid to practical considerations.

A preoccupation with time has been noticeable in a number of aspects of religious and official practice. It featured in many of the questions that diviners put to the turtle shells or yarrow stalks; it is seen in the government's responsibility for promulgating an accurate calendar; and correct timing was of vital importance both to emperors who hoped that their dispensation would accord with the rhythms of the universe and to officials who were obliged to adhere to schedules in implementing their duties. In intellectual terms this concern necessarily stimulated attention to mathematics and astronomy.

Early Chinese mathematics is characterized by its dependence on algebraic terms to denote general relationships, rather than on expression by means of geometry. The *Jiu zhang suan shu* or *Textbook of Calculations in Nine Sections* is probably the world's earliest comprehensive treatise on arithmetic. The work drew on results achieved during the Warring States period (481 or 403–221 BC); it reached its present form of compilation towards the start of the Christian era, and it deeply affected Chinese mathematical thought thereafter. By the third century AD the book's identification of π as 3 had been refined to 3.14159. For the immediate purposes of speedy calculation, the abacus was probably in general use by the fifteenth century. It had been evolved from considerably earlier origins.

From an early period gnomons were used to mark the position of the shadows cast by the sun, and thereby to permit a record to be made of the passage of time. The gnomon was fixed to a square plate, on which a graduated circle had been marked, and with which an observer could measure the interval that had passed since sunrise. Instead of the twenty-four hours of the western system, the Chinese divided day and night into twelve double hours, which were together further divided into a total of 100 periods. From the Han period at least, a form of water clock was also used to measure time and its passage.

Early astronomical observation depended perhaps on the use of the sighting tube, or on a pair of gnomons whose line provided a means of identifying the movements of certain stars. From perhaps the fourth century BC catalogues of the stars were being compiled in lists which no longer survive. From the first century BC the armillary sphere was taking shape, with its sets of rings that would eventually make it possible to observe the position of a particular star. A report of AD 89 refers to the obliquity of the ecliptic, which was then calculated at an equivalent of 24°; early in the fourth century AD Chinese astronomers had discovered the principle of the precession of the equinoxes; as far as may be known, observation of the stellar explosion of 1054 which gave rise to the Crab Nebula in Taurus was recorded only by Chinese and Japanese astronomers.

Experiments in chemistry and alchemy arose from mixed motives, not least the hopes of producing the elixir of eternal life and of rendering base metals into gold. The masters of these practices developed special equipment with which certain substances could be sealed and certain conditions of temperature maintained; and indeed control of temperature was essential in metallurgy and the manufacture of ceramic wares. A knowledge of chemistry was of considerable significance in the steps taken to preserve the human body from decomposition after death, as is well known from the successful way in which this was achieved, just before 168 BC. By the Tang period alcohol was being distilled. The properties of a proto-gunpowder, which included sulphur and saltpetre, with its readiness to ignite, were perhaps discovered by accident in the third or fourth century. Gunpowder itself was first used for military purposes, in weapons such as grenades, from the tenth century; in the early part of the twelfth century, as has been discovered recently, it was being used with bombards, the earliest form of cannon.

From texts found in a tomb of the second century BC much may be learned of the use of herbs for treating diseases, and of early distinctions that were drawn in diagnosis. Further information is forthcoming in the biographical accounts of a few physicians whose skills were sufficiently well known to merit recognition and inclusion in the Standard Histories. Hua Tuo, of the second century AD, was an accomplished surgeon who may have been able to apply some measure of anaesthesia to his patients. He also practised moxibustion and acupuncture, which had been evolving in the previous centuries. A treatise on these two subjects by Huangfu Mi (died 282) describes them both analytically and from the point of view of practical treatment. By the Song period Chinese physicians had discovered the secret of variolation – an early form of vaccination.

A SCIENTIFIC OUTLOOK AND ITS LIMITATIONS

Separate schools of physics, chemistry, biology or medicine were not included among the traditional institutes of learning or education; and the structure of Chinese society could not give rise to the growth of a scientific profession. Advances in knowledge were due to the initiative of a few pioneers, whether officials or not, whose interests lay in a number of different fields or disciplines. These included mathematics, with its application to astronomy and harmonics; observation of the phenomena of the heavens; the study of the human body and of remedies to cure its ills; the study of plants and pharmaceutics; and that of the physical, chemical and biological changes that are wrought in the phenomena of nature. Most of these pioneers must remain nameless, along with the larger number of those who applied discoveries and inventions to the problems of daily life on a major scale.

There is evidence enough to show how the habits of observation and readiness to take measurements had grown up from early times; and there were those who sought to formulate theories or hypotheses, and to see the value of seeking verification by controlled experiment; the full realization of the need to combine these approaches was finally reached in the nineteenth or twentieth century.

Traditional scholastic method and the love of categories were peculiarly well suited to the collection and classification of information. The unitary view of the universe, as consisting of the three interdependent estates of heaven, earth and man, lent support to attempts to understand the order of nature. From early times explanations of the seen world and its phenomena were conceived as a search for unity, or *dao*; and they were conditioned by the significance attached to the rhythms and cycles whereby changes were wrought; such cycles had been conceived in terms of either the Five Phases or the sixty-four hexagrams; eventually they were explained within the compass of a binary system, as formulated by Shao Yong (1001–77).

Within such schemes there ran certain fundamental ideas, such as that of the inevitable sequence of birth, death and rebirth; or the inherent ability of one living creature to be transformed into another of a different type; or the supposition that like things attract one another and repel their opposites. The concepts of Neo-Confucian thought, as formulated in the twelfth century, likewise affected the view of matter. For all the myriad things of the phenomenal world were seen as partaking of two elements: *li*, form or principle, which gave a particular object its character; and *qi*, energy, which controlled its physical shape and gave it power of movement; *shu*, the inherent numerical property, controlled the proportions of the object, and its relations to its neighbours.

In the absence of a compelling monotheism there was no insistence on the divine nature of creation, or on an essential distinction between creator and created. Creation was seen as a continuous process, which the observer could witness around him; without the shackles of received dogma or fundamentalist belief there was a readiness to pose questions that could strike at the root of reality. The Christian west has been beset by a greater need to reconcile the calls of faith and reason than that felt in the east; China has perhaps lacked the urge to formulate arguments and frame an analysis that such a conflict has stimulated.

The development of science owed much to the early tradition of maintaining records, whether of the phenomena observed in the skies or of the acts of established civil authorities on earth. The early emergence of printing, the skilled engraving of illustrations on wood blocks and the compilation of encyclopaedic works contributed substantially to the preservation and dissemination of knowledge and to refinements of classification.

Certain factors, however, which were fundamental to the growth of Chinese culture tended to reduce the scope or need for the type of analysis that moulded some of Europe's early philosophies. Reference has already been made to the absence of a compelling, rigorous search for definition, or of a traditional love of rhetoric, which did much to induce a respect for rationality in the west. The training that was given in imperial institutions was directed to prepare men for careers in the civil service, rather than to provide them with an all-round education; with its limited interest in practical skills, it could hardly engender a desire *rerum cognoscere causas*. For schooling was designed with an eye to the examinations; at its worst it could descend to learning texts by heart and to a readiness to repeat the accepted, orthodox interpretations of a passage. Pupils were enjoined to follow the opinions of the masters, without seeking explanations that might be branded as heterodox.

Historians were expected to record certain events, including those of natural disaster, in terms of the warnings that Heaven had vouchsafed to the ruler of mankind, and the treatment of such disturbances as omens may well have inhibited a sense of causation. Similarly, should an historian or other writer wish to criticize or protest at a decision of state, he must do so in veiled terms, if he wished to avoid a charge of *lèse-majesté*. As a study of history formed an integral part of the training of officials, here too there was room for stifling the growth of objectivity.

One of the achievements of the Han dynasty had been the establishment that imperial government was the norm; maintenance of such government, with the acknowledged retention of the mandate of Heaven, was the ambition of all pretenders to power until 1911. But despite modifications in the concept and its institutions, few questions were raised regarding some of its basic assumptions, such as the authority, rights and obligations of emperor, official or member of the public. Until the seventeenth century philosophers had rarely been called to set out a vindication of the operation of government by arguing that it was based on concepts of justice; in this respect too a failure to question basic principles may well have blunted a sense of enquiry.

Reliance on basic schemes may sometimes have been taken to excess, to the point that the observation of phenomena could become inhibited by adherence to set categories, within the scope of preconceived notions. In this way, for example, emotions, tastes and even parts of the human body could at times be so classified that they must accord either with the scheme of the Five Phases, or with a different scheme that depended on groups of six.

In addition, the attitude of established authority to Daoist activities and establishments was of some importance, in view of the major part that the latter played in scientific or proto-scientific experiment. Distrust arose from the Daoist rejection of the disciplines and institutions needed to control an empire, and from the frequency with which potential dissidents could live out their lives under the protection of a Daoist monastery. Exercises in alchemy, when practised in such circumstances, could easily be regarded as a threat to the validity of an official's administration. In a prevailing belief in the validity of many types of occult art, it was perfectly possible for men of letters to combine such modes of enquiry with a trust in Confucian learning; but retention of such beliefs could also discourage a search for rational understanding.

MOMENTS OF ADVANCE

Despite these difficulties, advances in scientific exploration have proceeded continuously, affected but little by major dynastic change. For a number of branches of knowledge it is possible to identify a moment of breakthrough, to name an individual whose personal genius or initiative accounted for a major discovery, or to suggest a period when activity was at its most productive point. The contributors to the *Huainanzi*, a text which was completed by 139 BC, explored the workings of nature in terms of the overriding unity of the *dao*. It was in the fifth to the ninth centuries that the most effective experiments in alchemy, and perhaps chemistry, took place, during the heyday of the Daoist religious establishments. There was a marked degree of attention to astronomy during the Song age, along with many other manifestations of intellectual brilliance; Chinese mathematics may have reached its highest point in the thirteenth century, with Qin Jiushao's (*c.* 1202–*c.* 1261) treatise that concerned the solution of cubic and other equations, and his work on the properties of circles and triangles.

Along with those many men of genius whose names were never recorded, there are some which should not escape recognition, in so far as their achievements pointed the way to new directions of scientific enquiry. Wang Chong (AD 27–*c.* 100) was a man of an independent frame of mind, ready to question the received dogma of his contemporaries. In his collected essays (the *Lunheng*, or *Disquisitions*) he sought to explain the reasons for natural phenomena such as a thunder-storm, and suggested how similar conditions could be reproduced with the use of fire, water and a furnace. But Wang Chong lived and worked outside the approved circles of learning; for long the radical way in which he looked at the problems of the natural world attracted but little attention.

Ge Hong (283–343) is known as one of the pioneers of alchemy who was thinking, teaching and working at a time when the Daoist religious establishments were gaining considerably in popularity. His written account of his ideas, entitled the *Baopuzi*, includes much that concerns the production of the elixir in its various forms, and the alchemist's hope of bringing about the interaction of *qi* (vital but invisible energy) with the material elements assigned to each of the Five Phases. And no account of Chinese science can omit reference to Zhu Xi (1130–1200). A pioneer in metaphysics, he drew together a number of his predecessors' ideas to form a comprehensive system of being and urged the importance of examining the nature of all the myriad objects of the created world.

Matteo Ricci's arrival in China in 1583 heralded a new departure in Chinese science. The ideas and inventions that he and his successor colleagues of the Jesuit Order introduced were quite new to the Chinese mind; once they had accepted that there was value in these concepts, the Chinese insisted that they should be described under the general term of the 'New Science' rather than that of 'Western Science'.

The Jesuits' main purpose lay in winning the souls of their hosts; to do so they chose the long-term plan of first impressing them with their intellectual powers, in order to gain their respect. This involved acquiring a familiarity with China's culture and history, so that they could support their arguments with Chinese ideas; it also involved demonstrating their own prowess and showing how this could benefit the work of the imperial order. Their task therefore lay in the practical help that they could offer rather than in the exposition of the theoretical side of European thought as it was then developing. They showed their superiority in the all-important matter of predicting eclipses; they applied the principles of geometry to an understanding of the motions of the planets; they introduced a circle which was divided into 360 rather than $365\frac{1}{4}$ degrees; and they set about the manufacture of clocks, telescopes and instruments used in observing the heavens. Owing to the doctrinal inhibitions under which they laboured, they were obliged to retain the concept of a geocentric universe until the middle of the eighteenth century.

Ricci himself died in 1610, witnessing the corruption and lack of stability that marked the final decades of the Ming dynasty. One of his more significant achievements may still be seen in the prints of the map of the world which he had prepared from 1584; this opened the eyes of his hosts to unimagined dimensions of the earth, and introduced them to names such as those of America with which they were as yet unfamiliar.

Father Adam Schall von Bell (1592–1666), who reached Macao in 1619, was called to Beijing in 1630 to assist in the work of regulating the calendar. In the year following the establishment of the Qing dynasty he was appointed director of the Astronomical Bureau, and he held that post until his death. In the meantime his missionary work had led him into an exposition of a fundamental difference between a Christian and a Chinese outlook. In a work which he published in 1626 he explained how the Christian God did not proceed from the Supreme Ultimate or from the primeval forces of *yin* and *yang*; rather was it God who had brought such things into being and commanded their operation. Father Schall also engaged in trying to convert the Shunzhi emperor (reigned 1644–61) to the Catholic faith.

Father Ferdinand Verbiest (1623–88) served as vice-president of the imperial Court of Mathematics from 1669, and the instruments that he made for the imperial observatory in the succeeding years may be seen in Beijing today. He followed the precedents set by his predecessors, by producing a more informative map of the world in 1674. In 1681 he supervised the manufacture of guns for the Qing armies, engaged at the time in campaigns against three Chinese dissidents, who were still challenging the authority of the Manchus. Father Verbiest published on a large scale in Latin, Manchu and Chinese; his works ranged from expositions of astronomy and the working drawings of his instruments to rebuttals of Chinese belief in occult powers and mantic practices. He was on familiar terms with the Kangxi emperor (reigned 1662–1722), being at one time engaged with him in daily discourse. Arrangements for his funeral were prescribed by the Board of Rites, in a manner deemed to be suitable for so highly honoured a guest.

In a treatise written in Chinese (*Kunyu tushuo*) that is dated in 1672, Verbiest set out to inform his readers of some of the facts, features and fables that they might encounter, should they venture beyond the limits of the Qing empire. He included illustrated descriptions of the Seven Wonders of the World, and of the strange animals to be seen in different parts of Europe, Asia, Africa and America. These latter can hardly have failed to fascinate any reader who was familiar with the *Classic of the Mountains and the Lakes* (*Shanhai jing*), parts of which were already some 1,500 years old by Verbiest's time. A new edition of this book, with a fine set of woodcut illustrations, had appeared in 1667; dare it be asked whether a copy had reached Verbiest's hands, and inspired him with the idea of providing Chinese readers with comparable material for the west?

The self-questioning and the attempts at reassessment that followed the collapse of the Ming dynasty (1644) stimulated intellectual movements which rested on a new appreciation of scientific method. The attitude is seen most conspicuously in the 'school of Han learning' (*Han xue*) and its methods of studying Chinese literature and history. In reaction against the intellectual habits of their predecessors, some scholars deliberately attempted to undertake an objective study of early texts and their real evidence, irrespective of the political implications that had grown around them or their use as instruments of philosophical speculation. The school of Han learning concentrated on the collection and examination of textual evidence of all types, drawn from a variety of sources; for its members wished thereby to elucidate the original meanings of the classical and other works, devoid of the interpretation to which they had been subjected by some two millennia of erudition. Some distrusted the work of writers as early as the Han period; others were prepared to use such work as a basis for their own studies.

Inductive reasoning was in this way applied to the problems of the authenticity of early writings or some of their chapters; the Qing scholars were looking for evidence of forgery or interpolation, in order to recover what they believed to be an accurate original text. They began the study of phonetics, in the hope of reconstituting ancient pronunciations and applying these to the problems of poetry; and by comparing information given in different sources, they hoped to correct some of the inconsistencies that were all too obvious in the Standard Histories of the dynasties. In respect of philosophy, they wished to dislodge Zhu Xi (1130–1200) and other scholars of the Song and Ming periods from the pre-eminent place which they had attained.

As might be expected, the school of Han learning met with protests and criticism. Its protagonists were accused of excessive pedantry, or of a failure to comprehend the basic content of the works which they were subjecting to such minute scrutiny. But notwithstanding the bitter disputes that arose between those who espoused the cause either of Song or of Han learning, the new school engaged the attention of some of the most acute minds of the period, and exercised a profound influence on the future of several branches of scholarship and science. Yan Ruoju (1636–74) spent thirty years in examining the authenticity of parts of the *Book of Documents*; Dai Zhen (1724–77) applied the comparative methods that were being tried for textual criticism to questions of phonetic changes of the language; he also embarked on a study of mathematics and astronomy. Cui Shu (1740–1816) tried to apply the same methods to clarify the tales of mythology and their mixed references to China's early paragon rulers. In his edition of the Thirteen Classics, Ruan Yuan (1764–1849) left a heritage of learning that has ever since been a source of information for all those who study those works.

*

Private pioneer and official sponsor alike contributed to the advance of science. Some discoveries arose as a result of individual genius, some perhaps as the accidental result of a chain of circumstances; and in their early stages they were probably exploited on a local level rather than on a major scale. But once the governors of mankind had learned of the new knowledge with its techniques and its potential benefits, they could command subordinates to put it to practical use in a grand manner, calling on the corporate manpower and plentiful material resources that provincial offices could command. In this way, perhaps, the kings of Shang had ordered the manufacture of their precious bronze vessels, and the authorities of the empires had exploited the printer's secrets; and as will be seen below (Chapter XVII), it was officials of state who were able to undertake a number of enterprises to control China's wayward waters and alleviate the effects of flood.

At the same time, experiments and enquiry proceeded, often thanks to those who spurned a paid post in government or who chose to describe their findings in private rather than in official publications. Yi Xing was the religious name adopted by a Buddhist monk who lived from 683 to 727. Among other achievements he translated some of the Sanskrit *sūtras* into Chinese, but his principal contribution lay within the fields of mathematics and astronomy. He detected errors in some of the old star catalogues, and had a set of new instruments constructed; and the Dayan calendar that he drew up in 727 was based on more accurate calculations than those of the past.

Shen Gua (1031–95) stands out by way of exception even in the singularly brilliant age of the Song dynasty. He indeed enjoyed an official career, in the course of which he supervised hydraulic works, the reclamation of land and the prevention of floods. But he was also a polymath investigator, ready to initiate research in many fields of enquiry, including music, medicine, geography, animal and plant life and military science. Of his numerous writings his *Jottings of the Brook of Dreams* (*Meng qi bi tan*) is perhaps the best known; and as the title implies, the work was not of a form that was intended for presentation to the throne or for scrutiny as an official document. It is a work which includes an individual's notes of topics that interested him; and these ranged from the origin of fossils, to the invention of printing by means of movable type.

Gu Yanwu (1613–82), whose name has appeared in these pages before, was a steadfast loyalist of the Ming house whose ruin he had the misfortune to witness. In obedience to his conscience, he refused to serve the house that had defeated that of his fathers, and spent much of his time after 1644 on horseback, riding around the provinces, and noting much that he had observed in his *Daily Record* (*Rizhilu*); the resulting diary is a mine of detailed information for China's topography. His use of evidence of all types, such as that of inscriptions, and his analytical approach to the practical problems of history had much in common with the new critique of the school of Han learning.

XVII

PROBLEMS OF LAND
AND WATER

Mythology and religious ritual reflect the problems and dangers that have beset the greater part of the peoples of China in their daily occupation of wresting a living from the soil and their constant need to take precautions against crop failure, drought or flood. Quite apart from the well-known tales of Yu the Great and Shennong (see Chapter VI), there are accounts of deities or others who commanded powers that spelt the safety or the ruin of the inhabitants, and who therefore required propitiation.

He Bo, Lord of the Yellow River, demanded each year a sacrifice of girls, that his wrath might be assuaged, and the practice of paying this toll survived until Han times; later the myth became amalgamated with that of Feng Yi, who was capable of causing the rain to fall in times of need. For the Yangzi River area, Li Bing, an historical personage whose feats of engineering will feature below, figures in a similar myth; he was the hero who put to death the monster or spirit of the river which likewise demanded human, and later animal, sacrifice. The tale includes an account of a fight in which Li Bing worsted a pair of water buffalo, and the theme was taken up in Chinese drama; eventually Li Bing became an object of worship himself. Along with Shennong, mythology tells of Yandi, the sovereign who taught mankind to sow the fields; he collected the seed that a pair of red birds had let fall from their beaks while in flight; there followed the tilling of the land and the opening up of virgin soil.

That the problems which lay behind these myths were ever present in the minds of emperors and their officials needs little emphasis. The distinction between the primary occupations (*ben*) of agriculture and sericulture and the secondary occupations (*mo*) of the artisans and the shopmen had been recognized long before the imperial age, and was asserted by statesmen of different political attitudes; and the prime importance of agriculture is stressed repeatedly in imperial edicts. The government's long dependence on revenue which was collected in kind necessarily involved an interest in conditions of land tenure. From time to time questions of principle and policy arose. Statesmen considered whether the possession of the land should be left free of controls, thus allowing free enterprise to bring larger and larger areas under the plough; or whether it was justifiable to encourage more abundant production by a policy of allocating the land on a basis of equality, or by ordering enforced migrations so as to bring more and more soil under cultivation. Officials of the early kingdoms and of the empires were also concerned in the allocation of conscript labour to construct and operate waterworks, whether for irrigation or transport; a provincial governor might perhaps win his promotion by the successful completion of such a project.

THE GROWTH OF CEREAL CROPS

With beginnings that are now traced back to perhaps 5000 BC, the cultivation of cereals has retained its significance as the keystone of China's economy. The extent of arable and worked land as compared with the size of the population has long made it necessary to derive as much produce as possible, and the comparatively small size of some of the landholdings has spurred the individual farmer to undertake ever greater efforts. From the second century BC critics and moralists contrasted the large estates that lay securely in the hands of the rich with the exiguous plots from which the greater part of the inhabitants must needs find their subsistence, with little chance of respite from the hard labour that was involved. But pious protest could not prevent wealthy or well-established families from acquiring large landholdings, and there were times when some of the Buddhist monasteries were able to do so. Such estates could support the expensive equipment or machinery that the small farmer could not afford to install. Such considerations were not without their political and social implications.

From early experiments in farming the land as intensively as possible there emerged techniques that have characterized the Chinese way of life. Many of the more important advances had already been achieved by the end of the Song period, when they were being applied not only in the northern terrain, but also in the Yangzi River valley and beyond; because of dynastic fortunes, palace and officials were now situated in lands with which they were not familiar, and they were required to apply their administrative and intellectual skills to supply the new needs of a rapidly growing population.

Dry-field farming, suitable for millet, was the general practice in the north; wet-field farming, suitable for rice, was the practice of the south. Wheat and barley, which had been introduced into China from elsewhere, were being cultivated by the Shang period. In the early stages of dry-field farming, seed was sown broadcast over the land, and perhaps the first major change of a radical nature came with the systematic use of ridges and furrows in which crops could be tended and controlled more efficiently. The initiative for this innovation is ascribed to an official named Zhao Guo, who served the Han court towards the beginning of the first century BC. He had his furrows ploughed to a depth and width of a foot (that is, 23 cm); once his seedlings had sprouted, he gave them stability by shovelling down the soil from the ridges, until eventually the surface of the field was even; and he planned to alternate the positions of ridge and furrow each year. Zhao Guo's method had the further advantage of providing protection against the parched conditions of drought. He was ordered to give instruction in its use, and his method was duly put into operation not only in the metropolitan area but also as far afield as the sponsored military colonies established in the extreme north-west tip of the empire.

Rice was grown in wet fields, and there soon emerged the traditional process of nurturing the seedlings in separate beds before transplanting them into the paddy fields; along with the rice crops, the water gave the farmer the opportunity to raise water chestnut, and to breed his ducks. From the sixth century farmers were aware of the advantages of rotating their crops and using the land for alternate types of harvest; they would grow wheat in the winter, to be followed by rice, indigo or vegetables such as cabbage in the summer. In both north and south, much of China's terrain lent itself to the construction of terraced plots along the hillsides, to be used for dry farming in the loess areas and wet farming in the south.

Early references to these methods show that they were known long before the Song period, when they were being practised extensively; and it was in the Song period that agricultural methods advanced conspicuously. The changes were due partly to the deliberate stimulus of the government, now paying closer attention than ever before to the conditions that prevailed in the Yangzi River valley and beyond. Even before the enforced move to the south in 1127, officials were proposing financial measures to help the farmer, who was all too prone to fall into debt when buying his seed, and failing to satisfy his creditors at harvest time if there had been a crop failure. The introduction of new varieties of fast-growing rice from Champa in the eleventh century enabled some farmers to practise double cropping, already known for some centuries, on a greatly increased scale, particularly in the south. By the twelfth century the population and its needs had been growing steadily, as a result of the concentration of the government at its new capital of Lin'an and the development of commerce and manufactures in the neighbouring cities. The use of new types of fertilizer and new methods of irrigation, together with the increased output that the farmer could get from his new strains, helped to alleviate conditions that could easily become critical.

The earliest farmers had used a simple digging stick to plant their seed, and considerable advances had taken place by the Han period. Iron was by now in much more general use than it had been hitherto; the moulds in which ploughshares had been cast and which have come to light recently show that a variety of types were in use, some being specially shaped so as to increase the depth of penetration. Oxen had been used to draw the plough, it is now believed, from the Longshan period of the neolithic era; reliefs and paintings found in Han tombs show the use of plough with oxen, man and boy, and it is evident that by then animals were being put to far greater use than previously. Han artisans had also produced a device attached to the plough that directed the seed to drop systematically and economically where it was required. From Han times, winnowing fans were constructed with handles operated by means of a crank; by Song these were in general use. In the meantime some of the rich Buddhist establishments of the Tang period had been able to build the large-scale equipment for milling that individual farmers were perhaps not able to afford.

In general terms, the closer the fields lay to the metropolitan area, the greater chance there would be of adopting new farming methods or acquiring new types of equipment, and it is only to be expected that agricultural practice was subject to considerable variation. Recent archaeological finds from Yunnan province show that somewhat primitive methods were in use there during the Former Han period, before the full force of Chinese culture had reached those remote regions. The finds included some tools that were made of bronze, but there were no iron goods which had been made specifically for work in the fields, and it is likely that tools made of bamboo were in general use. Rice formed the main crop, but irrigational methods were primitive, and the use of plough oxen was probably unknown until the start of the Christian era.

Effective conservation of the harvest was a matter of prime concern both to the private farmer and to the official tax collector, who needed to ensure that the goods taken from the fields would survive in a good state of preservation. Ideally, at times a government would hope to establish large stores of grain, which had been bought up cheap at a time of glut and would be ready for sale at a reasonable price in time of famine; in such a way the farmer would not suffer at a time of over-production, and the local population would not be

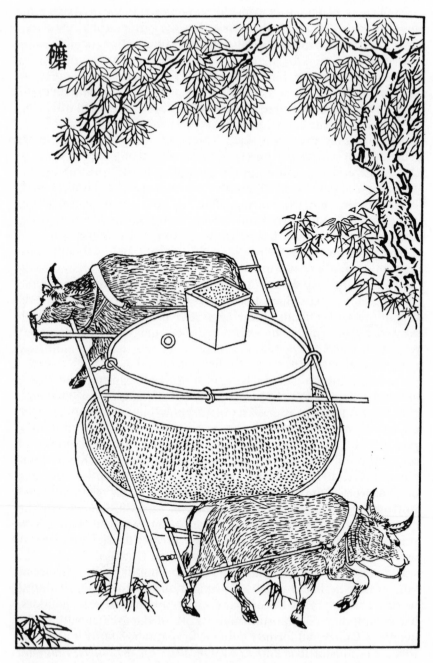

11. *Ox-driven grinding mill; Qing dynasty illustration to the* Tian gong kai wu *(see Fig. 9)*

faced with the excessively high prices that accompanied a shortage. Miniature clay models of granaries that were buried in Han tombs show the way in which they were designed; stout stilts raised the floor safely above the damp level and helped to deter rodents; vents provided a passage for air to prevent condensation. In addition to the rectangular styles, built of brick, there were also circular granaries, with walls of straw and a thatched roof. In a completely different way, grain could be stored in large pits, dug with careful attention in the loess, and sealed with clay, lime or ashes.

There was no shortage of written advice to guide the farmer in his schedules, or to instruct him in newly evolved methods of work or the use of new types of equipment with which he was unfamiliar. Almanacs, examples of which survive from the third century BC, laid down in a somewhat mechanistic way how success would attend the choice of the appropriate day in the calendar for ploughing, planting or harvesting; failure to do so could bring disaster. In the following centuries prescriptions of a somewhat more formal nature were taken shape in documents such as the *Ordinances of the Months for the Four Types of Person* (*Si min yue ling*), of the latter part of the second century AD. Such books gave practical advice on growing crops, preserving foods, brewing liquor or raising silk; they also reminded the farmer of his religious duties, such as the offerings that he should make in due season, or the reverence that he should pay to his forebears.

A somewhat more advanced text of the sixth century, the *Manual of Essential Matters for All People* (*Qimin yaoshu*), treats the same subjects in a fuller and more systematic manner. As might be expected, the advent of printing and the new techniques and tools of the Song period gave rise to the publication of books of a new degree of sophistication. The *Book of Agriculture* (*Nong shu*), which was completed before 1313, includes a much more comprehensive coverage of all aspects of the subject, with illustrations of new techniques and instruments, than anything seen hitherto. This was followed by the *Complete Agricultural Management* (*Nong zheng quan shu*), which was printed in 1639. Its author was a man who merits brief attention. A well-known figure in the world of politics, Xu Guangqi (1562–1633) was a convert to Christianity; and it was doubtless from the Jesuit fathers that he had gained his acquaintance with the agricultural work of contemporary Europe, and with crops such as sweet potatoes. Meanwhile the all-important daily work of the greater part of the people of China had formed a theme for painter, engraver and poet in a set of illustrations known as *Agriculture and Sericulture, Illustrated* (*Gengzhitu*). These twenty paintings, and their accompanying poems, date from *c.* 1145; they were engraved on stone some half-century later; and the whole work was reprinted on several occasions during the Qing dynasty, graced by the addition of the poems of no less than three emperors.

THE USES AND CONTROL OF WATER

Water and its age-old problems engaged the minds and attracted the attention of provincial officials, engineers, landowners and farmers. The results of their initiative in facing perennial difficulties and dangers are seen in the reservoirs built for storage, the canals dug for irrigation or transport and the ingenious devices which were evolved for pumping water from one level to another. Some of China's major and most long-lasting projects have been directed to the prevention of floods, and while the choice of a site for a city often depended on the availability of good supplies of water, the proximity of a river that might easily burst its banks demanded due precautions. The impressive list of projects undertaken to divert major waterways to stem their floods, of which no more than a few examples may be cited, starts at least as early as the third century BC.

It was at that time that the kingdom of Qin had taken possession of much of the upper part of the Yangzi River valley, in the province that is known today as Sichuan. Li Bing, the new governor, set himself to gain control of the Min River, a tributary of the Yangzi, and to exploit its waters on behalf of the inhabitants of what was potentially a highly fertile area. His project is known as the *Dujiang yan*; and as a result of the care with which it has been kept in order and renovated, Li Bing's scheme is operated until this day.

Li determined to split the river into two courses; he retained the main channel to carry the full press of water, variable as this was from season to season; he brought this channel under control by splitting off a secondary course, which was intended to serve the needs of irrigation; and in its turn this secondary channel was further divided and subdivided. Li Bing had separated his streams by using piles of stones; attempts that were made in the thirteenth and then the sixteenth centuries to supplement these with blocks of iron were not successful. As part of the work needed to dig the second channel, Li Bing had had to cut through rock to a width of some thirty metres.

Throughout the centuries the success of this project has depended on the regularity with which the requisite depths have been maintained in the various channels; until the end of the Qing dynasty such work was subject to inspection by provincial officials, who carried out their duty with considerable relish. A day that carried the hope of good fortune was chosen for the task; at dawn, the spirit of Li Erlang, that son of Li Bing who had helped to complete his father's work, received his due meed of worship, and the god of the river was seen to accept the sacrifices that he still demanded. Only then could workmen dismantle the barriers that had been set up to allow the repairs and maintenance to continue; and the mighty waters filled the channel with a rush, often inflicting casualties in the process.

The Yellow River is sometimes known as 'China's sorrow', owing to the frequency with which it can devastate much of the countryside. A breach that had occurred in 132 BC remained without repair until 109, and the following decades saw further occasions when the river burst its banks or disrupted its dikes. In 29 BC Fei Tiao introduced effective measures, after yet further trouble; with some 500 boats he evacuated the dispossessed inhabitants – some 97,000 persons according to the record – from those areas that had suffered worst; and within thirty-six days he had successfully constructed a new set of dikes, rising from midstream. He had had canisters filled with stone dropped to the river bed directly from his fleet of boats.

This successful feat gained official recognition and imperial praise; for the expression 'Pacification of the River' (*Heping*) was chosen as the regnal title by which the years 28–25 BC have ever afterwards been known and enumerated. But the overall results may have been only short-lived; failure to control the river's vagaries, or to survive its change of course, may well have been one of the reasons why Wang Mang could not sustain his dynasty of Xin (AD 9–23) for more than a few years.

In many other instances an imperial government was able to muster sufficient resources to face these dangers. In AD 69 Wang Jing, a hydraulic engineer who enjoyed a fine reputation for his work, undertook to repair the Bian channel so as to preclude damage; with the large force of conscripts placed at his disposal he was able to build new dikes over a distance of perhaps 400 kilometres, with water-gates set at frequent and regular intervals.

But few things last for long in the lower reaches of the Yellow River valley, least of all the contrived works of man. If the effective force of government slackens at times of dynastic weakness, the absence of regular maintenance combined with the unstable condition of the terrain can destroy an earlier hydraulic project, or render it useless. By the middle of the fifth century AD the level of the land in one region had dropped by some three metres below the original position that it had held when a set of dikes had been built to retain the drainage channels. As a result the surviving walls of the old works were far too high to receive the discharge of any excess water from the main course of the Yellow River. So a scheme was put in hand to build a new set of dikes at a suitable height, partly alongside the course of the earlier lines, with careful attention to the levels. In this way effective use could be made of the waters for purposes of irrigation.

Canals had been built in China from the pre-imperial period, and attention has been paid above to the two occasions on which minor waterways were linked or extended to form the major systems of the Grand Canal (see pp. 12–13). Transport by water also depended on the installation of the means of controlling the flow, should it be necessary to pass from one level to another. From the first century AD vertical shutters or water-gates had been attached at a few points, to be raised so as to allow excess water to pass through, or to be lowered in order to hold it back. By the eighth century the efficient transport of tax grain and silk from the south to the north was becoming subject to considerable delays, in the absence of fully operative locks. By the tenth century these were being constructed in sufficient size to permit the retention of vessels while the level of the water was being changed.

China's wide rivers could form an effective barrier that faced travellers by land, and they required the construction of bridges. From references in early literature it would seem that suspension bridges had been in use since the Han period, being developed from a simple use of a pair of ropes that could form a cable line. The Chinese landscape presents numerous examples of such bridges, built either with a single span or, as was sometimes necessary, with a series of spans resting on pillars that lay athwart the river. One of the most famous of these bridges, and one of the most ambitious, is that of eight spans that crosses the Min River, very close to the works undertaken by Li Bing. Probably this had been in existence some decades before an official traveller named Fan Chengda (1126–93) described how he had crossed the bridge in c. 1177; at the time a strong wind may have been blowing, and the bridge was swaying up and down, to the consternation or even terror of both Fan himself and those who accompanied him on that day.

These bridges were built mainly of rope or bamboo, without the use of iron, and they rested on piers of rock or granite. At a later date chains of wrought iron were used in place of rope. Other bridges, such as the great rainbow bridge that spanned the river of the Song capital city of Kaifeng, were built on the cantilever principle. The earliest known example of a bridge that was built of stone was that placed on the east side of the Han capital city of Luoyang. This was the point at which the grain barges would unload their cargoes, and by AD 135 the bridge was doing duty in conveying the heavily laden carts that took the grain to safe custody within the city. But perhaps it is the still extant stone bridge of Li Chun which calls for greatest admiration. It was built in about AD 610 to a length of some forty metres with an arch that took the traveller across the Jiaoshui River (Hepei); the beauty and grace of this bridge are difficult to surpass.

Much of China's manpower has been used to raise water to feed the growing seedlings of the paddy fields or the terraces of the hills. In this respect the initiative of the artisan and the engineer has long kept pace with the farmer's needs, providing him with devices that could be operated continuously, with least possible expenditure of manpower. Pumps took the form of an endless chain of scoops or flat boards, which were constantly lowered into stream or pond; and as they were raised they drove before them a supply of water that would then gush forth upon the fields of the upper level or fall into the tubes that led to an aqueduct. Human labour, of one or more peasants, operated the chain; or perhaps an ox plodded wearily around a circular path, tethered to a large wheel that was set horizontally, being geared to the shaft that worked the chain of pumps. At times it was possible to harness the force of the current to drive the mechanism.

Devices of this type brought water to the streets of Luoyang city in the first century AD; by the Tang and Song periods they were commonplace. Of a somewhat more complex nature was the noria. Here a series of scoops or buckets was attached to a wheel whose diameter was sufficiently large for its lowest segment to rest below the water level, and its uppermost segment to reach the height of a pipeline that strode across the fields on stilts. In this way the scoops raised the water directly from the river, before discharging it where it would flow to its destined home, perhaps to a reservoir that had been carefully framed in a land-locked valley, sealed by a man-made dam where necessary. If they were established over a fast-running river, no manpower was required to keep these giant devices moving; should they be installed over stagnant ponds or slow-moving streams, man or animal could be called to assist. Some devices of this type may have been in use by the second century AD; they were in more general use by the tenth century.

But there were times when a Chinese general made deliberate use of a river's mighty power for less beneficial purposes. The accounts, fictional or factual, of the battles fought between the states of the pre-imperial period include references to the siege of Jinyang. The defence had held out for three months, when the general of the besieging army deliberately pierced the banks of the nearby river and inundated the city. The graphic account tells how the inhabitants took to living like birds in their nests; and a second reference adds the detail that aquatic creatures thrived in the waters that filled their cooking vessels. The text has a ring of fable or myth rather than fact; but there were other occasions when harsh reality entered in. To stave off the oncoming Manchu invaders in 1644, the inhabitants of Kaifeng opened the dikes to stop their advance; and in 1938 Chiang Kaishek's forces unleashed the full flood of the Yellow River as a desperate measure to bring the Japanese armies to a halt.

THE BLESSING OF THE RAIN

Religious rites, imperial edicts and secular literature alike reflect the farmer's crying need for rain to fall in its proper season. An extreme measure that may have been in practice in these early times required a shaman, or possibly the king, to offer himself in sacrifice; in this way the sun, whose fierce rays were parching the land, might be persuaded to relent, and thus allow the rain to fall. From the eighth century BC at least major festivals of prayer and sacrifice (yu) may have included the intercession of shamans and the performance of special dances. In addition, passages in literature allude to a myth that was probably already old at the time and which continued to affect belief, ceremony and allegorical writing for many centuries thereafter. The myth tells how rain falls thanks to the benevolent action of the dragon, who mounts the clouds and in so doing precipitates a downpour.

The great ceremony of intercession for rain continued to be observed during Han times. Simultaneously farmers and others were performing an act of sympathetic magic, whose efficacy depended on its imitation of the result that was desired. If, as it was believed, a fall of rain followed the appearance of a dragon, let model dragons be fashioned in clay and then arrayed in the fields, and surely the heavens would then open. By the first and second centuries AD this rite was being incorporated in the major ceremony of the yu in which senior officials of state took part.

Meanwhile intellectual developments were leaving their mark on these performances. Philosophers of the Han period were writing on the theme of the mutual attraction of things that are of similar character; in doing so they were propounding a rationalist explanation of a belief in the efficacy of sympathetic magic. This was a time when the movements of the universe were thought to follow the regular rhythms of yin yang and the Five Phases, and when formal acts were being regulated accordingly. An account of the means of attracting rain that is ascribed to Dong Zhongshu (c. 179–c. 104

BC) but which may well have been compiled some centuries later describes a highly complex series of procedures, in which the authentic initiative of the farmer has given way to standardized prescriptions.

Five forms of rite were prescribed, with variations that allowed for the five seasons of the year; for the existence of a fifth season had to be presumed, at midsummer, to fit the Five Phases of the major rhythms of the universe. The ceremonies included prayers and offerings; shamans were exposed to the heat of the sun, there to intercede on behalf of suffering humanity; and the great dance of the dragons took place. The dragons, between 50 and 90 feet long,* had been made of a flexible frame, covered in green, red, yellow, white or black clothing, according to the season at which the rite was being performed. For each season one of these effigies was accompanied by a series of smaller dragons, whose size and number depended on similar considerations, as did the choice of the actors who took part in the dance – eight youths in the spring, seven able-bodied men in the summer, five adults in midsummer, nine widowers in autumn and six elderly men in winter.

When the dance had been completed, holes were dug in the shrine where it had been performed so as to connect with the watercourses of the area; and thereafter a further act of ritual was performed, again depending on a belief in sympathetic magic. For in China, as indeed in Europe, it was thought that a shower of rain follows the croaking of frogs. Live frogs were therefore collected and let loose in tanks within the shrine; and lest anything be left to chance, the dimensions of those tanks conformed precisely with those thought to be characteristic of the season when the rite was being performed; so the tanks measured eight, seven, five and nine feet (Han) square, depending on their use at different times of the year. Towards the end of the ceremony, all possible ways of access, such as the gates on the south side, by which the influence of *yang*, the controller of heat and sunshine, might be able to penetrate the area, were closed; and on appropriate days, dragons that had been made of clay were exposed, in the hope that they would continue the good work of encouraging the rain to fall.

At later periods other steps were taken in the hope of persuading a reluctant god to let the rain fall; should he be unwilling to do so, he could be subjected to pressure, by indignities that were paid to his image; and if he persisted in failing to respond to prayer and entreaty, the angry worshippers felt justified in smashing that image, in punishment for his refusal to help them.

---

*I.e. Chinese (Han) feet; one foot = 23 cm.

Han Yu (768–824) was a man known for his literary accomplishments and the part that he played in public life. Writing in the early
part of the ninth century, he could call on the myth of the dragon
and the clouds as an allegory, to show how an emperor depends on
the ministers who serve him. The deep cry for rain and the immense
relief that farmer and provincial governor felt when their entreaties
were answered are seen in a beautiful piece of writing from the hand
of Su Dongpo (1036–1101), a native of Sichuan. This well-known
statesman and littérateur spent a chequered political career moving
in and out of favour, and being finally banished to the remote island
of Hainan. Su Dongpo wrote how sustained drought had eventually
been relieved by a persistent downpour. Officials rejoiced in their
courtyards; merchants broke into song in the market-places; the
farmers rejoiced in their fields; the hearts of the distressed were
lightened; and the sick were cured of their ailments. With deep
thanks, Su Dongpo chose to name the summer house that he had
just built so as to commemorate this happy event. He summoned
guests to celebrate and wrote a song for the occasion. Were the
heavens to rain down pearls or jade, he wrote, there would be no
clothing or food for the cold and the hungry; and he reminded his
audience that the gift of the rain comes not from the emperor nor
from the governors of his provinces, nor yet from the creative force;
it is the gift of those sources that must for ever be dark, mysterious
and unnamed.

*

River, waterfall and lake often form essential elements in the landscapes of the Song period. Those who planned the layout of Tang's
capital of Chang'an deliberately drew a serpentine river into the city
to beautify its streets; the Song cities of Lin'an (Hangzhou) and
Suzhou owe much of their character to their adjoining lakes and
their network of canals; and the beauties of a garden in a residence
of the Song period depend on the skilful combination of water with
the other elements of nature. Much of the farmer's effort lay with
the control or manipulation of water; such preoccupations stand
revealed in the many graceful woodcuts of the manuals that illustrate
the daily lives of so many of China's inhabitants.

XVIII

COMMERCIAL PRACTICE

Concentration on agriculture played a highly significant part in determining how the Chinese developed in a characteristic and distinctive manner as compared with the various peoples of Central Asia. Thanks to the relatively settled way of life that this occupation implied or even demanded, there emerged the principal forms of religious practice, intellectual development, political institutions and social structure; it was these habits that fostered the development of the arts and the growth of scientific and technological skills.

Such results depended as much on the hard labour and constant cares of the great majority of the population as on the intellect and ingenuity of those backed by sufficient wealth or privilege with which to enjoy the pursuits of leisure. But trade and manufacture were essential elements of communal life, alike for the peasant engaged in his daily work in the fields, the priest or monk who served the shrines and temples of his village or city and the townsman who could concentrate his heart and mind on the gentle work of scholar, artist or philosopher. They all depended on the artisans, whether to turn out the implements needed to tend their crops, to provide the furnishings and ornaments that filled their holy places or to produce the printed books and equipment required in their studies.

Along with the artisan or manufacturer, the tradesman likewise played a key role in their lives; for, but for his activities, there might well be no means of distributing some of the necessities of life, the utilities that distinguished a civilized from an uncivilized people or the luxuries whose production stimulated the efforts of the artist. Such distribution could itself be complex and could raise problems of principle and practice, whose solution formed part of China's achievement.

THE FUNCTION OF TRADE

Commerce was essential to the operation of government and to the conduct of daily life; but it formed a focus for political dispute and was marked by tension and compromise. Traditionally, officials who

263

had been nurtured on the Confucian ethic could afford to express a lofty moralist claim that trade took the lowest place in the hierarchy of human occupations; in practical terms such officials could well find themselves obliged to engage in commercial transactions in the course of their duties.

From early times moral principles were called into question. There were statesmen or philosophers who believed that it was not right for human beings to profit from the sufferings or shortages that beset their neighbours, let alone to exploit such opportunities for personal gain. Some believed that imperial government should rightly take a part in the sale and distribution of the necessities of life. Others, who recognized that trading was an inescapable activity in the harsh world of reality, none the less maintained that it was improper for the organs of state to compete with individuals who were engaged in these undertakings. They also held that salaried officials of government should not engage in profitable undertakings, which should properly be left for those who were not thus privileged. Such discussions took their place within the scope of a much wider debate that concerned the right of a government to interfere with the activities of the individual. In extreme terms, the difference lay between those who wished to leave individuals as free as possible to pursue their own chosen occupations without restriction, and those who insisted on the need of an imperial government to organize human effort corporatively in the major interests of the whole community.

In practical terms, tension could arise between the conflicting interests of a government and those of some of the major well-established clans. This would occur at times when a strong imperial government, perhaps of a newly founded dynasty, was embarking on policies to co-ordinate its efforts and make best use of its resources. Should they go to the point of attempting to control or even to exploit commercial possibilities, such measures could well prejudice the interests of the leading families of the provinces and destroy their opportunities for profiteering. But often enough a compromise could be found. Alive to the value of professional skills, a government might well wish to call on the services of a rich magnate, who had enjoyed long experience in commercial or industrial undertakings and enriched himself in the process. Should a minister of state suggest doing so, he would by no means feel inhibited from affirming that his main objectives lay in promoting the welfare of the people of China, in a manner that conformed with the ideals of the Confucian ethic. For their part, the rich iron-masters, landowners and leaders of the city's guilds would find it well worth their while to co-operate with officials, to the great advantage of both parties.

The work named the *Mengzi* includes the sayings attributed to a teacher (Meng Ke or Mencius) of the fourth century BC; at a much later date it was adopted as one of the principal treatises of Confucian teaching. The work was compiled at a time when iron had been in use for some centuries and had already left its mark on China's economic development. The work includes a clear recognition that the occupations of farmer, artisan and tradesman are interdependent, and stresses the need for their co-operation. By the imperial age, the principle had gained general acceptance, while giving rise to considerable controversy regarding the proportionate importance that each type of production merited.

There were other reasons why this situation could hardly remain stable. Burdened with the increasing responsibilities that the scale of imperial government demanded, officials came to resent the easy way in which some of the merchants had been able to acquire wealth. For, as part of their regular duties, officials were obliged to arrange for the collection and transport of large cargoes of bulky and perishable material such as grain; and they had perforce to rely on the unwilling effort of conscript labour for the fatiguing work that was involved. The merchants, by contrast, could make most of their profits from dealing in smaller consignments of goods such as hardware that were not subject to wastage; and they conducted their trade with the help of supporters or servants whose livelihood was bound up with the success that attended their efforts. Nor did the advancement of a merchant's interests depend on the whim of an emperor or a turn of political fortune whereby an official could be brought to ruin.

Ambivalent attitudes towards trade were developing. Even from the Warring States period (481 or 403–221 BC) some restrictions may have been imposed on the social status to which they could aspire. Imperial Han regulations which may have been intended to be more symbolic than effective forbade them from wearing garments of silk, or from riding on on horseback. Merchants were subject to higher taxes than others; their sons were not allowed to enter the ranks of the civil service; and they could not become landowners. But sometimes the merchants could dispose of resources that were not available elsewhere, and in such circumstances officials would be glad to call on their help. In this way a merchant could be rewarded for arranging to deliver large consignments of grain to a remote corner of the empire that lay beyond the easy reach of the official; his reward lay in the bestowal of honours that would enhance his social status.

There were other ways in which an imperial government took part in manufacture or trade. It called on magnates to organize the state's monopolies of the iron and salt industries; it took sole control of the minting of coin; it attempted to arrange for the distribution of staple goods on an equable basis. Such measures were not adopted without raising the fundamental question of whether the state was entitled to engage in such profitable undertakings, or whether these should be more properly left to private enterprise.

THE CONDUCT OF TRADE

In the early empires much of China's grain and cloth, whether woven in silk or hemp, found its way into the local, provincial or central stores that had been stocked by the tax-gatherers. At times officials received a proportionate part of their salaries in these goods, at an agreed value that was set against payments in cash. Should a highly paid senior official receive more than he needed, he would obviously wish to dispose of the surplus by sale; and there was no lack of merchants who would be ready to profiteer from such opportunities in times of shortage, when deals could be struck quickly and without the difficulties that officials suffered in handling these materials.

But trade was mainly concerned with manufactured goods that served the needs of daily life or formed the luxuries that the wealthy could afford. Merchants dealt in the iron tools used in the fields or in the kitchen, or in the jades, gold and silver of a rich man's home. They sold the potteries, porcelains and lacquer wares that graced the altar of a shrine or the banqueting halls of the palace; they dealt in consumable items such as preserved foods, alcoholic liquor and sweetmeats. In the large emporia which served the needs of the new sophisticated standards of the Tang and Song periods, townsmen could buy varieties of vegetables, fruit and tea; oils, sugar and spices were on sale, together with the products of the fisheries, and textiles of hemp, ramie and silk made in the cottage industries. There was scope for dealings in the timber that was needed for boats and houses; for the paper and brushes that a scholar official required; and for two types of commodity on which so much of China's achievement depended and with which artist and craftsman had been glad to display their virtuosity – the sticks of ink with their moulded ornamentation, and the stone slabs on which those sticks were ground. Vases and platters of *cloisonné* enamel reached the markets of the Yuan and Ming periods; from the eighteenth century the pawn-broker's shop or office was making its presence felt with increasing regularity.

In early imperial times, officials were present to control some of the transactions of the specially designated market-places of the cities. By the Tang period these same areas were being used as a venue for entertainments, public performances and competitions. The *hang* ('row') system was also developing, whereby purveyors of the same type of commodity, be it, for example, bales of silk, candles or coffins, plied their trade in the same row or street, thereby providing purchasers with a wide choice and encouraging brisk competition. Although such a system was by no means universal, vestiges survived until after the end of the imperial era.

The thrust of private enterprise is seen conspicuously in the growth of the guilds, which were taking a greater and more prominent part in public life and in the organization of trade, particularly in the last century of the Qing dynasty. Since the Song period the guilds had been growing up spontaneously in the towns, as associations of men who shared an interest in common. These were members of families from the provinces who were tempted to seek their fortunes by moving from the countryside to the towns. They had been ready to forsake the protective companionship of their village or clan, to undertake more lucrative work as artisans or craftsmen; in so doing they might easily expose themselves to the oppression of those families or establishments for whom they worked and whose powers could hardly be challenged. They therefore formed their own groups, where they could converse with their own fellows in their own native dialect, partake in the communal worship of their own gods and set up a base to welcome further emigrants arriving from their villages and families. Some of these guilds founded charitable trusts or educational services whereby they could foster their sense of individuality and provide for their future well-being.

By the nineteenth century the characteristic features of the guilds had altered; they now depended less on sharing a common place or origin, or descent from the same clan; they relied more on membership of the same occupation. The guilds represented a particular type of trader or manufacturer, and they had acquired sufficient authority to regulate commercial practices, and to supervise the conduct of trade in the interests of fair dealing. A weak or disorganized government was glad to co-operate with their leaders, and at times of official laxity to lean on them for work such as the collection of tax. In this way, as the population of the cities grew, the guilds came to exercise a far greater influence on public life, almost to the point of forming the municipal authority over a city. It was some of the guilds that gave the lead to the Chinese in the introduction of western methods of finance.

At the same time the growing strength of the clans and their organizations was affecting the conduct of trade in the country, and here again there was a noticeable willingness to compromise and to sustain an ambivalence. The gentry or leading families of the countryside would be the first to assert that their way of life and social status depended on their profession of the Confucian virtues. But despite the view of trade that had become entrenched in the traditional Confucian view of social status, the country magnates were ready to compromise with such lofty ideals and to engage in commerce so as to keep their communities on a viable economic footing.

Imperial governments imposed, or tried to impose, their will in three principal aspects – the regulation of weights and measures, the establishment of monopolies for certain industries and the control of foreign trade.

Various units of measurements had come into use in different parts of China during the Spring and Autumn period (722–481 BC). At the time when the kingdom of Qin was expanding its strength and consolidating its government, Shang Yang (*c.* 390–338 BC) is credited with introducing a standardized system, as specified by the authorities of state, and the imperial governments were glad to follow this precedent. Treatises in the Standard Histories of the dynasties, which doubtless call on basic documents of state as their source, specify the units that were used for measurements of length, volume, weight and area, and there is no shortage of material evidence to support these theoretical statements. Basically, the standards were defined in terms of the size of grain kernels, which would be likely to produce a reliable average, if taken in sufficient quantity. The evidence includes foot-rules, carefully graticulated in the ten inches of the Chinese foot (23 cm at the start of the Christian era) and in tenths of the inch. There are also bronze weights and measures of capacity, usually inscribed with a note that defined the unit and authorized its use as a standard.

Different scales, sometimes in accordance with a decimal progression, were used to relate smaller to larger units. Over the centuries there was a tendency for the size of the units to increase (for example, the Chinese foot rose from 23 cm in Han times, to nearly 30 cm in Tang and 32–35 cm in Qing). But complexity entered in, as it was by no means uncommon for two approved sets of measurement to be in use simultaneously, the one for official transactions and the other for popular dealings. The system also included some refinements for which there was not always a great call. Thus minuscule linear measurements were needed in designing astronomical instruments or in the sighting devices attached to the trigger of a crossbow; small fractions of units of volume were used to compound medicines, if for few other commodities of daily life.

During the Spring and Autumn period the dukedom, and later

the kingdom of Qi, which was situated in the modern province of Shandong, acquired a new measure of strength and wealth, largely by exploiting its resources of iron and salt. According to the tradition, which may be based as much on fantasy as on fact, during the seventh century BC control of these necessities of life came into the hands of the duke and his ministers, on advice that had been proferred by Guan Zhong. Certainly during the second century BC the Han governments were ready to call on Guan Zhong's work as a precedent, at a time when they were actively trying to intensify their control over the population, to increase the riches of the empire and to extend its territories. From 120 BC magnates and others who had been operating some of these mines on a private basis were appointed to act as assistants to ministers of state, and in 119 BC monopolies were set up to control the production and distribution of the products. Forty-eight agencies were established to oversee the work of the iron mines and foundries, and thirty-four at the sites where salt was mined from the rock or collected from the sea. The commissioners were charged to raise much-needed revenue during the course of distribution.

In this way it was planned to divert the profits of these undertakings from private hands and to enrich the government, and for a short time the production of alcoholic liquor also came under state control, perhaps for the same reasons. But complaints were soon heard about the quality of the iron goods that were being turned out and the refusal to reduce the price for items that were of especially poor finish. Retention or abandonment of the monopolies formed a controversial issue in politics; and although they were still operating until the latter part of the first century AD, it cannot be told with what efficiency these industries were managed. When the Tang government determined to establish monopolies of state, they were confined to the production of liquor and salt. Different economic conditions prevailed at the time (758), and the salt commission rose to become one of the dominant financial organs of the empire, torn asunder as it then was by the rebellion of An Lushan.

From the early days of the empires, governments had been aware of the need to control the export of certain goods. In addition to the danger of detracting from China's own resources, there was the fear of enriching her potential enemies, or supplying them with weapons that they themselves were unable to make. Other considerations, however, could make themselves felt. The goodwill of some of the leaders of the Central Asiatic communities might depend on China's willingness to supply them with silk; and the Chinese were themselves anxious to retain an assured source of horses of good quality from the north. Nonetheless a belief in China's self-sufficiency was an essential element of a long-standing political creed. Imperial pride could not admit openly that the Son of Heaven tolerated, let alone needed, to conduct trade with other peoples. Should officials propose such exchanges or historians record them they would need to describe them under the suitably euphemistic terms of a foreigner's submission of tribute or the emperor's bestowal of gifts on his visitors.

Early in imperial times (188–180 BC) a ban prevented the export of metal wares or female stock animals to some of the peoples of the south. Shortly afterwards one of the characteristic and regular tasks that devolved on the garrison of the north-west was that of controlling points of access and subjecting outgoing travellers to an inspection of the goods that they carried. At the same time, governments were soon to permit, tolerate or even encourage caravans to set out annually with cargoes of silken bales, some of which were destined to reach the Mediterranean world. Middle men supervised the trade; in return China received the horses that she needed or those warm woollens whose comforts were provided by the shaggy sheep of Central Asia.

The colourful way of life of the Tang city of Chang'an owed much of its character to those trading parties who brought their goods from the western world for sale in the city's markets or for the delectation of the court. Attitudes varied in later times, particularly after the end of the Mongol dynasty (Yuan: 1260–1368). Although the Mongols, now retired to the fastnesses of the steppe, were anxious to enjoy the benefits of Chinese goods, the Ming emperors were far from willing to encourage contacts, and in refusing to do so they may well have aroused feelings of disappointment and animosity. The new walls of the Ming dynasty acted as an effective barrier to a renewal of commercial ventures.

By the nineteenth century a very different situation was prevailing in the south, following the intrusion of European traders and the extension of diplomatic activities by the western powers. Since 1760 western traders had been allowed to pursue their occupations, thanks only to the gracious permission of the emperor. They had done so under the supervision of a special guild of Chinese merchants, known as the Cohong, which was responsible for the proper behaviour of those foreigners who had been admitted within the empire. All communications that foreign merchants wished to make with the Chinese authorities were passed through the hands of the Cohong, and the traders were subject to considerable restrictions of movement.

The Cohong had worked with the East India Company; but a change took place early in the nineteenth century, when adventurers or private firms were able to exploit opportunities to promote the sale of opium. With the marked increase in the volume of this pernicious trade, there followed the first armed clash between China and the western powers, in the form of the Opium War (1839–42); and the treaty of Nanking, which brought this episode to a close, opened a new chapter in trading relations. By the terms of the treaty foreigners were no longer obliged to work through the intermediacy of the Cohong; instead they gained the right to conduct their trade without restriction or molestation in five specified ports, including Guangzhou (that is, Canton) and Shanghai. By the end of the empire, similar concessions had been made elsewhere, with the result that there were no less than fifty designated 'treaty ports', where foreigners were allowed to reside and conduct their business.

These concessions were of far-reaching importance. The cities became international centres with a cosmopolitan flavour, such as had grown up some twelve centuries previously in Chang'an. China gained from the stimulus that was given to trading initiative; many Chinese took advantage of the opportunities to learn from personal experience the niceties and mysteries that lay behind the management of business in the western world. The system of the treaty ports was yet another example of a Chinese ability to compromise, in a manner that suited all parties. The Chinese could claim that the foreigners were still subject to imperial sovereignty, being restricted to operate in certain designated towns; the foreigners had acquired facilities for a lucrative trade that were recognized as legal, together with the support of a diplomatic, consular and naval presence. By exercising jurisdiction over his own nationals the consul of a European power could both satisfy Chinese officials that their regulations were being obeyed and promise his own countrymen a measure of security. The extra-territoriality to which the treaty of Nanking had given birth in 1842 was, in the beginning, of as much benefit to the Chinese as it was to the foreigner.

THE MEDIA OF EXCHANGE

The development of a coinage gave rise to questions of both principle and practice. Statesmen discussed whether members of the public should be permitted to mint coin, or whether this should be controlled as a monopoly of state. There were times when an official submitted a memorial arguing that, in view of the inequalities that were bound to arise, the use of coin should be restricted and replaced as much as was possible by dealings in commodities. On occasion the question arose of the respective advantages of a multi-denominational currency in place of the more regular coinage with units of one denomination only. In practical terms the expense of minting coin was by no means inconsiderable; with the growing complexity of Chinese trade, supplies of copper or silver were not always sufficient to satisfy the needs of both business man and tax collector. Shortages of staple goods, only too likely in times of flood or drought, could easily stimulate an inflation, as could the uncontrolled issue of paper money, once the age of printing had dawned.

Such conflicts and difficulties may be traced from the earliest experiments. In the Shang-Yin period, the rare cowry shell was used as an item of exchange, as it was in other parts of the world, and the problem of whence these could be obtained in large quantity has yet to be solved. Followed as this was by the emergence of bronze coins, the cowry nonetheless survived as a monetary unit in some of the more remote parts of China as late as 100 BC.

With the bronze and the iron ages, it seems that rare and valuable utensils that were made of those materials acted as a medium of exchange. Before long, replicas of such tools were being made specifically for the purpose. Bronze spades circulated as currency in the kingdoms of the west and the north-west, and bronze knives in those of the east. By the time of the Warring States (481 or 403–221 BC) a marked tendency had set in whereby the size of these replica tools was reduced and their shape conformed with certain standards; in some cases the coins bore a crude inscription that identified the place of minting. At the same time the bronze disc coin, which was destined to become China's standard form of currency, had made its appearance. Somewhat exceptionally, small gold ingots which were minted in the kingdom of Chu circulated in the area of the Yangzi River valley.

The introduction of a standard circular coin in the Qin empire brought these complexities to a close, and by *c*. 120 BC it had been finally resolved that coin should be minted by the state, and not by private hands. The regular coin of the Han empire, known as the 'cash' (*qian*), was cast with a square hole in the centre, and inscribed with a note of its nominal weight (*wu shu*, that is 3.25 grams). To prevent clipping or the use of illegal tender, various designs were adopted for the cash, including some that were cast with a specially wide and thick rim. The purpose of the hole was twofold; it saved the use of metals, and it enabled users to thread a cord, presumably of leather, so as to assemble a 'string' of cash. In this way the string, nominally of 100 coins, was quoted as a unit of currency; in the Song period the same principle gave rise to the string whose nominal value was that of 1,000 coins.

To numismatists these early Chinese coins lack the aesthetic appeal of those of Greek, Hellenistic or Roman origin. Accustomed to their own simple cash, Chinese officials who were serving in the outposts of empire in Central Asia made a point of reporting on some of the foreign coins that were circulating in Bactria or Kashmir and which had fallen into their hands. For they had seen, perhaps with some astonishment, coin struck with the portrait of an alien ruler, or with the device of a mounted charger. Their reports duly found their way into the Standard Histories.

Gold ingots were also in use in Han times, on a somewhat limited scale. Bearing a nominal value of 10,000 cash, they were probably exchanged at a somewhat lower rate that was subject to fluctuation; and they could be used only for major transactions. But use of a different type of valuable for the submission of certain dues to the government has given rise to a misapprehension. When the noblemen presented themselves at court, they were at one time (c. 120 BC) required to include a gift of a piece of rarely seen white deerskin, thereby enriching the emperor's private collection of valuables. But the deerskin in no sense constituted an early experiment in 'paper money'; supplies were limited rather than obtainable at will, and the commodity was never used as a unit of general circulation.

If the later, and perhaps anachronistically written, accounts were to be believed, a number of valuable items such as horn, hide and jade had been used as media of exchange in the remote past. Such a precedent, whether of fact or fiction, was invoked in support of attempts to introduce a multi-denominational currency, during Wang Mang's short-lived empire (AD 9-23). But his complex systems (one of which included no less than twenty-eight units) failed to win confidence or popularity, at a time when political and social norms were subject to question. In the absence of stable dynastic government, from the end of the second century AD there was a tendency to use bolts of silk as a substitute for coin; occasionally an experiment was made with coin cast of iron rather than bronze.

With the strength of a newly founded dynasty, the Tang governments reasserted the use of the copper cash, minting new models that were considerably larger than those of their Han predecessors. The coins were turned out in sufficient quantity to form the principal medium of exchange, and an inscription recorded the reign period in which they had been minted. But difficulties arose, not only in the growing scarcity of copper and the expense of manufacture, but also in the conveyance of large sums across the provinces in safety; it was from such causes that paper money came to be evolved.

Both officials and merchants had been working under restrictions; the tea merchants wished to transfer the profits that they had made by sales in the north to their home base in the south; the provincial authorities in the south needed a safe way of remitting money to the capital in the north. Following the use of privately arranged promissory notes, there emerged the 'flying cash' (*fei qian*) which was issued by the government in the ninth century. These notes had started as instruments of credit which entitled the bearer to draw cash from a designated office or seat of commerce. Real paper money, with notes that circulated freely as items of currency, developed during the tenth century, at the time when printing was about to come into its own. Starting in the independent kingdom of Shu, in the south-west, the practice was adopted on an empire-wide scale after the reunification by the Song dynasty, and by the eleventh century it was operating widely. The paper money of the Song dynasty was issued in various denominations. The notes were printed either in monochrome or in coloured patterns of red and blue; their legend named the year and number of the issue, thereby showing the time limit within which they were legal tender.

The emergence of paper money is an excellent example of an experiment that was tried in a limited manner at a time of dynastic disunity, and was adopted with far greater implications once a single regime had been established. At first the issues of notes were controlled, by means of entry on a register, or as a direct return after the receipt of public moneys. But by 1072 notes were being printed to excess, irrespective of the backing that they needed, and the inflation that duly set in soon reached alarming and uncontrollable proportions. The government of the Yuan dynasty (1260–1368), however, achieved considerable success in curbing these tendencies. Paper money became the sole form of legal tender, with copper, silver and gold being demonetized; some of the notes printed for the Yuan treasury circulated outside China.

With the Ming dynasty there came a return to other currencies. In both the Tang and Song periods gold and silver had been used for large transactions, including gifts and bribes, at both official and popular levels; with the increased volume of business of the Song period, the use of these valuable metals had extended widely. By the sixteenth century there had also been a growth in the silver reserves; notes were no longer in circulation, and the use of silver as one of the main items of currency could cause considerable distress. Writing in the seventeenth century, Gu Yanwu (1613–82) described in bitter terms the hardships that could be involved, if farmers or peasantry were forced to find silver with which to pay their taxes. For at the best of times supplies could be short and subject to interruption; silver could simply not be prized from the countryside, and it was by no means uncommon for villagers to sell members of their family into slavery as a means of meeting their debts. During the nineteenth century notes were reissued on a comparatively small scale in times of emergency; units of foreign currencies, such as the Mexican dollar or money that had originated in Hong Kong, Japan or America, were circulating in the provinces of the Qing empire.

*

Despite all the protestations of those who wished to emphasize primary at the expense of second occupations, a thriving trade made its essential contribution to the growth of Chinese culture. As in other respects, so here major change may be traced to the Song period.

Opened from *c.* 100 BC, but in no sense in permanent use, the Silk Roads had seen the exchange of goods and important ideas between east and west; but they had not permitted the establishment of direct contacts between the officials and inhabitants of Chang'an or Luoyang on the one hand, and those of Rome, Byzantium or Alexandria on the other. The new routes that were opened from the Song age onwards brought a new emphasis and new opportunities, whereby east and west would be unable to avoid relations with each other, whether as partners or as rivals. China's centre of balance had moved to the central and southern parts of the empire, and it was there that the new rich emporia were arising. As the population increased, so did the demand for more manufactures; and as the workshops turned out more and better articles for daily life or for adornment, so the printing presses kept up a steady supply of banknotes for use as ready money. When the European entrepreneurs arrived in the nineteenth century, they found markets that promised a considerable potential and a population that was well accustomed to the sound of bargaining.

EPILOGUE

Europe owes its civilization to the Judaeo-Christian tradition, to the spirit and genius of Greece and to the systematic ordering of human life by Rome. Greece left a heritage of a love of beauty, a search for wisdom and the compelling need to define goodness; Rome showed how to formulate enduring values of law, to impose order and discipline on a community and to harness human energies so as to reach a commonly accepted objective. China fulfilled the same function for East Asia, associating human endeavour with universal patterns of existence, demonstrating that things of beauty outlast those intended solely for material use and framing exemplary forms for human conduct.

Higher concepts of humanity emerged in China thanks to the search for permanent values, the incidence of conflict and the readiness to compromise. Tension arose when Buddhist ideas penetrated Chinese views of the world; reassessment followed the shock of a foreigner's easy victory over the native tradition. Compromises emerged between Chinese and alien, between native practices and the faith of an outsider and between official and unofficial types of leadership. Due partly to the prevailing view of the unitary nature of the universe, closer relationships between sacred and profane, myth and fact, astronomy and astrology survived in China with greater strength than elsewhere. Throughout, there has been an underlying tension between two fundamental attitudes or ideas: of *li*, the ordered and regulated way of life sponsored by officials; and *dao*, the unrestrained or even boisterous behaviour of individual hermit or mystic. Each of these approaches to life has produced major elements in the Chinese tradition; so too has the harmony or reconciliation of the two, symbolized in the intertwined figure of *yin* and *yang*.

In many respects myth has been of as much importance as, or of greater importance than, reality. For, despite all the claims that thanks to the blessing vouchsafed by Heaven the Chinese forms of government kept mankind in safety, few periods of fifty years ever passed without dynastic discord, leading often to destruction, violence or bloodshed. But the myth maintained that the rule of man always passed correctly and legitimately from one holder of the mandate to his successor. It was axiomatic that the golden rule of the Heaven-blessed monarchs of the past had witnessed perfect concord and sufficiency; no mention should be made in this connection of those unavoidable shortages of food or clothing that provoked envy and dispute.

It was a myth that the highly structured and complex institutions of imperial government had been evolved in the dim mists of the past and that they formed a model for all ages to come; the myth ignored the constant need to adjust to changed circumstance and to provide for the growing sophistication of man's ways. Emperors or their advisers might claim that the just government which they practised assured prosperity and eliminated the danger of oppression; they would prefer to ignore the delays in implementing administrative decisions, or the temptations of some officials to profit personally in the course of imposing imperial orders. The Son of Heaven could certainly boast that he commanded all the resources that his people required, or that he could deny the essentials of life to his tribute bearers, but other truths prevailed. The Han emperors were ready or even glad to import horses from the steppes of Asia. The belief expressed by Commissioner Lin in 1839 that other countries could not survive without supplies of tea, rhubarb and silk from China failed to deter a British government from its supercilious attitude towards Chinese authority.

*

As an historian's point of view differs from that of his colleagues, so too does his way of dividing China's history into periods. In dynastic and political terms, the events and processes that are of major significance and which introduced change are easy to recognize. They include the establishment of the first empire in 221 BC; the alien occupation of the north in AD 317; and the reassertion of strength by the Sui and Tang emperors in the sixth and seventh centuries. In time (1127) there followed the flight of the Song house to the south, with the foundation of non-Chinese regimes in the north. The native Ming dynasty established its rule over the whole of China in 1368, to be overtaken by the Manchu conquerors in 1644; and the demise of the Qing dynasty in 1911 heralded the eventual introduction of new political ideas that had been formulated in the reading room of the British Museum.

Such events must be set against other changes that were of equally strong significance. In economic terms these included the construction of the two versions of the Grand Canal, c. 600 and c. 1300; the evolution of a monetary system, starting with the use of cowry shells in the Shang-Yin dynasty, depending on printed banknotes in the eleventh century, and supported by western-style business in the last decades of the imperial era. The introduction of new types of crop and new agricultural techniques during the Tang and Song periods and the growth of manufactures, industries and imports in the nineteenth century form equally important landmarks.

Religious developments likewise gave rise to major change. The worship that the early kings had paid to a supreme power was celebrated as an official cult of state by the Han emperors and their successors. Han China saw the arrival of Buddhism and the growth of Daoist religion. Islam had reached China by the eighth century; the most significant attempts to convert high-ranking Chinese to Christianity took place in the Ming and Qing periods.

In intellectual terms a few periods witnessed key developments whereby the Chinese tradition was nurtured, enriched or reasserted with new strength. Ethical concepts and political ideas took shape in the Warring States period (481 or 403–221 BC). In Han times there emerged the concept that the temporal rule of the emperors formed an indispensable element of the universe and its operation, seen as this now was in the light of *yin yang* and the theory of the Five Phases. In the twelfth century and later, philosophers were to reassess the Confucian view of man and the interpretation of the classical texts in the light of the Buddhist message and metaphysical speculation of a new type. A further and radical reassessment of Chinese values and political theory followed the disaster of 1644; European concepts that affected the view of state and person took hold in China in the latter part of the nineteenth century.

Historians of different frames of mind have chosen to set these changes within their own preferred framework, or to explain them within the context of preconceived ideas of periodization. To some it may seem more advisable to shun such definitions, with the reflection that the Song period, 960–1279, was of seminal significance in most aspects of Chinese life; for it was those centuries which separated the age of the early empires from accommodation to modern needs. From Song onwards the Chinese became subject to much more direct exposure to some of the dominating elements of non-Chinese ways of life. It was in Song that ancient usages reached their peak and many art forms their finest achievements.

*

In common with a number of other nations, China has recently chosen to embrace a new way of life, whose forms originated outside her own borders and whose origins lie in a completely different set of ideals and traditions than her own. The insistence on monotheism that the Jesuits and others brought was strange to a people accustomed to worship a plurality of gods. China's history had evolved a different view of loyalty and heroism from that of the west, with its call for an unfamiliar form of government that depended on popular acclaim. Europe's intellect had drawn extensively from the habit of analysis and definition and the requirement to explain a policy or to defend a proposal in public; mastery of rhetoric had also contributed to the legal procedures of the west, and to the establishment of a body of law whose authority transcended that of those who actually wielded power.

It is therefore hardly surprising to find a marked contrast in the characteristics of public life of traditional and contemporary China. Occasions when the Confucian ideal has manifestly failed to maintain a stable China or to prevent the outbreak of violence have, alas, been only too frequent; but it is nothing less than tragic that since the resolute rejection of that ideal and its values in 1919, no intellectual framework has emerged that is adequate to take its place. Constitutions, elected assemblies and revolutionary committees take the place of the chancelleries of imperial sovereignty. Education is designed to provide a vocational training for doctors or engineers rather than to prepare an emperor's subjects to compete for a place in the civil service. The head of state and his ministers take decisions of policy without the support or comfort of religious sanction. *Das Kapital*, *The Origin of Species* and Lenin's works form the framework of their minds rather than the *Book of Documents* or the *Analects of Confucius*. For the general public, books and newspapers are printed in the commonly accepted vernacular rather than in the polished forms of language loved by men of letters. Social cohesion depends no longer on the leadership of clan or guild but on membership of the same branch of a political party, or on employment in the same factory. Electricity saves much of the back-breaking labour of the fields or the haulage of goods by human hands; and business is conducted according to the methods of the western world.

For all these differences the enduring gifts of the past survive to enrich the contemporary world. Despite severe natural disasters, dynastic turbulence and a surrender to foreign pressures, time and again China has retained her integrity, and her basic cultural unities have remained unimpaired. At the time of writing (June 1989), when China's destiny is once again open to question, it might seem over optimistic to hope that, fragile as they may well be, some of China's traditional values and creations may yet survive recent cataclysms. But, however different they may be from the compositions of the twentieth century, the poetry, art and literature of the Han, Tang, Ming or Qing ages cannot evade attention by those who seek to identify the enduring parts of the humanities, or to understand how China's gifts must rank among the most noble and precious heritages bequeathed to man.

NOTES FOR FURTHER READING

In general the list of titles that follows has been restricted to books written in the English language and to editions which can be obtained without undue difficulty. In many cases further guidance may be sought from the bibliographies that are included in many of the books to which attention is drawn.

For a general survey of the scope of Chinese civilization, see Brian Hook (ed.), *The Cambridge Encyclopedia of China* (Cambridge: Cambridge University Press, 1982). Raymond Dawson (ed.), *The Legacy of China* (Oxford: Clarendon Press, 1964), and Arnold Toynbee (ed.), *Half the World: The History and Culture of China and Japan* (London: Thames & Hudson, 1973), include valuable essays on particular aspects of China's development. Useful reference books include: *The Times Atlas of China* (London: Times Books, 1974); Herbert A. Giles, *A Chinese Biographical Dictionary* (Shanghai: Kelly & Walsh, 1898); William H. Nienhauser Jr (ed.), *The Indiana Companion to Traditional Chinese Literature* (Bloomington: Indiana University Press, 1986); and Charles O. Hucker, *China: A Critical Bibliography* (Tucson: University of Arizona Press, 1962).

I: THE GIFTS OF NATURE AND THEIR PROBLEMS

For a general account of China's geography, see T. R. Tregear, *A Geography of China* (London: University of London Press, 1965), and R. R. C. de Crespigny, *China: The Land and its People* (Melbourne: Thomas Nelson, 1971). Detailed maps of the provinces of modern China will be found in *The Times Atlas of China*, together with maps which illustrate the territorial extent of successive dynasties, the diversity and spread of the population, the distribution of economic resources and enterprises and the lines of communication of modern times. For kingdoms or empires of pre-modern times and their administrative divisions, see Albert Herrmann, *Historical and Commercial Atlas of China* (original edition, Cambridge, Mass.: Harvard University Press, 1935; new edition, ed. Norton Ginsburg, Chicago: Aldine, 1966).

In *Cultural Atlas of China* (Oxford: Phaidon, 1983), Caroline Blunden and Mark Elvin relate geographical and economic factors to cultural and political growth, with a wealth of maps and illustrations. For problems of communications and their solution, see Joseph Needham, *Science and Civilisation in China*, volume 4, part III (Cambridge: Cambridge University Press, 1971); for the development of agriculture, see volume 6, part II, of the same series, by Francesca Bray (1984). In *China's Sorrow: Journeys around the Yellow River* (London: Century, 1985), Lynn Pan describes the economic and geographical diversity of modern China with some of its historical implications.

II: KINGDOMS AND EMPIRES: MOMENTS OF DYNASTIC CHANGE

III: DYNASTIC SUCCESSION AND ITS DIFFICULTIES

For short general histories of China, see L. Carrington Goodrich, *A Short History of the Chinese People* (original edition 1943; London: Allen & Unwin, 1948 and subsequently); Jacques Gernet, *A History of Chinese Civilization*, translated by J. R. Foster (Cambridge: Cambridge University Press, 1982); and Witold Rodzinski, *The Walled Kingdom: A History of China from 2000 BC to the Present* (London: Fontana, 1985). Fuller accounts of particular periods will be found in volumes as they appear in *The Cambridge History of China* (Cambridge: Cambridge University Press, 1979–).

A number of controversial problems that concern the beginnings of Chinese culture are studied in David N. Keightley (ed.), *The Origins of Chinese Civilization* (Berkeley, Los Angeles and London: University of California Press, 1983). For a general survey of archaeological evidence, see Kwang-chih Chang, *The Archaeology of Ancient China* (New Haven, Conn., and London: Yale University Press, revised fourth edition, 1987). For political and institutional development, see Jacques Gernet, *Ancient China: From the Beginnings to the Empire*, translated by Raymond Rudorff (London: Faber, 1968). Specialist studies of the Shang-Yin period may be found in Li Chi, *Anyang* (Folkestone: Wm Dawson & Son, 1977); David N. Keightley, *Sources of Shang History: The Oracle-Bone Inscriptions of Bronze Age China* (Berkeley, Los Angeles and London: University of California Press, 1978); and Kwang-chih Chang, *Shang Civilization* (New Haven, Conn., and London: Yale University Press, 1980).

Jessica Rawson, *Ancient China: Art and Archaeology* (London: British

Museum Publications, 1980), covers the period from the neolithic to the Han dynasty; Wen Fong, *The Great Bronze Age of China* (New York: Metropolitan Museum of Art/Knopf, 1980), that from Shang of Qin. For the Zhou, Spring and Autumn, and Warring States periods, see Cho-yun Hsu, *Ancient China in Transition* (Stanford, Calif.: Stanford University Press, 1965); Herrlee G. Creel, *The Origins of Statecraft in China*, volume 1 (Chicago and London: University of Chicago Press, 1970); Henri Maspero, *China in Antiquity*, translated by Frank A. Kierman Jr (Folkestone: Wm Dawson & Son, 1978); and Li Xueqin, *Eastern Zhou and Qin Civilizations*, translated by K. C. Chang (New Haven, Conn., and London: Yale University Press, 1985).

Monographs on particular aspects of and incidents in dynastic history include: Derk Bodde, *China's First Unifier: A Study of the Ch'in Dynasty as Seen in the Life of Li Ssu 280?–208 BC* (Hong Kong: Hong Kong University Press, 1967); Michael Loewe, *Crisis and Conflict in Han China 104 BC to AD 9* (London: Allen & Unwin, 1974); Rafe de Crespigny, *The Last of the Han* (Canberra: Australian National University, 1969); Woodbridge Bingham, *The Founding of the T'ang Dynasty: The Fall of Sui and Rise of T'ang, a Preliminary Survey* (Baltimore, Md: Waverly Press, 1941); Edwin G. Pulleyblank, *The Background of the Rebellion of An Lu-shan* (London: Oxford University Press, 1955); Morris Rossabi, *Khubilai Khan: His Life and Times* (Berkeley, Los Angeles and London: University of California Press, 1988); Ray Huang, *1587: A Year of No Significance: The Ming Dynasty in Decline* (New Haven, Conn., and London: Yale University Press, 1981); Douglas Hurd, *The Arrow War: An Anglo-Chinese Confusion 1856–1860* (London: Collins, 1967); Mary Clabaugh Wright, *The Last Stand of Chinese Conservatism: The T'ung-chih Restoration, 1862–74* (New York: Atheneum, 1966); Henry McAleavy, *A Dream of Tartary: The Origins and Misfortune of Henry Pu Yi* (London: Allen & Unwin, 1963).

For relations between the Chinese empires and other peoples, see chapters in various volumes of *The Cambridge History of China*; also: John King Fairbank (ed.), *The Chinese World Order: Traditional China's Foreign Relations* (Cambridge, Mass.: Harvard University Press, 1968); Owen Lattimore, *Inner Asian Frontiers of China* (Boston, Mass.: Beacon Press, 1962); L. Boulnois, *The Silk Road*, translated by Dennis Chamberlain (London: Allen & Unwin, 1963); Ying-shih Yü, *Trade and Expansion in Han China: A Study in the Structure of Sino-Barbarian Economic Relations* (Berkeley and Los Angeles: University of California Press, 1967); Arthur Waley, *The Opium War through Chinese Eyes* (London: Allen & Unwin, 1958).

IV: MAN AND HIS NEIGHBOURS: SOCIAL DISTINCTIONS

For traditional social structure, see chapters in Henri Maspero, *China in Antiquity*; Etienne Balazs, *Chinese Civilization and Bureaucracy: Variations on a Theme*, translated by H. M. Wright (New Haven, Conn., and London: Yale University Press, 1964); Cho-yun Hsu, *Ancient China in Transition*; and Herrlee G. Creel, *The Origins of Statecraft in China*. In *Han Social Structure* (Seattle and London: University of Washington Press, 1972), T'ung-tsu Ch'ü presents translations of passages of original source material, preceded by a lengthy introduction, which concern the main aspects of society in the early empires. In *Slavery in China during the Former Han Dynasty 206 BC–AD 25* (Chicago: Field Museum of Natural History, 1943), Clarence Martin Wilbur fastens on one particular aspect; Patricia Ebrey studies the fortune of a single clan over succeeding centuries in *The Aristocratic Families of Early Imperial China: A Case Study of the Po-ling Ts'ui Family* (Cambridge: Cambridge University Press, 1978); more general aspects are treated in Michael Loewe, *Everyday Life in Early Imperial China during the Han Period 202 BC–AD 220)* (London: Batsford, 1968; reissued New York: Dorset Press, 1988).

In *Conquerors and Rulers: Social Forces in Medieval China* (Leiden: E. J. Brill, 1952), Wolfram Eberhard draws attention to some of the problems that arise when parts of China come under the control of non-Chinese leaders. For the background of social divisions during the medieval dynasties, see Arthur Waley, *The Life and Times of Po Chü-i 772–846 AD* (London: Allen & Unwin, 1949); Jacques Gernet, *Daily Life in China on the Eve of the Mongol Invasion 1250–1276*, translated by H. M. Wright (London: Allen & Unwin, 1962); and Edward A. Kracke Jr, *Civil Service in Early Sung China 960–1067* (Cambridge, Mass.: Harvard University Press, 1953). Essays by Hui-chen Wang Liu and Denis Twitchett in *Confucianism in Action*, ed. David S. Nivison and Arthur F. Wright (Stanford, Calif.: Stanford University Press, 1959), concern aspects of clan organization. In *The Ladder of Success in Imperial China: Aspects of Social Mobility, 1368–1911* (New York and London: Columbia University Press, 1962) Ping-ti Ho analyses the competitive nature of the examination system in the Ming and Qing periods; translations of some of the novels that are mentioned in Chapter XI shed considerable light on social distinctions, particularly for those dynasties. Other studies of social structure in the Qing period include Maurice Freedman, *Lineage Organization in Southeastern China* and *Chinese Lineage and Society: Fukien and Kwangtung* (London: University of London, Athlone Press, 1958 and 1966), which draw attention to the religious implications; and

T'ung-tsu Ch'ü, *Local Government in China under the Ch'ing* (Cambridge, Mass.: Harvard University Press, 1962).

V: THE SPOKEN AND THE WRITTEN WORD

Different aspects of the spoken dialects and the system of writing are treated in Bernhard Karlgren, *Sound and Symbol in Chinese* (first published 1923; reprinted London: Oxford University Press, 1946); Paul Kratochvíl, *The Chinese Language Today: Features of an Emerging Standard* (London: Hutchinson, 1968); Geoffrey Sampson, *Writing Systems: A Linguistic Introduction* (London: Hutchinson, 1985); and Jerry Norman, *Chinese* (Cambridge: Cambridge University Press, 1988). For a radically different theory regarding the origin and growth of the Chinese script, see Arthur Cooper, *The Creation of the Chinese Script* (London: China Society, 1978).

For a study of an early attempt by a European to explain the system of writing, see Knud Lundbaek, *T. S. Bayer (1694–1738), Pioneer Sinologist* (London and Malmö: Curzon Press, 1986). See also Tsuen-hsuin Tsien, *Written on Bamboo and Silk: The Beginnings of Chinese Books and Inscriptions* (Chicago and London: University of Chicago Press, 1962), for the development of written records. For dialects and the languages of the minority peoples, see S. Robert Ramsey, *The Languages of China* (Princeton, NJ: Princeton University Press, 1987).

VI: BELIEFS, HOPES AND FEARS

For a general account of the figures and themes of Chinese mythology, see Anthony Christie, *Chinese Mythology* (London: Newnes, 1968; second edition 1983); or E. T. C. Warner, *Myths and Legends of China* (London: Harrap, 1922, with subsequent reprints). In *Essays on Chinese Civilization* (Princeton, NJ: Princeton University Press, 1981), Derk Bodde reprints an earlier article 'Myths of Ancient China' (1961), which treats the subject analytically. For detailed studies of various aspects, see Marcel Granet, *Danses et légendes de la Chine ancienne* (Paris: Alcan, 1926); and Wolfram Eberhard, *Folktales of China* (London: Routledge & Kegan Paul, 1965).

For beliefs and practices, see D. Howard Smith, *Chinese Religions* (London: Weidenfeld & Nicholson, 1968); Laurence G. Thompson,

Chinese Religion: An Introduction (Belmont, Calif.: Dickinson, 1969); and Marcel Granet, *The Religion of the Chinese People*, translated by Maurice Freedman (Oxford: Blackwell, 1975). Detailed studies of particular subjects may be seen in Derk Bodde, *Festivals in Classical China: New Year and Other Annual Observances during the Han Dynasty 206 BC–AD 220* (Princeton, NJ: Princeton University Press: Chinese University of Hong Kong, 1975); Stephan D. R. Feuchtwang, *An Anthropological Analysis of Chinese Geomancy* (Vientiane: Vithagna, 1974); and Michael Loewe, *Ways to Paradise: The Chinese Quest for Immortality* (London: Allen & Unwin, 1979). For the interchange of religion and philosophy, see Michael Loewe, *Chinese Ideas of Life and Death: Faith, Myth and Reason in the Han Period (202 BC–AD 220)* (London: Allen & Unwin, 1982); for the social implications, see C. K. Yang, *Religion in Chinese Society* (Berkeley and Los Angeles: University of California Press, 1967); and books by Maurice Freedman as cited above for Chapter IV. An interpretation of Chinese religion that is written from a European point of view will be found in J. J. M. de Groot, *The Religious System of China*, six vols. (Leiden: E. J. Brill, 1892–1910; reprinted Taipei: Literature House, 1964). Daoist religious practices are studied in John Lagerwey, *Taoist Ritual in Chinese Society and History* (New York: Macmillan Publishing Company and London: Collier Macmillan Publishers, 1987).

Translations of the early Daoist mystical writings will be found in Arthur Waley, *The Way and its Power: A Study of the Tao Te Ching and its Place in Chinese Thought* (London: Allen & Unwin, 1934); A. C. Graham, *The Book of Lieh-tzu* (London: Murray, 1961); and A. C. Graham, *Chuang-tzu: The Seven Inner Chapters and Other Writings from the Book Chuang-tzu* (London: Allen & Unwin, 1981). For accounts of Daoist religious beliefs and exercises, see Henri Maspero, *Taoism and Chinese Religion*, translated by Frank A. Kierman Jr (Amherst: University of Massachusetts Press, 1981); Max Kaltenmark, *Lao Tzu and Taoism*, translated by Roger Greaves (Stanford, Calif.: Stanford University Press, 1965); and Kristofer Schipper, *Le Corps Taoïste corps physique–corps social* (Paris: Fayard, 1982). For Buddhism, see Arthur Wright, *Buddhism in Chinese History* (Stanford, Calif.: Stanford University Press, 1959); Kenneth K. S. Ch'en, *Buddhism in China: A Historical Survey* (Princeton, NJ: Princeton University Press, 1964); and E. Zürcher, *The Buddhist Conquest of China* (Leiden: E. J. Brill, 1959). In chapter 16 of *The Cambridge History of China*, volume I, Paul Demiéville analyses the metaphysical and religious elements introduced into China by Daoist and Buddhist teaching and their interaction with each other.

For the introduction of Christianity to China, see Vincent Cronin, *The Wise Man from the West* (London: Hart-Davis, 1955); and Jacques

Gernet, *China and the Christian Impact: A Conflict of Cultures*, translated by Janet Lloyd (Cambridge: Cambridge University Press, 1982).

VII: THE INTELLECT AND ITS POWER

General accounts of Chinese philosophers and their ideas, including translations of passages of primary material, will be found in Fung Yu-lan, *A History of Chinese Philosophy*, translated by Derk Bodde, two vols. (London: Allen & Unwin, 1952); Wm Theodore de Bary, *et al.*, *Sources of Chinese Tradition*, two vols. (New York and London: Columbia University Press, 1960); and Wing-tsit Chang, *A Source Book in Chinese Philosophy* (Princeton, NJ: Princeton University Press, 1963). For translations of works included in the classical canon, see under Chapter XI below.

Studies of particular aspects or figures include: Arthur Waley, *Three Ways of Thought in Ancient China* (London: Allen & Unwin, 1946); David L. Hall and Roger T. Ames, *Thinking through Confucius* (New York: State University of New York, 1987); Kung-chuan Hsiao, *A History of Chinese Political Thought*, translated by F. W. Mote (Princeton, NJ: Princeton University Press, 1979); D. C. Lau, *Mencius* (Harmondsworth: Penguin, 1970); Hellmut Wilhelm, *Change: Eight Lectures on the 'I Ching'* (London: Routledge & Kegan Paul, 1961); David McMullen, *State and Scholars in T'ang China* (Cambridge: Cambridge University Press, 1988); A. C. Graham, *Two Chinese Philosophers: Ch'eng Ming-tao and Ch'eng Yi-ch'uan* (London: Lund Humphries, 1958); Carson Chang, *The Development of Neo-Confucian Thought* (London: Vision Press, 1958); and Joseph R. Levenson, *Confucian China and its Modern Fate: The Problem of Intellectual Continuity* (London: Routledge & Kegan Paul, 1958). For the application of Chinese thought to other parts of East Asia, past and present, see Wm Theodore de Bary, *East Asian Civilizations: A Dialogue in Five Stages* (Cambridge, Mass., and London: Harvard University Press, 1988).

VIII: IMPERIAL SOVEREIGNTY

For the development and application of imperial power, see essays by various scholars in S. R. Schram (ed.), *Foundations and Limits of State Power in China* (London: School of Oriental and African Studies, and Hong Kong: Chinese University Press, 1987); *The Cambridge History of China*, volume I, chapter 13; and Ray Huang, *1587: A Year of No Significance.* Translations of key documents, including the essays of Ban Biao and Huang Zongxi, will be found in Wm Theodore de Bary *et al.*, *Sources of Chinese Tradition.*

IX: THE ORGANS OF GOVERNMENT

X: OFFICIALS AND THEIR DUTIES

Descriptions of the organization of imperial government for all the major dynasties have not yet appeared. Studies of certain periods may be found in Hans Bielenstein, *The Bureaucracy of Han Times* (Cambridge: Cambridge University Press, 1980); Charles O. Hucker, *The Traditional Chinese State in Ming Times (1368–1644)* (Tucson: University of Arizona Press, 1961); Sybille van der Sprenkel, *Legal Institutions in Manchu China: A Sociological Analysis* (London: University of London, Athlone Press, 1962). For local government, see T'ung-tsu Ch'ü, *Local Government in China under the Ch'ing* (Cambridge, Mass.: Harvard University Press, 1962); for organs of surveillance, see Charles O. Hucker, *The Censorial System of Ming China* (Stanford, Calif.: Stanford University Press, 1966); for organization of the armed forces, see Michael Loewe, *Records of Han Administration*, two vols. (Cambridge: Cambridge University Press, 1967). Specialist studies of particular problems of administration appear in John L. Bishop, *Studies of Governmental Institutions in Chinese History* (Cambridge, Mass.: Harvard University Press, 1968); and S. R. Schram (ed.), *The Scope of State Power in China* (London: School of Oriental and African Studies, and Hong Kong: Chinese University Press, 1985).

Few studies of prominent Chinese officials or men of letters fail to touch on their training and their careers in the service. Detailed accounts of institutional arrangements and their effect on individuals may be seen in David McMullen, *State and Scholars in T'ang China*; John W. Chaffee, *The Thorny Gates of Learning in Sung China: A Social History of Examinations* (Cambridge: Cambridge University Press, 1985); Ping-ti Ho, *The Ladder of Success in Imperial China*; Ichisada Miyazaki, *China's Examination Hell: The Civil Service Examinations of Imperial China* (New York: Weatherhill, 1976); and Johanna M. Menzel, *The Chinese Civil Service: Career Open to Talent?* (Boston, Mass.: D. C. Heath, 1963). For Dong Yu's view of education, see *Sanguozhi* (Beijing: Zhonghua shuju, 1959), p. 420, note 3.

For legal codes and procedures, see A. F. P. Hulsewé, *Remnants of Ch'in Law* (Leiden: E. J. Brill, 1985), and *Remnants of Han Law*, volume I (Leiden: E. J. Brill, 1955); Wallace Johnson, *The T'ang Code: Volume 1, General Principles* (Princeton, NJ: Princeton University Press, 1979); Derk Bodde and Clarence Morris, *Law in Imperial China Exemplified by 190 Ch'ing Dynasty Cases* (Cambridge, Mass.: Harvard University Press, 1967); and Sybille van der Sprenkel, *Legal Institutions in Manchu China*. Liu Zongyuan's description of the descent of officials on a village will be found in his essay ' "Camel" Guo the Tree-Planter'.

Documents illustrating the work of the servicemen on the Han defences are presented in Michael Loewe, *Records of Han Administration*; for a study of the development of the various wall systems, see Arthur Waldron, *The Great Wall of China: From History to Myth* (Cambridge: Cambridge University Press, forthcoming 1990). For an illustrated description, see Luo Zewen *et al.*, *The Great Wall* (London: Michael Joseph, 1982).

XI: LITERATURE AND SCHOLARSHIP

For general accounts of Chinese literature, see Burton Watson, *Early Chinese Literature* (New York and London: Columbia University Press, 1962); and Ch'en Shou-yi, *Chinese Literature: A Historical Introduction* (New York: Ronald Press, 1961). Fuller information on particular authors or works may be found in William H. Nienhauser Jr (ed.), *The Indiana Companion to Traditional Chinese Literature*.

Various reprints have been made of parts of the pioneer *The Chinese Classics*, translated by James Legge (first published, in part, London: Trübner, 1861). Later versions of some of these works include Arthur Waley, *The Book of Songs* (London: Allen & Unwin, 1937); and *The I Ching or 'Book of Changes': The Richard Wilhelm Translation Rendered into English by Cary F. Baynes* (third edition, London: Routledge & Kegan Paul, 1968).

For translations of basic philosophical writings, see Arthur Waley, *The Analects of Confucius* (London: Allen & Unwin, 1938); D. C. Lau, *Mencius*; Burton Watson, *Basic Writings of Mo Tzu, Hsün Tzu and Han Fei Tzu* (New York and London: Columbia University Press, 1967; also available in separate volumes); Arthur Waley, *The Way and its Power*; and Alfred Forke (trs.), *Lun-hêng. Part I: Philosophical Essays of Wang Ch'ung; Part II: Miscellaneous Essays of Wang Ch'ung* (second edition, New York: Paragon Book Gallery, 1962).

Translations of select pieces of prose and poetry have been collected as follows: E. D. Edwards, *Chinese Prose Literature of the T'ang Period (AD 618–906)*, two vols. (London: Probsthain, 1937–8), and *The*

Dragon Book (London: William Hodge, 1938); Lin Yutang, *The Importance of Understanding* (London: Heinemann, 1961); Cyril Birch (comp. and ed.), *Anthology of Chinese Literature from Early Times to the Fourteenth Century* (Harmondsworth: Penguin, 1965); Arthur Waley, *Chinese Poems* (London: Allen & Unwin, 1946); and J. D. Frodsham, *An Anthology of Chinese Verse* (Oxford: Clarendon Press, 1967).

For separate collections of poems or of named poets, see David Hawkes, *The Songs of the South* (Harmondsworth: Penguin, 1985); Arthur Cooper, *Li Po and Tu Fu* (Harmondsworth: Penguin, 1973; reprinted, 1986); Arthur Waley, *The Life and Times of Po Chü-i*; G. W. Robinson, *Poems of Wang Wei* (Harmondsworth, Penguin, 1973); and Anne Birrell, *Popular Songs and Ballads of Han China* (London: Unwin Hyman, 1988).

Translations of select rhapsodies (*fu*) appear in Burton Watson (trs.), *Chinese Rhyme-Prose Poems in the Fu Form from the Han and Six Dynasties Periods* (New York and London: Columbia University Press, 1971); and David R. Knechtges, *Wen Xuan or Selections of Refined Literature*, two vols. (Princeton, NJ: Princeton Unviversity Press, 1982–7).

Essays in W. G. Beasley and E. G. Pulleyblank, *Historians of China and Japan* (London: Oxford University Press, 1961), provide a critical assessment of Chinese historiography. For studies of one of China's first named historians and his works, see Burton Watson, *Ssu-ma Ch'ien: Grand Historian of China* (New York: Columbia University Press, 1958), and *Records of the Grand Historian of China*, two vols. (New York: Columbia University Press, 1961). For studies of a few outstanding figures of Chinese literature, see Lin Yutang, *The Gay Genius: The Life and Times of Su Tungpo* (London: Heinemann, 1948); and James T. C. Liu, *Ou-yang Hsiu: An Eleventh-Century Neo-Confucianist* (Stanford, Calif.: Stanford University Press, 1967).

Translations of some of the major Chinese novels will be found as follows: Pearl S. Buck, *All Men are Brothers* (London: Methuen, 1933); Clement Egerton, *The Golden Lotus*, four vols. (London: Routledge, 1939); Arthur Waley, *Monkey by Wu Ch'eng-an* (London: Allen & Unwin, 1942); and *The Story of the Stone*, volumes 1–3, translated by David Hawkes, volumes 4–5 by John Minford (Harmondsworth: Penguin, 1973–86).

XII: THE CREATION AND CIRCULATION OF BOOKS

For the development of written records and books, see Tsuen-hsuin Tsien, *Written on Bamboo and Silk*. The emergence and growth of printing are described in Thomas Francis Carter, *The Invention of Printing in China and its Spread Westward* (second edition, New York: Ronald Press, 1955); Denis Twitchett, *Printing and Publishing in Mediaeval China* (London: Wynkyn de Worde Society, 1983); and J. Needham *et al.*, *Science and Civilisation in China*, volume V, part 1, *Paper and Printing*. For the production of some of the major literary collections, see Michael Loewe, *The Origins and Development of Chinese Encyclopaedias* (London: China Society, 1987).

XIII: THE CAPITAL CITIES OF THE EMPIRES

For the evidence of the earliest cities of China and their features, see Kwang-chih Chang, *Shang Civilization*, and Li Xueqin, *Eastern Zhou and Qin Civilizations*. The Han capital cities of Chang'an and Luoyang are described in Wang Zhongshu, *Han Civilization* (New Haven, Conn., and London: Yale University Press, 1982); and Hans Bielenstein, *Lo-yang in Later Han Times* (Stockholm: Museum of Far Eastern Antiquities, 1976).

For studies of various aspects of Chinese cities, see Mark Elvin and G. William Skinner (eds.), *The Chinese City between Two Worlds* (Stanford, Calif.: Stanford University Press, 1974); and G. William Skinner (ed.), *The City in Late Imperial China* (Stanford, Calif.: Stanford University Press, 1977). Jacques Gernet, *Daily Life in China on the Eve of the Mongol Invasion 1250–1276*, and Michael Loewe, *Everyday Life in Early Imperial China during the Han Period*, include descriptive details of life in the Southern Song capital of Lin'an (Hangzhou) and the Han capital of Chang'an (Xi'an) respectively. Perhaps the best source of photographs of Beijing as it was at the close of the imperial era will be found in Donald Mennie, *The Pageant of Peking* (Shanghai: Kelly & Walsh, 1920); see also L. C. Arlington and William Lewisohn, *In Search of Old Peking* (Oxford: Oxford University Press, 1935; reprinted 1987); and Lin Yutang, *Imperial Perking: Seven Centuries of China* (London: Elek, 1961). A study of the traditional gardens that adorned major cities from the Song period onwards may be found in Maggie Keswick, *The Chinese Garden: History, Art and Architecture* (London: Academy Editions, 1978). The reference to the growth of the vine and lucerne will be found in *Han shu* (Beijing: Zhonghua shuju, 1962), 96A, p. 3895.

XIV: TOMBS AND THEIR TREASURES

Considerable information about the burial habits and styles of the kings of Shang is provided in Kwang-chih Chang, *Shang Civilization*, and Li Chi, *Anyang*; in *Eastern Zhou and Qin Civilizations*, Li Xueqin gives an account of the evidence for the succeeding centuries of the pre-imperial period. A particular set of royal graves and their contents is treated in *Zhongshan: tombes des rois oubliés* (Paris: Galeries Nationales du Grand Palais, 1984). Susan L. Caroselli (ed.), *The Quest for Eternity* (San Francisco: Los Angeles County Museum of Art, 1987) provides a valuable introduction to the whole subject of funerary habits and furnishings. For the Han period, see Wang Zhongshu, *Han Civilization*; Michèle Pirazzoli-t'Serstevens, *The Han Dynasty*, translated by Janet Seligman (New York: Rizzoli, 1982); and, for the underlying beliefs, motifs and iconography of Han funerary habits, Michael Loewe, *Ways to Paradise: The Chinese Quest for Immortality*.

A number of illustrated monographs in Chinese treat some of the recently excavated major tombs such as those of the first Qin emperor, and Wang Jian, or at sites such as Mawangdui, Mancheng or Yinan; others concentrate on the frescoes found at a tomb in Holingol, or in the mausoleums of members of the Tang imperial family. Monographs of this type in English include *The Chinese Bronzes of Yunnan*, foreword by Jessica Rawson (London: Sidgwick & Jackson, and Beijing: Cultural Relics Publishing House, 1983); and Ann Paludan, *The Imperial Ming Tombs* (New Haven, Conn., and London: Yale University Press, 1981). A selection of some of the more important recent finds from tombs is presented in Qian Hao, Chen Heyi and Ru Suichu, *Out of China's Earth: Archaeological Discoveries in the People's Republic of China* (London: Muller, and Beijing: China Pictorial, 1981).

XV: THE ARTS

The following items are chosen from a large number of books which serve to introduce readers to Chinese art. They may be supplemented by the catalogues which accompany exhibitions held from time to time in Europe, North America or Japan. Specialist and scholastic articles on particular topics appear in periodical publications such as *Arts Asiatiques* (Paris), *Artibus Asiae* (Ascona) and the *Bulletin of the Museum of Far Eastern Antiquities* (Stockholm). A series of illustrated handbooks to different art forms has been published by the National

Palace Museum, Taipei, Taiwan, based on its holdings.

For a general view of the arts of China, see Michael Sullivan, *A Short History of Chinese Art* (London: Faber, 1967); Jessica Rawson, *Ancient China: Art and Archaeology*; Laurence Sickman and Alexander Soper, *The Art and Architecture of China* (Harmondsworth: Penguin, 1956); and William Watson, *Style in the Arts of China* (Harmondsworth: Penguin, 1974). For technical terms, see S. Howard Hansford, *A Glossary of Chinese Art and Archaeology* (London: China Society, 1972); and Margaret Medley, *Handbook of Chinese Art* (third edition, London; Bell & Sons, 1977).

Suggested readings for particular art forms follow:

Jade

S. Howard Hansford, *Chinese Carved Jades* (London: Faber, 1968), and *Chinese Jade throughout the Ages* (London: Victoria & Albert Museum, 1975).

Bronze

Li Xueqin, *The Wonder of Chinese Bronzes* (Beijing: Foreign Languages Press, 1980); Wen Fong (ed.), *The Great Bronze Age of China* (New York: Metropolitan Museum of Art/Knopf, 1980).

Ceramics

Basil Gray, *Early Chinese Pottery and Porcelain* (London: Faber, 1953); Soame Jenyns, *Later Chinese Porcelain: The Ch'ing Dynasty (1644–1912)*, and *Ming Pottery and Porcelain* (London: Faber, 1951 and 1953); Margaret Medley, *The Chinese Potter: A Practical History of Chinese Ceramics* (Oxford: Phaidon, 1976).

Painting

Arthur Waley, *An Introduction to the Study of Chinese Painting* (originally published 1923; reprinted New York: Grove Press, 1958); Osvald Siren, *Chinese Painting: Leading Masters and Principles*, seven vols. (London: Lund Humphries, 1956–8); Peter C. Swann, *Chinese Painting* (New York: Universe Books, 1958); Roderick Whitfield, *In Pursuit of Antiquity: Chinese Paintings of the Ming and Ch'ing Dynasties from the*

Collection of Mr and Mrs Earl Morse (Princeton, NJ: Art Museum, Princeton University, 1969); Cécile and Michel Bourdoley, *Giuseppe Castiglione: A Jesuit Painter at the Court of the Chinese Emperors*, translated by Michael Bullock (London: Lund Humphries, 1971).

Calligraphy

Chiang Yee, *Chinese Calligraphy* (second edition, Cambridge Mass.: Harvard University Press, 1954); Lothar Ledderose, *Mi Fu and the Classical Tradition of Chinese Calligraphy* (Princeton, NJ: Princeton University Press, 1979); Frederick W. Mote and Hung-lam Chu, *Calligraphy and the East Asian Book*, ed. Howard L. Goodman (Boston and Shaftesbury: Shambhala, 1989).

Buddhist Sculpture and Painting

Michael Sullivan, *The Cave Temples of Maichishan* (London: Faber, 1969); Terukazu Akiyama and Saburo Matsubara, *Arts of China: Buddhist Cave Temples: New Researches* (Tokyo: Kodansha International, 1969); Anon., *The Flying Devis of Dunhuang* (Beijing: China Travel & Tourism, 1980).

Architecture

Andrew Boyd, *Chinese Architecture and Town Planning 1500 BC–AD 1911* (London: Alec Tiranti, 1962).

Textiles

Cyril C. E. Blunt, *Chinese Fabrics* (Leigh-on-Sea: F. Lewis, 1961); and *Joseph Needham Science and Civilisation in China*, volume 5, part IX, *Textile Technology: Spinning and Reeling*, by Dieter Kuhn (Cambridge: Cambridge University Press, 1988).

Lacquer

Le Yu-kuan, *Oriental Lacquer Art* (New York: Weatherhill, 1972).

XVI: THE ADVANCEMENT OF SCIENCE AND ITS APPLICATIONS

The most detailed account of the development of science and technology will be found in Joseph Needham *et. al.*, *Science and Civilisation in China* (Cambridge: Cambridge University Press, 1954– ; fifteen vols. published to date, with nineteen further vols. envisaged). For a summarized version of these findings, now in course of publication, see Colin A. Ronan, *The Shorter Science and Civilisation in China* (Cambridge: Cambridge University Press, 1978). Sung Ying-hsing, *T'ien-kung k'ai-wu: Chinese Technology in the Seventeenth Century*, translated by E-tu Zen Sun and Shiou-chuan Sun (University Park, Pa, and London: Pennsylvania State University Press, 1966), describes the techniques of a number of regular occupations of Chinese life and includes woodcuts from original editions of the book. Some of the basic philosophical and mathematical ideas of Chinese science are explained in Ho Peng Yoke, *Li Qi and Shu: An Introduction to Science and Civilization in China* (Hong Kong: Hong Kong University Press, 1985). For a short overview of the scope and development of science, see Nathan Sivin's chapter in Leo A. Orleans (ed.), *Science in Contemporary China* (Stanford, Calif.: Stanford University Press, 1980).

Monographs on particular topics include: Joseph Needham *et al.*, *Heavenly Clockwork: The Great Astronomical Clocks of Medieval China* (second edition, Cambridge: Cambridge University Press, 1986); Lu Gwei-Djen and Joseph Needham, *Celestial Lancets: A History and Rationale of Acupuncture and Moxa* (Cambridge: Cambridge University Press, 1980); Joseph Needham, *The Development of Iron and Steel Technology in China* (Newcomen Society, 1958; reprinted, Cambridge: Heffer & Sons, 1964); and the following works by Nathan Sivin: *Chinese Alchemy: Preliminary Studies* (Cambridge, Mass.: Harvard University Press, 1968); *Cosmos and Computation in Early Chinese Mathematical Astronomy* (Leiden: E. J. Brill, 1969); and *Traditional Medicine in Contemporary China* (Ann Arbor: Centre for Chinese Studies, University of Michigan, 1987). See also Shigeru Nakayama and Nathan Sivin (eds.), *Chinese Science: Explorations of an Ancient Tradition* (Cambridge, Mass.: MIT Press, 1973).

For a translation of the *Lunheng*, see Alfred Forke, *Lun-hêng*, parts I and II (originally published 1907 and 1911; reprinted New York: Paragon Book Gallery, 1962). For the context within which the Jesuit fathers brought western science to China, see Jacques Gernet, *China and the Christian Impact*, translated by Janet Lloyd (Cambridge: Cambridge University Press, 1985).

XVII: PROBLEMS OF LAND AND WATER

Many of the topics mentioned in this chapter are discussed in detail in the volumes of *Science and Civilisation in China* (see especially volume 6, part II, *Agriculture*, by Francesca Bray); and in Sung Ying-hsing, *T'ien-kung kai-wu*. For agriculture, see also Cho-yun Hsu, *Han Agriculture: The Formation of Early Chinese Agrarian Economy 206 BC–AD 202* (Seattle and London: University of Washington Press, 1986), which includes translations of early source material on the subject. Conditions of travel and communications are vividly described in G. R. G. Worcester, *The Junkman Smiles* (London: Chatto & Windus, 1959); and Lynn Pan, *China's Sorrow: Journeys around the Yellow River*. Han Yu's allegory appears as his essay *Zashuo (yi)*; Su Dongpo's essay is entitled *Xi yu ting ji*.

XVIII: COMMERCIAL PRACTICE

Essays on certain aspects of the economic role of the state are included in S. R. Schram (ed.), *The Scope of State Power in China*. For a major study of this subject, see Mark Elvin, *The Pattern of the Chinese Past* (London: Eyre Methuen, 1973). Financial aspects are considered in Wang Yü-ch'üan, *Early Chinese Coinage* (New York: American Numismatic Society, 1951); Lien-sheng Yang, *Money and Credit in China: A Short History* (Cambridge, Mass.: Harvard University Press, 1952); and D. C. Twitchett, *Financial Administration under the T'ang Dynasty* (Cambridge: Cambridge University Press, 1963). For economic relations with westerners, see John King Fairbank, *Trade and Diplomacy on the China Coast: The Opening of the Treaty Ports 1842–54* (first published 1953; reissued, Stanford, Calif.: Stanford University Press, 1969).

CHARACTER INDEX
(Entries in this list are limited to items
that are of particular importance)

An Lushan 安祿山
An Shigao 安世高
Anyang 安陽

ba gua 八卦
Ban Biao 班彪
Ban Gu 班固
Banpo 半坡
Baopuzi 抱朴子
Beijing 北京
Bei tang shu chao 北堂書鈔
Bencao gangmu 本草綱目
Bi Sheng 畢昇
Bo Juyi 白居易

Cai Lun 蔡倫
Chan 禪
Chang'an 長安
Chao Cuo 晁錯
Chen 陳
Chen Menglei 陳夢雷
Chengdu 成都
Chengzi'ai 城子崖
Chiang Kaishek 蔣介石
Chongqing 重慶
Chu 楚

Chuci 楚辭
Chu xue ji 初學記
Chunqiu 春秋
Ci Xi 慈禧
Congshu 叢書
Cui Shu 崔述

Dabaotai 大葆臺
Dadu 大都
Dai Zhen 戴震
dao 道
Daodejing 道德經
daojia 道家
Dao zang 道藏
Daxue 大學
di 帝
Dian 滇
Donglin 東林
Dong Yu 董遇
Dong Zhongshu 董仲舒
Dong Zhuo 董卓
Dunhuang 敦煌

Emei 峨眉
Ennin 圓仁
Erligang 二里岡

299

Mo Di 墨翟

Nanjing 南京
neige 內閣
Nong shu 農書
Nügua 女媧

Ouyang Xiu 歐陽脩
Ouyang Xun 歐陽詢

pailou 牌樓
Pangu 盤古
Pan Geng 盤庚
Panhu 槃瓠
Penglai 蓬萊
Pinyin 拼音
Piyong 辟雍
po 魄
putonghua 普通話

Qi (kingdom) 齊
qi 氣
Qiang 羌
Qianlong 乾隆
Qimin yaoshu 齊民要術
Qin 秦
Qin Jiushao 秦九韶
Qing 清
Qu Yuan 屈原

ren 仁
Rizhilu 日知錄
Ruan Yuan 阮元

Ruizong 睿宗
rujia 儒家
Rulin waishi 儒林外史

Sanguozhi yanyi 三國志演義
Sanmen 三門
Sanxingdui 三星堆
sha 煞
Shang 商
Shangjun shu 商君書
Shanglin 上林
Shangshu sheng 尚書省
Shang Yang 商鞅
Shaogou 燒溝
Shao Yong 邵雍
Shazitang 沙子塘
shen 神
Shen Gua 沈括
sheng 省
Shennong 神農
shi nong gong shang 士農工商
Shiji 史記
Shijing 詩經
shu 數
Shuihu zhuan 水滸傳
Shujing 書經
Shun 舜
Shundi 順帝
Shuowen 說文
Si ku quan shu 四庫全書
Si min yue ling 四民月令
Si shu 四書
Sima Guang 司馬光

INDEX

(Figures in italic refer to pages which carry maps)